Intervention in the 1980s

DATE DUE

INTERVENTION IN THE 1980s

INTERVENTION IN THE 1980s

U.S. Foreign Policy in the Third World

Edited by
Peter J. Schraeder

Lynne Rienner Publishers ■ Boulder/London

Published in the United States of America in 1989 by
Lynne Rienner Publishers, Inc.
1800 30th Street, Boulder, Colorado 80301

and in the United Kingdom by
Lynne Rienner Publishers, Inc.
3 Henrietta Street, Covent Garden, London WC2E 8LU

Library of Congress Cataloging-in-Publication Data
Intervention in the 1980s.
Bibliography: p.
Includes index.
1. Intervention (International law). 2. United States—Foreign relations—Developing countries. 3. Developing countries—Foreign relations—United States.
I. Schraeder, Peter J.
JX4481.I558 1989 341.5′8 88-32200
ISBN 1-55587-070-8
ISBN 1-55587-071-6

British Cataloguing in Publication Data
A Cataloguing in Publication record for this book
is available from the British Library.

Printed and bound in the United States of America

To my wife,
Mary

Contents

Tables

Acknowledgments

The genesis of this book is the personal desire shared by the eighteen contributors to write a systematic analysis of U.S. interventionist practices in the Third World. More specifically, *Intervention in the 1980s* offers a comprehensive overview of the origins, tools, and constraints of U.S. intervention, with special emphasis placed on analyzing U.S. policies during the post–World War II period. As editor of this volume, I have the distinct pleasure of acknowledging those who contributed to its successful completion. At the same time, however, I accept full responsibility for any remaining deficiencies in the book.

First and foremost, I wish to thank the contributors who, in the process of writing and revising these original submissions, cheerfully and quickly responded to what often must have seemed to be an endless string of queries and requests for revisions and updates. Second, all eighteen of us inevitably enjoyed the support of numerous individuals—administrative staff, colleagues, family members, and students—who were crucial in contributing to the final product but whose numbers preclude personal recognition on these pages. To all these individuals, we extend a heartfelt thank you.

Certain individuals, however, deserve special thanks. Michael Smith, both friend and colleague, was there at the beginning and was influential in sorting out the ideas and themes that eventually would become this book. John Creed, another friend and colleague, provided invaluable advice concerning the revision and clarification of the entire manuscript. At Lynne Rienner Publishers, Steve Barr was crucial in keeping the project on schedule, while Beverly Armstrong's editorial skill enhanced the readability and coherence of the ideas presented. Especially appreciated is Lynne Rienner's encouragement and patience as this project slowly made its way to fruition.

In many respects, this book is the product of my years spent in the Department of Government and International Studies at the University of South Carolina. Funds provided by the department and most notably by the West Foundation during 1987–1988 were significant aids and are greatly appreciated. My professors at the University of South Carolina were especially important in my development as a student of U.S. foreign policy. In particular, Charles W. Kegley, Jr., and Jerel A. Rosati cultivated my interest in comparative foreign policy theory and empirical analysis, while Paul M. Kattenburg, with his numerous years of experience in the U.S. State Department, fostered my appreciation for policy relevant analysis. Finally, Mark W. DeLancey's love for Africa and patient guidance nurtured my interest in U.S. foreign policy toward Africa in particular and the Third World in general.

Most important, however, has been the loving support of my wife, Mary. Mary has acted at various times as typist, editor, critic, and, most of all, friend, providing words of encouragement when the light at the end of the tunnel seemed dim indeed. In short, without her there would have been no book.

Peter J. Schraeder

About the Contributors

DOUG BANDOW is a nationally syndicated columnist for the Copley News Service and a senior fellow at the Cato Institute. He served from 1981 to 1982 as a special assistant to President Reagan, where he handled military manpower and international development issues. The author and coeditor of several books, including *U.S. Aid to the Developing World: A Free Market Agenda* (1985), he is currently writing a book on the U.S. defense commitment to South Korea.

TED GALEN CARPENTER is director of foreign policy studies at the Cato Institute. An expert on defense and foreign policy issues, his work has appeared in the *Wall Street Journal*, the *New York Times*, *Harper's*, *Reason*, and other publications. He is the editor of *Collective Defense or Strategic Independence?: Alternative Strategies for the Future* (1989) and is currently writing a book examining the impact of U.S. foreign policy decisions on domestic liberty.

GWENDOLEN M. CARTER is adjunct professor of political science and African studies at the University of Florida. A specialist on southern Africa, she has devoted more than four decades to researching, teaching, and writing about the region. She is the author and editor of dozens of books and articles including *Southern Africa: The Continuing Crisis* (1979) and *International Politics in Southern Africa* (1982). Her most recent work is *Continuity and Change in Southern Africa* (1985).

STEPHEN DAGGETT is a senior analyst for the Committee for National Security and has written extensively on the U.S. military budget and defense policy planning process. His work has appeared in *Foreign Policy*, *Arms Control Today*, and the *American Defense Annual*, as well as in various military publications, including *Army Times, Air Force Times,* and *Navy Times*. His current research centers on Soviet strategic defense and space programs and the U.S. Strategic Defense Initiative.

R. HUNT DAVIS, JR., is professor of history and former director of the Center for African Studies at the University of Florida. From 1980 until 1988 he served as editor of the *African Studies Review*. The author of *Bantu Education and the Education of South Africans in South Africa* (1972) as well as several articles dealing with modern South African history, his work has appeared in *African Affairs,* the *International Journal of African Historical Studies,* the *Journal of African Studies,* and other publications.

CHARLES F. DORAN is professor of international relations at the Johns Hopkins School of Advanced International Studies. The author of more than fifty scholarly articles and books on international politics and political economy, his research encompasses security policy; domestic and interstate conflict; and commercial, environmental, and energy resource questions. His most recent books include *Systems in Crisis: New Imperatives of High Politics at Century's End* (1989) and *Intersecting Parallels: Intervulnerabilities in Trade and Politics at the 49th* (1989).

KIMBERLY A. ELLIOTT is research associate for the Institute for International Economics in Washington, D.C. She has coauthored several studies on the roles of trade and sanctions in U.S. foreign policy, including *Trade Protection in the United States: 31 Case Studies* (1986) and *Economic Sanctions Reconsidered: History and Current Policy* (1985).

LLOYD C. GARDNER is Charles and Mary Beard Professor of History at Rutgers University, where he specializes in the history of U.S. foreign policy. His most recent books include *A Covenant with Power: America and the World from Wilson to Reagan* (1984), *Safe for Democracy: The Anglo-American Response to Revolution 1913 to 1923* (1984), and *Approaching Vietnam: From World War II Through Dienbienphu* (1988).

ERIC HOOGLUND is adjunct professor of Middle East Studies at the Johns Hopkins School of Advanced International Studies and was senior analyst (1986-1988) for the Iran Revolution Project at the National Security Archive, Washington, D.C. His five years in Iran conducting scholarly research and teaching included the revolutionary period 1978–1979. An editor of *Middle East Report,* his major works include *Land and Revolution in Iran, 1960–1980* (1982) and *The Iranian Revolution and the Islamic Republic* (1986).

CHRISTOPHER C. JOYNER is associate professor in the department of political science at the George Washington University. Specializing in international law and world politics, he is the author of numerous articles on the international legal implications of U.S. intervention in the Third World. His works also include *The Antarctic Regime* (1987) and the upcoming *Antarctica and the Law of the Sea*.

RICHARD J. KESSLER is former associate at the Carnegie Endowment for International Peace. He has made numerous trips to the Philippines, has served as a visiting research fellow at the University of the Philippines, and has published numerous articles on U.S. foreign policy toward Asia and the Philippines, including the forthcoming book *Repression and Rebellion in the Philippines*.

MICHAEL T. KLARE is director and associate professor of the Five College Program in Peace and World Security Studies based at Hampshire College. He is the defense correspondent of *The Nation* and author of numerous articles on U.S. military policy, and his books include *Beyond the "Vietnam Syndrome"* (1981), *American Arms Supermarket* (1985), and the recently coedited *Low-Intensity Warfare: Counterinsurgency, Proinsurgency, and Antiterrorism in the Eighties* (1988).

PETER KORNBLUH is an information analyst at the National Security Archive in Washington, D.C. He specializes in U.S. policy toward Latin America and is author of *Nicaragua: The Price of Intervention* (1987) and coeditor of *Low-Intensity Warfare: Counterinsurgency, Proinsurgency, and Antiterrorism in the Eighties* (1988).

HARRY PIOTROWSKI is associate professor in the History Department at Towson State University. His specialty is the history of U.S.-Soviet foreign policy, especially as it pertains to the Third World. His most recent work is the coauthored *The World Since 1945: Politics, War, and Revolution in the Nuclear Age* (1988). He is currently working on a study of the origins of the cold war.

HARRY HOWE RANSOM is professor emeritus of political science at Vanderbilt University. A noted scholar of foreign and defense policymaking and strategic intelligence, he has written numerous articles and books, including *The Intelligence Establishment* (1970), *Can American Democracy Survive Cold War?* (1963), and *Central Intelligence and National Security* (1958).

JEREL A. ROSATI is associate professor of government and international studies at the University of South Carolina and was director of the foreign policy section of the International Studies Association. A specialist in the beliefs of political leaders and in the foreign-policy-making process, he is author of *The Carter Administration's Quest for Global Community: Beliefs and Their Impact on Behavior* (1987) and coeditor of *The Power of Human Needs in World Society* (1988).

PETER J. SCHRAEDER, the editor of this volume, is a doctoral fellow at the University of South Carolina. A scholar in international studies, African studies, and U.S. foreign policy in the Third World, he worked in Djibouti for the U.S. State Department and has taught and carried out research under the auspices of Somali National University in Mogadishu, Somalia. He is the coauthor of *Cameroon* (1986) and *Somalia* (1988) and is currently working on a book titled *Crisis and Incrementalism: Continuity and Change in U.S. Intervention in Africa,* as well as a general study on Djibouti.

TONY THORNDIKE is professor of international relations at the North Staffordshire Polytechnic, Stoke-on-Trent, England. Extensive travel and research in the Caribbean region have informed his numerous articles and books, on the Caribbean in general and Grenada in particular, including *Grenada: Politics, Economics and Society* (1985) and the coauthored *Grenada: Revolution and Intervention* (1984).

Acronyms

AFL-CIO	American Federation of Labor-Congress for Industrial Organization
AID	Agency for International Development
AIOC	Anglo-Iranian Oil Company
ANC	African National Congress (South Africa)
ANS	Armée Nationale Sihanoukienne (Cambodia)
ARENA	Nationalist Republican Alliance (El Salvador)
ASEAN	Association of Southeast Asian Nations
CARICOM	Caribbean Community
CDB	Caribbean Development Bank
CENTO	Central Treaty Organization
CGDK	Coalition Government of Democratic Kampuchea (Cambodia)
CIA	Central Intelligence Agency
CINCLANT	commander in chief of the U.S. Atlantic Command
COSATU	Congress of South African Trade Unions
CPP	Communist Party of the Philippines
CPSU	Communist Party of the Soviet Union
DCI	director of central intelligence
DDP	deputy director for plans
DIA	Defense Intelligence Agency
ESF	Economic Support Fund
FBI	Federal Bureau of Investigation
FDN	Nicaraguan Democratic Force
FMLN	Faribundo Martí Front for National Liberation (El Salvador)
FNLA	National Front for the Liberation of Angola
FSLN	Sandinista National Liberation Front (Frente Sandinista de Liberacion Nacional) (Nicaragua)

FY	fiscal year
GAO	General Accounting Office
GDP	gross domestic product
GNP	gross national product
ICJ	International Court of Justice
IFDP	Institute for Food and Development Policy
IMF	International Monetary Fund
INF	intermediate-range nuclear forces
ITT	International Telephone and Telegraph
JCS	Joint Chiefs of Staff
JDA	Joint Deployment Agency
KPNLF	Khmer People's National Liberation Front (Cambodia)
LIC	low-intensity conflict
LIDs	Light Infantry Divisions
MBA	Military Bases Agreement (Philippines)
MILGROUP	military group
MPLA	Popular Movement for the Liberation of Angola
NAM	Non-Aligned Movement
NATO	North Atlantic Treaty Organization
NDU	National Defense University
NICs	Newly Industrializing Countries
NIEO	New International Economic Order
NJM	New Jewel Movement (Grenada)
NLF	National Liberation Front (Vietnam)
NNPA	Nuclear Non-Proliferation Act
NP	National party (South Africa)
NPA	New People's Army (Philippines)
NPT	Non-Proliferation Treaty
NRP	New Republic party (South Africa)
NSA	National Security Agency
NSAM	National Security Action Memorandum
NSC	National Security Council
NSDD	National Security Decision Directive
NSSD	National Security Study Directive
NSSM	National Security Study Memorandum
OAS	Organization of American States
OECS	Organization of Eastern Caribbean States
OIDP	Overseas Internal Defense Policy
OPC	Office of Policy Coordination
OPEC	Organization of Petroleum Exporting Countries
OSO	Office of Special Operations
OSS	Office of Strategic Services
PF	Patriotic Front (Zimbabwe)
PFP	Progressive Federal party (South Africa)

PHILCUSA	Philippine Council on U.S. Aid
P.L. 480	Public Law 480
PLA	People's Liberation Army (PRC)
PLO	Palestine Liberation Organization
PPBS	Planning, Programming, and Budgeting System
PRA	People's Revolutionary Army (Grenada)
PRC	People's Republic of China
PRG	People's Revolutionary Government (Grenada)
psyops	psychological operations
RDF	Rapid Deployment Force
RENAMO	Mozambique National Resistance
RN	Nicaraguan Resistance
SALT	Strategic Arms Limitation Talks
SAVAK	National Security and Information Organization (Sazman-e Attelaat va Amniyat-e Keshvar) (Iran)
SEALs	sea-air-land commandos
SEATO	Southeast Asian Treaty Organization
SWAPO	South West African People's Organization (Angola)
UCLAs	Unilaterally Controlled Latino Assets
UDF	United Democratic Front (South Africa)
UN	United Nations
UNITA	National Union for the Total Independence of Angola
UNO	United Nicaraguan Opposition
USIA	United States Information Agency
USSR	Union of Soviet Socialist Republics

■ Part 1

INTRODUCTION

□ 1

Concepts, Relevance, Themes, and Overview

Peter J. Schraeder

As U.S. policymakers approach the end of the 1980s and the United States prepares to enter the twenty-first century, the time seems ripe for a critical assessment of nearly forty years of U.S. interventionist policies in the Third World. The primary purpose of such an assessment is to clarify and analyze critically the shortcomings of past and current U.S. foreign policy in the hope that an understanding of past mistakes may provide the basis for a more enlightened foreign policy of the future. This is no mere academic exercise. Ill-conceived past policies have had severe consequences for U.S. society as a whole, the most notable example being U.S. involvement in the Vietnam War. The secondary purpose of this appraisal is to contribute to the ongoing debate in official policymaking circles, academia, and within the general population as to what should constitute a proper U.S. foreign policy in the Third World. It is only by reasoned debate that a policy consensus—the basis for an effective foreign policy in a democracy—can be achieved. This chapter is devoted to defining key concepts, pointing out the relevance and importance of studying U.S. intervention in the Third World, discussing the major themes around which the book is designed, and providing an overview of the chapters that follow.

■ KEY CONCEPTS

Analysis of U.S. intervention in the Third World first requires a brief explanation of what is meant by "intervention" and "Third World." Both concepts are widely used and are potentially confusing, meaning many different things to many different people.

"Intervention" is most commonly understood to mean the use of military force by one state to interfere in the internal affairs of another state. A classic example would be the Reagan administration's invasion of Grenada in 1983 to overthrow the unpopular military government of General Hudson Austin. This narrow definition may be expanded to include the use of economic force by one state to interfere in the internal affairs of another, such as the U.S. adoption of economic sanctions in 1986 to pressure the South African regime to change its system of apartheid. In an even broader sense, intervention may be defined as any form of outside influence on, or interference with, the domestic policies of a country. It has been argued, for example, that President Jimmy Carter's official declaration in 1979 of U.S. support for the presidential aspirations of South Korea's Lieutenant Colonel Chun Doo Hwan actually prompted Chun to assume the presidency by military force.[1] In the extreme, the definition of intervention could even include the absence of foreign policy behavior in some situations. For example, if Israel were attacked simultaneously by and subjected to an extended military conflict with all of its Arab neighbors, complete U.S. neutrality most likely would ensure Israeli defeat. Although the United States would not have physically intervened, its inaction—contrary to Israeli expectations—would be crucial in determining the outcome of the conflict.

For the purposes of this book, intervention is defined in a broad sense as the purposeful and calculated use of political, economic, and military instruments by one country to influence the domestic politics or the foreign policy of another country. Four important aspects of this definition stand out. First, intervention is seen as purposeful and calculated, underscoring the intentional nature of the act. Second, intervention entails a wide choice of instruments ranging from the extension of economic and military aid to economic sanctions, covert action, paramilitary interference, and, finally, direct application of military force. Third, attempts to influence a regime's domestic or foreign policies need not be restricted to efforts to change those policies but may also support a given regime in order to insulate it from change. Finally, intervention is not limited to affecting the domestic politics of a given country but can be undertaken to affect that country's foreign policy as well. This broad definition of intervention is adopted to capture the richness of U.S. actions in the Third World.

"Third World" is a popular label for the majority of the world's countries in Africa, Asia, Latin America, and the Middle East that belong neither to the First World (the United States and other industrialized capitalist nations, including Australia, Canada, Japan, and Western Europe) nor the Second World (the Soviet Union and the industrialized communist countries of Eastern Europe). The concept of a Third World arose from these countries' wish to pursue a third, "nonaligned" path of development during the cold war period, independent of the political-military wishes of either the Soviet Union or the United States. Implicit in this approach was a desire to draw attention to the economic inequalities between the industrialized North (including both the First and Second Worlds) and the developing South (the Third World) and to the need for a restructuring of North-South economic relations through plans like the New International Economic Order (NIEO).[2]

Several characteristics further distinguish the Third World from the industrialized North.[3] Third World countries, typically former colonies, exhibit low levels of industrialization, lack well-developed infrastructures in terms of transportation, energy, education, and social services, and exhibit large inequities in the distribution of wealth and resources. Moreover, they are saddled by high rates of population growth, are unable to bring the majority of their populations into the formal economy, and rely on a monocrop or monomineral export to sustain their economies. Most important, the combination of these factors contributes to the economic and political fragility of Third World regimes, making their systems highly vulnerable to external economic, political, and military intervention.

Despite the common label and similarities of underdevelopment, the countries of the Third World do not represent a coherent, unified, or homogeneous group but are, rather, a highly heterogeneous set of countries divided along numerous lines—ideological, ethnic, religious, and economic.[4] Among Third World countries, one finds Marxist, socialist, and capitalist orientations toward development. Some countries, such as Nigeria, comprise several competing ethnic groups that, as was evident during the 1960s, can provide the basis for secessionist or civil wars. At the other extreme are countries, such as Somalia, that have only one ethnic group and have resorted to war to reunify peoples of that group who were incorporated into neighboring territories during the colonial period. Third World countries are also distinguished by religious differences—for example, predominantly Hindu India and predominantly Muslim Pakistan. In fact, deep divisions *within* major religions have sometimes exacerbated traditional rivalries. Among the factors contributing to the bloody Iran-Iraq war has been the animosity between the dominant Sunni Muslim regime in Iraq and its Shiite counterpart in Iran. Finally, there are major differences in economic levels of Third World countries. Some countries may be members of the oil-rich Organization of Petroleum Exporting Countries (OPEC) or be one of the Newly Industrializing Countries (NICs) (such as Brazil, South Korea, and Taiwan); others belong to what the World Bank has termed the Fourth World, or the "poorest of the world's poor" (such as Bangladesh). In short, although the concept of a Third World is a useful distinction for an analysis of U.S. intervention, one should not lose sight of the characteristics that divide the countries included in this grouping.

■ RELEVANCE OF STUDYING U.S. INTERVENTION IN THE THIRD WORLD

U.S. scholars and policymakers have in general paid greater attention to U.S. foreign policy toward the industrialized countries of Western Europe and the West, as well as toward the Soviet Union and other industrialized communist countries, to the detriment of the study of policy toward the Third World. Yet, the study of U.S. foreign policy in the Third World—and, in particular, of U.S.

interventionist practices there—has become increasingly important during the last forty years. Increased attention to, and scrutiny of, U.S. intervention in the Third World is warranted for five reasons:

1. *The Third World constitutes an increasingly important focal point for U.S. trade and investment.* According to the U.S. Department of Commerce,[5] imports from Third World countries in 1984 totaled $122.1 billion, or 35.3 percent of the $345.3 billion in total U.S. imports. Similarly, U.S. exports to the Third World in 1984 were 36 percent of total U.S. exports, earning $76.5 billion for the U.S. economy (out of total earnings of $213.1 billion). Moreover, U.S. direct private investment in the Third World during 1984 exceeded $50 billion, or 23.5 percent of total U.S. private investment in the world. These investments earned nearly $7 billion for U.S. private industry, nearly 32 percent of all U.S. profits earned from overseas private investment.

This gradual shift in U.S. financial interests is perhaps best reflected by the changes in the extension of U.S. government foreign grants and credits overseas since the end of World War II. From 1945 to 1955, the lion's share of U.S. grants and credits were targeted toward the reconstruction and economic rehabilitation of war-torn Western Europe. Delivered under the sponsorship of the Marshall Plan, over 63 percent (nearly $34 billion) of U.S. government grants and credits went to Western Europe. By 1984, however, Western Europe was receiving a mere 1.8 percent of these resources, whereas the various regions of the Third World were the recipients of nearly 90 percent. Although Western Europe and the other industrialized countries remain the premier economic partners of the United States, there can be no doubt that the Third World has become—and will continue to be—increasingly important in the economic calculations of U.S. policymakers.

2. *The Third World is a theater for conflict of increasing scope and intensity.* Prior to 1945, the center of conflict in the world was Europe—two world wars were fought there in the first half of the twentieth century. In the second half of this century, however, the major portion of conflict moved to the Third World. Although the Third World has served as a battlefield for U.S.-Soviet ideological competition during the last forty years, increasingly significant has been the rise of regional powers attempting to pursue strategies of regional hegemony, often through the use of military force. This trend toward the diffusion of power away from the superpowers has been complemented by the growing salience of nationalism, ethnic strife, and religion in contributing to conflict in the Third World. A cursory overview of Third World conflict in 1988 turns up wars between Cambodia and Vietnam, Iran and Iraq, and Libya and Chad; domestic uprisings in the search for national self-determination by black nationalists in South Africa, Palestinian nationalists in the Middle East, and Tamil separatists in Sri Lanka; and civil wars in Afghanistan, Angola, El Salvador, Ethiopia, Nicaragua, and the Philippines. Indeed, the origins and theater

of any future world war involving the United States very likely could be in the Third World.

3. *U.S. strategic planning is being reoriented toward the Third World.* U.S. strategic thinking in the 1980s has begun to question the traditional emphasis on preparing for a conventional, full-scale military conflict with the Soviet Union and has focused more on the rise of "low-intensity conflict" (LIC) in the Third World and the need for the United States to reorient its military capabilities to deal with this "unconventional" threat. Secretary of Defense Caspar Weinberger captured this growing sentiment within the U.S. national security bureaucracy in his 1987 annual report to Congress:

> Today there seems no shortage of adversaries who seek to undermine our security by persistently nibbling away at our interests through these shadow wars carried on by guerrillas, assassins, terrorists, and subversives in the hope that they have found a weak point in our defenses . . . these forms of aggression will remain the most likely and the most enduring threats to our security.[6]

The Pentagon, with strong support from the Reagan administration, has supervised the development of LIC doctrine and the expansion of U.S. projection forces—the army's Green Berets, the navy's SEALs (sea-air-land commando forces), the U.S. Central Command (formerly Rapid Deployment Forces), and similar groups—to prepare U.S. armed forces for dealing with five major types of operations in the Third World: counterinsurgency, proinsurgency, peacetime contingency operations, terrorism counteraction, and antidrug operations. As Michael T. Klare argues in Chapter 3, just as a growing emphasis on counterinsurgency during the 1960s led to increasing U.S. involvement in Vietnam, so the current evolution in strategic thinking ensures that LIC "will be an increasing U.S. strategic concern of the 1990s, potentially leading to ever-increasing U.S. involvement in regional conflicts."

4. *Official recognition of U.S. strategic interests in the Third World provides the basis for increased U.S. intervention.* The United States currently maintains a worldwide network of bases, allies, and client states in which nearly half a million U.S. troops are stationed at 374 military bases, many of which are in the Third World. This worldwide network, when coupled with the designation of particular Third World countries or regions as "vital" to U.S. strategic interests, provides the basis for potential U.S. intervention to safeguard these interests. The Carter Doctrine, for example, identifies the continued flow of oil from the Persian Gulf as one of the paramount strategic interests of the United States, to be defended with U.S. military force if necessary; the doctrine provided the basis for the 1987 Reagan administration policy of reflagging Kuwaiti oil tankers in the Gulf. Analysts have cited other examples of paramount U.S. strategic interests, both past and present, including the maintenance of an open and free Panama Canal, continued U.S. access to leased bases in the Philippines, continued Western access to strategic minerals in south-

ern Africa, and the maintenance of Western control over strategic maritime "choke points" (such as the Cape of Good Hope in southern Africa).[7]

Although individuals from all points of the ideological spectrum agree that the United States has strategic interests worth defending in the Third World, differences arise over where they are, their relative level of importance, and the proper means of maintaining their integrity. For example, although the conservative Committee on the Present Danger considers the Persian Gulf to be a region of vital strategic importance to the United States and favors the Reagan administration's policy of reflagging Kuwaiti oil tankers, policy analysts from the libertarian Cato Institute have questioned both the strategic value of the Gulf to the United States and the reflagging policy. Even when schools of thought agree upon a region of vital strategic importance to the United States (such as Central America), policy prescriptions often differ greatly. Whereas the Committee on the Present Danger favors expanding U.S. support for the contras to overthrow the Sandinista regime in Nicaragua, the Cato Institute views such a policy as counterproductive to long-term U.S. foreign policy interests in the region.[8] Despite these differences, the fact remains that the official designation of areas of vital strategic importance provides the basis for increased U.S. intervention in the Third World.

5. *U.S. intervention in the Third World has had a spillover effect into U.S. society.* Perhaps the most important reason for studying U.S. intervention in the Third World is to understand the effects it has had on U.S. institutions and society. In the case of the Vietnam War, for example, the wiretaps initiated to uncover who had leaked highly sensitive information concerning secret U.S. B-52 bombing raids into Cambodia gradually mushroomed into the Watergate scandal, which drove Richard Nixon from the presidency.[9] The Iranian hostage crisis revealed the seeming impotence of the Carter administration in protecting U.S. citizens abroad, contributing to President Carter's ultimate defeat and the subsequent election of Ronald Reagan in the 1980 presidential elections. U.S. intervention in Nicaragua under the Reagan administration led to the Iran-contra affair, which led to further straining of relations between the executive branch and Congress over the proper role each should play in the foreign-policy-making process. In short, U.S. intervention in the Third World has contributed to U.S. domestic crises of legitimacy.

Moreover, the study of U.S. foreign policy in the Third World will aid in clarifying and understanding past U.S. failures and in providing the basis for formulating future policy prescriptions. The most destructive of these failures was U.S. involvement in Vietnam: Social costs included over 200,000 American casualties (including nearly 60,000 dead) and the erosion of the social fabric of U.S. society; experts have estimated that the cumulative economic costs of carrying out the war exceeded $156 billion.[10] Vietnam was not unique, but rather is indicative of a foreign policy whereby the United States intervened in more than seventeen major Third World civil wars during the post–World War II period.[11]

Foreign policy failures are not endemic to a particular president or political party but may be found in all administrations: Presidents Dwight D. Eisenhower and John F. Kennedy organized and carried out the unsuccessful Bay of Pigs invasion of Cuba in 1961; Lyndon B. Johnson became increasingly mired in a losing war in Vietnam; Nixon expanded the Vietnam War to Cambodian territory, prompting ever greater unrest in the United States; Gerald R. Ford involved the United States in a losing civil war in Angola; Carter continued a faulty policy toward Iran and the shah that ended in disaster; and Reagan suffered a major policy defeat in Lebanon when terrorists killed several hundred U.S. Marines with a truck bomb. Only by understanding the past—cognizant that no two case studies are exactly alike—can one look to the future.

■ MAJOR THEMES

Five themes serve as the guiding principles and intellectual underpinnings of the nineteen chapters of this book:

1. *Overemphasis in U.S. foreign policy on what has been titled the globalist perspective*. The globalist vision, which has dominated U.S. foreign policy in the Third World during the post–World War II period, stresses the central importance of East-West confrontation at all levels of the international system, relegating Third World countries to the role of pawns in the greater East-West conflict. Revolution and conflict are thought fundamentally to result not from oppressive social conditions within the Third World country in question, such as lack of land reform and government indifference to human welfare (although these are recognized as contributing factors), but rather from communist aggression led by the Soviet Union. This globalist logic assumes that radical revolutionary regimes (for example, Cuba), along with the Soviet Union, can successfully export revolution to other areas of the Third World and conjures up visions of falling dominoes once a radical regime has established itself in any given region (Vietnam in Southeast Asia; Nicaragua in Central America). Typical of this type of thinking was President Reagan's characterization of revolutionary conflict in the early years of his administration: "Let us not delude ourselves. The Soviet Union underlies all the unrest that is going on. If they weren't involved in this game of dominoes, there wouldn't be any hotspots in the world."[12]

But history does not support this proposition. Successful revolutionary movements usually fight at first with weapons acquired locally, often from opposing forces; external arms generally do not arrive until the guerrillas have proven themselves on the battlefield.[13] For example, Fidel Castro received Soviet military support only after the Cuban revolution was won, and Vietnam's Ho Chi Minh initially armed his forces with Japanese and French arsenals captured during World War II. In fact, when Castro attempted to export revolution to Central America during the 1960s, he met with failure: The guerrilla forces were easily defeated because of their inability to attract a major following. The example of the Sandinista-led revolution in Nicaragua during the 1960s is especially instructive. Although the Sandinista National Liberation Front (FSLN) received Cuban arms during the 1960s, this aid was discontinued in the early 1970s and did not begin again until the insurrection against Somoza was *already* well under way.[14]

This is not to say, however, that the Soviet Union and radical revolutionary regimes cannot exacerbate or profit from revolutionary upheaval within a given Third World country. Rather, this evidence underscores the misplaced emphasis on the Soviet Union and its allies as deus ex machina or as catalysts for regional turmoil, once the social, economic, and political conditions for revolution are ripe. As distinguished specialists on Central America have noted,

> . . . those who point to external assistance as responsible for exploiting internal problems often miss the depth of these internal problems. It is not poverty and inequality that suddenly get ignited by outside arms and ideas; it is the brutal suppression of attempts at nonviolent reform by oligarchs and officers that moves numbers of people to pick up arms and risk their lives to make revolutions. By pointing to insurgents who seek outside arms, policymakers in Washington mistake symptoms for causes and justify aid for the very military and security forces whose opposition to reform generated armed insurgency in the first place.[15]

2. *Desirability of a U.S. foreign policy that emphasizes a regionalist perspective*. Rather than placing undue emphasis on the Soviet Union and its allies as the chief provocateurs of conflict and instability in the Third World, the regionalist approach emphasizes the regional economic, cultural, political, and historical roots of these upheavals. Several internal conditions have led to the downfall of numerous Third World regimes: increasing income gaps between rich and poor; accumulation of vast wealth by the ruling family through personal control of major aspects of the economy; accentuated mass poverty (from already low levels) in the rural areas and urban shantytowns; limited access to basic social services; lack of meaningful political participation for the majority of the population; exclusion of the rising middle class from sharing in the political and economic benefits of the ruling class; lack of equitable land reform; and government suppression of peaceful attempts at reform.[16]

Focus on the regional or internal causes of a particular conflict lends importance to that conflict in its own right and renders it amenable to resolution based on regional or internal structural change. For example, in the case of mounting guerrilla insurgency in Rhodesia (now Zimbabwe) during the late 1970s, the Carter administration supported Great Britain's initiatives in pressuring the white minority regime of Ian Smith to accept universal suffrage and transition to black majority rule—even though this ensured a regime dominated by the Patriotic Front, a coalition of two guerrilla groups led by avowed Marxists and supplied by the Soviet Union and the People's Republic of China (PRC). By avoiding the traditional U.S. reflex to attribute the growing guerrilla conflict to Soviet-Cuban interference and to back the beleagered government, the United States correctly perceived that alleviation of the conflict depended on internal political and economic reforms and that its influence could aid in bringing such a settlement about. The United States was rewarded for pursuing this policy. Despite the Marxist rhetoric of Zimbabwe's Prime Minister Robert Mugabe, he has clearly followed a pragmatic policy of socioeconomic reform and maintained extensive links with the West.[17]

The regionalist logic may be applied to many other examples. In El Salvador, as has been argued persuasively, continued guerrilla insurgency is fueled by lack of agrarian reform and by political repression.[18] In the Horn of Africa, the arbitrary colonial drawing of boundaries significantly contributed to the Somalia-Ethiopia conflict over the Ogaden region. In the Middle East, conflict between Iran and Iraq is fueled, in part, by opposing and hostile interpretations of Islam (Shiite for the former and Sunni for the latter). In short, the argument of regionalist logic is that, although the importance of Soviet involvement in a particular region must be recognized, the East-West dimension of a conflict should be deemphasized in favor of its regional dimension. By overplaying the East-West dimension of a Third World conflict, the United States is usually forced to take a side, unnecessarily and unproductively alienating one or more of the belligerents.[19]

3. *Increasing nonviability of military force in achieving long-term U.S. foreign policy goals in the Third World.* The international system and the role of direct military intervention therein by the major powers has changed substantially since the end of World War II. First, one is struck by the way unwritten norms governing the use of military force have been altered in the post–World War II period. For example, when the government of Nicaragua did not pay its debts in the 1930s, the United States sent in its marines to force payment. Yet, it is extremely difficult to conceive of Washington in 1989 dispatching the marines should either Mexico or Brazil decide to default on its substantial loan repayment to the West in general and to the United States in particular. As the interdependence theorists correctly have noted, although military force is "ultimately necessary to guarantee [national] survival" and is therefore a "central component of national power," it is "often not an appropriate way of achieving other goals (such as economic and ecological welfare) that are becoming more important."[20]

A more important constraint is found in the evolution of the Third World itself, whereby former colonial empires have evolved into a system of independent states of widely varying and increasing levels of power. Although the major powers of the colonial era, including the United States, still predominate militarily within the international system, there can be no doubt of the increasing diffusion of power within the system as individual Third World countries acquire more sophisticated weapons systems. As one author has noted:

> Compared to the situation that the colonial powers found in the heydays of imperialism, when a small flotilla of gunboats could manhandle an ancient civilization or conquer disorganized territories, many of today's Third World states wield much more formidable degrees of organized power. . . . While most Third World states may not yet be powerful enough to guarantee their own sovereignty, it has certainly become more problematical for foreign powers arbitrarily to impose their will upon them.[21]

U.S. involvement in the Vietnam War is especially instructive. Whatever lessons may be drawn from U.S. intervention in Vietnam—indeed, there are as many conflicting interpretations as there are days in a month[22]—two themes in particular stand out: (1) Even the most sophisticated levels of military technology make victory against popular revolutionary nationalism, at the least, highly unlikely and, at the most, prohibitively costly; and (2) the American people are not willing to support protracted, direct U.S. military intervention in the Third World. Although the latter condition could potentially change sometime in the future, the former is likely to persist.

4. *U.S. inability to control Third World nationalism*. U.S. intervention against revolutionary nationalism in the Third World is based upon the assumption that revolutionary elites are extremely vulnerable to the political wishes of a dominant external power (such as the Soviet Union) in the sense of becoming a "tool" for international communism. *The Pentagon Papers*, for example, dismissed the possibility that Ho Chi Minh or Mao Zedong could be both nationalists and communists.[23] Despite the more sophisticated view of the fragmented nature of international communism that exists in Washington in the 1980s—a result primarily of U.S. recognition of the enduring Sino-Soviet split—U.S. policymakers still view with suspicion Third World leaders seeking close relationships with the Soviet Union. This "tool-for-communism" thesis is dubious at best. Although Soviet allies such as Cuba surely follow the Soviet lead when such a course is viewed in Cuba's own national interests, these common interests should not be construed as Soviet control or ability to dictate policy. History is replete with examples of former so-called Soviet client states—including China, Egypt, Ghana, Indonesia, Somalia, and Sudan—that have expelled the Soviets when the Soviet presence became inimical to the client states' foreign policy interests. In Third World politics, self-interest and nationalism are stronger than ideological affinity.

The importance of nationalism and self-interested elites in stemming Soviet influence in the Third World is also relevant to U.S. special relationships with various Third World regimes. As is suggested by Panamanian General Manuel Noriega's purported sharing of U.S. military secrets with Cuba, his involvement in the international drug trade, and his clear defiance of U.S. demands in 1988 that he step down, U.S. client states may act against the wishes of Washington. Some authors have argued that, in fact, a case of "reverse dependency" often exists in which the United States falls prey to the demands or interests of the client state.[24] Indeed, a more apt description of Third World elites is that they are relatively autonomous actors who may act contrary to the wishes of either the Soviet Union or the United States.

The failure of U.S. policymakers to comprehend their limited power in controlling Third World nationalism has been especially acute concerning its populist revolutionary variant. Despite Castro's political and economic excesses by Western standards, there should have been little doubt in Washington in 1959 that his revolution generated mass support and ignited Cuban nationalism. Rather than accept the legitimacy of Castro's revolution, the United States attempted to isolate the regime diplomatically, initiated a trade embargo, authorized assassination attempts, and ultimately managed the unsuccessful Bay of Pigs invasion of the island in 1961 by CIA (Central Intelligence Agency)-trained exiles. Rather than overthrow Castro, these actions served as focal points whereby Castro strengthened his position on the island by whipping up "anti-yankee" nationalism and painting those elements still opposed to his rule as mere lackeys of U.S. imperialism. The lesson to draw from this—which should become the guiding principle for U.S. relations with revolutionary nationalism—is simple: "When a regime has any large degree of popular support and legitimacy, a foreign state's force, pressure, and propaganda directed against the country may only cause the people to rally around their government."[25]

5. *Need for greater U.S. tolerance of social change in the Third World, regardless of ideology.* Despite the heritage of the United States as a revolutionary nation that fought against oppression and external control, U.S. policymakers have consistently failed to understand the growth of this phenomena in the Third World. Although the original intent of the Monroe Doctrine, as enunciated in 1823, was to protect Central American revolutions from external influence, these revolutions, and the economic and political instability that accompanied them, were increasingly viewed by U.S. policymakers as injurious to U.S. interests.[26] This regional antirevolutionary propensity became globalized and fused with a virulent anticommunism as the United States embarked on an ideological competition with the Soviet Union at the end of World War II. The net result is that all U.S. administrations in the post–World War II period have been hostile in varying degrees to revolutionary change in the Third World, combining antagonism toward radical regimes with support for traditional authoritarian allies, often with dire consequences for U.S. foreign policy.

The key to U.S. tolerance of social change is recognition that opposing ideologies should not automatically preclude mutually beneficial relationships and that similar ideologies should not automatically provide the basis for strong U.S. support. Indeed, growing U.S. ties with Marxist Mozambique, despite U.S. conservative calls to support a noncommunist guerrilla insurgency titled the Mozambique National Resistance (RENAMO),[27] demonstrate that fruitful relationships can be sought with revolutionary communist regimes. To the contrary, the downfall of Fulgencio Batista's Cuban regime and the fallout then experienced by the United States underscores the dangers in supporting a traditional dictator who, although joining the United States in its anticommunist crusade, rules through a repressive regime marked by immense social inequality.

■ OVERVIEW

This book is divided into five major sections. The first three provide analysis concerning the origins, tools, and constraints on U.S. intervention in the Third World, and the final two comprise the case studies and a concluding essay.

Part 2, "Origins of Intervention," begins with Lloyd C. Gardner's chapter on the evolution of the interventionist impulse. Gardner shows how the American revolutionary spirit and western continental expansion spawned a mythic belief in the universalism and innocence of the U.S. cause, which led to extracontinental expansion in the early part of the twentieth century and the globalization of U.S. intervention in the Third World in the immediate post–World War II period. Michael T. Klare, in Chapter 3, continues this historical perspective, tracing the origins and evolution during the post–World War II period of the military doctrine of low-intensity conflict (LIC). Klare also examines the application of LIC to direct and indirect U.S. military involvement during the 1980s and beyond in five types of operations in the Third World: counterinsurgency, proinsurgency, peacetime contingency operations, terrorism counteraction, and antidrug operations. He notes that U.S. military strategy in the 1980s rests on two fundamental assumptions: (1) Vital U.S. interests are threatened by radical and revolutionary violence in the Third World; and (2) the United States must be prepared to use military force to protect its vital interests in the Third World. In Chapter 4, Charles F. Doran examines the nature of the globalist-regionalist debate surrounding the proper role of U.S. intervention in the Third World. Whereas globalists stress "the primacy of East-West confrontation at all levels of international political behavior, in all parts of the international system," regionalists emphasize "the dilemmas of North-South relations, the idiosyncracies of politics and culture within the various geographic regions, and the comparative autonomy of the struggles that go on within and between the states inside each of these regions." The differences between these divergent perspectives are discussed within three broad categories: the origins of change and stability; foreign policy purpose; and foreign policy strategy and means.

Part 3 centers on the different instruments of intervention that have been employed by the United States in the pursuit of foreign policy goals in the Third World. Each author explores how Washington's use of a particular instrument has changed or evolved during the post–World War II period, presents the field of case studies in which it has been employed, and asks why it has been successful or unsuccessful. In Chapter 5, Doug Bandow examines Washington's use of official economic and military aid to Third World governments in pursuit of

U.S. foreign policy goals. Kimberly A. Elliott, in Chapter 6, reviews fifty-four cases of U.S. implementation of economic sanctions, defined as the "deliberate government-inspired withdrawal, or threat of withdrawal, of *customary* . . . trade or financial relations." In Chapter 7, Harry Howe Ransom examines U.S. covert intervention in the Third World, including assassination plots, coups d'état, election intervention, and propaganda or psychological warfare. In Chapter 8, Peter J. Schraeder examines Washington's use of paramilitary intervention, or external economic and military aid to an armed insurgency intent on overthrowing a government deemed inimical to U.S. foreign policy interests. This interventionist tool is made use of by the Reagan Doctrine—U.S. support for guerrilla insurgencies attempting to overthrow Soviet-supported Marxist regimes in Afghanistan, Angola, Cambodia, and Nicaragua. Ted Galen Carpenter, in Chapter 9, reviews Washington's use of the ultimate interventionist tool: direct U.S. military force in the Third World.

Part 4 consists of four chapters centering on the domestic and international constraints inhibiting successful U.S. intervention in the Third World. In Chapter 10, Jerel A. Rosati presents an analysis of the U.S. domestic environment, exploring how a domestic consensus built upon the twin themes of anticommunism and containment of the Soviet Union has favored an interventionist Third World policy led by the executive branch during much of the post–World War II period. U.S. involvement in Vietnam shattered this consensus, however, making it increasingly difficult for presidents to continue implementing interventionist policies and leading "to such crises of leadership and legitimacy as Watergate, the Iran hostage crisis, and the Iran-contra scandal." In Chapter 11, Stephen Daggett analyzes significant barriers to the effective application of U.S. force that persist in the U.S. government—especially within the military establishment—despite recent efforts by some elements of the political leadership and by parts of the military to prepare for armed responses to conflict in the Third World. Factors discussed include the interplay between bureaucracy and ideology, priority of large-war planning in the military establishment, bureaucratic politics, and interservice rivalries. In Chapter 12, Harry Piotrowski argues that the evolving structure of the international system increasingly inhibits successful U.S. intervention in the Third World. He focuses on resurgent nationalism and anticolonialism, indigenous applications of Marxism-Leninism, communist polycentrism, proliferation of both conventional and nuclear weapons, the rise of regional powers, and the relative decline of U.S. economic and military power. In Chapter 13, Christopher C. Joyner examines the role of international law and of the internationally accepted norms of intervention and nonintervention. Joyner argues that U.S. policymakers have adopted "convenient legal license to interpret international law such that it serves their own interests as a supportive foreign policy instrument rather than as a force of restraint conducive to a greater public world order."

The case studies presented in Part 5 provide an overview of U.S. interventionist practices in five Third World countries. Each case study includes a description of the historical nature and evolution of the particular country's relationship with the United States, the instruments that the United States has adopted in pursuit of specific foreign policy goals, why these have been successful or unsuccessful, and general lessons that may be drawn from U.S. involvement. In Chapter 14, Eric Hooglund examines U.S. intervention in Iran, ranging from the landing of 30,000 U.S. troops in that country during World War II, to U.S. involvement in the 1953 coup d'état that restored the shah to power, to U.S. relations with the revolutionary and Islamic fundamentalist government of the Ayatollah Khomeini. In Chapter 15, Richard J. Kessler focuses on the U.S.-Philippine relationship as it evolved from colonialism at the end of the nineteenth century to development of the patron-client relationship with President Ferdinand Marcos and culminated in the democratic revolution led by Corazon Aquino. Peter Kornbluh, in Chapter 16, analyzes the equally extensive U.S.-Nicaraguan relationship, focusing on how the United States has dealt with what it perceived to be radical revolution led by the Sandinistas in Washington's backyard. Indeed, Washington's support for the contras provided the principal battlefield for the U.S. military's LIC strategy and served as the test case for the Reagan Doctrine. In Chapter 17, Tony Thorndike examines the October 25, 1983, U.S. direct military intervention in Grenada to overthrow the Marxist revolutionary government of General Hudson Austin. In Chapter 18, R. Hunt Davis, Jr., and Gwendolen M. Carter examine U.S. policy toward the apartheid regime of South Africa, tracing its evolution from U.S. complacency and quiet willingness to work with the white minority regime in the 1960s to increasing intervention as U.S. domestic groups have successfully lobbied for the imposition of economic sanctions. In the final chapter, Peter J. Schraeder draws several conclusions concerning U.S. intervention in the Third World.

■ Part 2

ORIGINS OF INTERVENTION

2

The Evolution of the Interventionist Impulse

Lloyd C. Gardner

From the first stirrings of nationhood in the middle of the eighteenth century, Americans fixed their gaze outward. It could hardly have been otherwise. Born into an empire that had achieved preeminence among world powers by defeating the French in the Great War for Empire, 1754–1763, leaders in the thirteen colonies on the Atlantic coast expectantly looked forward to exploiting that position to add new lands and wealth to British North America. When London blocked westward expansion, the colonial elite transformed themselves into American nationalists and risked a war of independence rather than abandon their pretensions. Even in the darker moments of the American Revolution, visions of a new empire of liberty extending northward to Canada, southward to Central America and the Caribbean, and westward across the continent fired the cause with a belief in what would be called, in the middle of the following century, the United States' Manifest Destiny.[1]

Fervent belief in Manifest Destiny ensured rapid expansion beyond the initial confines of the thirteen colonies as French and Spanish claims were eliminated by the Louisiana Purchase and the 1819 Trans-Continental Treaty, the British relinquished Oregon, the Mexicans were forced to yield up California, and Russia sold Alaska. By 1900, moreover, Manifest Destiny included expansion beyond the North American continent and produced the Monroe Doctrine, Caribbean hegemony, and acquisition of an island chain across the Pacific to outermost Asia. At the end of World War II, what had been foretold by the American Revolution seemed fulfilled. A French diplomat noted dourly, in 1945, that the United States appeared to interest itself "in everything that was taking place" and further stated that at the recent graduating exercises at Annapolis the new naval officers had "dipped their rings in a vase of water from the seven seas, whereas previously the water for this ritual had come from the Atlantic, the Pacific, and the Caribbean."[2]

■ THE REVOLUTIONARY SPIRIT AND WESTERN EXPANSIONISM

Private fortune and public responsibility went hand in hand in early American expansionist visions. And like other challengers to old ways, Americans had a tendency to believe a special virtue accompanied their ambitions. But prospects for the colonies in commerce and westward expansion suddenly dimmed when London made it clear that the mother country had no intention of turning the West over to the colonials to do with as they pleased. Major disputes arose as Britain pursued colonial reorganization in an effort to make the colonies pay the costs of their own defense, including those associated with the recently concluded Great War for Empire and the continuing conflict with native American Indians. This policy gave rise to suspicions that the mother country was even indifferent to the dangers of "creeping Catholicism" from culturally different French Canada.

What had only yesterday seemed a glorious banner—the British Union Jack—now appeared to symbolize repression and corruption. The bolder colonials were soon debating independence in courthouses and taverns. Behind the irksome restrictions London imposed on colonial trade and the mother country's suddenly timid attitude toward the Indians—it was now being said—lurked a calculated effort to deprive the colonies of their future.

Nearly two hundred years later, Secretary of State Dean Acheson explained how the Founding Fathers had arrived at the conclusion that independence was the only solution. "The whole mercantile system was irritating," he began a brief postprandial lesson for fellow diplomats,

> whereby trade had to go through the center at London and could not take place directly between the colonies and other trading points. . . . At every point they were met by restrictions imposed on the ruling, powerful, directing groups by a government which was far away and, most important of all, had shown its inability to govern. . . . What happens when people who want to resist want support? They generalize their position. They don't ask support to fight against timber restrictions. They talk about taxation without representation, and each generalization leads to broader generalizations. Until finally they get to the broadest generalization; which is that all men are created equal.[3]

So it seemed at the time to Benjamin Franklin. Like the Virginia planter George Washington, Franklin had heavy investments, both material and spiritual, in western lands. The Philadelphia printer, who by 1767 had risen to high office as deputy postmaster for the colonies, and who was regarded on both sides of the Atlantic as perhaps the best thinker the new world had produced, had developed a powerful vision of what settlements in the Illinois country would yield the Americans, with or without their British forebears. Occupation of that territory, he lectured correspondents in the mother country, would allow the holder to raise a force, "which on occasion of a future war, might easily be poured down the Mississippi upon the lower country, and into the Bay of Mexico, to be used against Cuba, or Mexico itself."[4] Even before they called upon the world to bear witness to the justice of their cause, by officially separating the thirteen colonies from British control in the Declaration of Independence on July 4, 1776, colonial leaders had authorized an attack on British Canada, ordering a hastily assembled army to march northwards in 1775 to overthrow British rule.

The Canadian invasion, like the wars resulting from the French and Russian revolutions, was motivated as much by ideological factors as by military questions. And although the American Revolution did not witness the same profound social upheavals as those in France or Russia, the urge to carry forward its ideals on bayonets gradually melted into what in the nineteenth century would come to be known as Manifest Destiny. In that narrow sense, the "revolutionary spirit" lasted longer in the United States than it did after the Napoleonic Wars or after Stalin's consolidation of Bolshevist Russia into socialism in one state.[5]

As ambassador to France, a key post in the Revolutionary War, Benjamin Franklin devoted himself tirelessly to the game of nations in order to achieve both Canada and the Mississippi for an envisioned American empire on the North American continent. During the protracted peace negotiations, he was adamant that the Mississippi be the new country's western boundary. When the treaty was ready, Franklin and the other negotiators bragged that although the new nation's allies, France and Spain, had sought to "coop up" the Americans, the treaty boundaries "appear to leave us little to complain of and not much to desire."[6]

Actually, the Americans desired a lot more. Franklin had even suggested that it would be "advisable" for the British to cede Canada if they wanted to gain the goodwill of the United States. London laughed at such pretensions. When the Americans came to their senses, they would see that their only option would be to buy their way back into the empire, at least economically, with such concessions as king and Parliament might deem proper for the privilege of trading with His Majesty's subjects in the home islands or anywhere else in the empire.

The shock of independence in a world dominated by mercantilist theory and still-powerful empires did, in fact, sober the Americans. Until things were straightened out at home, it was now argued by those who demanded a strong central government, it was necessary to put aside thoughts of Canada, Florida, and the West Indies. Those who met at the Federal Constitutional Convention in Philadelphia in 1787 to remedy the supposed excesses of individual state action, as George Washington would put it, were divided on many questions. But they all saw a new constitution as an absolute necessity for foreign policy. The Founding Fathers granted the executive powers therein that only a few years before would have been unthinkable, as is clearly demonstrated by the weak federal government established under the original Articles of Confederation ratified in 1781.

The controversial "imperial presidency" was not an invention of post–World War II occupants of the White House. The U.S. Constitution, as every president from Washington on understood, gave the executive a decisive edge over Congress in making foreign policy. When he assumed office in 1801, President Thomas Jefferson declared that the nation had escaped tyranny (which he blamed on Federalist excesses) only because of its large territory. Albert Gallitin, Jefferson's secretary of the treasury, who knew a good deal about frontier democracy, agreed absolutely: "If the cause of the happiness of this country was examined into, it would be found to arise as much from the great plenty of land in proportion to the inhabitants . . . as from the wisdom of their political institutions."[7]

In 1803, Jefferson annexed the Louisiana territory to the United States—almost an empire unto itself—and for $15 million provided the nation with unlimited navigation of the Mississippi River, thereby assuring control of the restless westerners and a strategic position for projecting U.S. power and democracy abroad. Jefferson embodied the fervent belief in the U.S. cause: "Our southern defensive force can take the Floridas, volunteers for a Mexican army will flock to our standard, and rich pabulum will be offered to our privateers in the plunder of their commerce and coasts. Probably Cuba would add itself to our confederation."[8]

A chronicler of the westward movement, Patricia Nelson Limerick, noted that although historians have come to terms with the legacy of slavery, they have yet to do so with the legacy of conquest by which Americans moved across the continent:

> To most twentieth-century Americans, the legacy of slavery was serious business, while the legacy of conquest was not. . . . Conquest took another route into national memory. In the popular imagination, the reality of conquest dissolved into stereotypes of noble savages and noble pioneers struggling quaintly in the wilderness. These adventures seemed to have no bearing on the complex realities of twentieth-century America.[9]

The rationales for U.S. expansionism are not unique; similar stereotypes and rationalizations (which Limerick insightfully calls foundations for an "Empire of Innocence") are notable throughout European writings on Africa and Asia. Not uniqueness, but the deceptive ease of conquest sets the U.S. historical tradition apart, providing Americans with both a false sense of security about their past and an illusory notion that all foreign policy questions are somehow capable of being resolved expeditiously—like Jefferson's straightforward solution to the threatened closing of the port of New Orleans: Buy Louisiana.[10] That sense of security and belief in a unique American innocence, exalted by all U.S. presidents, is captured in President Ronald Reagan's second inaugural address in 1985, in which he called upon Americans to heed the "echoes of our past" to meet the challenges of the future: "The men of the Alamo call out encouragement to each other; a settler pushes west and sings his song, and the song echoes out forever and fills the unknowing air. It is the American sound: It is hopeful, bighearted, idealistic—daring, decent and fair. That's our heritage, that's our song. We sing it still. For all our problems, our differences, we are together as of old."[11]

After direct conflict between the United States and Great Britain in the War of 1812, which did not exactly conform to these legendary accounts, and which required promoting some rather dubious victories to boost confidence and erase the memory that the British had burned Washington, the United States found itself in the fortunate position of being able to take advantage of revolutions in Central and South America. The successful quest of Latin American nations for independence from Spain and Portugal allowed the United States to detach Florida from Madrid by diplomatic pressure (and less well known military pressure exerted by Andrew Jackson) and then boldly to announce the Monroe Doctrine in 1823. The doctrine declared that henceforth the Western Hemisphere was closed to European colonization and that European states must refrain from intervening in Latin American affairs. Though the Monroe Doctrine was unenforceable without the British fleet standing behind U.S. rhetoric of regional hegemony, the legend grew that the United States had put an end to European intriguing in the Western Hemisphere and had intervened successfully in world politics to protect democracy against repression.

All revolutions spawn a mythic belief in the universality of their cause and the dangerous conviction that the world eagerly awaits an opportunity to participate in its fulfillment. In the case of the French Revolution—and later, the Russian Revolution—this myth was dispelled rather soon. Attempts to universalize those revolutions through territorial expansion, behind the slogans "Liberty, Equality, and Fraternity" and "All Power to the Soviets," met with overpowering resistance at those nations' borders. Not so in the case of the United States. The Mexican War of 1846, even with its vested and ambiguous origins in the slave controversy and its blatantly imperialist character (indeed, an incident was manufactured to bring on the war: U.S. forces occupied Mexican-claimed territories), because of the ease of the U.S. conquest, confirmed basic aspects of the American belief in the nation's Manifest Destiny and in the Empire of Innocence.

The men at the Alamo fit into the legend of an Empire of Innocence, but the reality of the Mexican War a decade later rested upon an opportunistic view that Mexico was about to disintegrate, and the time was right to gain California. According to the last president of the short-lived Texas republic, Anson Jones, war resulted when President James K. Polk decided to "consummate views of conquest which had been entertained probably for years, bringing down an army and a navy upon us, when there was not a hostile foot, either Indian or Mexican, in Texas; not (as afterwards became apparent) to *protect* Texas . . .

but to insure a *collision* with Mexico."[12] In the 1848 Treaty of Guadalupe Hidalgo, which ended the war, Mexico was forced to cede two-fifths of its territory to the United States.

Until the American Civil War in 1861, wrote historian Henry Adams (the first of his illustrious family to find irony history's most compelling lesson), the nation's foreign affairs had encompassed a single general principle: "the steady absorption of all the neighboring territory."[13] The ease of expansion had permitted Americans to carry forward the revolution while maintaining a "loose and separately responsible division of government."[14]

Lincoln preserved the Union, the first truly defensive move of the U.S. empire since the Revolutionary War, only by using every power granted by the Constitution against a "foreign" power. His secretary of state, William H. Seward, declared that a Confederate success would so upset "the equilibrium of the nations, maintained by this republic,"[15] that no one could be sure that mankind would even have another chance. Seward further stated:

> Dissolution would not only arrest but it would extinguish the greatness of our country; it would drop the curtain before all our national heroes. . . . Public prosperity would give place to retrogression, for standing armies would consume our substance; and our liberty, now as wide as our grand territorial dimensions, would be succeeded by the hateful and intolerable espionage of military despotism.[16]

It was Seward, of course, who negotiated in 1867 the Alaska purchase from Russia—nearly 600,000 square miles, the single largest addition to U.S. territory since the Louisiana Purchase. According to Seward, adding Alaska to an expanding United States was necessary for commercial purposes. Time and again he would say that it had become the objective of the United States to contest for "the commerce of the world, which is the empire of the world."[17]

Having purged itself of the debilitating influence of slave power through defeat of the South's attempt at secession from the Union, the United States could go forward with commercial expansion unencumbered politically and uplifted morally by the terrible blood sacrifice of war and martyrdom. Seward had foreseen all this in an 1852 speech on the great commercial future of the United States in Asia:

> Who does not see that this movement must effect our own complete emancipation from what remains of European influence and prejudice, and in turn develop the American opinion and influence which shall remould constitutions, laws, and customs in the land that is first greeted by the rising sun? Sir, although I am no socialist, no dreamer of a suddenly coming millennium, I nevertheless cannot reject the hope that peace is now to have her sway.[18]

■ EXPANSION BEYOND THE NORTH AMERICAN CONTINENT

Seward's purchase of Alaska represented a thrust into Asia that prefigured events of three decades later once considered accidental byproducts of the 1898 Spanish-American War. Since the 1850s, U.S. policymakers had wanted to get Spain out of Cuba. Unfortunately for expansionists, the larger aims of diplomacy became enmeshed in the "filibustering" expeditions operating out of New Orleans at midcentury, including the ill-fated and confused attempt of William Walker to conquer Nicaragua for a new slave state and the attempt to purchase Cuba for the same reason.[19]

The time was still not right for such expansion immediately after the Civil War. Political conflicts during Reconstruction (the reorganization and reintegration of the defeated Confederacy with the Union) were a vital factor in curbing the expansionist impulse and prevented President Ulysses S. Grant from achieving his goal of annexing Santo Domingo, a former Spanish colony in the Caribbean. Grant's ambitions were caught in a political cross-fire between conservative and radical views: Whereas conservatives opposed annexation on the grounds that the "colored" peoples of the Caribbean and Central America—unlike the Native Americans of the U.S. West—would not be a "vanishing race," radicals, also opposed to annexation, felt that such efforts would divert the government from its primary task of Reconstruction. In short, both groups had little taste for taking on new racial problems when they could not solve ones closer to home. But when Cuban nationalists rose up against Spain in the 1890s, the situation had changed. Eager for commercial expansion in both the Caribbean and the Pacific, U.S. leaders championed the revolutions against Spanish colonial rule in Cuba and in the Philippines.

War came when the United States demanded revenge for the 1898 sinking of the U.S.S. *Maine* in Havana Harbor, an incident blamed on the Spanish, whose culpability was never proved and was later disputed. The fruits of U.S. victory included Cuba, Guam, the Philippines, and Puerto Rico. The brief "imperialist" debate of 1898–1900, when Americans divided over the question of what to do with Cuba and the Philippines, ended when the administration of William McKinley convinced enough people that its foreign policy objectives—protection of U.S. economic and security interests—did not require extensive additions of territory or the incorporation into the U.S. political system of large numbers of "subject peoples" of "alien race."

The Cuban question, for example, was resolved rather quickly by U.S. adaptation of the European protectorate form of imperialism, though it was never recognized as such. Unlike direct colonial control, protectorate status means that the territory retains nominal sovereignty and its people do not become citizens of the conquering nation. The work of General Leonard S. Wood and the U.S. Army in improving health conditions in the former Spanish colony eased the minds of those who still felt any qualms about the terms whereby Cuba was granted its semiindependence.

Cuba became the model for a series of U.S. interventions in the Caribbean area in the first two decades of the twentieth century; these interventions were designed to protect the interests of U.S. property holders (actual and projected) and the entrances to a long-planned isthmian canal. "The people ask me what we mean by a stable government in Cuba," General Wood wrote the secretary of war, Elihu Root. "I tell them that when money can be borrowed at a reasonable rate of interest and when capital is willing to invest in the Island, a condition of stability will have been reached."[20] When the nominally independent Cuban government accepted a treaty guaranteeing the United States the right to intervene to restore order, the troops that had been sent to the island to overthrow Spanish misrule came home. But they returned whenever danger threatened. Under the terms of the Platt Amendment as inserted into the American-Cuban Treaty of 1903, the United States retained the right to keep a military base on the island—it is still there (Guantanamo Bay)—and the right to oversee Cuban financial matters, at least in regard to foreign debt. Similar treaties, establishing "customs house" protectorates, were also sought with Haiti, Nicaragua, and Santo Domingo. When these sometimes failed, as in Haiti in 1915, the U.S. Marines came back—to stay as long as a decade, or more.

President Woodrow Wilson's policies, although paved with good intentions, followed in the interventionist path established by his predecessors. Rejecting crude bids by Haitian politicians to avoid U.S. intervention by awarding economic concessions to selected interests, Secretary of State William Jennings Bryan declared: "While we desire to encourage in every proper way American investments in Haiti, we believe that this can be better done by contributing to stability and order than by favoring special concessions to Americans."[21] Yet, while Wilson waged war against the Central Powers to secure the right of self-determination for small countries under the hegemony of Germany and Austria, U.S. forces intervened throughout the Western Hemisphere to establish reliable governments. Mexico became a test case for Wilson's oft-stated belief that he could teach the Latin Americans to elect good men who would pursue the same goals as elected leaders in advanced industrial societies. But, having sent the marines to Vera Cruz in 1914 and General John Pershing into northern Mexico in 1916, Wilson came to realize that stability usually was not enhanced by foreign bayonets.

World War I gave these hemispheric interventions a strongly strategic cast in much historical writing about the era. But this was often post facto rationalization. Robert Lansing, Bryan's successor, had before the outbreak of the war authored a memorandum on the modern meaning of the Monroe Doctrine, which summed up U.S. concerns about the security of the Western Hemisphere. The presumed right to intervene under the Monroe Doctrine should not be lightly abandoned, said Lansing. "With the present industrial activity, the scramble for markets, and the incessant search for new opportunities to produce wealth, commercial expansion and success are closely interwoven with political domination over the territory."[22]

If Cuba served as the prototype for hemispheric intervention, retaining the Philippines, deemed essential to gaining access to the vast market of China, involved a more complicated procedure. The suppression of Philippine guerrillas under General Emiliano Aguinaldo's leadership proved costly in a number of ways. Defeating Spain had taken three months; establishing U.S. rule took 125,000 soldiers and cost $160 million. In the process 5,000 U.S. soldiers and an estimated 200,000 Filipinos died, some from wounds and most as a result of a war-induced famine.

One of the last barriers to the full realization of the imperialist program—the U.S. Constitution—was removed as an obstacle by a series of rulings between 1901 and 1904: the "insular cases," whereby the U.S. Supreme Court accepted the McKinley administration's arguments that the Constitution did not follow the flag (that is, occupants of conquered territories did not enjoy the rights of U.S. citizens). This issue had been hidden under the surface since the debate over the annexation of Santo Domingo in Grant's day. If, as had been the case in westward expansion, new territories had to become states, all sorts of problems arose to confront the expansionists—the race question, for one. Wide powers to rule newly acquired territories were needed, powers that might deny occupants the rights of U.S. citizens under the Constitution, the attorney general argued, because in the future the United States might need to become involved "in Egypt, the Sudan, Central Africa, or a spot in the Antarctic Circle, or a section of the Chinese Empire."[23]

Expansionist voices drowned out the doubters. Typical of the time was an editorial in the *Army and Navy Journal,* which proclaimed about the Philippine action: "While it is true that a people have a certain right to say what shall be done in a political way on their own soil, it is equally true that a narrow-minded race have not the right to shut out from use by other peoples vast natural resources."[24]

Wilson strove mightily during the peace negotiations at the end of World War I to reinvigorate a "liberal" worldview that would produce agreement among the industrial nations to exercise collective self-restraint in dealing with places like China, thereby removing, he hoped, the basic causes of the tragic cycle of imperial competition, war, and violent revolution. Essential to this worldview was recognition of the principle of self-determination and the creation of the League of Nations. These two themes were embodied in the Treaty of Versailles, the most important of five treaties ending World War I. Wilson believed that once the industrial powers—following his leadership—established the rules of the game, the increasingly dangerous situation between the industrial powers and the rest of the world could be ameliorated. After the war, Wilson told a delegation of Mexican newspaper editors that all nations would be held to strictly accountable standards of behavior, "because so soon as you can admit your own capital and the capital of the world to the free use of the resources of Mexico, it will be one of the most wonderfully rich and prosperous countries in the world."[25]

Wilson's effort to be in the world but not of it produced such paradoxes as U.S. intervention in Mexico before World War I and in Siberia in 1918, as the war came to an end—both in the name of making the world safe for democracy. Having tried out something similar in Mexico, with far less than satisfactory results, U.S. troops were sent to Asian Russia both to check Japanese imperial ambitions and to support spontaneous efforts by local governments to resist revolutionary leader V. I. Lenin's efforts to consolidate the Russian Revolution. Good sense prevailed—especially as the Bolsheviks eliminated their rivals—and U.S. military intervention in Russia came to an end. But a picture of communist intrigues had been established, and, very soon, Washington policymakers were blaming their failures in Mexico and elsewhere on Soviet-inspired communist agents who, it appeared, were capable of influencing the course of political affairs in every far-off place around the globe.

U.S. withdrawal from European political affairs following the failure of the Treaty of Versailles to gain Senate approval signaled a change in approach—but not isolationism, as was once commonly argued.[26] Seeking to untangle centuries of European diplomacy, now overlaid with revolutionary passions, the Wilsonians had lost their way. Not wanting the responsibility for enforcing the peace treaty's punitive clauses against Germany, largely out of fear of destroying the only reliable barrier blocking a perceived expansionist Soviet Union, the United States used its new financial power in an independent attempt to reshape world politics, much as British economic power had been exercised in the aftermath of the French Revolution and the Napoleonic Wars.[27]

The plan to use financial power fell victim to accumulated ills, with the Great Depression and the subsequent collapse of worldwide financial markets applying the coup de grace to a half-realized vision of Wilsonian internationalism. A similar working relationship with the Japanese, an effort to curb competition in the Pacific area, also broke down under the strain of the depression. Of all the policies initiated in the 1920s, only President Herbert Hoover's retreat from overt interventionism in Central America lasted and became the Good Neighbor policy during President Franklin D. Roosevelt's domestic reform program known as the New Deal.

Isolationism is a better description of both the atmosphere and the policy trends of the 1930s than it ever was of the decade following World War I. But Adolf Hitler's ambitions for domination over Europe finally exceeded what the European democracies could afford to give away simply to keep the peace. With war looming in 1939, Dean Acheson spoke at Yale University on the U.S. predicament. The principal source of trouble, Acheson noted, was Britain's faltering economic power. "We can see that British naval power no longer can establish security of life and investment in distant parts of the world, and a localization of conflict nearer at home."[28]

■ GLOBALIZATION OF INTERVENTION

Ever since the promulgation of the Monroe Doctrine, U.S. policies had been at least partially underwritten by British naval power. World War II put an end to that support. U.S. policymakers, inheriting the fruits of a fallen Europe-centric system that had been dominant in international affairs since the sixteenth century, perceived the Soviet Union as a distinctive challenge to U.S. goals in the postwar world. This perception fueled an intense ideological competition that came to be known as the cold war. U.S. leaders welcomed the opportunity to take on this challenge. President Harry S. Truman reconfirmed that message in the speech he delivered before Congress on March 12, 1947, asking for $500 million to aid Greece and Turkey, the former threatened by a communist insurgency. Truman said that it "must" be U.S. policy to support all nations seeking to resist "attempted subjugation by armed minorities or by outside pressures."[29] The sweeping nature of Truman's new doctrine, both in regard to its extent—apparently global—and in respect to the assumption that it would be possible to determine when "attempted subjugation" was under way (as opposed to indigenous revolutionary tumult), caused some concern even within a Congress that was militantly anticommunist and anti–Soviet Union.

Dean Acheson tried to reassure the Senate Foreign Relations Committee that the administration was aware of the limits on intervention or, as it would soon be called, "containment," but committee members were not so sure. Senator Alexander Wiley confessed, for example, that he was "in doubt as to which way to go," and Senator Walter F. George pondered the implications of leaving the United Nations on the sidelines in favor of unilateral action:

> I do not see how we are going to escape going into Manchuria, North China, and Korea and doing things in that area of the world. . . . [W]e have got the right to exercise commonsense. But I know that when we make a policy of this kind we are irrevocably committing ourselves to a course of action, and there is no way to get out of it next week or next year. You go down to the end of the road.[30]

George's prescience did not lead the committee to oppose Truman, partly out of concern for the consequences in an unsettled world (even if the Soviets were *not* planning a campaign of subversion, might not a split in the U.S. government be too tempting to resist?); partly because the cold war had not yet shifted from Europe, with its traditional boundary lines, to the soon-to-be-called Third World; and partly because Americans now had the atom bomb, which added to the frontier-days legend of the ease of conquest.

The Korean War not only proved Senator George right, it also reinforced the Truman Doctrine worldview. The invasion of South Korea by the "communist" North, like the Chinese Revolution of 1949, was interpreted, wrongly and tragically, as an extension of Soviet power across the Eurasian landmass. Americans were predisposed to see in both events the Kremlin's dark hand, stretching out to take into the Soviet domain not only the Chinese but, beyond those vast borders, the industrial workshops of Asia, Japan, and the raw-materials areas of former European colonies.

The interventionist impulse, as it developed in the 1950s and 1960s, also worked from the premise of "nation-building." U.S. leaders, from the end of World War II to the fall of Saigon in 1975, justified intervention in the Third World as defense against communist expansion and convinced themselves that they best understood the needs of newly emerging areas. After all, the world system they had created to replace the wornout prewar structure that collapsed before the Japanese onslaught at Singapore in 1942 had originated in the first successful example of revolutionary nationalism: the American Revolution of 1776.

Presidents Harry S. Truman, Dwight D. Eisenhower, and John F. Kennedy celebrated U.S. exceptionalism without embarrassment as well as with a good deal of pride. Theirs was a nation with a privileged history: a history that had seen the United States progress across the North American continent largely uncontested, brushing aside overextended European empires, opening up the prairies and interning the remnants of Indian tribes, and swooping up vast mineral resources as they went along—finally, to make of the nation a land rich beyond previous human experience.

The one era in U.S. history that challenged certain of these assumptions, the Great Depression and New Deal years, was only a bad memory. After the almost traumatic experience of the limited experiment in self-containment during the early New Deal, U.S. policymakers, from the time of World War II to the 1980s, vowed never to return to isolationism, economic or political. Blocking Soviet expansionist thrusts was crucial, but U.S. leaders also undertook to restructure the world capitalist system on stronger foundations. The United States, said Dean Acheson around the time the Truman Doctrine was formulated, now found itself "far more dependent upon exports than before the war to maintain levels of business activity to which our economy has become accustomed." The nation's aid programs would have to be concentrated "in areas where it will be most effective in building world political and economic stability, in promoting human freedom and democratic institutions, in fostering liberal trading policies, and in strengthening the authority of the United Nations."[31]

If U.S. economic aid was to be concentrated in certain areas, the scope of interventionist operations to protect the security of this "free world" system could not be so restricted. The basic charter for U.S. covert operations around the world may be found in a policy paper prepared for the National Security Council (NSC) in early 1950. This famous paper (NSC-68) was drafted in the wake of the Soviet atom bomb, which signaled the end of the U.S. nuclear monopoly, and of the Chinese Revolution. Its authors had tried to strike a balance between the limits imposed on the means a free society might use without doing violence to its basic institutions and the requirements of meeting the challenge posed by the USSR's ability to exploit a still-chaotic world situation:

> In a shrinking world, which now faces the threat of atomic warfare, it is not an adequate objective merely to seek to check the Kremlin design, for the absence of order among nations is becoming less and less tolerable. . . . The integrity of our system will not be jeopardized by any measures, covert or overt, violent or non-violent, which serve the purpose of frustrating the Kremlin design, nor does the necessity for conducting ourselves so as to affirm our values in actions as well as words forbid such measures, provided only they are appropriately calculated to that end and are not so excessive or misdirected as to make us enemies of the people instead of the evil men who have enslaved them.[32]

From that paragraph written in 1950 to the oral testimony of Lieutenant Colonel Oliver North in the summer of 1987 in justification of the Iran-contra affair is no great leap, even if it is not exactly a straight line. In certain well-known instances, such as Vietnam in the 1950s and Chile in the 1970s, U.S. actions extended measures permitted under NSC-68 to the prevention of democratically elected regimes. In the case of Vietnam, Secretary of State John Foster Dulles simply ruled out all-Vietnamese elections in 1956 as required under the 1954 Geneva Agreement ending the Vietnamese war against the French. In the case of Chile, Secretary of State Henry Kissinger was reported to have said, "I don't see why we need to stand by and watch a country go communist due to the irresponsibility of its own people."[33]

In a discussion with congressional leaders at the height of the first Vietnam crisis in 1954 (how was the United States to respond to imminent French defeat at Dienbienphu at the hands of the communist insurgents?), President Eisenhower provided an explanation of what the United States sought with these interventions.

> The President said that every individual is the center of the universe so far as that individual is concerned; in the same manner, every nation is the center of the universe in working out its own problems. Yet, in a general sense . . . it is correct to say that the United States is the central key, the core of democracy, economically, militarily and spiritually. Consequently in simple terms, we are establishing international outposts where people can develop their strength to defend themselves. Here we are sitting in the center, and with high mobility and destructive forces we can swiftly respond when our vital interests are affected. We are trying . . . with these programs to build up for the United States a position in the world of freedom of action. . . . One of our greatest hopes . . . is to get our troops back home. As we get these other countries strengthened economically, to do their part to provide the ground forces to police and hold their own land, we come closer to the realization of our hopes. . . . [W]e cannot publicly call our Allies outposts . . . [but] we are trying to get that result.[34]

Eisenhower always had feared the consequences of a permanently mobilized society. He had sought to prevent that danger and its consequence, the dominance of the military/industrial complex, leading to financial insolvency as well as to political malaise. In the event, the reverse happened. The globalization of the interventionist impulse and its synthesis with an anticommunist ideology presaged not the demobilization of U.S. society during the postwar period, but rather the dominance of a national security culture increasingly committed to intervention abroad. The application of this interventionist ethos in the Third World (most noted by U.S. involvement in the Vietnam War), would, as the following chapters attest, have significant implications for both U.S. foreign policy and the U.S. domestic political system in the postwar period.

☐ 3

The Development of Low-Intensity Conflict Doctrine

Michael T. Klare

The U.S. Commission on Integrated Long-Term Strategy reported in January 1988 that nearly "all the armed conflicts of the past forty years have occurred in what is vaguely called the Third World" and that, although these conflicts may be less threatening than an all-out U.S.-Soviet confrontation, "they have had and will have an adverse cumulative effect on U.S. access to critical regions, on American credibility among allies and friends, and on American self-confidence." Because Third World challenges to U.S. interests are multiplying, moreover, "in the coming decades the United States will need to be better prepared to deal with conflicts in the Third World."[1]

The notion that U.S. interests are facing increased pressure in the Third World and that new military initiatives are needed to resist these threats became a prominent theme in U.S. strategic thinking in the late 1980s.[2] With the signing of an accord on the elimination of intermediate-range nuclear forces (the INF Treaty) and the accompanying decline in U.S.-Soviet tensions, many strategists have focused their attention on the growing incidence of "low-intensity conflict" (LIC)—that is, conflict falling below the threshold of full-scale combat between modern armies. "Since the end of World War II," Secretary of Defense Frank C. Carlucci wrote in 1988, "ambiguous aggression in the form of low-intensity conflict has become an increasing threat to our interests, as well as those of our allies and friends."[3]

To counter this challenge, Secretary Carlucci recommended an increase in U.S. military and economic aid to threatened allies in the Third World, along with a significant buildup of U.S. "power projection" forces—forces intended for rapid insertion into distant Third World areas. As part of this effort, Carlucci also urged the further expansion of U.S. Special Operations Forces—the army's Green Berets, the navy's SEALs, and similar groups—plus continued U.S. support for anticommunist guerrillas in the Third World. Such measures were essential, he argued, because "LIC is one of the most serious challenges we face today, and our survival and well-being depend on how we comprehend the threat and respond to it."[4]

Such alarmism, and the attendant calls for improvements in U.S. interventionist capabilities, has been a recurring phenomenon in post–World War II U.S. history. Although nuclear issues and the U.S.-Soviet arms race have dominated the strategic landscape, regional conflict in the Third World has been a persistent concern of U.S. policymakers. This preoccupation with regional conflict reflects the large increase in U.S. trade with and investment in the Third World, along with a growing fear that Third World unrest and insurgency represents an essentially autonomous threat (that is, autonomous from the Soviet military threat) to U.S. interests. "Both an expansion of U.S. interests in the Third World and an increase in Third World conflicts have forced us to focus more attention there," Defense Secretary Caspar Weinberger declared in 1984. "Our economy and the economies of our allies are . . . especially susceptible to disruption from conflicts far from our shores."[5]

The ascendancy of such views in U.S. strategic thinking has been accompanied historically by increased U.S. military involvement in regional Third World conflicts. Because the United States appears to be in the initial stages of such a period today, it is important to examine the evolution of U.S. interventionist policy since World War II and its resurgence—in the form of LIC doctrine—in the 1980s.

■ THE TRUMAN DOCTRINE, KOREA, AND VIETNAM

In the years immediately following World War II, U.S. foreign policy was focused largely on the East-West struggle in Europe. Most of the early cold war crises arose from conflicting U.S. and Soviet positions on the postwar political order in Eastern Europe and on the status of Berlin. And, with the demobilization of the large U.S. armies established in the 1942–1945 period, U.S. strategy came to depend more and more on the use of nuclear weapons to offset the purported Soviet advantage in nonnuclear, "conventional" forces.

But although East-West issues dominated strategic thinking in the late 1940s, North-South concerns were not entirely absent from the political-military landscape. Indeed, two of the earliest crises of the postwar period—the emergence of a Soviet-backed republic in Azerbaijan (a northern province of Iran) and the civil war in Greece—were largely the products of revolutionary and separatist pressures indigenous to the Third World. That such events were generally perceived through the lens of East-West conflict (a pattern that has recurred periodically ever since) should not prevent us from seeing them as part of a succession of Third World upheavals.

The Greek civil war of 1946–1949 played an especially pivotal role in the evolution of U.S. policy. Although viewed by many historians as a quintessential expression of cold war hostilities, the Greek conflict actually had much in common with the Vietnam War both in military and political terms. Because the U.S. public was weary of war by 1946, and leary of involvement in what was essentially viewed as an internal Third World conflict, the administration of Harry S. Truman encountered considerable domestic resistance to its plans for aiding the conservative forces in Greece. And because this resistance was seen as a significant obstacle to the emerging policy of containment—which envisioned active U.S. military efforts to prevent further communist gains on the Soviet periphery—President Truman was determined to use the Greek affair to mobilize public support for a policy of global interventionism.[6]

To achieve a transformation in public attitudes, Truman sought to portray all conflicts in the world—whatever their origins—as manifestations of a global struggle between light and dark, tyranny and freedom. On March 12, 1947, he articulated this theme in a major speech on U.S. military aid to Greece. Suggesting that the spread of communism to *any* corner of the globe posed a significant threat to U.S. security, the president affirmed—in what was subsequently dubbed the Truman Doctrine—that "it must be the policy of the United States to support free peoples who are resisting attempted subjugation by armed minorities or by outside pressures." Although this policy was initially to be applied solely to Greece and Turkey, Truman made it clear that it would be extended to other nations when and if he deemed it necessary.[7]

Propelled by the crusading rhetoric of the Truman Doctrine, Congress approved the president's request for substantial military aid to anticommunist forces in Greece. In succeeding years, U.S. policymakers sought to amend the doctrine to allow for the *direct use* of U.S. forces (as distinct from the provision of military aid) in resisting Soviet/communist gains abroad. Such a policy, indeed, was explicitly proposed in National Security Council Memorandum No. 68 (NSC-68), a secret strategy paper drawn up by Paul Nitze of the NSC in 1950. Nonetheless, most Americans continued to oppose the direct use of U.S. troops in Third World conflicts.[8]

With the fall in 1949 of Chiang Kaishek in China, however, the public mood began to change. Angered by heavy-handed Soviet moves in Eastern Europe, and alarmed by the communist victory in China, many public figures began to call for a more vigorous struggle against international communism. Some of this fear and anger also was directed against those Americans who were said to have contributed to the success of communism abroad, either through espionage or by their failure to adopt a more aggressive anticommunist stance. This sort of paranoia, popularly known as McCarthyism (after the most prominent crusader against domestic communists and "fellow travelers," Senator Joseph R. McCarthy of Wisconsin), helped to generate a new mandate for the use of military force in combating future communist advances in the Third World.[9]

This commitment was soon put to the test in Korea. On June 25, 1950, North Korean forces crossed into the South in what appeared to be naked communist aggression against a U.S. ally. Although many troubling aspects of the Korean crisis were not considered at the time (including the possibility, supported by considerable evidence, that the South Koreans themselves provoked the conflict),[10] the president immediately invoked the Truman Doctrine and ordered U.S. forces to resist the North Korean attack. At first, most Americans supported President Truman's action, especially when it appeared that General Douglas MacArthur would succeed in forcibly "liberating" North Korea from communist rule. But when communist China entered the conflict, thereby introducing a significant risk of nuclear confrontation, senior U.S. leaders recoiled from further escalation and chose instead to fight a conventional campaign restricted to the Korean peninsula. This decision, along with the introduction of large numbers of Chinese forces, produced a bloodly and frustrating stalemate on the ground—which, in turn, provoked considerable public discontent in the United States.

In the wake of the frustrating Korean conflict, President Eisenhower adopted a new, scaled-down defense posture, which relied to a great extent on the threat of "massive retaliation" (with nuclear weapons) to deter Soviet probes in the Third World. In line with this "New Look" policy, Eisenhower ordered a substantial cut in U.S. conventional capabilities, particularly the army's ground forces and the navy's surface fleets. For the next half-dozen years, East-West issues dominated the strategic landscape, as President Eisenhower presided over a major buildup of nuclear forces; only at the end of his tenure, with the 1958 U.S. landing in Lebanon and the accompanying Eisenhower Doctrine (authorizing U.S. military action to prevent a communist takeover of Middle Eastern countries), did he envision a direct U.S. military role in regional, nonnuclear conflicts.[11]

As the 1950s drew to a close, some U.S. strategists began to question the logic of Eisenhower's New Look posture. These dissidents, led by General Maxwell D. Taylor of the army, charged that massive retaliation was an inappropriate and ineffective response to the many insurgencies and low-level military challenges facing the United States around the world. "While our massive retaliatory strategy may have prevented the Great War," Taylor wrote in *The Uncertain Trumpet,* "it has not maintained the Little Peace: that is, peace from disturbances which are little only in comparison with the disaster of general war."[12] In order to provide a credible, realistic response to such "disturbances," Taylor called for a significant expansion of U.S. nonnuclear forces. Such a buildup, he argued, would permit the president to implement a strategy of "flexible response"—that is, the use of whatever type of forces, nuclear or nonnuclear, would constitute the best response to any given challenge.

Taylor's views were embraced by John F. Kennedy, then a senator, who pledged in the 1960 presidential campaign to mount a more vigorous U.S. military response to communist probes in the Third World. After his election, Kennedy invited General Taylor and like-minded strategists to join his administration and to implement their military ideas. Taylor was named security adviser to the president and, later, chairman of the Joint Chiefs of Staff (JCS), and the strategy of flexible response became the cornerstone of a massive buildup of nuclear and conventional forces. In initiating this buildup, Kennedy placed special emphasis on the development of forces and tactics for "counterinsurgency" —that is, for the defeat of revolutionary guerrilla upheavals (or, as they were known at the time, "wars of national liberation").

The Kennedy approach to counterinsurgency was spelled out in a number of secret NSC documents, including National Security Action Memorandum No. 124 (NSAM 124), dated January 18, 1962, and NSAM 182, dated August 24, 1962. NSAM 124 affirmed that "subversive insurgency . . . is a major form of politico-military conflict equal in importance to conventional warfare," and directed the various agencies of the government (such as the NSC and CIA) to develop coordinated plans for resisting this threat. NSAM 182 provided for the adoption of an Overseas Internal Defense Policy (OIDP) that was to govern U.S. counterinsurgency operations in threatened Third World countries. Drawing on the British counterinsurgency experience in combating communist guerrillas in Malaya from 1948 to 1956 and U.S.-backed operations against the communist Huk guerrillas in the Philippines during the mid-1950s, the OIDP called for coordinated political, economic, and military efforts intended to mobilize popular support for the established government while isolating the guerrillas from the rural populace. Although the brunt of these efforts were to be borne by agencies of the host regime, the OIDP allowed for the direct employment of U.S. military forces at "higher levels of insurgency."[13]

To test the Pentagon's new weapons and tactics, and to demonstrate the effectiveness of counterinsurgency strategy, President Kennedy authorized a substantial increase in the U.S. military presence in South Vietnam. In justifying this move before Congress, General Taylor affirmed in 1963 that "here we have a going laboratory, where we see subversive insurgency, the Ho Chi Minh doctrine, being applied in all its forms." To perfect U.S. defense against such threats, he noted, "we have recognized the importance of the area as a laboratory [and] have had teams out there looking at the equipment requirements of this kind of guerrilla warfare."[14]

Although perceived initially as a laboratory, Vietnam soon turned into something rather more significant. For, having designated Vietnam as a proving ground for counterinsurgency, it became essential for the United States to avoid defeat lest U.S. failure in Indochina encourage revolutionaries in *other* countries to undertake guerrilla campaigns of their own. Hence, U.S. counterrevolutionary credibility was put on the line, and it became more and more difficult to contemplate retreat, especially when U.S. counterinsurgency efforts fell apart following the overthrow of Vietnamese President Ngo Dinh Diem in 1963. As suggested by Taylor in 1964,

> . . . the failure of our programs in South Vietnam would have heavy influence on the judgements of Burma, India, Indonesia, Malaysia, Japan, Taiwan, the Republic of Korea, and the Republic of the Philippines with respect to U.S.

> durability, resolution, and trustworthiness. Finally, this being the first real test of our determination to defeat the communist wars of national liberation formula, it is not unreasonable to conclude that there would be a corresponding unfavorable effect upon our image in Africa and Latin America.[15]

This perception of Vietnam's critical importance created an excruciating dilemma for U.S. officials: Orthodox counterinsurgency doctrine assumed that the host nation would assume primary responsibility for both political and military operations against the guerrilla insurgency, but in Vietnam (as in other Third World countries aided by the United States), the government was so alienated from the general population that it was incapable of sustaining an effective politico-military campaign without substantial outside help. As the United States ultimately discovered in Vietnam, counterinsurgency cannot work when the prevailing regime lacks popular support for the antiguerrilla effort. In such cases, an increasing number of U.S. troops must be substituted for unreliable indigenous forces in order to save the regime from collapse. On this basis, Kennedy and his successor, President Lyndon B. Johnson, deployed more and more troops in Vietnam in what became an ever-expanding (and ultimately futile) test of U.S. military "credibility."[16]

■ THE POST-VIETNAM ERA

In the wake of Vietnam, U.S. citizens and policymakers sought to prevent any repetition of such a fiasco by imposing a number of important restrictions on U.S. military involvement in regional Third World conflicts. These restraints, inspired by the "Vietnam syndrome" (a clear and pervasive reluctance on the part of American citizens to support U.S. intervention in local, Third World conflicts), included the abandonment of conscription, a substantial reduction in U.S. military aid to unstable Third World governments, and, under the War Powers Act of 1973, a legislative ban on the extended deployment (without congressional approval) of U.S. troops abroad.

Recognizing the depth of public opposition to involvement in regional Third World conflicts, U.S. strategists focused most of their attention in the 1970s on defense issues in Europe. Charging that Moscow had used the Vietnam interregnum to build up its nuclear and conventional capabilities in Eastern Europe, Presidents Gerald R. Ford and Jimmy Carter called for a major buildup of U.S. forces in the North Atlantic Treaty Organization (NATO). Significant funding increases were requested for the modernization of U.S. armored forces and for the deployment in Europe of a new generation of "theater" nuclear weapons (the weapons that were later eliminated by the INF Treaty). At the same time, spending on the Special Forces and other Third World–oriented capabilities was reduced.

This European focus was attractive to the military for a variety of reasons: It was easy to sell to Congress (because it had no taint of Vietnam and hinged on opposition to a traditional enemy, the USSR); because U.S. troops could not fight the Soviets in Europe with Vietnam-oriented equipment, it required a vast modernization of U.S. ground and air capabilities (thus producing lucrative contracts for the U.S. defense industry and thereby satisfying important domestic constituencies); it underscored an old-school style of military management (one that favored the tank generals of World War II rather than the counterinsurgency experts of Vietnam fame); and it simplified military recruiting in an all-volunteer setting (West Germany being a much more attractive posting than Vietnam). For all these reasons, preparation for a European conflict became the central concern of U.S. defense planning in the mid-1970s.

The existence of the Vietnam syndrome did not, however, entirely discourage those U.S. strategists who sought to enhance U.S. power and influence in the Third World. To get around the impediments described, National Security Adviser (later Secretary of State) Henry Kissinger and his colleagues devised what may be called the "post-Vietnam strategy" of indirect intervention. This strategy eschewed the direct use of U.S. combat forces in regional Third World conflicts but employed other means for exercising U.S. power. In particular, this strategy entailed: (1) the extensive use of arms transfers and military aid to bolster the defense capabilities of friendly Third World countries (the policy known as the Nixon Doctrine); (2) the extensive use of covert operations to manipulate the political environment of selected Third World countries (most evident in the U.S. campaign of 1971–1973 to undermine the Chilean regime of President Salvador Allende); and (3) the cultivation of surrogate gendarmes to guard U.S. interests in critical Third World areas (the most important such surrogate was Iran under the shah). Together, these measures constituted the major thrust of U.S. policy toward the Third World in the immediate post-Vietnam period.[17]

It cannot be said, therefore, that interventionism disappeared entirely from the repertoire of U.S. policy in the 1970s. But there certainly was a decreased level of *direct* military involvement in Third World conflicts, as exemplified by the U.S. failure to directly intervene in the Angolan civil war of 1975–1976 (in which U.S. involvement was precluded by the Clark Amendment to the Defense Appropriations Bill for Fiscal Year [FY] 1976), in Iran during the collapse of the shah in 1978–1979, and in Nicaragua during the overthrow of Anastacio Somoza in 1979.

Although strongly supported by most Americans, this aversion to direct intervention in regional Third World conflicts was criticized by some strategists who viewed it as a retreat from global power and leadership. For these strategists, U.S. preoccupation with East-West issues in Europe was distracting Washington from significant military perils arising in other critical areas. In particular, they warned of mounting threats to Western control over Third World sources of energy supplies and strategic minerals, coupled with growing political and social unrest—threats that they believed required a direct U.S. military response. To overcome the U.S. public's continuing resistance to such a response, these critics obscured the indigenous nature of these disputes by painting an alarming picture of aggressive Soviet expansion in the Third World. "The Soviet Union clearly created an important new threat to Western interests during the 1970s—a capability to project military power into areas far from the Soviet Union," Admiral Elmo R. Zumalt warned in 1980. Moreover, "Moscow's willingness and ability to exploit Third World crises have complicated U.S. efforts to maintain stability in the Third World."[18]

Despite such warnings, East-West concerns dominated U.S. military planning for most of the 1970s. In 1979, however, the pendulum began to swing back to Third World concerns in response to four critical events: (1) the fall of the shah of Iran, whose departure from the scene eliminated a crucial pillar of the Nixon Doctrine; (2) the emergence of revolutionary governments in Nicaragua and Grenada, heralding a new wave of guerrilla upheavals in Central America and the Caribbean; (3) the Iranian hostage crisis, which produced an emotional public outcry in the United States and generated strong demands for U.S. military retaliation against Third World terrorists; and (4) the Soviet invasion of Afghanistan, which culminated a series of Soviet and Cuban thrusts into Africa and the Middle East, most notably in Angola and Ethiopia. In response to these challenges, the Carter administration undertook a major review of U.S. strategy in the Persian Gulf and the Third World in general. What emerged from this review was a consensus that critical U.S. interests in the Third World were at risk and that the United States should take stronger action to protect these interests. As suggested by National Security Adviser Zbigniew Brzezinski in April 1979, the United States was recovering from "a very deep philosophical-cultural crisis" induced by the Vietnam War and was now ready to "use force when necessary to protect our important interests."[19]

In June 1979, following a series of secret NSC meetings, the new interventionist consensus was translated into several key presidential decisions: (1) a commitment to the use of U.S. military power to protect key economic resources in the Third World (especially oil); (2) the activation of the Rapid Deployment Force (RDF), an assortment of units from all four military services earmarked for intervention in the Third World; (3) the acquisition of new basing rights in the Indian Ocean area (notably in Oman, Kenya, and Somalia); and (4) the permanent deployment of a carrier battle group in the Indian Ocean.[20] These decisions were made in June 1979—prior to the onset of the Iranian hostage crisis in November of that year and the Soviet invasion of Afghanistan in December—but were not announced to the U.S. public until President Carter's State of the Union Address of January 23, 1980. In this address, Carter affirmed Washington's readiness to use military force in protecting the oil flow from the Persian Gulf. "Let our position be absolutely clear," Carter declared. "An attempt by any outside force to gain control of the Persian Gulf will be regarded as an assault on the vital interests of the United States of America, and such an assault will be repelled by any means necessary, including military force."[21] This announcement, soon dubbed the "Carter Doctrine," continues to govern

U.S. military action in the Persian Gulf.

These moves were not, however, sufficient to overcome public dissatisfaction with the president's performance during the Iranian hostage affair and other international crises, and so Carter lost to Ronald Reagan in the 1980 election. President Reagan subsequently moved much further in implementing a policy of resurgent interventionism; it should be noted, however, that much of what he did—especially with respect to the RDF and the expansion of U.S. power projection capabilities—was initiated by President Carter during his last months in office.

Although Reagan certainly owed a debt to the interventionist buildup initiated by Carter, it is undeniable that he placed much more emphasis on the use of force to advance U.S. foreign policy objectives in the Third World. In early policy declarations, Reagan denounced the Vietnam syndrome as "a temporary aberration," and vowed to enhance U.S. capacity for intervention abroad.[22] Moreover, the $2-trillion military buildup launched by the Reagan administration in 1981 gave high priority to the expansion of U.S. power projection capabilities, particularly the army's Special Forces, the navy's carrier and amphibious fleets, and the air force's long-range airlift units.[23] In defending this buildup, Defense Secretary Weinberger declared in 1981 that "we and our allies have come to be critically dependent on places in the world which are subject to great instability," and therefore the United States must "urgently [acquire] a better ability to respond to crises far from our shores, and to stay there as long as necessary."[24]

This buildup was accompanied, moreover, by a conspicuous readiness to use force in overseas conflict situations. "Over the last 18 months," Richard Halloran of the *New York Times* observed in January 1984, "President Reagan has clearly stepped into the front ranks of those American Presidents who, since World War II, have been willing to employ military force as an instrument of national policy." Often disregarding the cautionary advice of his military advisers, Reagan deployed U.S. troops or advisers to Central America, Grenada, and Lebanon, authorized air strikes against Libya, and sent a powerful naval fleet into the Persian Gulf. Such action, Halloran wrote, places Reagan "in a league with President Truman, who sent forces to fight in Korea, and Presidents Kennedy and Johnson, who led the United States into the war in Vietnam."[25]

■ LOW-INTENSITY CONFLICT

The revived U.S. commitment to intervention in the Third World during the 1980s is largely encapsulated in the doctrine of low-intensity conflict, or LIC, as it is known in military circles. In military terms, LIC connotes the low end of the "spectrum of violence," embracing terrorism, guerrilla warfare, counterinsurgency, ethnic and border conflicts, show-of-force operations, and what the Pentagon deceptively calls "peacetime contingency operations." Furthermore, under Reagan, low-intensity conflict took on broader significance, representing a new policy of military intervention in Third World areas. Indeed, U.S. military strategists speak of the "doctrine of low-intensity conflict," and new military manuals, tactics, and forces have been created in accordance with this doctrine.[26] The LIC doctrine rests on two fundamental assumptions:

1. *Vital U.S. interests are threatened by radical and revolutionary violence in the Third World.* Perhaps no figure has stated this view with greater urgency than Lieutenant Colonel Oliver North, who told the Select Committee on the Iran-Contra Affair in June 1987 that extraordinary measures of the sort he employed were justified because "this nation is at risk in a dangerous world."[27] North was very clearly influenced by other theorists of low-intensity warfare, including Pentagon counterinsurgency expert Neil C. Livingstone. "Unfulfilled expectations and economic mismanagement have turned much of the developing world into a 'hothouse of conflict,' capable of spilling over and engulfing the industrial West," Livingstone told senior officers at the National Defense University (NDU) in 1983. Although the Soviets may not be directly responsible for this disorder, they view guerrilla warfare "as a means of undermining the West, wearing it down, nibbling away at its peripheries, denying it the strategic minerals and vital straits critical to its commerce." This being the case, U.S. policymakers must recognize that "what is at stake [in low-intensity conflict] is nothing less than the survival of our own country and way of life."[28]

2. *The United States must be prepared to use military force to protect its vital interests in the Third World.* In the view of the U.S. theorists, the threat posed by LIC is equivalent to an all-out assault by the Soviet Union and its allies and must be countered, therefore, by vigorous U.S. political and military action. "Police actions, peacekeeping missions, and counterinsurgency . . . are all part of the same long, continuous war," Livingstone argued in 1983, "a war composed of many small, often nameless battles of short duration in dozens of different venues against an unchanging enemy and its proxies and surrogates." Accordingly, "the security of the United States and the rest of the Western World requires a restructuring of our warmaking capability, placing new emphasis on the ability to fight a succession of limited wars and to project power into the Third World."[29]

These assumptions, although not always expressed in such explicit terms, form the core of U.S. doctrine on LIC. Added together, they provide a potent rationale for intervention. This rationale, moreover, has been given formal recognition by the Reagan administration, as indicated by Secretary of State George Shultz's comments to participants in the Pentagon's LIC conference held in 1986:

> We have seen and we will continue to see a wide range of ambiguous threats in the shadow area between major war and millennial peace. Americans must understand . . . that a number of small challenges, year after year, can add up

> to a more serious challenge to our interests. The time to act, to help our friends by adding our strength to the equation, is not when the threat is at our doorstep, when the stakes are highest and the needed resources enormous. We must be prepared to commit our political, economic, and if necessary, military power when the threat is still manageable and when its prudent use can prevent the threat from growing.[30]

On this basis, the United States has developed an elaborate body of doctrine for low-intensity warfare. This doctrine envisions direct or indirect U.S. military involvement in five types of operations:

1. *Counterinsurgency,* or U.S.-backed political and military efforts to isolate and suppress revolutionary guerrilla movements in the Third World. (These U.S. efforts are also identified as "foreign internal defense".) In line with the tenets of "classical," 1960s-style counterinsurgency, LIC doctrine stresses the efforts of host-nation military and civilian personnel in "winning the hearts and minds" of rural peasants. Such operations, generally described in the doctrinal literature as "military civic action" and "psychological operations" (psyops), are intended to convince disaffected peasants that the established government is sensitive to their needs and concerns. Military operations, in such a setting, are aimed at driving the rebels away from populated areas without causing excessive destruction to the civil infrastructure.

As the United States found in Vietnam, however, it is easier to promulgate such policies than to carry them out in practice. Typically, the United States is asked to assist in counterinsurgency operations only in the case of governments that have so abused and exploited the rural peasantry that no amount of good deeds (civic action) and public relations (psyops) will suffice to arouse public support. In such cases, the incumbent regime tends to rely increasingly on military action to crush dissent, and this, in turn, tends to feed the insurgency—thereby increasing the pressure on Washington to step up U.S. involvement. This dynamic appears well under way in El Salvador and the Philippines, where the United States is supporting major counterinsurgency efforts.[31]

2. *Proinsurgency,* or U.S. paramilitary support for anticommunist guerrillas who seek to overthrow pro-Soviet governments in the Third World (see Chapter 8). Such efforts, which include covert and overt support for the anti-Sandinista contras, fall under the Reagan Doctrine. Other U.S.-backed proinsurgency campaigns are under way in Afghanistan, Angola, and Cambodia.

3. *Peacetime contingency operations,* or any limited short-term use of military power as an instrument of U.S. foreign policy. Such actions may include the rescue of U.S. citizens caught in overseas war zones; "show-of-force" operations intended to signal U.S. displeasure with the behavior of a particular regime (by threatening direct intervention); "peacekeeping" operations designed to restore order in war-torn countries or to separate two warring parties; and punitive strikes against governments that support terrorism or otherwise threaten U.S. interests. Examples of such U.S. operations include the 1983 in-

vasion of Grenada, the 1983–1984 mission in Beirut, and periodic naval exercises in the Gulf of Sidra (claimed by Libya) and the Persian Gulf.[32]

4. *Terrorism counteraction,* or the use of military force to prevent or deter terrorist attacks on U.S. personnel or facilities abroad. Although the emphasis here is on preventative measures, U.S. policy—as spelled out in National Security Decision Directive No. 138 (NSDD 138) of April 3, 1984—allows for retaliatory strikes against terrorist groups (and their supporters) identified as being responsible for attacks on U.S. citizens and facilities. "The United States . . . will not use force indiscriminately," National Security Adviser Robert C. McFarlane avowed in 1985. "But we must be free to consider an armed strike against terrorists and those who support them, where elimination or moderation of the threat does not appear to be feasible by other means."[33] Such strikes were conducted on April 14, 1986, against the headquarters of Libyan leader Colonel Muammar Qaddafi.

5. *Antidrug operations,* or the use of military force to interdict the flow of illegal drugs into the United States or to locate and destroy narcotics plantations and laboratories located in other countries. Until fairly recently, U.S. law and policy precluded the use of U.S. military force in law-enforcement functions of this sort; under a presidential directive signed by President Reagan in April 1986, however, the Department of Defense was empowered to play a direct role in antidrug operations. Specifically, the Pentagon was authorized to conduct aerial and naval surveillance of suspected drug traffickers and to plan and support strike operations against drug laboratories and processing facilities in foreign countries. A large-scale action of this sort—Operation Blast Furnace—was conducted in the cocoa-growing Chapere area of Bolivia in 1986.[34]

All of these activities entail a significant role expansion for the U.S. military, pushing them into fields once reserved for diplomatic, police, and customs personnel; all, moreover, entail a significant risk of escalation. Counterinsurgency may lead to direct U.S. involvement in a protracted guerrilla war if local government forces collapse in the face of superior insurgent capabilities (as occurred in Vietnam in 1965); proinsurgency may invite U.S. intervention to defend a U.S.-backed insurgent group that faces defeat on the battlefield; and peacetime contingency, terrorism counteraction, and antidrug operations could ignite a regional conflict of unforeseeable breadth, duration, and intensity.

■ THE IMPETUS FOR INTERVENTION

For those familiar with the evolution of U.S. military policy in the post–World War II period, the policies of the 1980s will suggest many parallels to the Kennedy period of the early 1960s. Then, as now, U.S. policymakers perceived a growing threat from low-intensity conflict in the Third World; then, as now, U.S. policymakers prescribed an increase in interventionist activity as the response to this threat. Whether or not the United States will again, as in 1965, find itself deeply embroiled in a debilitating Third World conflict remains to be seen. What does seem evident, however, is that low-intensity warfare will be an increasing U.S. strategic concern of the 1990s, potentially leading to ever-increasing U.S. involvement in regional conflicts.

Aside from the heightened risk of intervention, what other conclusions may be drawn about the context of U.S. policymaking? This survey of postwar U.S. policy reveals a striking degree to which North-South issues—particularly issues raised by U.S. military involvement in regional Third World conflicts—have dominated the strategic agenda and shaped the public mood. Consider, for example, the fact that all five of the postwar military doctrines—those of Presidents Truman, Eisenhower, Nixon, Carter, and Reagan—concerned U.S. intervention of one sort or another in the Third World. Indeed, the very prominence of these North-South issues appears to contradict the common wisdom that East-West security issues constitute the dominant paradigm of U.S. security policy. What, then, accounts for the persistent importance of North-South conflict issues?

First, there is what might be termed the bureaucratic factor—the tendency of any large organization to perpetuate itself even when the conditions for its emergence no longer prevail. Having been established to meet the postwar military threat from Moscow, the mammoth U.S. military establishment will naturally manufacture urgent reasons for its expansion on the North-South axis of conflict when the East-West axis appears less threatening. Thus, if the current rapprochement between Washington and Moscow results in a diminished requirement for nuclear weapons and Europe-oriented systems, Americans are likely to be barraged with propaganda on the need to beef up U.S. defenses in the Persian Gulf, Asia, and the Caribbean.

Second, there is an inevitable spillover effect from the cold war itself. Because popular anticommunist beliefs in the United States periodically have produced an almost uncontrollable compulsion to "do something" of an aggressive and punitive nature, and because "doing something" in Europe poses an unacceptable risk of nuclear annihilation, U.S. policymakers have periodically lashed out at hostile Third World powers as a substitute for confronting the Soviet Union itself. Typically, such aggression has also been fueled by other factors—factors originating in the antagonism between the United States and radical Third World regimes—but the intensity and virulence of these conflicts (consider Korea, Vietnam, and Grenada) is to a significant degree produced by frustrated anti-Soviet (or, in an earlier period, anti-Chinese) hostilities.

Beyond these factors, however, it is important to note that the United States often has intervened in Third World conflicts for reasons that have little to do with U.S.-Soviet competition. The United States exercised de facto dominion over Latin America long before the Bolsheviks rose to power in Russia, and what we are witnessing in the 1980s in Central America is as much a reassertion of hegemonic will as it is a manifestation of East-West rivalry. Indeed, the

United States has acquired substantial economic interests in the Third World since the 1940s, and the protection of these interests has become an increasingly central concern of U.S. defense planning—hence, the Carter Doctrine, which still drives U.S. involvement in the Persian Gulf.[35]

Finally, it seems more and more evident that the U.S. public and much of its leadership view Third World radicalism with much greater anxiety than they do Soviet communism. Although no one should ever underestimate the intensity of anti-Sovietism in U.S. society, there is no denying that Soviet President Mikhail Gorbachev's ascendancy and the ongoing U.S.-Soviet summit meetings have taken some of the sting out of cold war hostility. Gorbachev has dined at the White House, has been received with considerable warmth by many U.S. leaders, and has been given respectable treatment by the U.S. press. Compare this behavior with the treatment given such figures as Qaddafi and the Ayatollah Khomeini—neither of whom has a nuclear arsenal aimed at the United States, but who are considered personae non grata in Washington, whereas Gorbachev is given a royal welcome. True, Libyan- and Iranian-sponsored terrorism has endangered some American lives, but surely Moscow has been accused of crimes far more heinous than anything attributed to Qaddafi or Khomeini. The hostility to radical Third World leaders derives, therefore, from fears or instincts that lie outside of the conventional calculus of U.S. national security interests.

Why, then, the special hostility reserved for Third World adversaries? There is no clear-cut answer, but perhaps it has something to do with the vast imbalance in wealth between North America and the developing countries—and the fear that Third World terrorism and insurgency is fundamentally inspired by a desire to readjust that balance in a more equitable fashion. Thus, in an unusual 1977 RAND Corporation study that articulated what many policymakers have left unsaid, Guy Pauker warned that the United States "faces the possibility of a breakdown of global order as a result of sharpening confrontation between the Third World and the industrial democracies." This confrontation, he wrote, is largely a result of the inescapable fact that "the gap between rich and poor countries is so wide that no solution satisfactory to both sides is likely to emerge." And, as domestic pressures in the poor countries continue to mount, "the North-South conflict . . . could get out of hand in ways comparable to the peasant rebellions that in past centuries engulfed large parts of Europe and Asia, spreading like uncontrolled prairie fires."[36]

Such imagery, as we have seen, permeates the literature on low-intensity conflict. It suggests that the United States is under assault from a variety of Third World rebels and revolutionaries and that only through military action can it avert the breakdown of global order. Lost in this alarmist picture is any effort to appreciate the heterogeneous character of Third World conflict or to consider nonmilitary solutions to outstanding North-South disputes. There may, indeed, be significant threats to U.S. interests in the Third World, but if the United States abandons diplomacy and negotiation for military intervention, it will almost certainly find itself enmeshed in a series of grueling Third World conflagrations.

□ 4

The Globalist-Regionalist Debate

Charles F. Doran

Much of the debate surrounding U.S. foreign policy in the Third World in the post–World War II period may be subsumed in the dialogue between the globalists and the regionalists. These two perspectives on foreign policy are not mutually exclusive on all points of conduct, legitimacy, and style, nor are they unique to the setting of U.S. foreign policy. To some extent, other governments and societies, are also preoccupied with these questions of priority and emphasis in terms of East-West and North-South. But globalist-regionalist perspectives certainly characterize much of analysis in the 1980s about where U.S. foreign policy ought to head and about how it ought to get there.

Defining such broad persuasions about foreign policy priority is not easy, and such definition should not be undertaken casually. The globalists stress the primacy of East-West confrontation at all levels of international political behavior, in all parts of the international system. All of international relations is seen through the lens of Soviet-U.S. relations and, indeed, as a virtual outgrowth of bipolar relations. The regionalists emphasize the dilemmas of North-South relations, the idiosyncracies of politics and culture within the various geographic regions, and the comparative autonomy of the struggles that go on within and between the states of these regions. More than just a divergent interpretation of the nature of the contemporary international system, these two perspectives involve divergent interpretations about the meaning and origin of contemporary international politics, differences that can be separated into three broad categories: (1) the origins of change and stability; (2) foreign policy purpose; and (3) foreign policy strategy and means.

■ ORIGINS OF CHANGE AND STABILITY

The fundamental difference in perspective between the globalists and the regionalists is in understanding the meaning and origins of social and political change.[1] Other policy distinctions are important but derivative. Although some elements of this difference in social understanding are timeless and universal, other elements are quite parochial in the temporal sense and are an outgrowth of the East-West struggle and contemporary North-South debates.

☐ Order Maintenance from the Top Versus Self-Determination at the Bottom

A presumption of the globalists is that order starts at the top of the international system.[2] If war breaks out there, it is very likely to become major. Thus, a premium is placed upon effectively "managing" relationships at the top of the systems hierarchy among the leading states. It is further assumed that order-maintenance, especially in a bipolar system (one in which two major powers are dominant), is never easy but is feasible. Because of the relative directness of communication, the continuity of probe and counterprobe, and the high quality of information available to each party, surprise and uncertainty are kept to a minimum. Small crises having their origin at the top of the system are not allowed to get out of hand. This has been the general experience of superpower relations in the post–World War II period, including the Berlin Crisis (1948), the Cuban missile crisis (1962), the October War (1973), and the problems of oil transport through the Persian Gulf (1987–1988).

The globalists, likewise, are troubled about the danger of confrontations among small powers that eventually percolate to the top of the system and become unmanageable.[3] The relationship between Austria-Hungary and Serbia (and, particularly, Germany and Austria-Hungary) in 1913 come to mind, but one could as easily point to the American colonies in the 1760s as a source of problems for France and Britain, to Korea in 1903 for Russia and Japan, or to Vietnam in the post-1945 period for China, the Soviet Union, and the United States. Thus, the inclination of the globalists is to attempt to control local and regional wars or to attempt to defuse the conditions of such wars before they ignite. It is true that these efforts often entangle the United States more deeply in the domestic and external affairs of small allies and client states than is otherwise preferable. But the alternative, according to globalists, is to stand aside, to do nothing, and to see the regional confrontations smolder into wider confrontations that may become even more problematic.

Opposed to this analysis on almost every point is the regionalist interpretation. From the regionalist perspective, a stable world system is best described as a system of interdependence among states with autonomous and unfettered foreign policies. The greatest threat to world order comes from oppression from the top.[4] The aftermath of colonialism (direct external governmental control of the colony's foreign policy) and perhaps imperialism (indirect external cultural, economic, or political influence over states abroad) is held to be proof of the failure of a hierarchical world order. Major states at the top of the system have no greater insight into the maintenance of world order, or any greater capacity to achieve it, than do smaller states. All states are equal in international legal attributes and in membership to bodies like the United Nations. All states have a right to the full expression of their grievances, in international bodies such as the World Court or in regional bodies such as the European Community. Growing interdependence between states assures a more stable international environment in which to carry out individual foreign policy preferences.

Thus, according to the regionalist perspective, suppression of legitimate foreign policy grievances from the top of the global hierarchy is the principal source of extensive (global) warfare.[5] This suppression creates frustration and hostility toward global powers that lead to open military challenge. The United States, it is argued, should understand this message better than most states as it was born during the eighteenth century in rebellion against oppression by a state at the top of the international system. The American colonies revolted against what were seen as the unjust, coercive, and exploitative policies of Great Britain. Whether from a liberal or a Marxist persuasion, these arguments often expressed by regionalists—sometimes favoring a "multipolar" conception of world order (several autonomous, comparatively equal regional centers of power); sometimes supportive of the thesis of growing interdependence among states—often reflect the way governments and opinion elites within regions appear to look at the world system.[6]

In short, the globalists implicitly favor order-maintenance from the top of the international system because they fear the escalation of wars on the periphery to eventual conflagrations at the center. Regionalists implicitly reject this concept of systemic stability, arguing that the greater danger is that a confrontation of major powers at the center is likely to spill war onto the periphery. Causation of extensive, global instability, they argue, moves from center to periphery rather than from the periphery to center. Moreover, regionalists object to efforts to control stability from the top of the system that become oppressive and even exploitative, creating the most dangerous conditions of all for aggravated rebellion and warfare within regions as well as between regional actors and the major states at the top of the system.

□ Soviet Meddling Versus Indigenous Causes of Conflict

Many contemporary globalists, perhaps most, believe that the Soviet Union is behind most important regional turmoil, if not as deus ex machina, then as a catalyst once the conditions for revolution and communist takeover seem ripe. In the view of these writers and analysts, the Soviet Union seeks to expand its power into new areas of geostrategic opportunity.[7] Its national capability is rising. Its capacity to project naval power throughout the world has grown significantly since the 1970s. It is the only country that can mortally wound the United States militarily; thus, every Soviet advance and marginal political achievement becomes a relevant factor in the overall military balance. Despite the possibility of Soviet-U.S. cooperation, the globalist perceives East-West conflict in a bipolar system as essentially zero-sum (that is, a Soviet gain represents a U.S. loss, and vice versa).

According to this version of globalism, a shift in the balance of power between the West and the Soviet Union is likely to have a significant impact upon world order and upon accepted rules of international behavior. Both neutrals and allies are likely to feel this negative change. The Soviets understand coercion and use it skillfully. The quality of the relationship between East Germany or Poland and the Soviet Union is not the same as the relationship between Brazil or Mexico and the United States, for example. The Soviet Union uses elite manipulation, party control, direct military intimidation, and economic bribery in a way that is far more constraining than anything employed by the United States, even assuming that each superpower has an equivalent interest in international political stability. A system in which the Soviet Union was more dominant would be a system, according to the globalists, that allowed for much less freedom—individual freedom within subordinate states, external freedom for the foreign policies of dependent polities.

In the view of the globalists, the greatest threat to U.S. interests stems from the Soviet Union and its principal allies. The Soviet Union has never given up its commitment to support "wars of national liberation," least of all in the 1970s interval of détente.[8] Hence, the Soviets aim to replace noncommunist governments with communist regimes and expand Soviet military bases of subversion into countries that are vulnerable or receptive. Although the Soviets cannot be credited with every stimulus to revolution or guerrilla warfare, they normally are found not far behind much organized opposition and will attempt to coopt or exacerbate whatever turmoil may exist in areas governed by noncommunist regimes. By contrast, they are quick to use whatever means are available, including force, to put down revolutionary activity within their own orbit. *Glasnost* may have permitted the superficial expression of pluralism, but the Soviet political leadership internally and externally continues to leave room only for strict control and one-party dominance.[9]

Regionalists are no more fond of the Soviet brand of world order than are globalists, but they see world politics through a more complex political lens. They see the primary source of regional instability as emergent within societies and internal to regions themselves. External catalysts of such instability are regarded as clearly secondary in importance. If access to guns and military hardware were the deciding factor in regional instability, these could be purchased on the black market or taken from government armed forces units. But the deciding factor, as regionalists see the matter of internal stability, is the effort of organized political movements and parties—some of them Marxist-Leninist, some of them not—to cope with governments heavily burdened by maladministration and indifference to human welfare. As population pressures grow and stagnant economies fail to meet the needs of large sectors of society, the conditions for guerrilla activity and other forms of violent opposition to government will increase.[10] Not carried out by illiterate peasants or an unemployed urban proletariat, but led by frustrated, belligerent members of the middle class, either within the army or outside it, most violent political change is perpetrated by individuals who seek to gain power for themselves in the name of transforming oppressive social conditions. Most massive social upheavals, according to the regionalists, are pragmatic and homegrown. Political freedom is often a forgotten variable. So is economic efficiency, as governmental control is substituted for whatever private enterprise may exist. But the response to indigenous problems, in the eyes of most regionalists, should still be indigenous, not imported from abroad.

Regionalists also lament the lack of knowledge globalists portray about the complexity of cultural, social, and political differences within regions.[11] For example, to understand the relationship between Iraq or Syria and the Soviet Union, one must understand the extent to which domestic communist parties have been subjected to repression and the extent to which governing elites (representing minority communal groups) have been able to stay in power by maintaining an internal equilibrium among offsetting Moslem orthodoxies. Radicalism has many fathers. Shiite Moslems may not have as much in common with the Palestine Liberation Organization (PLO) as with Iranian nationalists, and the Kurds (largely nomadic peoples on the USSR's southern border living in sections of Iraq, Iran, and Turkey), for historical as well as ethnolinguistic reasons, may reject both.[12] One of the most telling regionalist challenges to the globalists is that the latter often do not have the facts of social, political, and cultural organization upon which to make sound policy judgments concerning regional politics.

In sum, the regionalists recognize the overwhelming importance of indigenous factors in contributing to internal social and political unrest within regions. For them, the solution to such unrest must take into account internal regional dynamics and cleavages. In this vein, solutions are more likely to come from within regions than be imposed from outside. The Soviet Union is perceived as only one of the many possible stimuli of societal turmoil and rarely the most relevant. Indeed, according to regionalists, unless long-term indigenous factors are addressed, stability will not be possible in many areas of geostrategic interest to the United States.[13] Concentrating upon what the Soviet Union may or may not do is exactly the wrong way to make foreign policy that is regionally sensitive and, therefore, reasonably successful.

In contrast, the globalist is skeptical about many regionalist claims, not on grounds of factual understanding but on grounds of political interpretation. The globalist sees revolution as quite different from social unrest.[14] Revolution in the contemporary international system is likely to be Marxist-Leninist for many reasons, not the least of which is that most of the leaders of significant guerrilla movements have received their training either in Moscow or Havana.

Change as Orderly Political Process Versus Inevitable Destabilization

Globalist ideas stress the necessity for orderly political change—first, to permit significant economic development; second, to create at least the possibility of the growth of democratic institutions. Globalists tend to see the purpose of economic and military aid, for example, as creating the conditions whereby growth and development become possible.[15] They point out that, even in communist societies, a top priority is placed upon orderly political processes. Why should the allegedly more conservative noncommunist routes to political and social development be less supportive of a stable environment in which to carry out economic enterprise than the communist route?

For the globalist, orderly processes of development are not sufficient, but they are necessary. To use sad examples, Haiti under Papa Doc Duvalier may have been "orderly" in a narrow political sense, just as Albania is "orderly" from another political persuasion. But neither Haiti nor Albania have displayed much economic growth or development. Political order is necessary for economic achievement; indeed, from the viewpoint of liberal economic development theory, it is the most fundamental task of government. In the absence of political order (that is, in the atmosphere of continued social turmoil, civil war, or revolution), little progress can be made toward sustained economic achievement, as most attention is turned toward the struggle to remain in power or the struggle merely to survive.

But political order alone is not enough. As South Korea demonstrates for the globalist camp, substantial economic growth for the individual citizen must be accompanied by increasing access to the wealth produced. Likewise, welfare and social services ought to be provided broadly. Yet, throughout this process efficiency and equity are trade-offs—a proper balance must be maintained for each step of the development process. Without a modicum of political order, the government will be unable to deliver benefits to the society; without delivering social and economic benefits, maintenance of political order increasingly will have to rely on coercion. For the globalist looking at the problems of economic development in the Third World, it is difficult to ignore the high correlation between cultural cohesion, political order, entrepreneurship, and economic growth among the Newly Industrializing Countries (NICs), such as Hong Kong, Taiwan, and, despite student unrest, South Korea. Remove political order as a variable from this equation and the record of the NICs would have been far less impressive.

For the regionalist, economic growth and development are inevitably destabilizing, and it is the wise government that prepares for this and allows a certain level of such turmoil to proceed.[16] Governments on the right (such as the former Somoza family regimes in Nicaragua or regimes in Liberia) that place so much emphasis on maintaining order through coercion and neglect to create the proper atmosphere either for economic enterprise or for adequate schooling and governmental services discover they have neither growth nor long-term stability.[17] Similarly, governments on the left, such as China, North Korea, and Vietnam, have discovered that the ideological structures of authoritarian control and central planning have denied the opportunities for growth and economic development. Only room for decentralized enterprise, responsiveness to market signals, and economic entrepreneurship and risk will enable an economy to move forward at its potential, at least beyond the phase of heavy industrialization accompanied by the severest austerity.

The regionalist, likewise, is aware of what empirical research has pointed out concerning the impact of foreign assistance on the recipient polity. The effect of foreign assistance in the short run may be that it is not smoothly or effectively absorbed by the society. As it destroys old practices and allegiances, new ones may not easily be fashioned. Serious political instability may result.[18] For example, a road built deep into the rainforests along Brazil's Amazon River may open up new stresses and strains to development, as villagers are able to migrate to Brasilia and the influences of industrialization are carried to individuals living in the rural areas.[19]

In short, whereas globalists tend to be suspicious of instability of any variety, preferring to believe that modernization can proceed quietly and without confusion, regionalists recognize that modernization and economic development place enormous strains on any society, strains that for the most part are probably unavoidable. Yet, the globalist maintains that instability, however endemic to the development process, is nonetheless antithetical to economic enterprise and growth. Instability may be inevitable, but it is not desirable. Those Third World governments that learn to manage instability, often with initial outside help, while creating the conditions under which both import-competing and export industries can prosper, are the governments that will experience the highest levels of per capita income in the twenty-first century.

■ FOREIGN POLICY PURPOSE

Apart from their opposing understandings of the origins of social and political change, regionalists and globalists differ regarding the values and preferences they would bring to foreign policy conduct. They differ in how they perceive foreign-policy-making priorities and in the scope of the responsibilities to be assumed by good government abroad.

□ Maintenance of World Order Versus Economic Development

Globalists believe that the maintenance of order and security is the highest priority a government can establish for itself.[20] They also believe that security is a specialized function of government requiring substantial resources and great attention. All the techniques, strategies, and instruments commonly associated with security and order-maintenance, therefore, are given a high priority in relations with Third World countries.

The globalist tends to believe that any government committed to order-maintenance responsibilities probably has its hands full without assuming a variety of other functions better left to other national governments or to business firms or to local communities. Foreign assistance is thus a servant to order-maintenance objectives and is supplied with emphasis placed upon distributing military as opposed to economic aid to ward off problems made evident by crisis. By straying from the primary task of order-maintenance (providing economic assistance to achieve development objectives), government policy-makers probably will perform this function less well, according to the globalist, and will end up convincing themselves that they have, in fact, replaced the local government as the primary purveyor of services, leadership, and economic incentive. By restricting assistance to order-maintenance functions and the distribution of military aid, globalists believe they are setting limits upon U.S. commitments and are neither misleading nor overpromising benefits to foreign governments.

In contrast, the regionalist tends to adopt a very different mind-set. The number one problem facing Third World governments is sufficiently rapid economic progress to offset the growth of population and the rise in public expectations.[21] Likewise, the regionalist believes that Americans ought to be concerned both on humanitarian and practical political grounds with the problems of broadly shared economic development.

Because, as the regionalist perceives, the existence of deep social inequality in repressive Third World countries is one of the key contributors to revolution, the United States can only achieve its objective of stability and security through the proper attention to meaningful economic growth and development. In the absence of such meaningful growth and development, revolution and war, slippage toward regimes with an extreme leftist orientation, and political realignment are the evident consequences in polities as diverse as Ethiopia and Nicaragua. Given these negative consequences, the regionalist cannot understand how a rich society with global interests such as the United States would not put a very high priority on assistance for economic growth and development.

To put a finer edge on the argument, the regionalist believes that a preoccupation with local balances of power, alliances, military security, and arms considerations cannot achieve order and security for the United States or for countries within more isolated areas.[22] This approach to foreign policy conduct is narrow-minded and bound to fail in its objectives. The principal analytic problem is that the globalist has misplaced causation. War and communist revolution spring from deeper economic and social problems within developing societies.

Only by addressing these can the security and stability of the United States be obtained.

□ Containment of Soviet Expansionism Versus Cultivation of Third World Ties

Equally controversial for regionalists and globalists is the decision to place priority on East-West or on North-South questions. The regionalist tends to prefer long-term policy elaboration to achieve "positive" goals, such as broadly shared economic development, whereas the globalist takes a foreign policy position that often amounts to crisis management. The globalist, therefore, may be more predisposed to treat East-West questions in which response to problems rather than foreign policy initiation is more fitting, whereas the regionalist is more conditioned to the type of North-South problems in which the solutions are seen as long-term and which require the initiation of foreign policy programs.

Starting from the assumption that the Soviet Union is the principal U.S. rival and security threat, the globalist reasons that this justifies supporting insurgencies against Soviet-backed regimes. The irony here is that this East-West concern quickly may drag the unwary government into a quagmire such as Vietnam. The costs of direct military intervention are replaced by the costs of protracted guerrilla warfare.[23] Conversely, the regionalist may stress improved ties to individual Third World countries based upon a strategy of broadly shared development as a way to build a foundation for avoiding serious security problems (domestic instability and revolution) in the long run. Yet, the regionalist who actually faces foreign policy implementation may discover that many Third World governments are more interested in arms aid and security problems than they are in economic aid and the esoterics of growth and development.[24]

The regionalist criticizes the notion of Soviet containment as not only irrelevant to more important issues but unworkable in practice, as the Soviet Union is in no sense "contained" by U.S. actions in the Third World. Indeed, the regionalist argues that factors indigenous to the Third World, such as nationalism, constrain the Soviets just as effectively as they have constrained the United States. The globalist rejects as empty and moralistic the notion of "improving ties" to the Third World, claiming this amounts to placing foreign policy emphasis where the international political "action" is not, and that there is no way of cementing ties for the future in any consistent, or cost-acceptable manner.

□ Defense of Democratic Values Versus Evenhandedness in Human Rights

Globalist logic would suggest that democracy is a superior form of government, that true democracies are few in number (and, in some cases, may be on the political endangered-species list), and that alliances among such governments are likely to be necessary for reinforcement. Some globalists with idealist tendencies, however, maintain that democracy and economic development are strongly related and that only poor governments or governments in troubled intervals are likely to be drawn toward totalitarianism.[25]

It is implicit in the globalist outlook that U.S. ties to nondemocratic governments are also mandatory, either to prevent retrenchment in numbers or to assist in the nascent shift toward representative government. Those globalists who do not believe that democracy is inevitable, no matter how virtuous this form of government is, generally lean toward rightist regimes more than leftist ones, rationalizing this behavior under a hundred guises but, in practice, promoting the argument that "once communist, always communist," while also assuming that rightist generals sometimes can be overthrown. Totalitarian (that is, communist) governments are considered immutable; authoritarian governments (that is, traditional dictatorships) are thought to be capable of redemption. The globalist tends to make foreign policy on the basis of conclusions about the form of government, its institutions, and, most of all, its commitments.[26]

By contrast, regionalists, perhaps because they are closer to some of the regimes about which they speculate, perhaps because they are at once more pragmatic and more skeptical than most globalists, tend to dismiss much of the discussion regarding governmental form, constitutions, institutions, and even formal treaty commitments. What regionalists focus on is behavior, the track record of actual performance. For most regionalists, the human rights record is a very meaningful record of behavior, and they tend to follow this record intently, assisted by analyses that they or organizations such as Amnesty International are able to provide.[27] As the record varies across regimes of the same type, and across comparable historical intervals, great familiarity with individual societies is needed for this type of judgment, a situation in which the craft of regional specialization provides obvious rewards.

A further demand made by most regionalists is that the treatment of human rights be evenhanded. Governments that are allies should receive the same scrutiny as those that are not. Governments on the far right should be evaluated just as carefully as those that may be on the far left. Although intellectually honest, such analysis is sometimes revealed to be politically awkward.[28] How does one accuse a favorite uncle of larceny, especially when he may be contributing to the family welfare in terms of security?

But true regionalists, again because of their greater expertise in comparative government and politics than in international relations and foreign policy, tend to insist that no international standard is likely to be effective unless it is evenly applied across polities. Here the globalists, often experts on international relations, disagree, because they would prefer to compare the human rights record not so much across states as across the overall policy record of the individual government, quite a different situation.[29]

■ STRATEGY AND MEANS

A priori, regionalists and globalists may disagree about foreign policy goals without disagreeing about the strategy to implement those goals or about the means employed in the strategy.[30] Observed debate, however, suggests that there is no more agreement about strategy and means than there is about foreign policy objectives.

□ Intervention Versus Constructive Nonintervention

Ever since British Lord Robert Stewart Castlereagh sought to institute a strategy of nonintervention, following the Napoleonic Wars (1801–1814) and the Congress of Vienna (1815), to be abided by by all of the major powers in order to prevent France from using intervention as a means of once again threatening the peace of the Central European system, governments periodically have opted for a strategy that sets limits on intervention or outlaws it altogether. Although this strategy in its contemporary U.S. form allegedly has roots in Wilsonian ethics, President Woodrow Wilson in actuality intervened repeatedly in the Caribbean and Central America in an effort to promote political stability. Yet, the principle of nonintervention, akin in some ways to that of the self-determination of peoples, is an idea that tends to divide globalists and regionalists.

Regionalists are very skeptical of great-power intervention. They see all too often a frightening great-power ignorance of the politics and culture—even geography—of the target state. One is reminded of the Kennedy fiasco in the Bay of Pigs, in which the Cuban swamps and mountain ranges had not been properly delineated. More than this was the invaders' naive anticipation of rebellion by the populace against Castro. Regionalists also question the significance of external ties to local insurrection, removing one of the substantial globalist justifications for intervention. Regionalists know the negative impact intervention has on regional public and elite opinion and the criticism intervention evokes when outside force is used ostensibly to promote self-determination and representative government.[31] The regionalist also may argue the moral position that one cannot lament Soviet intervention in Eastern Europe while practicing intervention in Central America or the Caribbean. Most important, the regionalist believes that indigenous nationalism is stronger than the affinity for communism backed by Soviet aid and advisers. The examples of abrupt ruptures of relations with the Soviet Union by Egyptian leader Anwar Sadat and Somalia's Siyad Barre, despite both leaders' supposed economic and military dependence on the USSR, are cited by regionalists as proof of the resilience of local nationalism and the reversibility of ties once a country has aligned itself with the communist bloc.

A very telling criticism of intervention from the regional perspective is the nature of politics inside the target state *after* intervention. Although communist revolution may have been deterred, democracy is often nowhere in evidence, social progress is absent, and human rights continue to be trampled. For the most part, the polity is forgotten as long as it is no longer perceived as a threat. Even if foreign assistance is augmented, corruption eats up that assistance in such fashion that the polity is worse off than it was prior to the intervention. Hence, the record of economic and social progress following intervention is scarcely a matter of which the intervening state may be proud, in part because the main objective was military success and not a program of political and economic development founded on a pluralist party structure.

Yet, the globalist will hesitate to reject intervention as a foreign policy instrument.[32] The issue for the globalist is not the type of government a polity freely chooses for itself, but whether it (1) seeks to destabilize the countries around it through exported revolution; and (2) invites the Soviet Union to expand the Soviet military presence within the region and the quite substantial Soviet capacity for intelligence operations and subversion. In terms of contemporary U.S. foreign policy practice, the globalist sees these considerations as central in determining whether intervention is justified or not.[33] Although in some cases agreeing with these conditions, the regionalist may object that the problem is to determine when these conditions prevail in advance of their actual occurrence.

□ Utility of Force Versus Economic and Cultural Instruments

A closely associated argument involves whether force or noncoercive instruments are the more effective. Without reviewing the lengthy literature on this subject, suffice it to say that the utility of force is more apparent to the globalist than to the regionalist. Perhaps the correct judgment is that the globalist puts too much confidence in the utility of force as both a deterrent and a defense, and the regionalist puts too little.

The globalist is accustomed to thinking in terms of nuclear strategic weaponry and large standing armies. But within Third World regions, domestic stability and external stability are even more intertwined and less separable than among advanced industrial countries because the polity is more fragile and subject to foreign manipulation.[34] Subconventional warfare is more common than conventional. From the regionalist perspective, noncoercive instruments—such as cultural ties, economic assistance, and political cooperation—have a very long reach. The limits of military intervention are apparent both because of the risks of military failure and the political costs of military success. Thus, the regionalist often tends to reject force as the arbiter of regional politics.

The administration of foreign aid is the fulcrum over which this policy debate stretches. The globalist finds domestic political support in Congress for combined packages of military and economic aid awarded during crisis intervals when some form of communist threat seems imminent. The regionalist tends to want to divide economic and military aid and to provide economic aid in peacetime when the capacity to absorb this aid is greatest. Military assistance remains a crisis instrument. The problem for the regionalist is that the votes just have not existed in Congress for the equivalent amount of financial aid in the absence of crisis; nor, however much Third World governments want overall foreign assistance, are they prepared to value economic over military help.[35] Perhaps this is why, in addition to comparative availability, the Soviet Union provides so much military aid to its dependents and so little true economic assistance.

☐ Traditional Alliance Association Versus Basic Human Needs

Finally, regionalists and globalists differ on the proper instruments of association and involvement in the Third World. The globalist tends to favor traditional alliance association: hence, the creation of multilateral defense organizations such as the Central Treaty Organization (CENTO) and the Southeast Asian Treaty Organization (SEATO).[36] But these organizations collapsed of their own weight because of internal disputes among the members. Or, more precisely, collapse of these multilateral alliance systems occurred because the external threat they were designed to offset was less compelling to the members than internal political, cultural, communal, and ideological differences within the region. Similarly, the United States has attempted to rely on client governments like the shah of Iran or Ferdinand Marcos of the Philippines, whose rules eventually decayed into corruption and repression that contributed to domestic unpopularity and the regimes' overthrow. Far from acting as regional stabilizers, these regimes ultimately were unable to foster development and to govern effectively. Indeed, as some subsequent regimes (Iran's Khomeini, Nicaragua's Sandinistas, and Libya's Qaddafi) attempted to exploit dissociation with the pro-U.S. policies of preceding governments, disparagement of ties with the United States became the modus vivendi for local rule.

Regionalists, conversely, have been much taken by the campaign to address basic human needs.[37] In terms of foreign policy means, the essence of the needs approach is very simple. The failure of traditional U.S. policy as favored by the globalist has been attributed to working at the wrong level—namely, the systemic or governmental levels. Basic human needs are individual. Thus, the regionalist often urges that U.S. foreign policy focus upon the requirements of the individual citizen regarding nutrition, shelter, health care, and education. The regionalist sometimes recommends that policy should outflank or circumvent often bureaucratically inefficient and corrupt local govenments to bring resources directly to the individuals most in need of them.

But to the frustration of the regionalist, the reaction of the polity supposedly benefiting from the basic human needs approach is often starkly negative. Foreign governments are accused of intervention and imperialism.[38] Far from reaching the poorest members of the recipient society, assistance is left to "rot in the sun," as in Ethiopia, or fails to find adequate local transportation. Local citizens are intimidated and fear participation in basic human needs programs.

A reasonable judgment is that the globalist often views relations with Third World countries as too highly institutionalized and subject to management by formal arrangements with governments internal to the region. The globalist response is too political. By contrast, the regionalist response, although correctly targeted in terms of who would benefit, is sometimes rather naive in terms of mechanics of distribution and implementation. The regionalist, thoroughly aware of the shortcomings of local bureaucracy, eventually recognizes that outsiders must work with local governments at the risk of not being able to work at all. But the regionalist approach is sometimes not political enough.

■ THE DEBATE IN PERSPECTIVE

Although the globalist and the regionalist perspectives are not complete opposites, nor are they unrelated to other pressing aspects of foreign policy conduct, the assumptions of both schools of thought do underlie much that is profound and even perhaps ambiguous about U.S. foreign policy behavior in the Third World. As an ideal type, neither of these perspectives corresponds perfectly to the outlook of any U.S. administration in the post–World War II period. Yet, administrations may be categorized in terms of their comparative enthusiasm for either interpretation. For example, the policies of both the Truman administration (1945–1953) and the Reagan administration (1981–1989) reflected the globalist interpretation, whereas policies of the early years of the Carter administration (1977–1978) and certain aspects of those of the Kennedy administration (1961–1963) favored a regionalist approach. Differences are even discernible within each administration, as certain officials and policymakers became known for their globalist or regionalist emphasis. In the Carter administration (1977–1981), National Security Adviser Zbigniew Brzezinski favored a globalist orientation, whereas UN Ambassador Andrew Young and Secretary of State Cyrus Vance emphasized regionalist approaches. Over time, administrations have even changed in outlook concerning these perspectives. In general, the Carter administration began with a strong regionalist commitment. But that commitment was supplanted by a globalist outlook as events in Afghanistan, Nicaragua, and the Horn of Africa seemed to involve more and more of an East-West orientation. The strong globalist outlook of the Reagan administration was already in the making before the Republicans took office. Perhaps, overall, U.S. foreign policy in the post–World War II period has shown a tendency to be globalist in interpretation. The degree to which these perceptions corresponded to objective evaluation is a function of a great many factors, some of which I have attempted to assess in this chapter.

The tension between globalist and regionalist outlooks is central to any discussion of intervention in the Third World by the great powers, including the United States. Although persons of goodwill and intellectual honesty will differ on the validity of these perspectives, the shortcomings of each and strengths of each are worthy of examination by an informed U.S. public. U.S. foreign policy can only be conducted on the basis of broad consensus. Such consensus can only be formed through reasoned debate about priorities as different as those embodied in the globalist and regionalist outlooks.

■ Part 3

TOOLS OF INTERVENTION

□ 5

Economic and Military Aid

Doug Bandow

Since World War II, the United States has provided $196.5 billion in *bilateral* (that is, government-to-government) economic assistance. Most of this money officially has been intended to promote economic development in other nations, either by underwriting specific projects or augmenting foreign treasuries. The United States has also extended roughly $118.6 billion in bilateral grants and loans to recognized governments (in contrast to guerrilla movements) for avowed security purposes. The largest program is Military Assistance Grants, which provides cash to other nations to enhance their defense. Moreover, the largest share, 25 percent or more, of the $232.1 billion worth of *multilateral* (that is, international organization–to-government) economic assistance during the post–World War II period has come from the United States. Almost 75 percent of that money has gone through the World Bank and its two affiliates, the International Development Association and the International Finance Corporation. Other assistance has been channeled through the three regional development banks, the United Nations Development Program, and other UN agencies.

This flood of cash has thrust the United States into the affairs of virtually every other nation on earth, and, increasingly since the end of World War II, those nations comprising the Third World. In fact, although the United States most directly and effectively asserts its power through military force, foreign assistance has affected far more countries on a more frequent basis. However, the benefits of the $373.1 billion (roughly $825 billion in 1988 dollars) spent on foreign aid since World War II are less clear: Many developing states have been moving backward economically; well-subsidized U.S. allies have been overthrown; and funds have continued to flow to nations that regularly oppose U.S. interests abroad.

■ EVOLUTION OF THE FOREIGN AID PROGRAM[1]

The first official U.S. foreign aid bill was passed in May 1812; it provided $150,000 in disaster relief to Venezuela following an earthquake. Although certainly a substantial 7.5 percent of the nation's $20 million budget at the time, it was not until World War II that foreign aid became a significant tool of U.S. intervention in the Third World. As President Harry S. Truman's administration demobilized much of the military—which had numbered 12 million—at the end of the war, it turned to foreign assistance to augment the U.S. arsenal for overseas intervention. In the late 1980s, the United States grants and lends roughly $15 billion annually to other nations, both bilaterally and multilaterally.

The U.S. assistance program effectively began at the end of World War II with the Marshall Plan, though a few UN programs for rehabilitation and refugees preceded it. Between 1948 and 1952, the Marshall Plan consumed 15 percent of federal outlays, roughly ten times the burden of the much more diverse foreign aid program of the 1980s. The Marshall Plan theoretically was created for humanitarian purposes—to aid in the reconstruction of Europe—but the Truman administration also viewed U.S. assistance as a means to bolster Western Europe against the threat of both domestic communist revolutions and external Soviet invasion. The first official recipients of military aid were Turkey and Greece, and Greece was facing a serious communist insurgency at the time.

The role of foreign aid was greatly enhanced in 1949 when President Truman, in his inaugural address, advocated a much wider distribution of U.S. funds in his Point Four program. Truman proposed to make available to other countries the benefits of U.S. technical knowledge and to foster capital investment in developing countries. Five years later, Congress created the Food for Peace program in an effort to reduce U.S. crop surpluses and feed the hungry in developing nations.

Programs involving security aid were constantly changed, as Congress successively established the Mutual Defense Assistance Program, the Mutual Security Program, Supporting Assistance, and Security Supporting Assistance. The Agency for International Development (AID) was established by presidential executive order in 1961 to administer economic aid programs. In 1973, Congress passed the New Directions legislation, which instructed that economic assistance be used more to meet "basic human needs," through literacy and health-care programs, for example. A few years later, Congress enacted the Economic Support Fund (ESF). Though technically a form of economic aid, ESF in actuality functions as a type of military assistance by subsidizing nations deemed important to U.S. security, either because of the bases they offer (such as the Philippines) or their role as regional military surrogates for the United States (such as Israel and Pakistan). The other major defense programs are the Foreign Military Sales Credits Program, the Military Assistance Program Grants, and International Military Education and Training.

The United States has actively promoted multilateral assistance programs as well. The World Bank, established as one of the Bretton-Woods institutions in 1944, theoretically lends for the purposes reflected in its official name: the International Bank for Reconstruction and Development. Over the years, the bank added the International Development Association, which makes interest-free loans to poor states, and the International Finance Corporation, which extends credit to private and public firms in foreign nations. The UN, too, through several different programs, provides funds and technical assistance to underdeveloped states.

Though both economic and military aid have been constants of U.S. policy, the amount, recipients, and form of assistance have varied sharply. As is shown in Table 5.1, though spending has fluctuated over time, ranging between $40.9 billion in 1949 and $12.5 billion in 1976, it has steadily dropped as a percentage of U.S. gross national product (GNP). Aid consumed roughly 2 percent of GNP at the start of the 1950s but only 1 percent a decade later. In the early 1970s, the percentage of GNP devoted to foreign assistance dropped to roughly .7 percent; it was just .4 percent in the 1980s.

The beneficiaries of U.S. aid, as portrayed in Table 5.2, have also changed as U.S. strategic interests have evolved. This is just as true of development assistance, designed to promote economic growth, as it is of security aid, for economic assistance generally has been doled out in a manner thought to advance U.S. political and security interests. As a result, during the late 1940s and early 1950s the bulk of U.S. aid went to Europe, which was viewed as the region most vulnerable to communism. Between 1949 and 1952, annual U.S. assistance to Europe ranged between $25 billion and $33 billion. Once the major northern European nations, particularly Great Britain, West Germany, and France, began to recover, aid flows shifted toward poorer Greece and Turkey, which along with Spain and Portugal are the major European beneficiaries of U.S. funds in the late 1980s.

Asia was a distant second on the aid recipient list until Europe began to recover economically and the Korean War highlighted the threat of communist aggression in the Far East. In 1955, assistance to Asia totaled $9.2 billion and surged past that to Europe, $6.1 billion, which further declined in the 1970s. Throughout the mid-1950s and early 1960s, Asian assistance fell below $8.4 billion a year only once; the Vietnam War briefly pushed that figure above $15 billion. Moreover, during the war the United States provided an additional $40 billion—$8.4 billion in 1973 alone—through the Military Assistance Service Fund, which aided Vietnam and the U.S. allies that supplied troops in the conflict. But the collapse of Vietnam and Cambodia in the mid-1970s cut U.S. assistance to that region by more than half in 1974; in the 1980s assistance to Asia fell below $2 billion annually.

Throughout much of the 1960s, Latin America ranked second behind Asia as a recipient of U.S. aid money. There was a sharp but temporary increase—to $4 billion—in assistance during the mid-1960s as part of the Alliance for Prog-

TABLE 5.1
U.S. Foreign Aid as a Percentage of Gross National Product, 1946–1986

Year	Aid
1946	1.47
1947	2.88
1948	1.23
1949	3.21
1950	2.08
1951	2.30
1952	1.96
1953	1.36
1954	1.30
1955	1.02
1956	1.15
1957	1.10
1958	.89
1959	1.04
1960	1.03
1961	1.04
1962	1.16
1963	1.07
1964	.83
1965	.78
1966	.91
1967	.79
1968	.77
1969	.70
1970	.66
1971	.73
1972	.76
1973	.71
1974	.59
1975	.45
1976	.52
1977	.41
1978	.42
1979	.57
1980	.37
1981	.36
1982	.40
1983	.41
1984	.43
1985	.43
1986	.39

Source: Data provided by the Congressional Research Service, Washington, D.C.

TABLE 5.2
U.S. Foreign Aid by Major Region, 1946–1986[a]
(2–year averages, in billions of constant 1987 dollars)

Year	Europe	Asia	Middle East	Africa	Latin America	Totals
1946	13.217	2.239	.129	.049	.203	15.837
1947	30.744	6.677	.134	.009	.159	37.723
1948	11.101	4.023	.007	.003	.212	15.346
1949	33.338	6.646		.001	.131	40.116
1950	25.566	3.468	.059	.001	.141	29.235
1951	28.506	5.485	.137	.004	.083	34.215
1952	25.309	4.621	.683	.011	.344	30.968
1953	14.688	5.348	.700	.119	.603	21.458
1954	9.977	8.764	1.006	.144	.309	20.200
1955	6.074	9.185	1.141	.043	.527	16.970
1956	6.499	10.680	.971	.052	1.096	19.298
1957	4.695	10.828	1.394	.107	1.352	18.376
1958	5.105	6.751	2.050	.067	.857	14.830
1959	5.611	8.762	1.804	.299	.901	17.377
1960	5.025	10.430	1.959	.173	.878	18.465
1961	4.817	8.582	2.496	.850	2.010	18.755
1962	3.690	10.798	2.487	1.240	3.753	21.968
1963	3.764	9.722	2.442	1.013	3.559	20.500
1964	2.256	8.351	1.559	.872	3.999	17.037
1965	2.146	8.673	1.675	.784	3.273	16.551
1966	2.319	12.261	2.076	.962	3.540	21.158
1967	1.635	10.623	1.754	.974	2.559	17.545
1968	1.205	13.155	1.360	.679	2.727	19.126
1969	1.271	12.815	1.194	.801	1.494	17.575
1970	1.127	12.240	.549	.623	1.843	16.382
1971	1.180	14.052	2.359	.702	1.502	19.795
1972	1.392	16.508	1.832	.620	1.504	21.856
1973	1.088	15.589	1.681	.572	1.305	20.235
1974	.707	7.412	6.366	.689	1.125	16.299
1975	.531	5.768	2.992	.716	1.224	11.231
1976	.522	2.906	5.903	.552	1.089	10.972
1976[b]	.551	.834	1.912	.194	.262	3.753
1977	1.122	2.299	5.711	.754	.717	10.603
1978	1.532	2.326	5.527	.974	.780	11.139
1979	1.069	1.954	12.281	.883	.744	16.931
1980	1.160	1.723	4.694	1.167	.739	9.483
1981	1.177	1.627	5.353	1.180	.868	10.205
1982	1.599	1.590	5.523	1.286	1.195	11.193
1983	1.816	1.939	6.275	1.196	1.533	12.759
1984	2.192	2.076	6.301	1.355	1.755	13.679
1985	2.170	2.100	6.903	1.670	2.300	15.143
1986	1.853	1.840	6.831	1.119	1.714	13.347
Totals	271.352	293.689	118.228	25.527	56.928	765.724

[a]Figures do not include $120 billion focused on specific regions.
[b]Transition quarter (fiscal year shifted).
Source: Data provided by the Congressional Research Service, Washington, D.C.

ress; but once the specter of more Cuban-style revolutions receded, interest in the program waned, and a decade later aid to Latin America had fallen below that to Europe. Funding increased again in the 1980s, peaking at $2.3 billion annually in 1985 as a result of the Reagan administration's efforts to bolster the governments of El Salvador and its noncommunist neighbors. But when assistance fell by $600 million in 1986, Latin America fell behind Europe once more. (The administration also launched the Caribbean Basin Initiative to promote regional economic development; the program involved little money, however, and flopped badly when Congress imposed quotas on sugar imports, one of the Caribbean's most important export goods.)

Concern over Israel's security caused the Middle East, which between 1946 and 1973 had never received more than $2.5 billion in a single year, to catapult into the number two aid position, after Asia, in 1974. Two years later, with the end of U.S. aid to Vietnam and Cambodia, the Middle East became the largest regional recipient of aid; in fact, outlays for the Middle East escalated above $5 billion annually by the middle of the decade and spurted to $12.3 billion in 1979, largely as a result of the Camp David accords and the informal U.S. agreement to subsidize Egypt heavily as well as longtime ally Israel.

Aid to Africa has lagged far behind that to other regions. Only in the late 1950s did U.S. assistance rise above minimal levels; aid flows broke the $1-billion level only twice between 1946 and 1979. Even after African aid peaked at $1.7 billion in 1985, that continent was still the smallest regional recipient of U.S. help.

An examination of Table 5.3 shows that foreign aid priorities have also varied sharply over the years. Immediately following World War II, development and economic assistance accounted for the largest share of U.S. aid—$39.4 billion out of a total of $40.9 billion in 1949—though military assistance took first place at $20.2 billion in 1951, as the Marshall Plan was waning. With an occasional exception, including the years 1962–1965, security aid has stayed in the lead position, even after military assistance fell sharply from $13.3 billion in both 1972 and 1973 to $3.9 billion in 1977 after the collapse of Vietnam and Cambodia. The Reagan administration markedly increased military aid, pushing it above the $7-billion mark in 1984, though outlays fell somewhat in succeeding years.

Spending on food assistance, which is predominantly economic aid mixed with some humanitarian elements, has ranged from $1.6 billion to $5.5 billion between 1955 and 1986. During a few years, food aid actually exceeded development assistance, though the latter generally has been higher. Finally, aid given through the Economic Support Fund, which essentially provides economic aid based on security criteria, and its predecessor programs actually exceeded development aid in the mid-1950s, when it ran as high as $7 billion. Spending in this category fell throughout the 1960s and early 1970s, hitting a low of $1.4 billion in 1969, but climbed back above the $5-billion level by 1985, as it was used to pay de facto rent for bases in allied countries, as well as

TABLE 5.3
U.S. Foreign Aid by Major Program, 1946–1986
(2-year averages, in billions of constant 1987 dollars)

Year	Development Assistance	Food Aid	Other Economic Aid	Multilateral Development Banks	Economic Support Fund	Military	Total
1946			16.749	4.357			21.106
1947			37.670			.958	38.628
1948			14.333			1.638	15.971
1949	31.627		7.780			1.516	40.923
1950	18.343		5.657		.003	5.949	29.952
1951	11.896		3.729		.750	20.186	36.561
1952	8.489	.393	1.607		.908	20.844	32.234
1953	6.997	.018	1.350		2.013	12.633	23.011
1954	3.214	.318	.439		7.023	10.835	21.829
1955	2.628	2.421	.070		5.690	7.499	18.308
1956	1.645	3.802	.202		5.053	10.247	20.949
1957	2.223	4.844	.164	.146	4.716	8.209	20.302
1958	3.488	3.188	.091		3.196	6.313	16.276
1959	4.321	3.349	.073		3.382	8.994	20.119
1960	4.178	3.784	.065	.310	3.201	8.707	20.245
1961	4.937	4.419	.055	.282	3.235	8.112	21.040
1962	6.863	5.291	1.042	.647	3.014	7.781	24.638
1963	6.749	5.365	1.090	.450	2.270	7.466	23.390
1964	6.613	5.484	.658	.407	1.702	4.358	19.222
1965	6.061	4.872	.929	1.114	1.757	4.644	19.377
1966	6.156	5.414	.676	1.230	3.143	7.369	23.988
1967	5.529	3.262	.598	1.256	2.595	8.051	21.291
1968	5.108	4.308	.530	1.376	1.952	8.623	21.897
1969	3.839	3.630	.539	1.478	1.363	9.593	20.442
1970	3.997	3.322	.515	1.396	1.464	8.417	19.111
1971	3.560	3.404	.469	.497	1.583	12.154	21.667
1972	3.806	3.205	1.319	.372	1.623	13.313	23.638
1973	3.433	2.791	.556	1.934	1.561	13.371	23.646
1974	2.704	2.252	.717	1.883	1.482	10.655	19.693
1975	2.713	2.787	.580	1.645	2.572	4.214	14.511
1976	2.354	2.527	.429	.046	2.181	4.928	12.465
1976[a]	.797	.361	.149	.646	1.673	1.262	4.888
1977	2.547	2.149	.519	1.677	3.180	3.944	14.066
1978	3.140	2.067	.407	1.857	3.737	3.960	15.168
1979	2.850	1.993	.547	2.528	3.070	10.463	21.451
1980	2.640	2.046	.848	2.105	3.109	3.058	13.806
1981	2.558	1.997	.735	1.276	2.847	4.232	13.645
1982	2.502	1.585	.680	1.523	3.343	5.239	14.872
1983	2.595	1.588	.614	1.721	3.440	6.518	16.476
1984	2.827	1.487	.563	1.475	3.504	7.285	17.141
1985	3.059	2.330	.651	1.664	5.642	6.408	19.754
1986	2.447	1.810	.564	1.189	5.017	5.811	16.838
Totals	201.449	103.889	106.978	38.501	108.013	315.778	874.608

Source: Data provided by the Congressional Research Service, Washington, D.C.
[a]Transition quarter (fiscal year shifted).

to underwrite the Middle East peace treaty between Egypt and Israel.

Grouping foreign aid programs into the categories of economic/developmental and security/military (see Table 5.4) provides another way of viewing U.S. priorities over the years. Between 1946 and 1986, for example, U.S. aid devoted to economic/development priorities declined from 100 percent to 35.7 percent of the U.S. foreign aid budget, with this type of assistance predominating from 1946 to 1950, 1962 to 1966, and in three later isolated years. By the mid-1980s, security/military aid accounted for nearly two-thirds of U.S. foreign aid outlays, though the form of aid was changing sharply. Purely military assistance (that is, aid directly tied to defense uses), which actually accounted for more than half of all aid expenditures during some years in the early 1950s and 1970s, had fallen to about one-third in 1986, whereas the ESF (a more general form of assistance provided to strategic client states) had risen to almost one-third.

Finally, multilateral aid took on increasing importance during the 1960s and the 1970s, as bilateral development assistance levels were falling. However, multilateral assistance, which rose from $310 million in 1960 to $1.4 billion a decade later and $2.1 billion in 1980, never matched bilateral development aid levels. And, under pressure from the Reagan administration, multilateral assistance fell sharply from its $2.5-billion peak in 1980, ending up at just $1.2 billion in 1986. Thus, bilateral programs remained the far more important source of economic aid.

Though foreign assistance has been a traditional political target of conservatives, the Reagan administration, devoted to an interventionist foreign policy, boosted outlays from $13.6 billion in 1981 to $19.8 billion in 1985, a 37 percent real increase. As a share of GNP, foreign aid rose from .36 percent to .43 percent. However, the increase was distributed unevenly between the different programs, for the administration primarily viewed foreign aid as an adjunct of the defense budget. Outlays for bilateral economic/development assistance rose 14.4 percent, whereas security/military aid jumped 70.3 percent. Multilateral assistance increased too, though only after being cut sharply—39.5 percent—in 1981.

Spending rose, despite public dissatisfaction with foreign aid, largely because of congressional and presidential logrolling. The administration was able to garner large hikes in military aid by supporting smaller increases in the development assistance programs favored by liberals in Congress; in effect, the Democrats' price for supporting aid to El Salvador was more money for health projects in Africa. However, this high-budget consensus came to a dramatic end in 1986, after the huge budget deficit and the budget-balancing legislation known as the Gramm-Rudman-Hollings Act created strong pressure on Congress to cut outlays. Legislators quickly focused on foreign aid, which has never been popular with voters, as a place to make cuts; as a result, outlays fell 14.7 percent in 1986. Though the cuts were made across the board on economic and military programs, they nonetheless fell disproportionately on different geo-

TABLE 5.4
Distribution of U.S. Foreign Aid by Type, 1946–1986
(percent of total)

Year	Development	ESF & Precursors	Military
1946	100.0		
1947	97.6		2.5
1948	89.7		10.3
1949	96.3		3.7
1950	80.1		19.9
1951	42.7	2.1	55.2
1952	32.5	2.8	64.5
1953	36.4	8.7	54.9
1954	18.2	32.2	49.6
1955	30.0	31.1	41.0
1956	27.0	24.1	48.9
1957	36.3	23.2	40.4
1958	41.6	19.6	38.8
1959	38.5	16.8	44.7
1960	41.2	15.8	43.0
1961	46.1	15.4	38.6
1962	56.2	12.2	31.6
1963	58.4	9.7	31.9
1964	68.5	8.8	22.7
1965	67.0	9.1	24.0
1966	56.2	13.1	30.7
1967	50.0	12.2	37.8
1968	51.7	8.9	39.4
1969	46.4	6.7	46.9
1970	48.3	7.7	44.0
1971	36.6	7.3	56.1
1972	36.8	6.9	56.3
1973	36.8	6.6	56.5
1974	38.4	7.5	54.1
1975	53.2	17.7	29.0
1976	43.0	17.5	39.5
1976[a]	40.0	34.2	25.8
1977	49.2	22.7	28.1
1978	49.2	24.6	26.1
1979	36.9	14.3	48.8
1980	55.3	22.5	22.1
1981	48.1	20.9	31.0
1982	42.3	22.5	35.2
1983	37.5	20.9	39.6
1984	37.1	20.4	42.5
1985	39.0	28.6	32.4
1986	35.7	29.8	34.5

[a]Transition quarter (fiscal year shifted).
Source: Data provided by the Congressional Research Service, Washington, D.C.

TABLE 5.5
Recipients of Largest Amounts of U.S. Bilateral Aid, 1986
(total grants and loans in millions of U.S. dollars)

Country	Amount
Israel	3,621.0
Egypt	2,539.1
Pakistan	668.2
Turkey	618.5
Philippines	504.2
El Salvador	444.4
Greece	431.9
Spain	385.2
Honduras	197.7
India	197.0

Source: Data provided by the Congressional Research Service, Washington, D.C.

graphic regions. Congress chose largely to insulate Egypt, Israel, and some of the nations with U.S. military bases, concentrating the reductions on smaller aid recipients around the world. Among the ten countries receiving the largest amount of aid in 1986 (listed in Table 5.5), only India did not have a close security relationship with the United States. In fact, in early 1988 the State Department announced that it was ending assistance to a number of countries, including Fiji, Tanzania, and Mozambique, because of congressional cutbacks. Given the expectation of continued high deficits, foreign aid outlays are unlikely to grow much during the late 1980s and early 1990s. As a result, the primary political battle will be over distribution of foreign aid resources rather than spending increases.

■ THE EFFICACY OF FOREIGN AID

Does foreign assistance as a tool of intervention achieve its goals? That is a difficult assessment to make, in part because the various aid programs have several divergent objectives and may interact with each other in complicated ways. For example, although economic/development assistance is typically justified as fulfilling two major objectives—alleviation of human suffering in emergencies and disasters, and promotion of economic growth—every president since Dwight D. Eisenhower has also justified this form of assistance as supporting U.S. national security. President Reagan's first AID director, Peter McPherson, explained that the administration was pressing for large transfers to Central America to help "attack political and social unrest at their roots."[2]

Similarly, security/military assistance has two official purposes. The first is to help stabilize allied regimes, especially those facing armed insurgencies. The second is to enhance the military power of friendly states. However, this form of assistance is also thought to be a useful means of buying political favor for the United States.

Thus, the value of foreign aid as an instrument of intervention should be judged by its ability to relieve human suffering (humanitarian), promote economic growth (development), stabilize potentially unsteady societies (security), improve the defense capabilities of allied governments (military), and buy influence for Washington (political). It is not surprising that the U.S. foreign policy establishment, which has consistently supported financial transfers abroad, harbors few doubts—publicly, at least—about the efficacy of the $373.1 billion in foreign aid distributed during the post–World War II period. For example, Secretary of State George Shultz in 1983 formed the Commission on Security and Economic Assistance (informally known as the Carlucci Commission) to review "the goals and activities of United States assistance efforts." The commission concluded that "the [foreign aid] program makes an indispensable contribution to achieving foreign policy objectives."[3]

Yet, this conclusion rests on shaky ground. The commission itself admitted that it is not "clear that specific programs have been consistently effective with regard to any one objective"; nevertheless, it argued, "on balance" the programs have been a success.[4] In fact, there is substantial reason to question whether foreign transfers regularly fulfill any of their official ends, and there is substantial evidence that any successes achieved are largely ephemeral. The impact of foreign assistance on humanitarian, development, security, military, and political goals will be reviewed here in turn.

□ Humanitarian Goal of Relieving Human Suffering

There will probably never be a lack of need for humanitarian assistance. The Hunger Project, a New York–based organization whose goal is to eradicate world hunger, estimates that 13 to 18 million people die of starvation every year. Another half-billion are thought to be undernourished, and twice that number live in serious poverty. Life expectancies and infant mortality rates, though improving throughout the Third World, still lag significantly behind those in the industrialized West. Citizens of developing countries are also particularly vulnerable to natural and human-made disasters.

There is no doubt that at times foreign aid has helped meet serious humanitarian needs. AID manages a small general disaster assistance program, for example, that provides emergency goods and services. Among the beneficiaries of this disaster relief have been victims of drought in Africa, a cyclone in Bangladesh, fire in Burma, a volcano in Colombia, a cholera epidemic in Mali, an earthquake in Mexico, floods in Mozambique, a landslide in Peru, and civil strife in Sri Lanka. AID also offers predisaster planning and technical/managerial assistance to foreign governments and operates an early warning system that utilizes weather and geologic monitoring and forecasting technology to predict crop failures and potential famine. The application of this technology in the Horn of Africa, for example, was helpful in predicting crop shortages in 1987 and 1988 and in facilitating advance preparations for famine relief. It is hard to criticize short-term relief programs that respond to natural disasters.

Far more significant is the "Food for Peace" program (commonly referred to as P.L. 480), which grew out of a U.S. famine relief program in India in 1951. Created in 1954, Food for Peace has given away and sold, at reduced prices, 653 billion pounds of U.S. agricultural products to help feed starving Third World peoples. Despite its humanitarian intentions, however, the primary purpose of the program was (and continues to be) the cultivation of foreign markets to take price-depressing surpluses of agricultural products off the U.S. market (only 14 percent of food aid goes to disaster areas). Moreover, since the crops are sold at artificially low prices, U.S. competitors have charged that the United States is illegally "dumping" its surplus agricultural commodities on the international market. In short, Food for Peace has become a permanent subsidy for U.S. farmers, costing $1.5 to $2 billion annually, rather than supplying emergency assistance to needy foreign peoples.

The fundamental problem with the Food for Peace program is that large-scale transfers of cheap U.S. food products make it economically difficult for small producers in recipient countries to compete effectively, often forcing them out of business. As a result, concluded one internal AID audit, "the long-term feeding programs in the same areas for ten years or more have great potential" for creating disincentives to indigenous food production.[5] Similarly, complained one Third World observer, "Food for Peace became a stumbling block to development" as the United States offered and poor states accepted cheap food, despite "its impact on their farmers and on the fate of their agriculture and of their struggling economies."[6]

Specific examples of how well-intentioned projects have gone awry abound. Regular and large shipments of food to India bankrupted native farmers throughout the 1950s and 1960s, while farmers in Haiti do not bring their products to market during periods when Food for Peace food is distributed. In a more detailed example, analysts from the Institute for Food and Development Policy (IFDP) have highlighted the negative effects of extended Food for Peace aid on Colombia's domestic wheat industry:

> Between 1955 and 1971, Colombia imported from the U.S. over one million tons of wheat that could have been produced more cheaply locally. The marketing agency of the Colombian government fixed the price of the imported grain so low that it undercut domestically-produced wheat. This dumping resulted in 50 percent lower prices to Colombian farmers. From 1955 . . . to 1971, Colombia's wheat production dropped by 69 percent while its imports increased 800 percent. By 1971, imports accounted for 90 percent of domestic consumption.[7]

In fact, even well-meaning, short-term, disaster-related assistance may effectively undercut local producers in the recipient country.[8] Following the devastating 1976 earthquake in Guatemala, farmers—who in the previous year had enjoyed exceptionally high yields of corn and other grains—sought to sell their stockpiled grains to earn the cash necessary to rebuild their homes and farms. Yet, according to IFDP analysts, massive relief from the United States "helped to lower the prices for locally grown grain, just when farmers most needed cash for their grain. As a result, food aid *stood in the way* of reconstruction." Although IFDP does not oppose disaster relief, it warns that "even in short-term emergencies, relief food should be purchased, as much as possible, from local and national producers whose families' livelihood depends on their selling grain."[9]

In short, humanitarian aid is very much a double-edged sword: Although it can help relieve human suffering when limited to the short-term alleviation of natural disasters, long-term subsidized transfers of food aid may ultimately cause more harm than good. In this regard, Food for Peace often has been a better deal for U.S. farmers than for foreign recipients.

□ Developmental Goal of Promoting Economic Growth

The U.S. government makes bilateral loans and grants and provides technical assistance and advice, through AID, that is officially intended to encourage economic growth—the traditional rationale for most economic aid.[10] Several multilateral agencies, such as the World Bank, International Monetary Fund (IMF), and the United Nations Development Program, are also partially funded by the United States; they provide funds both for individual projects and general financial support.

Although U.S. taxpayers provide billions of dollars annually to poor countries to spur economic growth, there is little evidence that foreign aid has any significant beneficial impact on Third World incomes. Despite large doses of economic assistance, the average increase in the per capita GNP of developing countries fell steadily from 6 percent in the 1960s and 5 percent in the 1970s to 2.5 percent in 1980 and 1 percent in 1983. In 1986, real per capita GNP actually fell; a number of countries, particularly heavily indebted states and sub-Saharan African states, lost ground economically.

The lack of an obvious relationship between foreign assistance and economic growth is even more apparent in a comparison of the growth rates of individual nations with the amounts of aid they have received.[11] For example, of the twenty top recipients of U.S. funds between 1960 and 1985, twelve actually fell behind their neighbors economically during that twenty-five-year period.[12] Nor do overall aid levels correlate with economic growth. The recipients of the greatest amounts of total foreign assistance (from the United States, other individual donor nations, and international organizations) in 1986 were, in descending order, India, Israel, Egypt, Bangladesh, China, the Philippines, Pakistan, and Sudan. In terms of average growth rates between 1965 and 1986, however, these countries ranked far differently: China, Egypt, Israel, Pakistan, the Philippines, India, Bangladesh, and Sudan. The annual average growth rate varied between 5.1 percent and minus .2 percent.

An interesting case study is that of Tanzania, which has received more foreign aid per capita than any other nation. According to one observer, "its output per worker had declined 50 percent over a period of a decade," while "it had turned from an exporter of maize to an importer." Moreover, "nearly half of the more than 300 companies expropriated by the government ('nationalized') were bankrupt by 1975, with many of the remainder operating at a loss."[13] Although obviously an extreme example, this scenario has been repeated in varying degrees throughout much of the Third World.

There are many reasons why aid has so little impact on foreign growth rates. One point is that world economic forces and the openness of foreign markets have a far greater effect on the relatively small economies of developing states. Moreover, capital is not a dominant factor in economic development; more than two decades ago Harvard economist Simon Kuznets estimated that capital accounted for just one-fifth to one-seventh of the per capita income growth in industrialized states, which are more efficient users of capital than developing countries. Furthermore, the Third World, which by 1988 had amassed a $1.2 trillion debt, has had no problem arranging commercial financing for development projects. Indeed, "money—or the lack thereof—is not a significant constraint on development," according to analysts of the Development Group for Alternative Policies, an organization committed to the restructuring of U.S. foreign-aid practices in the Third World. "All too often, Third World agencies are overloaded with funds that they cannot effectively absorb and utilize."[14]

Of course, "development" requires more than the simple manifestation of a rising per capita GNP. Equally important is the building of a just society in which everyone, including the impoverished rural dwellers that usually make up the majority of Third World populations, has an opportunity to share in the benefits of economic development. Unfortunately, neither the U.S. government nor foreign ruling elites have generally pursued such a strategy, instead utilizing foreign aid to serve their own self-interests.

For example, despite AID's professed commitment to alleviate rural poverty, the reality remains that much U.S. assistance has a very different purpose—namely subsidizing domestic businesses by promoting U.S. trade and investment interests. This emphasis on serving U.S. interests was clearly reflected in a 1987 AID newsletter titled "Foreign Aid: What's in It For You":

> [Foreign aid is] a sound investment that benefits both Americans and the people of developing countries. To make certain this investment pays off, programs are carefully planned and carried out by experts who know what works and what doesn't. Most of the talent and tools needed in an ambitious foreign

> assistance program come from American business and industry. That's why 70 percent of the money appropriated for direct, or bilateral, U.S. assistance is spent here, not overseas. . . . In addition . . . fully one-half of the U.S. contribution to [multilateral development agencies] is spent on American goods. The benefits from foreign aid are shared throughout the nation. Business, research centers or universities in 49 states received foreign assistance contracts in 1985.[15]

The key to failed development strategies in the Third World is not external aid policies, however, but rather the way this aid is utilized by recipient governments. Indeed, the domestic policies of developing nations are of paramount importance. Although a detailed analysis of these factors is beyond the scope of this chapter, suffice it to say that no amount of assistance can overcome the stifling statism of so many nations—bloated government bureaucracies, money-losing state enterprises, price and production controls, and perverse monetary, fiscal, and credit policies—or force the reform of programs that benefit political and economic elites at the expense of the rest of the population.[16] Countries that, for example, steal from their farmers by requiring peasants to sell their crops at artificially low prices to state marketing boards cannot expect to increase per capita grain production and feed their people, irrespective of the number of irrigation projects being funded by AID and the World Bank.

Zimbabwe provides a notable example, underscoring the importance of sensible domestic policies in promoting agricultural development. Described by the Hunger Project as an "agricultural miracle," Zimbabwe's agricultural program made over 800,000 small-scale black farmers more productive by raising the once confiscatory prices paid by the government for their crops, as well as by extending other services to rural areas. According to one analyst, "These communal farmers, who once produced mainly for subsistence, now account for more than 50 percent of Zimbabwe's grain production, compared with less than 10 percent at independence." Unlike the majority of African countries, which increasingly depend on food imports, Zimbabwe "today is self-sufficient in food and sends excess as famine relief to neighboring states."[17]

☐ Security Goal of Stabilizing Unsteady Societies

Virtually all forms of assistance are assumed to promote the stability of allied states, many of which suffer from enormous problems of poverty, social unrest, and leftist insurgencies. And in the short term, at least, U.S. aid does advance this objective somewhat. That is, the governments of Egypt, Pakistan, Zaire, and other nations allied to the United States are strengthened by the receipt of millions or billions of dollars from Washington. Moreover, in some cases, such as El Salvador, which is threatened by a serious communist insurgency, massive U.S. aid may play a role in preventing a pro-American government from collapsing.

Foreign aid often appears to do more to undercut than promote U.S. security in the long run by discouraging incumbent regimes from adopting needed reforms, prompting them to cultivate support abroad instead of at home, and tying the United States to unsavory dictatorships. First, by subsidizing what are often authoritarian and corrupt regimes, U.S. assistance makes it easier for leaders to resist popular pressures for reform. President Ferdinand Marcos of the Philippines, for example, looted his country, wrecked the economy, and emasculated the military; yet generous U.S. aid, nearly $600 million between 1983 and 1985 alone, helped prop up his corrupt government (see Chapter 15). Second, U.S. aid encourages foreign leaders to look to Washington rather than to their own polities for legitimacy. Again, as long as Marcos was able to reap the financial benefits of U.S.-leased bases in the Philippines, his general inclination was to suppress increasingly vocal opposition. The result is potentially not only more brutal regimes but also less stable ones. Third, U.S. subsidies act as a public endorsement of brutal regimes that often seem destined to fall: Only the Reagan administration's last-minute abandonment of Marcos saved the U.S. reputation in the Philippines.

Marcos's 1986 overthrow, ultimately supported by the United States, seems to have reduced the likelihood of a communist revolution in the Philippines. By contrast, U.S. policy in Nicaragua, the subject of Chapter 16, proved a far greater disaster. Anastacio Somoza, confident of extensive U.S. economic and political support, created a personal kleptocracy and suppressed moderate democrats, radicalizing the opposition. U.S. aid did nothing to temper Somoza's greed, but it did inextricably link the United States to his venal autocracy; when Somoza was finally overthrown, Washington found itself confronted with a hostile revolutionary regime in his place.

Similarly, strong support for Shah Mohammad Reza Pahlavi of Iran—symbolic as well as financial—tarnished the U.S. reputation without restraining growing Iranian unrest with the shah's autocratic rule (see Chapter 14). U.S. aid may have purchased some temporary stability for what was viewed as a powerful U.S. surrogate in the Middle East, but in the long run U.S. intervention contributed to the creation of the revolutionary state that now threatens to unsettle the entire region.

The United States could face similar problems in Zaire, a longtime U.S. client state ruled by another corrupt autocrat. Although President Mobutu Sese Seko has, through the end of 1988, successfully survived a series of crises, his country is in disastrous economic shape and suffers from serious ethnic and regional divisions. U.S. aid, $80.4 million in 1986, may help Mobutu maintain his hold on power, but it is doing nothing to relieve the underlying pressures that could tear Zaire apart. If Mobutu should be overthrown, the United States might find itself facing a more unstable and less friendly government.

In fact, by helping authoritarian, anticommunist regimes hang on to power, U.S. foreign aid often conflicts with the United States' professed goal of promoting democracy abroad. Even the Carlucci Commission, which enthusiastically endorsed U.S. aid, acknowledged "the possibility that the assistance supplied will be used to suppress democratic forces."[18] This possibility raises fundamental moral issues that, unfortunately, are rarely seriously considered in the formulation of U.S. foreign policy. And aid to dictatorships has negative practical consequences for the United States as well, as democracies, however volatile, seem likely to be more stable and receptive to basic U.S. freedom values and political interests in the long run, even if they are not necessarily as supportive of the specific policy goals of a particular U.S. administration.

U.S. involvement in El Salvador's guerrilla war underscores the difficulties of achieving the stabilization of a client state through massive amounts of economic and military aid.[19] Despite approximately $3.3 billion in U.S. aid during the eight years of the Reagan administration (more than $1 million a day), El Salvador's guerrilla war is intensifying as the "politics of polarization" continue to undermine the fragile centrist policies of the ruling Christian Democratic party led by President José Napoleón Duarte. The right-wing Nationalist Republican Alliance (ARENA) is gaining ground and expected to win the March 1989 elections, while the leftist Faribundo Martí National Liberation Front (FMLN), still disenfranchised politically, is stepping up the guerrilla war. In fact, U.S. aid has had a destabilizing impact in at least two ways: It has strengthened the military vis-à-vis the civilian authorities, and it has funded a poorly designed land reform program (that did not vest ownership in the peasant operators) that proved disastrous and was later abandoned.[20]

In any case, U.S. funds could not overcome the most serious problem: that, according to diplomats and Salvadoran officials, Duarte "never had the power to stand up to the Army, the oligarchy, or the U.S. Embassy. He never had the courage to call a halt to corruption. And despite his good intentions, he never addressed the grave social inequities that fuel the conflict."[21] Increased pressure from both the right and the left, combined with the weakening of the ruling party and the growing power of the military, bodes ill for achieving peace in either the short or long term.

In short, handing out cash does not automatically promote social, economic, or political stability. On the contrary, U.S. aid often results in long-term instability by insulating ineffective and brutal regimes from serious domestic upheaval, and taints the United States by tying Washington to illegitimate autocrats. Even in the case of El Salvador, in which massive U.S. assistance to a centrist, democratic government has kept a pro-American regime from collapsing, U.S. policy is poised for disaster.

□ Military Goal of Enhancing the Defense Capabilities of Allied Countries

Although U.S. aid programs may have largely failed in promoting either economic growth or social stability, they have strengthened the defense of some nations.[22] There seems little doubt, for example, that the Foreign Military Sales Credits Program, by subsidizing the purchase of U.S. weapons, has enhanced the military preparedness of countries ranging from Egypt to South Korea. Yet, it is very hard to judge how important those improvements have been to the security of either the recipients or the United States. The Carlucci Commission admitted that "success is largely measured by what does not happen—the attack or insurrection that did not occur or did not succeed."[23]

Proving that U.S. aid prevented a war or insurgency is virtually impossible, especially as U.S. military assistance, aside from the unusually high levels of support for countries such as South Vietnam and El Salvador, has accounted for only a small proportion of recipients' defense spending. In fact, in some cases, U.S. aid probably displaced domestic military spending by the recipient regime rather than increased overall military outlays. South Korea, for example, received hundreds of millions of dollars annually in subsidized credit through 1986, even though its economy was growing faster than any other during the preceding decade. U.S. assistance merely allowed Seoul to devote more of its ample resources to activities other than defense.

Even if U.S. aid prompts the beneficiary to build a stronger military than it otherwise could afford, there may be no practical benefits for the United States. The size of many nations' militaries is irrelevant to U.S. security. Official military assistance has flowed to more than one hundred nations annually, far more than are strategically important in any meaningful sense. Countries such as Fiji face no serious security threats; Luxembourg plays a minor role in the European military balance; and what justification is there for giving security aid to neutral Austria and communist Yugoslavia?

True, in individual cases—Turkey, which is a member of NATO, but which has a poorly equipped military; El Salvador, which lies in the U.S. backyard and faces a dangerous communist insurgency; and Israel, which is considered by many to be the most valuable U.S. surrogate in the Middle East—military assistance may provide the United States with some security benefits. But, even then the cost may be prohibitive. (Israel, for example, received $3.6 billion in U.S. aid in 1986.) In far too many other cases, however, assistance does not appear to advance its official objectives, let alone do so in a cost-effective manner. Military aid outlays may have more than doubled between 1980 and 1985, but the United States seems no more secure as a result.

□ Political Goal of Buying Government Influence

The ultimate, but usually unstated, justification for all forms of foreign assistance is to gain political influence for the United States within a particular Third World country. The logic of foreign aid in this context is relatively simple: The greater the amount of U.S. economic and military aid to a Third World country, the greater that nation's willingness to comply with the foreign policy wishes of the United States. Economic and military aid provides "bargaining chips" to be used when discussing issues considered to be of importance to Washington.

Where U.S. assistance is high enough to turn a Third World country into a client state, such as in Vietnam during the 1960s or in El Salvador during the 1980s, the United States may enjoy considerable influence over the political, economic, and military policies of that country. This is not likely to be healthy for the long-term development or stability of that country, of course, but massive amounts of foreign aid will have gained some measure of temporary influence.

Lesser amounts of aid can reap political influence when the topic in question is of little or no importance to a particular Third World government, but assistance usually does not enable the United States to dictate foreign policy compliance when the ruling elite is strongly opposed to U.S. interference or meddling. In August 1988, for example, the Reagan administration pressured Costa Rica, El Salvador, Guatemala, and Honduras to ratify a U.S.-sponsored document denouncing Nicaragua's role in destabilizing the region. El Salvador and Honduras, which receive significant amounts of assistance from the United States and are closely tied to Washington's anti-Sandinista policies, agreed to Washington's demand. However, Costa Rica and Guatemala, which are also aid recipients, refused to make the desired declaration. Whether because of fear of Nicaraguan retaliation or genuine disagreement in approach, they resisted enormous U.S. pressure, including "veiled threats of economic reprisals," according to Guatemalan officials.[24]

There are many other examples of nations that have gone their own way despite generous U.S. assistance. Zimbabwe, for one, was a steady recipient of U.S. aid ($162.8 million between 1983 and 1985) but nevertheless moved toward a one-party socialist state and regularly opposed the United States in international forums (Zimbabwe abstained on the vote condemning the Soviet shootdown of Korean Airlines Flight 007 and sponsored an anti-U.S. resolution concerning Grenada, for example). The United States eventually slashed its assistance levels after Zimbabwean officials denounced U.S. policy in front of a U.S. delegation that included former President Jimmy Carter. And consider the case of longtime U.S. ally Morocco, which has collected more than $2.1 billion in U.S. assistance since World War II. King Hassan was long considered to be pro-Western, but he shocked U.S. officials by signing a short-lived Treaty of Arab-African Union with Libya, the Reagan administration's international enemy number one. Similarly, Somalia was the beneficiary of $41 million in U.S. aid in 1988. Although the United States is the primary external supporter of Siyad Barre's regime, the U.S. embassy could not gain permission to evacuate Americans from the northern portion of the country at the height of hostilities between government troops and guerrilla insurgents.

These examples, far from being "exceptions" to the general rule of the economic dependence–political compliance thesis, illustrate the wide latitude enjoyed by Third World elites despite their acceptance of aid from Washington. Even a State Department spokesman, although referring specifically to the U.S.-Somali incident, acknowledged that "foreign assistance gives very little leverage when you want one-for-one results." Nevertheless, he advocated continued aid: "The sign that you give is that you stick by your friends."[25]

The argument that aid brings with it political influence is called into question by simply reviewing which nations receive foreign aid. In 1988, the Reagan administration proposed giving money to eighty-seven countries that had voted against the United States at least two-thirds of the time in the UN; another thirteen would-be beneficiaries opposed the United States at least half of the time.[26] This may be an imperfect measure of the state of U.S. bilateral relations with other nations, but it nevertheless raises questions regarding the political benefits of U.S. foreign aid.

In reality, the State Department rarely supports a cut in funding because, in its view, either relations with the recipient nation are getting better, or they are getting worse. In either case, the recommended course of action is usually to *increase* aid in order to ensure the continuation of enhanced ties or to prevent the further slippage of the relationship. As a result, beneficiaries know that while they should let the U.S. ambassador occasionally visit the presidential palace, they can freely ignore U.S. advice.

An even more fundamental objection to the use of aid to gain political influence, however, especially when the recipient is a corrupt autocracy, is that there is no warrant for doing so unless fundamental national interests are at stake. Garnering support on a UN vote, resolving some commercial dispute involving a U.S. firm, and reducing the relative influence of Washington's international adversaries are all potentially worthy goals, but their value is limited: Forcing U.S. taxpayers to underwrite corrupt dictatorships is far too high a price to pay to score minor political points. There is a moral aspect of foreign aid policy that all too often seems to be lost in the rush to implement realpolitik.

Moreover, as discussed earlier, U.S. attempts to buy influence can backfire disastrously where the United States ties itself to a discredited regime that is toppled. The United States presumably had influence with the Somoza regime in Nicaragua, but the value of that access seems small compared to the problems of its relations with the Sandinista regime during the 1980s. Iran provides a similar example; less dramatic cases include Sudan, where U.S. favorite President Gaafar Mohammed Nimeri was overthrown, and the Philippines, where popular pressure is growing to close U.S. military bases.

■ FOREIGN AID IN PERSPECTIVE

Once the United States decided to try to enforce *pax americana* in the aftermath of World War II, foreign aid became an integral part of U.S. interventionist policies. Although military force was considered to be the ultimate guarantor of U.S. interests, financial and technical assistance was perceived as a less expensive and less intrusive means of reshaping the global order, especially throughout the Third World, in the U.S. image.

Over the years, foreign aid priorities have varied sharply, both in terms of recipients and types of assistance. The consistent theme underlying the program for four decades, though, has been a commitment to promoting U.S. economic, security, and political interests, however these are defined. Foreign aid has often been presented to the U.S. public and advertised to the world as selfless humanitarianism; in reality, nationalistic goals have always been dominant.

Throughout its history, foreign aid has been assumed to achieve its objectives. Indeed, its very name—foreign "aid" or "assistance"—implies that the program's overall results are salutary. Yet, the actual benefits of foreign aid for U.S. foreign policy are debatable. Temporary humanitarian assistance has alleviated some suffering, but aid programs like Food for Peace have often done more harm than good. Financial flows to poorer states have underwritten some good projects but have also left a string of expensive white elephants across Africa and other nations. And although there are few plausible success stories in which assistance has spurred economic growth, disastrous examples abound in which U.S. and other Western aid has subsidized corrupt, autocratic elites as they destroyed their economies in the pursuit of their narrow self-interests.

Foreign assistance is also viewed as a means of stabilizing Third World states that face social unrest, thereby advancing U.S. security interests. Yet, strengthening incumbent regimes that suppress moderate opposition forces may ultimately be destabilizing. U.S. support for dictatorships in Nicaragua, Iran, Haiti, and the Philippines only seemed to make their rulers more intransigent, thereby hastening their downfall. Some defense goals have been achieved through U.S. assistance, but the programs directed at enhancing the military prowess of other nations have often been devoted to countries that can afford to defend themselves or are of dubious strategic value. Moreover, although an unending stream of foreign aid may buy political influence with other countries, Washington's promiscuous use of assistance has ensured that most states receive funds irrespective of their actions. Most important, access bought today may very well lead to a closed door tomorrow, as revolutionary regimes turn against the United States for helping to keep a prior government in power.

Overall, foreign aid has been successful as an interventionist tool in one sense: It has thrust the United States into the affairs of the majority of other nations around the globe. But whether the impact of that involvement has been beneficial or has achieved official U.S. foreign policy goals is quite another question.

6

Economic Sanctions

Kimberly A. Elliott

Economic sanctions—defined here as the deliberate government-inspired withdrawal, or threat of withdrawal, of *customary* (rather than contractual) trade or financial relations between two or more countries—have enjoyed widespread application as an instrument of intervention. Such sanctions typically involve reducing or even eliminating the flow of goods and/or money between a *sender* country, the country imposing sanctions, and a *target* country. The first documented use of economic sanctions occurred in 432 BC when Athens, in retaliation for Megara's attempted expropriation of territory and the kidnapping of three women, issued the Megarian Decree—limiting entry of Megara's products into Athenian markets—thereby contributing to the outbreak of the Peloponnesian War between Athens and Sparta.

The United States has been the dominant user of sanctions in the twentieth century. As of autumn 1988, U.S. economic sanctions were in force against Chile, Ethiopia, South Africa, Haiti, Iran, Libya, Nicaragua, and Panama; in addition, long-standing trade embargoes were in place against Cuba, North Korea, and Vietnam. The United States has taken the lead in imposing sanctions in 69 of 103 episodes occurring between 1914 and 1983 and has targeted Third World countries in 48 of these, successfully 42 percent of the time in those Third World cases.[1] Closer examination of the record, however, reveals that the effectiveness of U.S. sanctions in the Third World declined substantially after 1973, even as the frequency with which sanctions were imposed greatly increased. The 103 cases on which my analysis is based are documented in a study published in 1985.[2] Although reference will be made to the conclusions of that broader study for comparative purposes, I focus in this chapter on the subset of 48 cases specifically pertaining to U.S. sanctions in the Third World.

■ EVOLUTION OF U.S. SANCTIONS IN THE THIRD WORLD

The United States first intervened in the Third World with economic sanctions in 1938 in concert with the United Kingdom. Both financial and trade sanctions were imposed over a period of nine years (1938–1947) to force Mexico to compensate British and U.S. oil companies for property that had been nationalized. Except for this case and another targeting Argentina (1944–1947), the fifty-two remaining cases listed in Table 6.1 (see the following section, "Success and Failure"), including six since 1983, occurred after the end of World War II, almost half in the 1970s alone. Although approximately 50 percent of the cases involved sanctions against Latin America, almost a quarter targeted the Middle East or South Asia, with the rest centering on countries in Africa and East Asia (four cases relate to the war in Vietnam).

In attempting to shape the postwar world to its liking, the United States did not hesitate to use economic leverage to coerce, even destabilize, uncooperative governments. Sanctions efforts in the first twenty-five years after World War II focused on moderating—or, failing that, overthrowing—nationalist, often left-leaning leaders in newly independent countries. In nearly half of the episodes in this period (ten of twenty-two), the United States sought to destabilize governments led by such leaders. Another third of these cases involved relatively modest goals, including several aimed at settling disputes over expropriated or nationalized property (also a source of conflict in half of the destabilization efforts). Sanctions twice accompanied U.S. military efforts and on two other occasions were used in attempts to influence military conflicts in which the United States was not directly involved.

One of the earliest cases grew out of U.S. dissatisfaction with Argentina's lack of cooperation in World War II against Germany. It evolved into an effort to destabilize Argentine President Juan Peron, initially because of his Nazi sympathies and, later, because of his nationalist rhetoric and general unwillingness to cooperate with U.S. foreign policy. As the cold war between East and West replaced the hot war between the Allies and the Axis as the focus of U.S. foreign policy, the United States frequently initiated sanctions efforts against leaders considered too independent and too leftist, such as Prince Souvanna Phouma in Laos, President Rafael Trujillo in the Dominican Republic, and Indonesia's President Achmed Sukarno. Others, such as General Phoumi Nosavan in Laos and Ngo Dinh Diem in Vietnam, were deemed a liability, not for ideological reasons, but because of excessive ambition or corruption, which was perceived in Washington as inhibiting the global fight against communism. And, when that fight erupted into violence in Korea and Vietnam, comprehensive economic sanctions, including trade embargoes and the freezing of financial assets, accompanied the military effort.

In several other destabilization cases, sanctions initially were imposed as a result of the nationalization or the expropriation of private property held by U.S.

companies or citizens in those countries. Such actions provided both the justification for intervention and confirmation of suspected anti-Western, anticapitalist tendencies on the part of the leaders of these countries. Sanctions efforts of this sort were directed against Prime Minister Mohammad Mosaddeq of Iran (1951–1953), who made the mistake of impinging on British and U.S. interests when he nationalized the oil industry, and President João Goulart of Brazil (1962–1964), who interfered with International Telephone and Telegraph's (ITT) interests in Brazil, as well as Cuba's Fidel Castro (1960–present) and President Salvador Allende in Chile (1970–1973).

Besides these cases and the case of Mexico, expropriation or nationalization of private property was the source of lesser conflicts in three other instances. The 1956 U.S. sanctions effort against Egypt, following nationalization of the Suez Canal, eventually escalated into military conflict, with Israel, the United Kingdom, and France uniting against Egypt. But the United States was interested primarily in settling the dispute over the canal and, in fact, used economic pressure to force Britain and France to disengage militarily. In the 1960s, U.S. economic leverage was brought to bear against both Ceylon (1961–1965) and Peru (1968–1974), once again to force compensation for the expropriation of assets of U.S. petroleum companies.

In addition to using sanctions to retaliate against perceived anticapitalist policies, the United States also imposed economic sanctions on at least three occasions in the mid-1960s in attempts to encourage the adoption of "appropriate" economic policies. It sought to influence Chile's copper pricing policy (1965–1966), primarily as part of its domestic efforts to fight inflation; manipulated food aid (1965–1967) to encourage India to shift resources to agricultural development; and briefly cut off aid to Peru (1968) because of its planned purchase of French fighter jets, which Congress did not think should be subsidized by U.S. aid dollars.

U.S. objectives in the Third World with respect to sanctions, at least in a relative sense, have been more modest since 1973 than in the earlier post–World War II period. Only 15 percent of the cases in this period involved destabilization efforts, one-third of the level in the earlier period. President Jimmy Carter's efforts to ease General Anastacio Somoza out of power in Nicaragua (1977–1979) were part of his campaign to improve human rights around the world, and President Ronald Reagan's subsequent efforts (1981–present) to destabilize Somoza's Sandinista successors signaled the chilling of détente, as did the militarily preempted sanctions against Grenada (1983). The Reagan administration's two other destabilization attempts involving economic sanctions, against Muammar Qaddafi in Libya (1978–present) and against General Manuel Noriega in Panama (1987–present), reflected growing U.S. concerns with fighting terrorism and drug smuggling. Finally, although U.S. sanctions against South Africa were significantly expanded in 1986 (from minor controls on exports of arms and related technology dating from 1962), no other major sanctions cases were initiated in this period.

With the cold war easing as a result of détente, the end of direct U.S. military involvement in the conflict in Indochina, and the later rapprochement with China, relatively more modest goals of improving human rights and deterring the proliferation of nuclear weapons dominated much of the 1970s. These issues were only briefly at the forefront of U.S. foreign policy, however, and faded quickly with the inauguration of President Reagan and the chilling of U.S.-Soviet relations in 1981. Although Reagan increased the use of sanctions against industrialized countries in an East-West context, his administration relied relatively more on military force, either direct or through the support of proxy forces, than on any economic lever in the struggle against Soviet influence. In the Third World, he followed the 1970s pattern of employing sanctions for relatively modest objectives, most prominently to deter drug smuggling and terrorism.

Congress initiated the strategy of using U.S. economic sanctions to promote human rights as a goal of U.S. foreign policy several years before President Carter, who is prominently associated with this effort, was elected. In December 1973, Congress amended the Foreign Assistance Act, adding a "sense of Congress" resolution that the president "should deny any . . . military assistance to the government of any foreign country which practices the internment or imprisonment of that country's citizens for political purposes."[3] The following year, Congress attached Section 502(b) to the Foreign Assistance Act, calling on the president to "substantially reduce or terminate" military assistance to any government that "engages in a consistent pattern of gross violations of internationally recognized human rights."[4] Frustrated by the Ford administration's reluctance to use security assistance as a lever to improve human rights, Congress amended the "sense of Congress" language to make it legally binding. Unable to override Ford's veto, Congress and the administration compromised on language whereby Section 502(b) is the "policy" of the United States.[5]

It is ironic that Chile's General Augusto Pinochet was one of Congress's first targets (1973–present) in the human rights campaign. Sanctions against his government were initiated just months after U.S. covert intervention and economic sanctions (1970–1973) had contributed to overthrowing Chile's left-wing leader President Salvador Allende. Other targets of economic sanctions imposed with the goal of improving human rights were Argentina (1977–1983), Brazil (1977–1984), Bolivia (1979–1982), El Salvador (1977–1981), Ethiopia (also involving an expropriation dispute, 1976–present), Guatemala (1977–1986), Kampuchea (1975–1979), Paraguay (1977–1981), South Korea (1973–1977), and Uruguay (1976–1981). Most of these sanctions were dropped in the late 1970s and early 1980s when several of the targeted countries elected civilian governments for the first time in many years.

The spread of nuclear weapons to countries that did not already possess them was another major concern, first of Congress and then of the Carter administration. In 1976, at the behest of Democratic Senators Stuart Symington and John H. Glenn, Congress amended the Foreign Assistance Act to require the suspension of economic and military assistance to countries buying or selling facilities for the enrichment or reprocessing of uranium (either of which could contribute to the development of nuclear weapons) unless the recipient was either a signatory of the Non-Proliferation Treaty (NPT) or had accepted "full-scope" safeguards (international inspection procedures designed to prevent nuclear weapons proliferation). In 1978, with the support of President Carter, Congress passed the Nuclear Non-Proliferation Act (NNPA), which required foreign buyers of U.S. nuclear materials or technology to submit to full-scope safeguards and allowed the United States to veto the retransfer or reprocessing of U.S.-supplied fuel. South Africa was the first target (1975–present) of export controls on nuclear materials, although the sanctions were driven as much by abhorrence of its system of apartheid as by its development of unsafeguarded enrichment facilities.[6] The United States subsequently imposed economic sanctions on Argentina (1978–1982), Brazil (1978–1981), India (1978–1982), Pakistan (1979–1980), South Korea (1975–1976), and Taiwan (1976–1977) because they refused to sign the NPT, submit to international inspection, were actively seeking sophisticated nuclear technologies, and/or had an apparent motive for the acquisition of nuclear weapons. Several of these cases also overlapped with those in which sanctions were imposed for human rights reasons.

A major foreign policy concern in the 1980s has been the spread of international terrorism. Although international efforts to combat terrorism were initiated after the 1972 massacre of Israeli athletes at the Munich Summer Olympics, terrorism did not become a frequent subject of economic sanctions campaigns until the late 1970s. In 1979, President Carter signed the Export Administration Act with an amendment proposed by Republican Congresswoman Millicent Fenwick attached. The Fenwick Amendment requires the State Department to identify countries that have "repeatedly provided support for acts of international terrorism" and to notify Congress of proposed exports to those countries that might "enhance the ability of such country to support acts of international terrorism."[7]

In accordance with the Fenwick Amendment, the State Department in 1980 cited Iraq, Libya, South Yemen, and Syria as supporters of terrorism. The Reagan administration State Department deleted Iraq from the list and added Cuba in 1982 and Iran in 1984. North Korea was added in 1987 for its suspected involvement in the downing of a South Korean airliner. Sanctions of varying degrees of severity were imposed against Iran (1984–present), Iraq (1980–1982), Libya (1978–present), and Syria (1986–1987). All trade with Cuba and North Korea had already been banned (in 1960 and 1950 respectively) by the time they were listed as supporters of terrorism, and sanctions against South Yemen would have been moot given the insignificance of its trade with the United States.

Discouraging drug smuggling is the most recent objective of economic sanctions and has attained prominence since the Reagan administration imposed sanctions against Panama (1987–present), especially in light of the indictment of strongman General Noriega on drug smuggling and money-laundering charges in Miami in February 1988. Congress had passed legislation conditioning U.S. economic and military assistance on cooperation with U.S. antidrug efforts in 1986, and, in addition to Panama, there have been rumblings about the alleged lack of cooperation from the Bahamas, Bolivia, Mexico, Paraguay, and Peru.

■ SUCCESS AND FAILURE

Despite the popular wisdom that "sanctions never work," economic coercion has been both a popular and somewhat effective tool of U.S. intervention in the Third World. Sanctions contributed to the advancement of U.S. foreign policy objectives in the Third World in twenty of forty-eight episodes.[8] Foreign policy goals, in this analysis, are changes actually and purportedly sought by the sender state in the political behavior of the target state.[9] Thus, the success of an economic sanctions episode—as viewed from the perspective of the sender country—is judged by two criteria: the extent to which the policy outcome sought by the sender was, in fact, achieved and the contribution to that achievement made by the sanctions (see Table 6.1).

A relatively simple index has been devised, scaled from 1 to 4, for each of these criteria:

Policy result:

1—*failed outcome,* as in the ongoing U.S. efforts (1960–present) to destabilize Cuba's Fidel Castro;

2—*unclear but possibly positive outcome,* illustrated by the U.S. effort to improve human rights in South Korea (1973–1977);

3—*positive outcome,* a somewhat successful result—for example, U.S. efforts (1938–1947) to force Mexico to pay compensation arising out of the nationalization of its oil industry; and

4—*successful outcome,* illustrated by Ceylon's settlement of expropriation claims by the United States (1961–1965).

Sanctions contribution:

1—*zero or negative contribution,* illustrated by the U.S. embargo against North Korea since 1950;

2—*minor contribution,* illustrated by the U.S. effort (1963–1966) to destabilize President Achmed Sukarno in Indonesia;

3—*modest contribution,* such as U.S. sanctions (1979–1981) against Iran during the hostage crisis; and

4—*significant contribution,* illustrated by the successful destabilization of President Rafael Trujillo in the Dominican Republic in 1960–1962.

The two indexes are multiplied together to get an overall success score; a rating of 9 or higher constitutes success. Success, by this definition, does not mean that the target country was vanquished by the denial of economic contacts or even that the sanctions decisively influenced the outcome. A score of 9 means that sanctions made a modest contribution to the goal sought by the sender country and that the goal was partially realized; a score of 16 means that sanctions made a significant contribution to a successful outcome. By contrast, a score of 1 indicates that the sender country failed to achieve its goals.

It is clear that economic sanctions cannot force a rival to surrender territory as easily as they can induce a country to pay compensation for expropriated property. Therefore, the cases were analyzed in terms of four categories of objectives: (1) modest goals, (2) destabilizations, (3) disruption of military adventures, and (4) major goals.[10] Although the "destabilization" and "disruption of military adventure" categories are relatively straightforward, "modest" and "major" are relative terms. In this instance, modest goals include settlement of expropriation disputes, deterrence of terrorism, improvement of human rights (including the restoration of democracy), prevention of nuclear proliferation, changes in economic policies, and interruption of drug smuggling. Examples of major goals include U.S. efforts to impair the military potentials of North Korea and North Vietnam and to force the Republic of South Africa to dismantle its racially based system of apartheid.

U.S. goals in 58 percent of the forty-eight episodes were modest and they succeeded 39 percent of the time. In 29 percent, the United States sought the destabilization of the target country's ruling regime and succeeded nearly 57 percent of the time. Overall, these two categories of objectives accounted for all but one of the successes, a case in the third category (disruption of military adventures) in which the United States interrupted economic and food aid (1963–1965) to pressure Egyptian President Gamal Abdel Nasser to remove troops from Yemen and halt aid to Congolese rebels, as well as to mute his anti-U.S. rhetoric. Efforts to influence the fighting between India and Pakistan in 1971 and halt Vietnamese intervention in Kampuchea failed (two of three such cases), as did the major sanctions campaigns against North Korea, North Vietnam, and South Africa.[11]

Besides the difficulty of the objective sought, a second major factor in success is the political and economic health and stability of the target. Third World target countries were, on average, less stable than target countries in the broader universe of 103 cases. Within the narrower subset, the health and stability of countries successfully targeted was typically lower still than that of countries against which sanctions failed. For example, although destabilization of a government would appear to be a relatively difficult goal to achieve, the success of sanctions in these cases may be explained in large part by the fact that the targeted regimes were often tottering even before the sanctions were imposed—for example, Allende's Chile in the early 1970s. In fact, in all but one of the successes—the replacement of Iranian Prime Minister Mosaddeq with the

TABLE 6.1
Cases of U.S. Economic Sanctions in the Third World

Target	Year(s)	Goal	Policy Result	Sanctions Contribution	Success Rating[a]
Mexico (with UK)	1938–1947	Settle expropriation claims	3	3	9
Argentina	1944–1947	Remove Nazi influence; destabilize Peron	2	2	4
North Korea	1950–*	Withdraw attack on South Korea	2	1	2
Iran (with UK)	1951–1953	Reverse nationalization of oil facilities; destabilize Mosaddeq	4	3	12
North Vietnam	1954–*	Impair military potential	1	1	1
Egypt (with UK and France)	1956	Ensure free passage through the Suez Canal; compensate for nationalization	3	3	9
Laos	1956–1962	Destabilize two governments; prevent communist takeover	3	3	9
Cuba	1960–*	Settle expropriation claims; destabilize Castro; disrupt military adventures	1	1	1
Dominican Republic	1960–1962	Cease subversion in Venezuela; destabilize Trujillo	4	4	16
Ceylon	1961–1965	Settle expropriation claims	4	4	16
South Africa (with UN)	1962–*	Dismantle apartheid; grant independence to Namibia	1	1	1
Brazil	1962–1964	Settle expropriation claims; destabilize Goulart	4	3	12
South Vietnam	1963	Ease repression; remove Nhu; destabilize Diem	4	3	12
Egypt	1963–1965	Deter military adventurism; stop anti-U.S. rhetoric	4	4	16
Indonesia	1963–1966	Cease "crush" Malaysia campaign; destabilize Sukarno	4	2	8
Chile	1965–1966	Reduce copper price	3	4	12
India	1965–1967	Change agricultural policy	4	4	16

continued

TABLE 6.1. Continued

Target	Year(s)	Goal	Policy Result	Sanctions Contribution	Success Rating[a]
Peru	1968	Prevent buying of French jets	1	1	1
Peru	1968–1974	Settle expropriation claims	3	4	12
Chile	1970–1973	Settle expropriation claims; destabilize Allende	4	3	12
India, Pakistan	1971	Stop military conflict	2	1	2
Uganda (with UK)	1972–1979	Improve human rights; destabilize Amin	4	3	12
Chile	1973–*	Improve human rights	2	3	6
South Korea	1973–1977	Improve human rights	2	2	4
South Africa[b]	1975–*	Deter nuclear proliferation	2	2	4
South Korea (with Canada)	1975–1976	Deter nuclear proliferation	4	4	16
Kampuchea	1975–1979	Improve human rights	1	1	1
Ethiopia	1976–*	Settle expropriation claims; improve human rights	1	1	1
Taiwan	1976–1977	Deter nuclear proliferation	4	4	16
Uruguay	1976–1981	Improve human rights	3	2	6
Guatemala	1977–1986	Improve human rights	2	2	4
Nicaragua	1977–1979	Improve human rights; destabilize Somoza	4	3	12
El Salvador	1977–1981	Improve human rights	2	3	6
Paraguay	1977–1981	Improve human rights	2	3	6
Argentina	1977–1983	Improve human rights	3	2	6
Brazil	1977–1984	Improve human rights	3	3	9
Libya	1978–*	End support for terrorism; destabilize Qaddafi	2	2	4
Brazil	1978–1981	Deter nuclear proliferation	2	2	4
India	1978–1982	Deter nuclear proliferation	2	2	4
Argentina	1978–1982	Deter nuclear proliferation	2	2	4
Pakistan	1979–1980	Deter nuclear proliferation	2	2	4
Iran	1979–1981	Return hostages	4	3	12
Bolivia	1979–1982	Improve human rights; prevent drug smuggling	2	3	6

continued

TABLE 6.1. Continued

Target	Year(s)	Goal	Policy Result	Sanctions Contribution	Success Rating[a]
Iraq	1980–1982	End support for terrorism	2	2	4
Nicaragua	1981–*	Destabilize Sandinistas	2	2	4
Suriname (with Netherlands)	1982–1988	Improve human rights; limit Cuban-Soviet influence	3	3	9
Grenada (with OECS)	1983	Destabilize Austin government	4	2	8
Zimbabwe	1983–1984	Stop anti-U.S. rhetoric	2	2	4
Iran[c]	1984–*	End support for terrorism; end war with Iraq	2	1	2
Syria (with UK)[c]	1986–1987	End support for terrorism	2	2	4
Zimbabwe[c]	1986–1988	Stop anti-U.S. rhetoric	2	2	4
Haiti[c]	1987–*	Improve human rights; hold elections	2	2	4
Panama[c]	1987–*	Stop drug smuggling; destabilize Noriega	2	1	2
El Salvador[c]	1988	Prevent amnesty for killers of U.S. advisers	4	3	12

* = Sanctions are ongoing.

[a]The success rating was derived by multiplying the two component indexes together; indexes are explained in the text. For a greater discussion of methodology, see Gary Clyde Hufbauer and Jeffrey Schott, assisted by Kimberly Elliott, *Economic Sanctions Reconsidered: History and Current Policy* (Washington: Institute for International Economics, 1985).

[b]This case is listed separately from the broader case against apartheid in South Africa that began in 1962 with the UN's call for voluntary sanctions. The U.S. did not really take the lead in that case until Congress forced the president's hand in the fall of 1985 and again in 1986. These later sanctions had not been imposed when the book was published, therefore the relatively minor sanctions imposed by the United States under the aegis of the UN were subsumed under that case.

[c]The rankings for these episodes are preliminary, as the cases occurred after *Economic Sanctions Reconsidered* was published and complete case studies have not yet been compiled.

shah—the target faced substantial economic and political problems.

Several other political and economic factors may be identified that might play a role in the outcome of a sanctions episode: (1) the presence or absence of companion policies, such as covert intervention or military force; (2) cooperation from one's allies; (3) the closeness of relations between sender and target prior to the imposition of sanctions; (4) the extension of offsetting assistance from third countries; (5) the degree of trade linkage between sender and target; (6) the costs to target and sender; and (7) the type of sanction. Each of these factors shall be considered in turn.

The United States applied noneconomic companion measures in addition to economic ones in one-third of the cases. Sanctions were a complement to the use of U.S. military force during the Korean and Vietnam Wars, whereas quasi-military maneuvers (such as moving an aircraft carrier into the Bay of Bengal during the fighting between Pakistan and India in 1970–1971) and covert intervention bolstered economic sanctions in other cases. Such companion policies were most prominent in destabilization efforts, in which they accompanied economic sanctions in ten of the fourteen cases. However, the presence of such measures is not terribly helpful in distinguishing successes and failures: Companion policies were present in almost as many destabilization failures (67 percent) as successes (75 percent). Economic sanctions contributed to the downfall of Idi Amin in Uganda (1972–1979) and of Anastacio Somoza in Nicaragua (1977–1979) without accompanying measures from the United States, although military pressure from Tanzania and indigenous rebels, respectively, obviously were the key deciding factors. To the contrary, the combination of complete trade embargoes, financial sanctions, and military measures have failed to dislodge popular revolutionary leaders in Cuba (1960–present), Libya (1978–present), and Nicaragua (1981–present). Furthermore, companion policies also do not appear to have played a significant role in cases other than destabilization efforts.

Another common perception contradicted by the evidence is that cooperation from allies is an essential component of a successful sanctions effort. Cooperation is typically sought in major sanctions efforts, although such efforts are unlikely to force fundamental changes in policy even if a relatively high degree of cooperation is attained. Obvious examples include the sanctions campaign against South Africa and the effort to destabilize Castro. As most of the cases discussed here involved modest objectives, international cooperation usually was not needed and often was not sought by Washington.

The warmth of presanctions relations between target and sender is important, however. First, it might be expected that the trade linkage (as measured by the ratio of target country trade with the sender to its total trade) would be higher between friends than between enemies. Second, it would also be expected that the willingness to change policies to accommodate an ally would certainly be higher than such willingness among countries whose relations are strained. Analyzing the set of cases reveals that in successful cases relations prior to the imposition of sanctions were more likely to be friendly—such as U.S. efforts to discourage the development of a nuclear-weapons capability in Taiwan (1976–1977) and in South Korea (1975–1976). In failed cases, relations had usually been more neutral and occasionally antagonistic, as with Libya even before 1978.

The sanctions effort may also be undermined if the target can convince a third country to come to its rescue, as even very high economic costs may be offset if another country is willing to step in with countervailing assistance. In the forty-eight episodes involving U.S. sanctions against Third World countries, offsetting assistance was three times as likely to have been a factor in failed cases as in those that succeeded. These cases usually involved targets in the struggle between the two superpowers, and the offsetting assistance frequently came from the Soviet Union or its allies, such as in the cases of U.S. sanctions against Cuba, Ethiopia, Nicaragua, North Korea, and Vietnam.

These factors are primarily political in nature; yet, in order to be able to inflict pain, the sender country must control something of value to the target, which in this case is measured by the target's value of trade with the sender as a ratio of the target's total trade.[12] Although the level of trade necessary to bestow coercive power still depends on the importance to the target of the policy change being demanded, a higher trade linkage should, on average, correlate positively with success. For example, 37 percent of Chile's total trade was with the United States in the mid-1960s when U.S. sanctions (1965–1966) were successfully imposed to influence Chile's copper-pricing policy. Conversely, only 5 percent of Iraq's trade was with the United States when unsuccessful sanctions were imposed (1980–1982) to discourage Iraq's alleged support for terrorism. Overall, evidence from the forty-eight cases shows that the trade linkage in successful cases was 27 percent as compared to 19 percent in failed episodes.

Other factors contributing to effectiveness are the economic costs to the target, as well as those that the sender must bear. There is no magic ratio of costs to target and sender that guarantees success. Rather, each cost variable is important independently. It is the degree of pain inflicted on the target economy balanced against the cost of complying with the demanded policy change that largely determines the effectiveness of the sanctions effort. From the sender's perspective, the higher the self-inflicted cost, the louder the protest from adversely affected domestic interests and the less sustainable the effort is likely to be.

As would be expected, the average cost to the sanctions target in the successful episodes was over 2 percent of GNP, whereas average cost in failures was only .7 percent of GNP. For example, the cost to Iran was nearly 4 percent of GNP in the (eventually) successful U.S. effort to get the hostages out of that country. To the contrary, cost was negligible in most of the failed cases of sanctions intended to deter nuclear proliferation, which typically involved fairly narrow export controls on nuclear fuels and technology that often could be obtained elsewhere. The cost to sender was less significant in these cases than in the total of 103 cases because the trade affected was usually of far less importance to the United States than to its target.

A final and very important factor contributing to effectiveness is the inclusion of financial sanctions. The economic and political effects of trade sanctions and financial sanctions differ in several ways. Trade controls are usually selective, affecting one or a few goods—for example, U.S. exports of nuclear technology. In such cases, the trade may only be diverted rather than cut off. Whether import (export) prices paid by (received by) the target country increase (decrease) after the sanctions are applied depends on the market in question. Often the price effects are very modest. By contrast, finding alternative financing may be harder and is likely to carry a higher price (in terms of the interest rate) and require greater credit security because of the uncertainties created by sanctions. Official development assistance may be irreplaceable. In addition, financial sanctions, especially involving trade finance, may interrupt a wide range of trade flows even without the imposition of explicit trade sanctions.

The economic effects of financial sanctions also tend to tilt the political balance in a more positive direction, from the perspective of the sender country. The pain from trade sanctions, especially export controls, usually is diffused through the target country's population. Financial sanctions are more likely to hit the pet projects or personal pockets of powerful government officials who are in a position to influence policy. On the sender's side of the equation, an interruption of official aid or credit is unlikely to create the same political backlash from business firms and allies abroad as an interruption of private trade.

The United States interrupted aid or other financial flows to Third World countries in forty-one of the forty-eight cases. Financial measures were employed in 95 percent of the successful episodes versus 79 percent of the failed cases. Moreover, financial sanctions without accompanying trade controls succeeded 50 percent of the time, whereas trade controls alone (export controls in six cases, export and import controls together in one) succeeded only once, when they contributed to Taiwan's decision to shut down a nuclear facility in which it was suspected of developing a nuclear reprocessing capability.

■ DECLINING SUCCESS AND SANCTIONS IN PERSPECTIVE

Despite the relative success that economic sanctions have achieved on average since the end of World War II, their effectiveness has declined substantially since the early 1970s. Approximately 64 percent of the episodes involving U.S. sanctions against the Third World between 1938 and 1972 were at least partial successes, compared to only 22 percent during the period 1973–1988. There appear to be four major reasons for this collapse in effectiveness.

The first is the relative decline of the U.S. position in the world economy. Immediately following World War II, the United States was the largest source for development assistance for newly independent Third World countries. Even well into the 1960s, the United States remained the primary source of development assistance and an important market for many developing countries, especially in Latin America. Since then, however, resource constraints in the United States, the recovery in Europe, and the emergence of Japan as a major economic player have made the United States just one aid donor and source of trade and finance among many. Moreover, with economic development has come reduced vulnerability for many potential targets. Perhaps, too, the relative decline of the United States and the post-Vietnam caution of U.S. leaders mean that target countries are less fearful that economic sanctions presage "something worse."[13]

A second reason for the greater success in the earlier period may have been a shift in the objectives that the United States hoped to achieve. Economic sanctions proved more effective in settling expropriation disputes and in campaigns to destabilize "undesirable" governments than in improving human rights, deterring nuclear proliferation, or combatting terrorism and drug smuggling. In addition, as 80 percent of the goals in the more recent cases were modest (compared to 32 percent in the earlier period), more important objectives, usually concerns about Soviet influence or strategic position, often superseded them. Moreover, although the goals may have been modest from the perspective of the United States, they were increasingly less so if viewed from the other side.[14] Stifling political opposition or keeping up with a rival thought to be pursuing a nuclear-weapons option were obviously far more important to military leaders in Argentina, Brazil, El Salvador, Pakistan, and elsewhere than continued economic assistance or nuclear technology from the United States.

A third and related trend is the growing assertiveness of Congress in foreign policy since 1973. Although it was the Hickenlooper Amendment, attached to the Foreign Assistance Act in 1962 by Republican Senator Bourke B. Hickenlooper, that provoked administration intervention in many of the expropriation disputes of the 1960s, that was a rare example of congressionally mandated economic sanctions. Increasingly in the 1970s, however, Congress has forced action on foreign policy priorities not shared by the executive branch through legislation constraining the president's discretion and requiring the use of economic sanctions in certain situations. The confused signals sent by administrations reluctantly imposing legislatively mandated sanctions, especially in the human rights and nuclear nonproliferation episodes, may have led target countries to believe (often correctly) that the sanctions would not be sustained.

The fourth major difference between the two periods is the form of sanctions imposed. Financial measures were part of the sanctions package in every episode prior to 1973 but were present in only 73 percent of the cases after that. The type of financial sanction used most frequently changed as well. Economic aid was the dominant choice in the earlier period, whereas military assistance was prominent in the later period, especially in the human rights cases where military governments were often the target. Given that many of these governments depended on force to maintain themselves in power, it is surprising that suspension or termination of military assistance—including training, police gear and other equipment—did not have more impact. As noted, however, these governments obviously perceived internal dissent to be the greater threat to their longevity.

Can the declining utility of economic sanctions be reversed? Although possible, the various factors that contributed to U.S. success in the earlier post–World War II period are continuing to move in a negative direction from the perspective of the U.S. government. Whatever administration follows that of President Reagan will be struggling to balance the still-large budget and trade deficits, which means the resource constraints on foreign economic and military aid will get tighter, and reluctance to interfere with trade flows for noncommercial reasons, especially in regard to U.S. exports, will grow.

But even after reaching sustainable fiscal and trade positions, it is highly unlikely that previous levels of U.S. dominance in the global economy can be restored. That dominance was inevitably a temporary phenomenon, the duration of which the U.S. government shortened when it adopted a policy of active reconstruction and development assistance for newly independent nations after World War II. These trends are accelerating. The European Community will be an even stronger economic competitor if it successfully completes the transition to a truly internal market by 1992. Japanese influence, rising out of its strong creditor position, will continue to grow for some time. The PRC is also emerging as a major player in the world economy, and the USSR may yet do so if the economic reforms espoused by Soviet President Mikhail Gorbachev can be sustained.

Nor will potential developing-country targets ever again be as vulnerable as they once were. The newly industrializing countries of East Asia—Hong Kong, Singapore, South Korea, and Taiwan—successfully adopted a strategy of export-led growth and have become important trading partners of the United States (as such, they may be subjected to sanctions for economic rather than political reasons), with growth rates that are the envy of the world. Many of the Latin American countries, favorite targets of the past, have also successfully penetrated the U.S. market, while diversifying their sources of supply for goods and finance.

Although the United States rightly recognized that it was in its interest to assist in the reconstruction and further development of the world economy after World War II, it does not seem to have recognized that the subsequent growth of healthy and powerful competitive economies would entail a parallel reduction in its leverage relative to other countries and, thus, in its ability to influence them. The circumstances in which U.S. economic leverage may be effectively applied have narrowed, and success will increasingly depend on the subtlety, skill, and creativity with which it is exercised.

[illegible]

[illegible] Helsinki [illegible]

[illegible]

□ 7

Covert Intervention

Harry Howe Ransom

Covert action is, by definition, a foreign policy instrument based upon secrecy and deception. Note the CIA's official definition: "Covert action is a special activity conducted abroad in support of United States foreign policy objectives and executed so that the role of the United States government is not apparent or acknowledged publicly. Covert action is distinct from the intelligence-gathering function. Covert action often gives the United States an option between diplomatic and military action."[1]

This one official paragraph captures the essence of and rationale for a policy of maintaining the ability to intervene covertly in the politics of Third World countries. The "special activity" referred to in official documents has included secret propaganda, manipulation of foreign electoral processes, overthrowing of governments, secret financial assistance, paramilitary operations, and assassination of political leaders. The secrecy required for covert action makes it difficult for an outside analyst to describe in authentic detail the past and, in particular, the recent application of this instrument. Often, only the the tip of the iceberg is visible. In describing such a variety of supposedly secret activities, one must, therefore, proceed by making inferences from known facts, speculating, or relying on undocumented accounts. At the same time, the pluralism of U.S. institutions and special interests makes secret-keeping a nearly impossible challenge for foreign policy decisionmakers and secret operators. Consequently, many, if not most, of past U.S. major covert operations have not remained secret.

■ EVOLUTION OF COVERT ACTION

The Truman Doctrine as enunciated in 1947 underscored the U.S. intention to contain Soviet communism around the globe and to protect noncommunist governments from communist subversive activities. The public side of this policy was economic and technical assistance, initially to Greece and Turkey, to strengthen capabilities for economic and political independence and self-defense. Yet, heightened U.S. fears in 1948 of an aggressive Soviet Union, fueled by the ruthless Soviet takeover of Czechoslovakia, the perceived communist threat to Italian independence in its 1948 elections, and accession to power of communist governments in Poland, Hungary, and other Eastern European countries, pursuaded Truman that containment required an additional, covert side. This included the organization within the CIA of a new unit, titled the Office of Special Operations (OSO), to conduct counterintelligence and espionage programs aimed at the Soviet Union. The initial covert policy of the OSO—which provided the foundation for later covert interventions in the Third World—was aptly described by Harry Rositzke, a CIA official at the time: "The Soviet Union was the enemy, and the 'Soviet target' our intelligence mission. We were professionally and emotionally committed to a single purpose. We felt ourselves as much a part of the American crusade against Stalin as we had against Hitler."[2]

President Truman signed a National Security Council directive (NSC 10/2) that set in motion several secret covert-action programs to contain communist expansion, carried out under the newly created Office of Policy Coordination (OPC). A vigorous internal debate occurred within the highest councils of government about the proper organization and control of covert actions. Despite State Department objections, the CIA, because of its existing capabilities and procedures for espionage through secret congressional funding, was chosen as the agency for covert action. Although such actions were assigned to the CIA, the State Department, Defense Department, and White House staff were expected to play the dominant role in policy controls. The problem of congressional consultation, however, which would come back to haunt the CIA with a vengeance, was ignored.

By the end of the Truman administration in 1952, and under the directorship of General Beedle Smith, the CIA's functions of espionage (OSO) and covert action (OPC) had been consolidated under a "deputy director for plans" (DDP). At this point the clandestine service was unified and began to grow and take on new assignments in the shadowy world of secret intervention. This occurred within the context of a consensus "communist containment" foreign policy for which there was strong bipartisan support. This policy required a major capability for secret intervention, primarily to counter Soviet support of Third World "wars of national liberation" around the globe.

Dwight D. Eisenhower, assuming the presidency in 1953, reaffirmed the need for a major covert-action capability. Eisenhower came into office on a platform of aggressive campaign rhetoric regarding containment—indeed, "rolling back"—of Soviet communism. The new administration was soon mounting covert actions to change the political climate in Iran, Guatemala, and elsewhere in the Third World. The temper of the times is illustrated by the words of a secret report to the president by a special Hoover Commission subcommittee in 1954. The report declared that "hitherto accepted norms of human conduct do not apply . . . to survive, long standing American concepts of 'fair play' must be reconsidered. We must . . . learn to subvert, sabotage and destroy our enemies by more clever, more sophisticated, and more effective methods than those used against us."[3] Hundreds of covert actions were undertaken throughout the Third World, ranging from propaganda through paramilitary actions to attempted assassinations. A national, bipartisan cold war consensus permitted these activities to go forward with little congressional knowledge or supervision. There was also little media exposure, because journalists and editors, in a spirit of wartime self-censorship, did not aggressively pry into secret operations. They adopted a government-knows-best attitude, in sharp contrast to that prevailing since the mid-1970s, when media passivity ended dramatically with almost constant investigations and disclosures about covert operations.

First came the Rockefeller Commission, an eight-member panel of conservative citizens (chaired by Vice President Nelson Rockefeller) that included Ronald W. Reagan. The commission, which limited its investigations to domestic intelligence activities as opposed to covert action abroad, concluded that the CIA had engaged in activities that were "plainly unlawful and constituted improper invasions upon the rights of Americans."[4] Its report cited such illegal conduct as opening of private mail, maintaining files on 300,000 individuals, infiltration of domestic groups, illegal break-ins, wiretaps, and investigations of tax records.

The Senate Select Committee to Study Government Operations with Respect to Intelligence, known as the Church Committee, was established in January 1975 to evaluate both the foreign and domestic activities of U.S. intelligence agencies. Its final report in April 1976 revealed that the CIA had conducted nearly 900 major and several thousand smaller covert-action projects since 1961, the vast majority taking place in the Third World. Although the report concluded that the impact of covert actions had been costly to U.S. foreign policy interests and reputation, it did not recommend the abolition of the covert-action function. Rather, it recommended that covert action be sharply restricted and that Congress assert a more aggressive monitoring of all future activity.[5]

The House Select Committee on Intelligence (Pike Committee) was organized in July 1975 to investigate allegations of illegal or improper intelligence activities by U.S. government agencies. In an unusual action, the full House of Representatives voted to suppress the Pike Committee's final report. The House had become convinced that the committee had acted irresponsibly with regard to some allegedly sensitive information that the president wanted deleted from the final report prior to publication. But the report was leaked to the press in February 1976.

The Pike Committee had analyzed all official covert-action approvals since 1965 and had concluded, contrary to popular beliefs, that the evidence gathered suggested that the CIA had not been a "rogue elephant," operating independently of presidential control or outside the boundaries of established foreign policy but, in fact, was responsive to the instructions of the president and his assistants.[6] The issue of covert intervention became not so much one of executive control as one of legitimacy, efficacy, or morality—in other words, a question of policy. Harry Rositzke, a veteran CIA officer, observed that the CIA had become as much a symbol of U.S. imperialism abroad and of secret government at home as the KGB, the CIA's rough equivalent in the Soviet Union.[7]

The Rockefeller Commission and Church and Pike Committees signaled the end of the cold war foreign policy consensus, influenced in part by disillusionment with the Vietnam War, the Watergate scandals, and revelations about U.S. intervention in Chile. In fact, a sign of the times was the 1974 congressional Hughes-Ryan Amendment, which explicitly prohibited use of the CIA for covert action unless the president had specifically certified its vital necessity for national security *and* had duly informed half a dozen congressional committees. This seemed to assure that covert action would rarely be undertaken in the future.

The hastily drawn Hughes-Ryan Amendment remained controversial throughout the administration of Jimmy Carter, as the president oversaw a massive reduction in covert-action budgets and staffs in which the number of covert actions in the Third World presumably were reduced. The Soviet invasion of Afghanistan in 1979, however, prompted renewed use of covert methods. In late 1980, Carter signed legislation, titled the Intelligence Oversight Act, that repealed the Hughes-Ryan Amendment. The act requires that the CIA and other U.S. intelligence agencies keep the two permanent standing intelligence committees of Congress fully and promptly informed of all secret intelligence activities—past, present, and anticipated—including sensitive, covert political interventions. Despite loopholes giving the president some discretion in extraordinary situations, a new national policy on covert action was established that seemed likely to reduce the future use of this secret instrument. Covert action was now to be a shared executive-congressional responsibility.[8]

The administration of President Ronald Reagan departed from the concept of shared responsibility, instead calling for "unleashing the CIA" from such inhibiting restrictions. Indeed, Reagan named William J. Casey, a veteran of the U.S. Office of Strategic Services (OSS) and covert operations in World War II, as director of the CIA and point man in an effort to reestablish covert-action programs on a par with those of the 1950s. A guiding program for the reinvigorated CIA was the Reagan Doctrine and its pledge to aid anticommunist guerrillas, which the administration was fond of calling "freedom fighters."

In the case of Nicaragua, the CIA became the instrument of "overt" covert action. This was because the CIA had become somewhat circumscribed by more aggressive congressional restrictions, such as the Boland Amendment prohibiting government efforts or expenditures to overthrow Nicaragua's government. Thus constrained by attempted congressional oversight, the White House turned to the National Security Council staff for a new and bizarre form of covert action. The actions of Lieutenant Colonel Oliver North and his associates brought upon the presidency a crisis in credibility and legitimacy that remains unresolved as of this writing. Indeed, the Iran arms-for-hostages deals and illegal diversion of funds to the contras placed the question of covert intervention at the center of national attention in 1987 and 1988. Congressional inquiries and efforts of investigative journalists suggest that secret foreign policies conducted by invisible and unaccountable governmental processes became the mode in the mid-1980s.[9] Questions and problems have been brought up regarding the place of covert actions in a constitutional democracy; these will be discussed later.

■ TYPES OF COVERT INTERVENTION

The covert action option for foreign policy implementation exists along a conceptualized "scale of coercion." It is one thing to give a little aid and comfort to U.S. friends in strategic Third World areas. It is quite another to change a regime by the direct action of plotting to overthrow its leader, perhaps by assassination. Indeed, the most extreme (coercive) form of covert action represents a foreign policy instrument just short of war. The four primary types of U.S. covert action to be discussed (in descending order of violence) are assassination plots, coups d'état, election intervention, and propaganda and psychological warfare. Paramilitary warfare, usually carried out covertly, and obviously located at the more coercive end of the spectrum, will be discussed in Chapter 8.

□ Assassination Plots

Political assassination of a foreign leader is the most extreme form of covert action and is usually part of a greater goal to change the existing government of the target country. Documented evidence provided by Church Committee investigators brought home the reality that assassinations had been regular instruments of U.S. foreign policy, a fact that came as a shock to many Americans. The finding of the congressional inquiry was that the CIA had been deeply involved in assassination plots during several decades of the cold war, despite the absence of any clear-cut proof of presidential authorization or concrete evidence that in any case an agent of the CIA "pulled the trigger."[10] It seems clear that a policy of "plausible denial" existed, leaving no paper trail implicating a president and no direct evidence that the CIA was directly involved in political murder.

Little doubt exists, however, that the CIA was to some degree involved in a number of assassination plots, including efforts to murder Fidel Castro in Cuba, Patrice Lumumba in the Congo, and Colonel Abdul Kassem in Iraq. The CIA also was associated with conspirators who plotted the death of Rafael Trujillo in the Dominican Republic, Ngo Dinh Diem in Vietnam, and General

Réné Schneider, army chief of staff, in Chile. The degree of U.S. complicity remains uncertain. Even less certain is whether such plots were authorized at the highest level—by the presidents themselves.

In the case of Castro, the Church Committee reports that the CIA began to plot his "elimination" as early as December 1959.[11] Earlier that year, Castro had turned to the Soviet Union, nationalized U.S. property (offering compensation in the form of 200-year bonds), and began exporting guerrilla teams to other Caribbean nations. By early 1960, Washington perceived Castro as directly challenging U.S. interests in the region, and the NSC's Special Group began discussing contingency plans for the overthrow of his government. It was soon clear that such plans included assassination. By the end of 1960, agents of the CIA had approached U.S. underworld leaders with the idea of placing a death contract on Castro, to be carried out by notorious U.S. mobsters or their agents. Other methods considered for doing away with Castro included various forms of poison from CIA labs, as well as poison pens, exploding seashells, a poison dart gun, and bacterial powder in a scuba-diving suit. Such plans were pursued during the administration of President John F. Kennedy. Obviously, none succeeded.

After the U.S.-supported Bay of Pigs landing in 1961 met with defeat, the president's brother, Robert F. Kennedy, insisted that the CIA continue its efforts to remove Castro from the scene. The renewed effort to kill Castro was directed within the CIA by William Harvey and bore the code name "Operation Mongoose." The Mongoose team, carefully monitored by Robert Kennedy, developed some thirty different plans to dispose of Castro, ranging from economic warfare to outlandish attempts at convincing Cuba's large Catholic population that Christ would return to Cuba in a Second Coming if they would rid themselves of their leader. Eventually it became clear that none of these schemes would work and nothing short of a U.S. military invasion could oust Castro. After the Cuban missile crisis in October 1962, the CIA was ordered to cease all covert operations in Cuba. We cannot know if this order was obeyed.

□ Coups D'État

The United States has been more successful, at least in the short-run, in staging coups d'état against foreign governments deemed inimical to U.S. interests. The first documented example in the post–World War II period was the CIA-directed overthrow in 1953 of Iranian Prime Minister Mohammad Mosaddeq and his replacement by Shah Mohammad Reza Pahlavi. The democratically elected Mosaddeq had nationalized the Anglo-Iranian Oil Company in 1951 and increasingly was perceived in Washington as falling under Soviet influence. Then, as now, the United States was interested in maintaining the flow of oil from the region.

Kermit Roosevelt, the grandson of President Theodore Roosevelt and a member of the CIA's covert operations branch, was put in charge of "Operation

Ajax." The plan was to overthrow Mosaddeq by an internal coup d'état, based upon intelligence assumptions that powerful groupings existed in the country that could be aided by the CIA. Within sixty days this was accomplished with the support of the Iranian army, a large segment of public opinion loyal to the shah, and the British intelligence services. The cost was small in both dollars (less than $200,000) and lives (the coup was virtually bloodless).[12] Unfortunately, the political leadership in Washington drew more about the efficacy of covert action than was warranted from this example. The heady wine of success led them to believe that this was a foreign policy tool that could be applied with equal success in other problem areas of the world. More important perhaps, as is discussed in Chapter 14, U.S. intervention in 1953 contributed to the fostering of a virulently anti-U.S. revolutionary regime some twenty-five years later.

A second example of U.S. covert intervention against a democratically elected leftist regime in the name of anticommunism—which, in the long run, would lead to dubious results—is Chile. During the Kennedy administration, the CIA had been very active in Chile, trying to shape favorable political outcomes, with considerable success. Kennedy, noting that Chile was a nation with a democratic tradition that had extended longer than a century (the last military coup d'état had been in 1925), hoped to make the country a model of democracy and capitalism in Latin America.

Under the administration of President Richard M. Nixon, however, Washington became aware that Salvador Allende, the leader of the Chilean left wing, was likely to win that country's 1970 presidential elections. Fearful of the prospect of a Marxist regime in South America, Nixon ordered the CIA to derail Allende's quest for the presidency. A "Track I" plan of covert intervention centered on manipulating the Chilean congressional vote through intense diplomatic and economic pressure, propaganda efforts, and subsidies of political groups opposed to Allende. The more nefarious side of U.S. covert intervention went under the heading of "Track II" and stressed the removal of Allende by a U.S.-induced military coup d'état. In 1973, Allende indeed was killed during a successful military coup d'état. Although the CIA apparently was not directly involved, the efforts of the Track I and II programs from 1970 to 1973 undoubtedly contributed to the outcome.[13] Chile's democratic system was replaced by a right-wing repressive regime that continues to hold power in 1989.

□ Election Intervention

Assassinations and coups d'état were the exception in the CIA's program of covert action during the cold war years. Other forms of covert action, such as interference with the electoral processes in areas of perceived strategic importance to the United States, were more common. In addition to the Chilean case, Italy, although not a Third World country, provided the classic *documented* example of U.S. intervention in the electoral process in target lands, and one that would become the blueprint for future U.S. intervention of this type in the

Third World. U.S. secret intervention in the 1958 Italian election was, in the words of its director, William Colby, "by far the CIA's largest covert political action program undertaken until then, or indeed, since."[14] CIA political operations chief in Rome in 1953, Colby stated that the Italian political scene was "an unparalleled opportunity to demonstrate that secret aid could help our friends and frustrate our foes without the use of force and violence."[15]

Colby's job was to ensure that NATO's line of defense was not breached by the possibility that a democratically elected Italian government headed by the nation's communist party would take power in 1958. Moscow was reportedly spending some $50 million per year to aid the Italian communists. The U.S. government assigned the CIA the task of secretly intervening in Italy to counter Soviet political action. A multimillion-dollar program was devised with the primary purpose of supporting Italy's center democratic political parties. This support was provided mainly in the form of direct payments for political activities, such as newsletters, leaflets, posters, and other propaganda material; staging congresses and public rallies; and membership drives, voter registration, and related political action. Additional CIA funds were allocated for supporting noncommunist trade unions, consumer and farmer cooperatives, cultural societies, youth groups, veterans' organizations, and a variety of local committees. In other words, CIA funds were used for a total penetration of Italian society in a massive secret effort to manipulate future political outcomes in keeping with the United States' perceived national interest.

The 1958 Italian national elections were a test of the efficacy of U.S. covert intervention. Yet, the results were inconclusive. Colby argued that covert political action in Italy was successful in terms of the long-term strategy of strengthening center democracy, deterring the growth of communist electoral strength, and eliminating the socialist-communist coalition. The Italians would possibly have produced such an outcome without U.S. intervention. In any case, U.S. covert election intervention, documented in an allied nation such as Italy, surely has taken place in Third World countries where possible leftist electoral victories were perceived as threatening U.S. interests. Indeed, one author has described various episodes of U.S. election intervention in countries as diverse as Brazil, British Guiana, the Dominican Republic, Ecuador, Jamaica, Laos, Lebanon, Nicaragua, the Philippines, and Vietnam.[16]

□ Propaganda and Psychological Warfare

The least coercive tool of covert action is propaganda/psychological warfare. Since the early 1950s, the United States has maintained a dual track for propaganda overseas: an open program, implemented by the United States Information Agency (USIA), and covert activities, most often performed by the CIA.

Congressional investigators have made public details of some covert propaganda activity. From these one can infer how such secret efforts are applied. For example, the Church Committee documented that U.S. covert action expenditures in Chile from 1963 to 1973 were targeted toward propaganda for elections and material support for political parties ($8,000,000), producing and disseminating propaganda and supporting mass media ($4,300,000), influencing Chilean interest groups (such as students and labor), and supporting private-sector organizations ($900,000).[17] This accounting demonstrates that propaganda efforts were combined with psychological warfare and political action to influence political outcomes believed to be favorable to the United States. Efforts were focused on aiding anticommunist forces within Chile with such programs as simple manipulation of the press, sponsoring of public opinion polls, placement of U.S.-written material in the Chilean media, and direct financial support of publications.

A 1977 survey in the *New York Times*[18] disclosed a number of details about the CIA's propaganda activities in the Third World at large. For example, at the peak of such activities, the CIA "Propaganda Assets Inventory" listed over 800 news and public information organizations and individuals that were on its payroll. Furthermore, the CIA secretly subsidized not only Radio Free Europe and Radio Liberty but also Radio Free Asia and Free Cuba Radio, as well as numerous social democratic magazines throughout the Third World, including *El Mundo Nuevo* in Latin America and *Quiet and Thought* in India. In Saigon, the CIA set up and financed the Vietnam Council on Foreign Relations, an organization designed to influence elite Asian opinions. Finally, the CIA maintained a major book-publishing program, which included the secret financing of over 200 English-language books since the early 1950s. As part of this effort, the CIA supported its own proprietary publishers, such as Allied Pacific Printing in Bombay and the Asia Research Center in Hong Kong.

■ COVERT INTERVENTION IN THE 1980s

For examples of covert action in the 1980s, the details are more sketchy and the evidence softer. We must rely on the writings of investigative journalists—Bob Woodward of the *Washington Post* is the outstanding recent example. His book *Veil: The Secret Wars of the CIA, 1981–1987* detailed a variety of covert actions taken by the Reagan administration to influence political events in selected Third World areas.[19] Woodward's work, full of intriguing particulars about secret operations, cites few sources and contains no footnotes. One major source cited is most unexpected and puzzling: William J. Casey, who was the director of the CIA from 1981 to 1987.

Accepting Woodward as a reliable source, one sees the CIA returning to a worldwide program of secret manipulation comparable in scope to activities in the 1950s and 1960s. For example, the Reagan administration, since 1981, has attempted to overthrow or weaken the regime of Libya's Muammar Qaddafi. A crucial aspect of this effort has been to assist Qaddafi's enemies both within Libya and in neighboring countries. Second, the United States initiated a major covert action in Chad beginning in 1981. The purpose of this program—which included arms, money, technical assistance, and political support—was to support Hissène Habré, Chad's former minister of defense, in his effort to overthrow the existing pro-Libya government. Finally, in 1982, the CIA, in coordination with Saudi Arabia, sponsored efforts by exiled Yemenis to conduct sabotage activities against the Soviet-dominated state of South Yemen on the Arabian Peninsula. The sabotage team was captured and tortured, ultimately confessing its CIA sponsorship. As stated earlier, these examples represent the tip of the iceberg of covert action, as scores of such activities remain invisible. In general, it is the failed secret operations that receive the most publicity.

One of the priorities of the CIA under the Reagan administration was combating international terrorism. Woodward claimed that the administration attempted to assassinate Lebanon's Sheikh Fadlallah, the fundamentalist Muslim leader of Hizbollah (Party of God), who was believed to be responsible for the three terrorist bombings of U.S. facilities in Beirut. Operations control was given to the Saudis, who, in turn, hired a British Special Air Services commando veteran. He, in turn, recruited members of the Lebanese intelligence service to direct the operation. The net result: an automobile laden with explosives detonated on March 8, 1985, within the vicinity of Fadlallah's high-rise apartment, killing eighty persons and wounding many more (Fadlallah escaped uninjured). After the bombing, Fadlallah's followers hung a "Made in USA" banner on the devastated building. Despite the attempt on his life, Fadlallah remained a problem. Changing course, the Saudis then apparently approached him with a $2-million bribe to cease attacks on Saudi and U.S. facilities. Fadlallah-supported attacks against Americans ceased.[20]

The most prominent aspect of the Reagan administration's covert activities revolved around the Reagan Doctrine and paramilitary support for anticommunist guerrilla insurgencies in Afghanistan, Angola, Cambodia, and Nicaragua. Although these activities are amply discussed in Chapter 8, three examples of direct CIA intervention relating to Nicaragua illustrate the problems that use of this tool have entailed for relations between Congress and the executive branch.[21]

The first example relates to the Reagan administration's decision to put counterrevolutionary pressure on the Sandinista government. The policy was implemented at a time when Congress was seriously divided over the issue. Many saw diplomacy as a better course to follow than aiding the Honduran-based contras, who sought to destroy the government in Managua. Senate and House intelligence committees became very involved in this policy. Not only had the House committee by law prohibited CIA efforts to overthrow the Sandinista government, but in January 1985 it issued a stinging report on other aspects of CIA-directed operations in Central America. The committee singled out for criticism the CIA-sponsored document *Psychological Operations in*

Guerrilla Warfare, labeled by the media as the "CIA Manual." After investigating the circumstances of the manual's production, the House Democratic committee majority concluded that the manual (1) violated the Boland Amendment by advocating overthrow of the Sandinistas; (2) violated presidential orders prohibiting assassination; (3) created profound embarrassment for the United States; (4) demonstrated that the CIA did not have effective procedures for controlling its agents; and (5) violated congressional spending guidelines placing a cap on aid to the contras. The report symbolized the new congressional posture of involving itself in CIA management issues.

The second example involves the CIA's direct role in the mining of Nicaraguan harbors. On April 10, 1984, CIA Director Casey was required to report to the full Senate on the harbor-mining project. Consequent to this briefing, the Senate voted eighty-four to twelve to prohibit future funds from being used for mining ports or territorial waters of Nicaragua. Again, Congress was involved in secret operational issues. Shortly thereafter, Casey met with the Senate Intelligence Committee and apologized to members for not keeping them properly informed. On June 6, 1984, Casey—with the president's approval—signed an agreement with the Senate committee pledging to follow precise procedures for fully informing the committee in the future, an agreement he apparently violated later.

The third example centers on the controversy raised in November 1986 by disclosure of arms shipments in 1985–1986 to Iran. This operation, which allegedly went forward under direct White House supervision and control, with CIA participation, was completely unknown to Congress until publicized in late November 1986. More than any other intelligence controversy since the beginning of the CIA, the arms-for-hostages (and diversion of funds to the contras) episode magnifies the national security dilemmas of the United States' constitutionally mandated separation of powers. In this case, the president claimed the right to withhold information, even from the congressional leadership, in the interest of the operation's security. Some congressional leaders have asserted that the president had violated legislative statutes designed to force the chief executive to consult in a timely manner with Congress—at least its leadership—on even the most sensitive of operations. Indeed, executive branch actions were in violation of the spirit if not the letter of the Intelligence Oversight Act of 1980, which required all intelligence agencies to keep the select oversight committees fully and promptly informed of all secret intelligence activities. The controversy produced a crisis for the Reagan presidency, threatening to produce a foreign policy stalemate between Congress and a president unwilling to give up independent, discretionary power in certain covert actions.

■ EFFICACY OF COVERT ACTION

How should the United States protect its foreign interests in the dynamic and unstable world of the 1980s? There is no question that the national interests of the United States are inextricably intertwined with events at the world's four corners. What happens in Grenada, Iran, Nicaragua, the Philippines, and South Africa—the five case studies of this book—can affect the welfare and security of the United States. Is covert intervention the most reliable instrument to protect these interests?

What are the arguments for and against covert action? Four basic arguments favoring its use are: (1) The United States should have a capability in certain situations that offers a choice between doing nothing and resorting to open military action; (2) the Soviet Union, through its KGB and other secret agencies, is engaged globally in covert action, and the United States must fight fire with fire; (3) the United States can sometimes assist friends and allies secretly when open assistance would be embarrassing to the recipient; and (4) the United States' complex political structure is an impediment to decisive, secret executive action in a crisis.

Major arguments against covert action include: (1) It is illegal, a violation of the United Nations charter or international law, and, in any case, immoral; (2) the covert act, designed to impose one's will on a foreign nation is, in effect, an act of war; (3) covert action, by definition, requires secrecy, but in an open democratic society, secrecy may be impossible; (4) it puts a severe strain on accountability, a requisite for democratic government; and (5) covert action dangerously distorts the intelligence function, often leaving leaders misinformed on foreign realities.

Covert action's most fundamental problem is its inherent incompatibility with the demands of U.S. constitutional democracy. A strong likelihood exists that a secret instrument of power will ultimately corrupt. The CIA was initially created for foreign information collection, analysis, and estimates—all noncoercive activities that are vital to keeping decisionmakers appraised of important events around the world. However, because some of its information was to be collected by espionage, the agency was clothed in extraordinary secrecy. Covert action required a similar secrecy, so, as a matter of administrative convenience, it too was assigned to the CIA. This unwise combination of the intelligence function with secret foreign policy implementation created enduring problems. On the one hand, U.S. constitutionalism demands policy accountability as a means for evaluating policy application. Yet, covert action requires that Congress and the public must be deceived by the executive branch. Indeed, Congress has accused the presidency of deceiving the public and Congress and of behavior so extreme as to elicit suggestions of impeachment. Members of the executive branch typically respond by accusing Congress of "micromanaging" foreign policy and encroaching on the president's claimed exclusive role in the conduct of foreign policy. Furthermore, executive branch officials constantly contend that Congress is unable to keep state secrets. An executive-congressional stalemate on foreign policy is threatened. Because secrecy and democracy are incompatible, the covert-action instrument of foreign policy has confronted U.S. foreign policy decisionmakers—executive and congressional—with the extremely difficult problem of weighing costs versus benefits in an uncertain world.

This review of the evolution of covert-action policy and organization and the citation of past examples of covert actions leads to certain tentative generalizations. First, covert action must be understood as existing on a scale of coercion that categorizes it penultimately as an activity just short of war. This is because its purpose is secretly to impose the will of one nation upon another. Some covert action is a form of secret aggression—indeed, sometimes terrorism. In particular, however, covert action may be seen as existing along a subscale of coercion, in a category of benign activity that does not represent aggressive, immoral, or illegal activity. In other words, some covert action may be acceptable, discreet behavior—acceptable, at least, in terms of international behavior. Such would be the case when friends of democracy are secretly aided, and no fundamental violence is applied to the principle of self-determination. But its acceptability within the U.S. democratic framework remains a dilemma because of the tension between secrecy and accountability and between the executive branch and Congress.

Second, to foster and strengthen truly democratic forces in a foreign nation with nonviolent assistance presents a different problem from fostering violent anticommunist counterrevolutionary action that leads to nondemocratic consequences or which places the United States in alliance with repressive, authoritarian forces. Too often U.S. covert action has produced such nondemocratic consequences as the early and later cold war "successes" of Chile, Guatemala, and Iran.

Third, whether or not foreign democracy can be fostered by U.S. covert action, such action has little chance of fulfilling its objective in the absence of a strong bipartisan foreign policy consensus within the United States. The cycles of isolationism-interventionism make this an inherent problem. When strong bipartisan support exists for clear foreign policy ends and means, covert action will be an unlikely choice. Yet, ever since World War II, U.S. presidents have been using covert action to seek foreign policy results they were unwilling—for a variety of reasons—to disclose publicly. Usually the reason for secrecy has been the absence of consensus about foreign policy ends and means within U.S. traditions and the institutional framework. In fact, the secret often has been kept from Congress and the public rather than from the target country or the adversary. Covert activities make extremely difficult the implementation of the design of the constitutional Founding Fathers, who intended that the president and Congress share the burden of foreign policy and its evaluation. When consensus exists, covert action, be it wise or unwise, at least stands a chance of remaining secret in its contemporary context.

Fourth, destabilizing foreign governments by covert action, as a foreign policy goal, is a risky enterprise for U.S. foreign policy, for the outcome usually cannot be accurately predicted or controlled. U.S. experience since World War II suggests that sending covert operators into action always risks the loss of policy control and guidance of these forces, with unpredictable and often undesirable consequences. For example, the 1983 "CIA Manual" suggested the hiring of professional killers and the selective assassination of Sandinista leaders in rural villages, despite executive orders prohibiting assassinations. Once set in motion, covert action agents operating under deep cover often cannot be effectively controlled by responsible authority. The Iran-contra affair demonstrates how politically accountable officials at home may be kept in the dark about certain secret operations, thus allowing these operations to proceed without executive supervision.

Finally, as of this writing, information and judgments about the Iran-contra covert action scandal of 1985–1987 remain incomplete. Criminal indictments against some major White House principals remain in process. At the very least, however, in the words of the presidentially appointed Tower Commission, "the arms sales in Iran [in 1985–1986] and the NSC support for the Contras demonstrate the risks involved when highly controversial initiatives are pursued *covertly* [emphasis added]."[22] One of the most serious risks, beyond policy failure, is the fostering of disrespect for the law by those sworn to see that the laws are faithfully executed. The Iran-contra investigations reveal a secret apparatus dangerously out of control. They also reveal the corruptive impact of secrecy, which invites serious violations of law and moral standards. One can agree with the Senate Select Committee on Intelligence, which recommended in 1976 that covert action should be used sparingly. It should be seen as an "exceptional act" to be underaken only when national security is in extreme jeopardy. One could go further to stipulate that covert action is an act of war to be used only when vital national interests are directly challenged. If covert action is needed to combat impending terrorist threats or, say, to prevent a nuclear war, then its use may be necessary. But the Reagan administration's return in the 1980s to an almost routine use of covert action must seriously be questioned.

Invisible government, based upon a doctrine of ends justifying means, had become a reality. If the United States is to serve as any kind of model for developing countries in the Third World, the decisionmaking process must be repaired in order to sustain democratic ideals. In the last analysis, covert action represents a cynical view of world politics. Its routine use rejects the ideal of a world of diversity, sustained by the rule of international law and order, based upon the consent of the governed.

8

Paramilitary Intervention

Peter J. Schraeder

Paramilitary intervention is defined as U.S. economic and military aid to an armed insurgency intent on overthrowing a government deemed inimical to U.S. foreign policy interests and represents a proxy utilization of force in situations in which policymakers have decided that direct U.S. intervention would be counterproductive. In short, use of this instrument allows U.S. policymakers to carry a war to the territory of another nation while at the same time avoiding the most costly aspects of that war—American casualties. The agents of U.S. paramilitary wars have included both existing guerrilla insurgencies and U.S.-organized exile invasion forces. Usually implemented covertly under the banner of anticommunism, paramilitary intervention generally has revolved around the provision of military weaponry through CIA-contracted airlines and the organization and training of insurgents by CIA personnel in allied nations adjacent to the target country.

This foreign policy instrument was used most often, though not exclusively, during the 1950s and early 1960s and included such varied cases as Angola, Cuba, Guatemala, Indonesia, Iraq, and Tibet. It was not until the 1980s, however, that paramilitary intervention became a comprehensive, coherent, and overt instrument of U.S. intervention in the Third World. During its time in office, the Reagan administration committed the United States to supporting guerrilla insurgencies attempting to overthrow Soviet-supported regimes in Afghanistan, Angola, Cambodia, and Nicaragua, all under the rubric of what has become known as the Reagan Doctrine.

■ THE PARAMILITARY OPTION FROM THE 1940s TO THE 1970s

In the cold war atmosphere of the late 1940s, President Harry S. Truman presided over the roots of future U.S. paramilitary intervention in the Third World.

Truman ordered the creation of covert links with partisan guerrillas in the USSR in a largely unsuccessful effort to obtain military intelligence, cooperated with the British in several unsuccessful attempts at infiltrating emigré Albanians into their homeland to organize guerrilla bands and overthrow the country's communist dictatorship, and authorized the training of Korean commando squads as part of U.S. direct military intervention in the Korean War. It was not until the administration of President Dwight D. Eisenhower, however, that the United States would vigorously pursue the overthrow of Third World governments through paramilitary intervention.

The Eisenhower administration's first paramilitary intervention resulted in the successful overthrow in 1954 of Guatemala's democratically elected and reform-minded Jacobo Arbenz Guzmán, a leader perceived by U.S. policymakers as leading Guatemala on a path toward communism.[1] Arbenz, attempting to promote broadly based development and build on reforms initiated in a 1944 middle-class revolution, formulated a land reform program targeted toward the largely landless rural farmer. The program immediately ran into problems because it included redistribution of 234,000 acres (95,000 hectares) of unused land owned by the United Fruit Company, a U.S. multinational company whose owners loudly protested these actions to the U.S. government. Arbenz also met with disfavor in Washington when he legalized the Guatemalan Communist party and brought a few of its leaders into the government. The Eisenhower administration's response was to formulate a covert psychological destabilization program, which included the creation of a paramilitary invasion force of 170 Guatemalan exiles (aided by air strikes carried out by CIA pilots) and the construction of a radio station to spread anti-Arbenz propaganda. Organized by the CIA at a mere cost of $20 million, the program succeeded in generating popular and military unrest, forcing a panicked Arbenz to flee; he was replaced by a military government led by Castillo Armas.

The inexpensive overthrow of Arbenz undoubtedly gave the Eisenhower administration (and future administrations) a false sense of power and of their ability to control the nature of Third World regimes through the paramilitary option. One must note that the United States was successful because the Arbenz regime represented a fragile democratic coalition with powerful domestic enemies—most notably a disenchanted military—that were all too happy to take control in exchange for U.S. economic and military support. Yet, this short-term "success" proved to be rather disheartening: The next thirty-two years would find Guatemala ruled by a host of repressive military dictatorships that would balk at any measure of social reform and thus fuel growing levels of guerrilla insurgency. Nonetheless, the Guatemalan case provided the model for future paramilitary interventions in the Third World.

A second intervention entailing an expanded version of the Guatemalan model was the CIA-organized paramilitary invasion of Cuba at the Bay of Pigs in 1961, designed to overthrow the revolutionary regime of Fidel Castro.[2] Castro's success in ousting the popularly hated and U.S.-supported regime of

Fulgencio Batista in 1959, his clear intent to reform Cuba's economy along socialist lines, and his support for revolutionary movements in the Western Hemisphere quickly incurred the wrath of Washington. Rather than accept the reality of a leftist regime ninety miles from U.S. shores, the United States attempted to overthrow Castro by initiating a trade embargo (which continues in 1989), authorizing assassination attempts, and ultimately training, equipping, and providing logistical support for nearly 1,500 Cuban exiles at bases in Nicaragua for a paramilitary invasion. Initially authorized under the Eisenhower administration, the invasion forces were given the green light by President John F. Kennedy.

Unlike the weak government overthrown in Guatemala, Castro's revolutionary regime enjoyed a large degree of support among the general population and especially within the military. Miscalculation within U.S. intelligence circles concerning the extent of Castro's popularity was one of the factors contributing to the invasion's failure (it was felt that if the exiles could maintain an invasion beachhead, popular rebellions, over time, would occur throughout the island).[3] Rather than lead to Castro's overthrow, the attempted invasion merely allowed Castro to whip up nationalist anti-U.S. feelings and subsequently strengthen his position on the island—the exact opposite of what the United States was trying to achieve. More important, Castro, who was completely isolated by the United States, had little choice but to turn to the willing embrace of the Soviet Union to ensure the longevity of the Cuban revolution in the face of possible future U.S. intervention. Ridiculing as "stupid" U.S. efforts to "drive Castro to the wall," Soviet Premier Nikita Khrushchev nonetheless relished the expected results: "Castro will have to gravitate to us [Soviet Union] like an iron filing to a magnet."[4]

A third leader targeted by the Eisenhower administration for overthrow through paramilitary means was President Achmed Sukarno of Indonesia.[5] Sukarno met with disfavor in Washington because he accepted communists into his cabinet, announced his intention of adopting one-party rule under "guided democracy," and, most important, was a leader of the nascent Non-Aligned Movement (NAM) in the Third World (hosting its first conference in Bandung, Indonesia, in 1955). As is well known, the Eisenhower administration (and particularly Secretary of State John Foster Dulles) vehemently rejected neutralism: Nations were either pro-Soviet or pro-United States, with nonaligned nations falling in the pro-Soviet category and ultimately being suspected of harboring procommunist tendencies.

Unlike the previous two cases, the vehicle for subverting Sukarno was paramilitary support beginning in 1956 for an existing secessionist movement that incorporated the Indonesian islands of Celebes, Java, and Sumatra. The covert CIA program included transfers of military weapons to the rebel government and CIA-piloted B-26 bombers flying support missions. Yet, when one of the U.S. pilots, Allen Pope, was shot down and captured by the Sukarno government in 1958—clearly establishing the CIA link—Eisenhower ordered the halt of the paramilitary program. Five months later, the rebel government collapsed. Although the withdrawal of U.S. support hastened the defeat of the rebels, the primary reason for the movement's failure was the lack of nationwide support for the secessionist generals and the clear superiority of military forces remaining loyal to President Sukarno.

A final paramilitary operation of the Eisenhower administration involved covert military support for Tibetan guerrillas fighting against communist China's attempts to consolidate control over the formerly independent territory. The case of Tibet is unique in that although Beijing considered it to be an integral part of China—indeed, it was a vassal state of China for centuries—the territory had functioned as an independent state since the beginning of the twentieth century, generating popular pressures for the maintenance of some semblance of autonomy from Beijing. U.S. support for the indigenous guerrilla movement, which lasted from 1956 to 1973, included the training of guerrillas in the United States, India, and Nepal, as well as direct resupply of military materiel into Tibet through CIA air support. Unlike the previous three cases, however, U.S. intervention was just a "holding" exercise against consolidation of rule by communist China, as U.S. policymakers agreed that it was highly unlikely that the Tibetans could achieve independence.[6]

U.S. support for the guerrillas was curtailed significantly in 1960 when Eisenhower ordered the cessation of violations of communist airspace (including the CIA resupply operations into Chinese-controlled Tibet) after the U-2 pilot Francis Powers was shot down over the Soviet Union. The subsequent decline of U.S. support during the 1960s (completely ceasing after the 1973 warming of Sino-American relations), was matched by the increasing inability of the Tibetan guerrilla forces to mount effective campaigns against the superior Chinese military forces. Despite achieving its short-term goal of harassing communist China, the covert program proved to be ultimately counterproductive when future administrations sought to achieve closer relations with the PRC.

In a twist to the paramilitary trend of the 1960s, the United States also became involved in organizing and funding rather substantial guerrilla armies in U.S.-allied Laos and South Vietnam to further the widening counterinsurgency war against communist guerrillas in both nations. In both cases, the CIA and U.S. Defense Department created autonomous guerrilla armies with the acquiescence of the host government, most notably among the Hmong ethnic groups in Laos (1960–1973) and the montagnards of South Vietnam's central highlands (1961–1970). As the creation of these guerrilla armies was part of overt military intervention in allied nations, they differ from the defined subject of this chapter. Yet, it is important to note that both efforts inevitably unraveled once the United States withdrew from Indochina and had, perhaps, all along worked contrary to U.S. regional strategic interests: Support of the ethnically based armies in essence created self-interested "nations within nations," defeating the primary U.S. goal of fostering unified, national governments capable of defeating highly motivated communist guerrilla insurgencies.[7]

Apart from U.S. operations carried out in Laos and South Vietnam, the paramilitary option during the 1950s (including intervention in Cuba in 1961) thus centered around three basic themes. First, the Eisenhower and Kennedy administrations sought the overthrow of leftist governments considered inimical to long-term U.S. foreign policy interests. The exigencies of the cold war struggle with the USSR ensured that the paramilitary option would be applied even to democratically elected (although leftist) regimes. Second, it was deemed critical by U.S. policymakers that the role of the United States remain hidden, therefore requiring covert action as carried out by the CIA. Most important, however, is that the president and his advisers maintained dominance in the policy process as they formulated covert interventionist policies with little or no oversight from Congress. As Harry Howe Ransom noted in the previous chapter, a "national, bipartisan cold war consensus permitted these activities to go forward with little congressional knowledge or supervision."

Yet, despite extensive use of the paramilitary option against leftist governments during the 1950s, no new operations were begun in the 1960s after 1961. Two reasons may be posited for this decline: Growing U.S. military involvement in the Vietnam War increasingly focused U.S. attention on Indochina to the detriment of other areas of the world, and the dramatic failure of the Bay of Pigs operation may have made policymakers reluctant to utilize the paramilitary instrument. The United States instead relied on more discreet forms of covert intervention, not resurrecting the paramilitary option until the early 1970s when it was applied against Iraq and Angola.

U.S. paramilitary intervention in Iraq was different from all the previous cases in that it was only an adjunct to (and at the request of) an ally's previously established program. In order to force a settlement in a territorial dispute with Iraq that would be favorable to Iran, Shah Mohammad Reza Pahlavi offered to provide military aid to a Kurdish group seeking to secede from Iraq.[8] Fearful that the shah would drop his military commitment once the border issue was resolved, the Kurdish leadership insisted upon a U.S. guarantee that aid would continue until independence was won. President Richard M. Nixon decided to help the shah and provided $16 million in covert aid over a three-year period (1972–1975). The intervention was highly successful; in return for the shah's guarantee that no further aid would be furnished to the Kurdish guerrillas (including U.S. aid), Iraq in 1975 recognized Iran's claims in the Persian Gulf and Shaat al-Arab waterway. In the absence of external aid, the guerrillas were decimated by Iraq in the months following the signing of the agreement.

Although in the short run, U.S. policymakers could be pleased that such a small investment had substantially helped an ally, the long-term effects were much more dubious in nature; four years later a revolution in Iran created an intensely anti-U.S. regime, and five years later Iraq would go to war in part to regain the Shaat al-Arab, starting a bloody regional conflict that, despite a truce and cessation of major hostilities in 1988, still is unresolved in 1989. The irony of the paramilitary campaign is that the United States in 1988 was leaning toward Iraq in the Iran-Iraq war (see Chapter 14).

The second paramilitary program of the 1970s, which served as the precursor of renewed emphasis on use of this tool during the 1980s, involved U.S. intervention in Angola's 1975 civil war. Three guerrilla groups had been fighting Portuguese colonialism in Angola since the 1960s: Agostinho Neto's Popular Movement for the Liberation of Angola (MPLA), backed by Cuba and the USSR; Holden Roberto's National Front for the Liberation of Angola (FNLA), backed by the PRC and Zaire; and Jonas Savimbi's National Union for the Total Independence of Angola (UNITA), backed by South Africa and the PRC. (The United States had maintained limited covert links with Roberto since the early 1960s and only began aiding Savimbi in 1975.) In 1974, Portugal announced it was divesting itself of its Angolan colony and convened a conference in Alvor, Portugal, with the heads of the guerrilla groups to work out a transition agreement. The conference was a great success; all three leaders became signatories to the Alvor Agreement, which outlined the nature and timetable for democratic elections and the formation of a tripartite transitional government in which power would be shared.

The administration of President Gerald R. Ford, however, had other plans. It has been asserted that, rather than risk a victory by the Soviet and Cuban-backed MPLA in free elections, the Ford administration provided Roberto's FNLA with over $300,000 in covert aid (funneled through neighboring Zaire), which prompted him to seek control militarily rather than risk defeat in agreed-upon elections.[9] Both South Africa and Zaire sent troops to aid the FNLA. The entire equation changed, however, when Cuba, in response to FNLA attacks and external intervention, introduced 30,000 combat soldiers into the conflict and emerged, along with the MPLA, victorious. In the wake of Vietnam and fearful of growing U.S. involvement that might result in miring U.S. combat troops in another distant guerrilla war, Congress passed the Clark Amendment in 1976 prohibiting any further aid to guerrilla forces in Angola, effectively terminating this paramilitary operation. The net result of the intervention was disturbing; chances for a peaceful transition and future democratic government were lost, and the Soviets and Cubans gained a major ally and foothold on the African continent—the exact opposite of what the Ford administration had been attempting to achieve.[10]

The most significant aspect of the Angola intervention was that it represented congressional assertion of oversight of U.S. foreign policy in general and covert intervention in particular. Harry Howe Ransom, in Chapter 7, has adequately explored the evolution of congressional-executive branch conflict over the covert action function during the post–World War II period. Let it suffice to note here that, from 1976 on, Congress would become an active player so far as U.S. paramilitary intervention in the Third World is concerned.

■ THE REAGAN DOCTRINE AND PARAMILITARY INTERVENTION IN THE 1980s

The Reagan Doctrine both intensifies and departs from past U.S. paramilitary intervention in the Third World. Whereas past administrations sporadically intervened to overthrow or harass leftist regimes, the Reagan Doctrine provides a comprehensive ideologically based program for arming insurgencies intent on overthrowing self-proclaimed communist Third World regimes.[11] In a significant departure from the 1960s and 1970s, when paramilitary operations were to be kept hidden from public view, the doctrine has become an openly announced policy of intervention in the name of democracy and anticommunism. As President Reagan proclaimed in his 1985 State of the Union Address: "We must stand by our democratic allies. And we must not break faith with those who are risking their lives—on every continent, from Afghanistan to Nicaragua—to defy Soviet-supported aggression and secure rights which have been ours from birth."[12] In fact, despite serious friction between the executive branch and Congress over aid to the Nicaraguan contras, Congress adopted public resolutions of support for administration policies in Angola, Afghanistan, and Cambodia. For the first time in post–World War II history, the United States publicly adopted and implemented a program that went beyond traditional containment and embraced instead the need to roll back already established communist Third World regimes. It is to the specifics of the four applications of this doctrine that we now turn.

□ Afghanistan and the Holy War of the Mujahedin

The Soviet Union invaded the bordering nation of Afghanistan in December 1979 with over 100,000 troops in what was intended to be a short-term exercise to prop up a communist regime threatened by a mounting guerrilla insurgency. Nearly nine years later, approximately 120,000 Soviet troops remained, the insurgency had intensified, and the Soviet-installed leadership of Babrak Karmal, unable to end the guerrilla war of attrition, had been replaced by the Soviet-blessed Najibullah. In an effort to end what he had called a "bleeding wound" costing the Soviets as much as $6 billion a year and over 30,000 casualties (what some U.S. policymakers have termed "the USSR's Vietnam"), Soviet President Mikhail Gorbachev announced on February 8, 1988, his determination to seek a negotiated settlement to the Afghan conflict. Moving beyond rhetoric, Afghanistan, Pakistan, the United States, and the USSR signed agreements (known as the Geneva Accords) on April 14, 1988, in which the Soviet Union pledged the complete withdrawal of Soviet troops by February 15, 1989.

Two factors cast a shadow over the seemingly productive peace process. First, the guerrilla forces opposing the Soviet occupation, popularly referred to as the "mujahedin" (holy warriors), rejected the peace accords, vowing to continue the guerrilla struggle against the departing Soviet troops as well as refusing to accept any power-sharing agreement with the Soviet-supported communist government. The communist regime is opposed by at least seven major resistance groups—united in a loose federation titled the Islamic Unity of Afghan Mujahedin—whose total strength numbers between 50,000 and 100,000 guerrilla fighters.

Second, although both the United States and the USSR have committed themselves to noninterference and nonintervention in Afghanistan, the Geneva Accords allow, in reality, for continued U.S. aid to the mujahedin as long as Moscow continues to arm the Kabul government. The Soviet Union was especially critical of U.S. intentions to continue to aid the mujahedin into 1989—claiming that U.S. aid violates the Geneva Accords—and thus temporarily suspended the withdrawal of its forces as of November 4, 1988 (although both Moscow and the Afghani government reiterated their adherence to the February 15 deadline).[13] In essence, both sides will contribute to continuing civil conflict in Afghanistan as the Soviets attempt to extricate their forces from a seemingly unwinnable situation at the lowest cost possible. Indeed, even if the Soviets do achieve the complete withdrawal of their forces by the February 1989 deadline, the basis is set for a continuing proxy war between a Soviet-supported Afghani government and the U.S.-supported mujahedin until either a negotiated end to the conflict is achieved or one side militarily prevails over the other.

The mujahedin's jihad (holy war) enjoys a large degree of regional support, receiving economic and military aid from such diverse nations as the PRC, Egypt, Iran, and Saudi Arabia. U.S. covert support for the guerrilla coalition, publicly supported by Congress in 1985 and actually begun in 1980 under the Carter administration, represents one of Washington's largest paramilitary undertakings. Intended to pressure the Soviet Union to withdraw from Afghanistan, this aid is funneled through neighboring Pakistan and, since 1986, includes the highly effective U.S. Stinger antiaircraft missile.[14] U.S. military and economic aid, totaling $750 million for the period 1980–1985, was $470 million in 1986 and $630 million in 1987.

Several circumstances seemingly legitimize extending U.S. aid to the mujahedin: According to accepted precepts of international law, the Soviet Union illegally invaded and occupied the country; the vast majority of the Afghani people desire a Soviet withdrawal; and the guerrillas enjoy a large degree of regional support and overwhelming international support. Indeed, proponents of aid cite the Geneva Accords and initial Soviet withdrawal of troops as evidence of the fruits borne by strong external paramilitary support of the guerrillas.

Yet, one writer has questioned whether or not U.S. policy in Afghanistan is "mired in success"; although the United States has promoted its short-term goal of fostering the withdrawal of Soviet troops, the future prospects of Afghanistan's political system and relations with the United States remain unclear.[15] One major problem is the factionalized nature of the guerrilla resistance. Four out of the seven factions that compose the guerrilla coalition espouse Islamic fundamentalism, rejecting any type of power-sharing agreement with the communist government headed by Najibullah. The other three guerrilla factions promote a more traditional Afghani nationalism and are more willing to negotiate some type of power-sharing agreement. The fundamentalists, however, who are based largely in Pakistan, receive the major portion of external military aid (including U.S. aid) and subsequently work counter to the U.S. goal of achieving a negotiated settlement. Moreover, the seven-party alliance as a whole is considered by many foreigners and a large majority of Afghanis to be a "corrupt" and "artificial" creation of Pakistan.[16] In short, it is highly possible that civil conflict will continue to dominate Afghanistan's political scene long after the expected withdrawal of Soviet troops, as competing factions jockey for total control of a future Afghani government.

A further point to consider is that the net result of even a negotiated withdrawal is unlikely to yield a democratic government in the Western tradition, even though the Reagan administration has portrayed the mujahedin as democratic freedom fighters. The dominant Islamic fundamentalist faction, for example, proclaims the need to create an Islamic republic and, in fact, is ideologically much closer to the teachings of Iran's Ayatollah Khomeini than to the democratic vision of the Reagan administration. In fact, Pakistan's leadership, whose country serves as the conduit of U.S. aid and which largely controls distribution of that aid, supports the radical fundamentalist Hezb-e-Islami guerrilla faction's bid to play the dominant leadership role in a postcommunist government.[17] Even if the nationalist faction were to gain power, it too rejects the need for a pluralist-type democracy in the Western sense.

□ Cambodia and Continuing Conflict in Indochina

The Vietnamese army invaded Cambodia in December 1978 to overthrow the Khmer Rouge government of Pol Pot, a Chinese-backed and internationally denounced communist regime that had slaughtered nearly 1 million of its own people over a three-year period beginning in 1975. Originally welcomed by the Cambodian people, the Soviet-backed Vietnamese installed a puppet government under the leadership of Heng Samrin. Ten years later, the Vietnamese still maintained an occupation army of over 100,000 troops to combat three guerrilla groups threatening the pro-Vietnamese regime.

The guerrilla groups are tied together in a loose coalition titled the Coalition Government of Democratic Kampuchea (CGDK) and include the Khmer People's National Liberation Front (KPNLF), led by former Prime Minister Son Sann (numbering roughly 8,000 fighters); the Armée Nationale Sihanoukienne (ANS), loyal to former head of state Norodom Sihanouk (boasting 18,000 guerrillas); and the feared Khmer Rouge, led by Khieu Samphan (controlling between 30,000 and 40,000 guerrilla troops). Yet, in contrast to the success attained by the mujahedin in Afghanistan, the three guerrilla groups in 1988 were no match for the Vietnamese army and the growing forces of the Heng Samrin regime.

Moreover, compared to U.S. involvement in Afghanistan, Washington's commitment to the CGDK is very limited. The Reagan administration gradually increased the levels of non-lethal covert aid extended to the noncommunist factions of the CGDK (KPNLF and ANS) from $5 million in 1982 to $12 million in 1985 and nearly $18 million in 1988. This covert aid was complemented by nearly $3.5 million a year in covert aid as authorized by Congress through the Solarz Amendment in 1985.[18] Yet, U.S. support for the guerrillas has been cautious, to say the least—obviously because of the still-strong memory of past U.S. intervention in Indochina—and has been forthcoming as a result of requests by allies in the region, most notably the PRC (which supports the Khmer Rouge), Thailand (whose territory borders Cambodia), and the Association of Southeast Asian Nations (ASEAN) (which backs the noncommunist factions of the resistance).

As in the case of Afghanistan, several factors seem to merit U.S. paramilitary aid to the guerrillas: According to international law, the Vietnamese illegally invaded and occupied the country; the Cambodian people desire a Vietnamese withdrawal; and the Vietnamese occupation is denounced both regionally and within the international system. Moreover, proponents of aid to the CGDK may note that Vietnam has announced that it intends to withdraw 35,000 troops from Cambodia by the end of 1988 and all remaining forces (estimated at 70,000) by March 1990 if a political settlement can be achieved between the three guerrilla forces and the Cambodian government.[19] Whether this intention is a result of military pressure and its drain on the Vietnamese economy (as seems to be the case for Soviet withdrawal from Afghanistan); of pressure by Mikhail Gorbachev—Vietnam's largest financial patron—who wishes to extricate the USSR from regional conflicts; or of enhanced Vietnamese confidence in the ability of the Heng Samrin regime to maintain itself in power (or a combination of all three) is difficult to decipher.

Regardless of Vietnamese intentions, the greatest problem for U.S. aid to the CGDK is that the Khmer Rouge constitutes the military backbone of the coalition. Even if U.S. aid is directed toward the noncommunist factions of the CGDK, their ultimate military victory (which is highly unlikely) could very likely mean a return to a communist, pro-Chinese regime headed by the Khmer Rouge. Offered a choice between continued Vietnamese occupation or a government headed by the Khmer Rouge, it has been suggested that the Cambodian people would choose the former.[20] Yet, nonsupport of the guerrillas also ensures a communist regime, albeit one largely controlled by Vietnam. The fact that both scenarios do not bode well for a democratic, noncommunist successor regime explains in part why the United States has been hesitant to commit significant sums of money to the guerrilla war.[21]

A related problem with the CGDK is the inherent incompatibility of the three major partners. Little cooperation is found between the guerrilla groups either militarily on the battlefield or in the political realm. In fact, in the military realm, the dominant trend in 1988 was one of growing clashes between the Khmer Rouge and the noncommunist factions of the CGDK. This infighting undoubtedly has hindered success on the battlefield and certainly has hindered political attempts at achieving a diplomatic solution to the conflict. Although the leaders of the three guerrilla factions and the Vietnamese-sponsored government met for peace talks in July 1988 for the first time since the Vietnamese invasion in 1978, they could only agree on the creation of a "working group" that would decide if any future talks would be possible.[22] It is ironic that the seeming impasse between the guerrilla factions has been paralleled by a gradual thawing of relations between the Soviet Union and the PRC, both of which desire to resolve the Cambodian issue. As the Soviets and the communist Chinese are the major material backers of the primary groups involved in the conflict, this growing trend toward cooperation could be influential in formulating and guaranteeing a future accord agreeable to all parties.

□ Angola and Resolution of the Cuban Dilemma

The military conflict in Angola is a continuation of the 1975 civil war in which the Soviet and Cuban-backed MPLA emerged victorious over the FNLA and UNITA guerrilla factions. At the end of 1988, the MPLA government continues to rely on over 50,000 Cuban troops and 2,000 Soviet advisers, in addition to its 50,000-strong army, to maintain the regime against Savimbi's UNITA guerrilla forces and repeated military interventions by the latter's regional patron, South Africa. Although unable to overthrow the MPLA government, the combined UNITA–South African forces have decimated Angola's economy. The MPLA stated quite frankly that, by the end of 1986, the continued struggle had cost the Angolan government close to $15 billion that otherwise could have been spent on development.[23] This figure could only have increased in 1987 and 1988.

The Reagan administration, denouncing Angola as a Soviet puppet in Africa and portraying Savimbi as a democratic freedom fighter, was handed congressional repeal of the Clark Amendment in 1985, thereby removing a major obstacle to providing military aid to UNITA under the auspices of the Reagan Doctrine. Congress subsequently voted in the same year to authorize the president to extend $15 million in covert paramilitary aid on a yearly basis to UNITA. The military aid, including Stinger antiaircraft missiles, is funneled to UNITA forces through Zaire. The primary goals of U.S. involvement in the paramilitary war are to achieve the withdrawal of Cuban forces from Angola and pressure the MPLA to accept a power-sharing role with UNITA.

U.S. support for Savimbi is fraught with negatives and contradictions. The major problem tarnishing Savimbi's guerrilla struggle (and U.S. foreign policy by association) is his obvious dependence on South Africa. The sensitive nature of the apartheid issue among black African countries originally contributed to regional recognition of the MPLA regime in 1975 and rejection of Savimbi's military struggle because of its association with South Africa.[24] Moreover, contradictory U.S. policies have sent confusing signals to both South Africa and black African countries: Whereas adoption of economic sanctions underscores U.S. opposition to South Africa's system of apartheid, support for UNITA, by association, supports South Africa's regional policies of destabilization. The irony of U.S. support for Savimbi is that the Ford administration, in the hopes of excluding the Marxist MPLA from sharing power in 1975, contributed to the unraveling of the Alvor Agreement and the possibility for peaceful transition to a democratic government. Although one can only speculate as to whether all three factions would have abided by the agreement (indeed, the opposite is very likely), U.S. (and other foreign) intervention effectively precluded this possibility. Most important, it was the ensuing civil war that led to the massive introduction and long-term presence of Cuban troops in Angola, the issue of greatest concern to the Reagan administration in Africa and the topic of intense regional negotiations led by the United States in 1988.

The key to achieving the removal of Cuban troops from southern Africa—the primary goal of the Reagan administration—lies not in placing military pressure upon the MPLA through UNITA but rather in resolving South Africa's continuing occupation of Namibia, a former League of Nations Trust Territory that acts as a buffer between southern Angola and northern South Africa. As South Africa has repeatedly utilized Namibia to invade Angola, the bargaining position of the MPLA has been that Namibia's independence, and therefore a withdrawal of South African troops, would decrease the security threat to Angola and allow the parallel withdrawal of Cuban troops. Yet, South Africa traditionally has resisted international pressures to grant Namibia independence, for fear that the Angola-based and Marxist-oriented South West African People's Organization (SWAPO) would dominate free elections and pose a direct security threat to South Africa's northern frontier.

The dominant trend in 1988 has been one of diplomatic resolution of the stalemate. On July 20, 1988, a U.S.-mediated accord among Angola, Cuba, and South Africa was made public in which all three nations agreed in principle to work toward Namibian independence as the basis for a withdrawal of Cuban troops. This initial step was enhanced by a preliminary peace accord outlined on November 15, 1988, which mapped out a timetable for the simultaneous withdrawal of Cuban and South African troops from Angola and Namibia, respectively, and acceptance of a UN-sponsored plan for Namibian independence. On December 22, 1988, two agreements—the Namibia Accord and the Angola Accord—were signed, thus formalizing these countries' acceptance of independence for Namibia and the withdrawal of Cuban troops. Although confidence is high that these accords will pave the way for the arrival of UN forces to oversee free elections in Namibia in 1989 or 1990, skeptics note that South Africa originally agreed in principle to the UN-sponsored elections in 1978, only to place one obstacle after another in the way of ultimate independence.[25]

The attainment of an enduring settlement is clouded, however, by lack of comprehensive negotiations concerning external aid to the UNITA guerrillas or the issue of national reconciliation in Angola (that is, power-sharing with UNITA, the second major goal of U.S. paramilitary support for Savimbi). The Namibia Accord, signed by Angola, Cuba, and South Africa, alludes to the UNITA issue by pledging the signatories to "respect the principle of non-interference in the internal affairs of the states of south-west Africa" and to "insure that their respective territories are not used by any state, organization, or person" in connection with acts of violence against any state of southwestern Africa. Yet, although South Africa, in accordance with the accord, announced its intention to cease aiding UNITA, the Reagan administration, not a formal signatory, pledged continued U.S. aid to Savimbi's forces. "There can be no military solution," noted Chester Crocker, assistant secretary of state for African affairs and the primary architect of the accord, affirming that U.S. aid would continue until there was an internal political settlement in Angola.[26]

The Angolan government, despite a proclamation of general amnesty for UNITA guerrillas due to take effect in early 1989, believes that once Namibia is independent, the question of UNITA will be more easily dealt with militarily than through some type of political compromise that decreases the power of the MPLA. This is clearly a concern for Savimbi, who is worried that both South Africa and the United States, in their haste to achieve the withdrawal of Cuban troops, will ultimately allow support for UNITA to fall by the wayside once Cuban troops are actually withdrawn. Yet, numerous African diplomats have warned that "an agreement on a Cuban troop withdrawal will only work if there is a political settlement in the Angolan civil war," and several African countries have been holding regional talks (apart from the U.S.-led talks) to reach such an agreement.[27] Similar to the example of Afghanistan, it is highly likely that withdrawal of foreign forces (in this case Cuban) will leave in place a continuing civil conflict.

☐ Nicaragua and the Contra War

Anastacio Somoza—one in a long line of popularly hated and U.S.-supported Nicaraguan dictators—was overthrown in 1979 by a broad-based revolution led by the Sandinistas. The Sandinistas, who are self-proclaimed Marxists, gradually centralized control over Nicaragua's political system, established close links with Cuba and the Soviet Union, and began providing assistance to other revolutionary movements in Central America, most notably in El Salvador. Although the Carter administration in its last year in office attempted to construct a productive relationship with the Sandinista regime (with debatable results), the Reagan administration entered office with a negative preconception of the revolution and a determination to prevent another Cuba in the Western Hemisphere. Perceiving Nicaragua as a beachhead for Soviet-led communist destabilization throughout Central America, support for the contras became the showcase for what paramilitary intervention could achieve under the Reagan Doctrine. Although official administration justifications for supporting the contras wavered between interdicting arms being sent to Salvadoran Marxist guerrillas, forcing the Sandinistas to democratize their system of governance, and limiting Soviet and Cuban influence in the region, the real aim seemed to be to overthrow the Sandinista regime.

As the paramilitary war against the Sandinistas is extensively discussed in Chapter 16, I will only highlight here several obstacles that hindered the successful carrying out of the Reagan administration's effort. First, among the four paramilitary wars carried out by the Reagan administration, U.S. support of the contras fueled the greatest amount of public debate and controversy and contributed to a virtual tug-of-war between the executive branch and Congress. In brief, although originally endorsing military aid in 1982 (only for the purposes of interdicting arms), Congress by 1988 had reduced U.S. support to limited amounts of humanitarian aid, and it was doubtful that any new appropriations would be made for 1989. Congressional cutbacks mirrored international opinion: The U.S. policy of supporting the contras has been declared illegal by the World Court, opposed by the majority of Nicaraguans, and disputed by a significant number of nations within Central America as well as within the international system. Equally important is that the contras themselves suffer several shortcomings that limit their effectiveness as a viable alternative to the Sandinistas: None of the contra leadership is respected in Nicaragua; they have been unable to enunciate an attractive alternative program of government; and they are discredited by continued atrocities in the rural areas.[28] Eight years of paramilitary warfare, although clearly able to wreak havoc within the Nicaraguan economy, have been insufficient to achieve the primary goal of overthrowing the Sandinista regime. In fact, it may be argued that U.S. paramilitary support for the contras has forced the Sandinistas to rely more heavily on Cuban and Soviet support and advisers, the exact opposite of U.S. foreign policy objectives in the region.

■ PARAMILITARY INTERVENTION IN PERSPECTIVE

Despite the sporadic nature of U.S. paramilitary intervention in the Third World, this brief overview of this tool's use in the post–World War II period provides the basis for several tentative conclusions. First, it appears that paramilitary intervention can be highly successful if the U.S. goal is to harass or otherwise disrupt the normal political or economic proceedings of a Third World country. There is no doubt that support for UNITA has contributed to severe disruption of Angola's economy or that support for Tibetan guerrillas delayed China's consolidation of control over the disputed territory.

If the goal of paramilitary intervention is to overthrow the government in question, however, the results have been less positive. Only in the case of Guatemala in 1954—a democratic government with powerful domestic enemies, most notably a disenchanted military—did the United States succeed in overthrowing a government considered inimical to U.S. foreign policy interests through paramilitary means. In all other cases, the paramilitary option has fallen short. This especially has been the case when the United States has attempted to overthrow leftist revolutionary regimes (such as Nicaragua's Sandinistas or Cuba under Castro) enjoying a large degree of popular support. Rather than overthrowing these types of regimes, U.S. intervention seems to stiffen their resolve and anti-U.S. rhetoric.

Yet, just as nationalism can be harnessed by revolutionary regimes to avoid defeat by counterrevolutionary paramilitary forces, so too can it be harnessed when the goal is withdrawal of a foreign occupation army. As witnessed by the USSR's intentions to withdraw Soviet forces from Afghanistan—regardless of the domestic configuration of a future Afghani regime (though the USSR will obviously continue to supply massive amounts of aid to keep the Najibullah government in power)—the combination of a popular guerrilla struggle with effective regional paramilitary support can make the costs of occupation potentially untenable in the long run. The key to success in Afghanistan, however, has not been the level of external aid but rather the widespread support that the guerrilla insurgency enjoys among the Afghani people. As is shown by the case of the contra war in Nicaragua, large infusions of external aid are insufficient for victory when the majority of the population rejects the legitimacy of the paramilitary group.

A further observation of paramilitary intervention is that it can lead to concessions by a Third World country, depending on the types of concessions sought. For example, Iran was able to achieve a desired border demarcation from Iraq through U.S.-guaranteed support of Kurdish guerrillas operating in Iraqi territory. Once this goal was achieved, support for the Kurdish guerrillas was dropped. Moreover, although U.S. support for the contras may make the Sandinistas think twice about sending arms to the Salvadoran guerrillas, it is not likely to force them to submit to something as important as dismantling their system of governance. Similarly, in the case of Angola, the MPLA has shown itself willing to negotiate the withdrawal of Cuban troops, but as of 1988 has refused to negotiate its dominant hold on political power. In short, the greater the importance or sensitivity of the demand sought, the lesser the likelihood that the target government will concede as the result of paramilitary intervention.

In addition, both the short-term and long-term effects of paramilitary intervention must be taken into account. In the case of Tibet, for example, although the short-term goal of harassing communist China seemed to be successful, the long-term effect proved ultimately to be counterproductive, as the United States sought to achieve closer relations with the PRC. In the case of Iraq, the coerced border demarcation provided one of the reasons for the bloody Iran-Iraq war. In the cases of Angola, Cuba, and Nicaragua, attempts at isolating these self-proclaimed Marxist regimes has left them little alternative—especially when confronting externally supplied guerrilla forces—than to seek an even closer relationship with Eastern bloc countries, the opposite of what Washington was attempting to achieve. The possibility of long-term results contrary to the original foreign policy objectives is not limited to paramilitary intervention but rather may be applied to all types of intervention.

The question of long-term results is especially important as concerns the democratic or undemocratic nature of a successor regime if the U.S.-supported guerrillas achieve their goal and assume power. The Reagan administration, for example, fondly referred to anticommunist guerrillas as democratic freedom fighters. As already stated, the success of paramilitary struggles in both Afghanistan and Cambodia could lead to radical Islamic fundamentalist and pro–Chinese communist governments in those two countries, respectively. In this regard, it is difficult to see how this promotes the cause of democracy or even pro-U.S. regimes. In the case of Guatemala, U.S. paramilitary success led to a litany of corrupt dictatorships and a cycle of guerrilla insurgency that has yet to reach its full conclusion. A democratic outcome in Angola or Nicaragua also is highly unlikely if either the contras or UNITA gain power, although it may be argued that these regimes would at least be more pro-U.S. than their predecessors.

Finally, the role of regional allies and the risks of escalation must be noted. In all the examined cases of U.S. paramilitary intervention, a regional ally bordering the target nation was imperative for training guerrillas and serving as a conduit for military aid. This situation provides the potential for future escalation, as the target nation, fed up with its neighbor's interference in its domestic affairs, may decide to eliminate guerrilla camps across the border or widen the war by mounting a full-scale invasion. The former scenario has occurred frequently; punitive strikes have been carried out by Nicaragua against contra bases in Honduras, by Vietnam against guerrilla camps in Thailand, and by Afghanistan against mujahedin guerrillas in Pakistan. What would or should be the U.S. response if the latter scenario were to take place, and a U.S. ally were invaded by the target of a paramilitary campaign? The invasion of Honduras by Nicaragua, for example, could provide the basis for direct U.S. military intervention in Central America with potentially disastrous effects. Indeed, the Reagan administration responded positively to a Honduran request for U.S. troops after Sandinista soldiers apparently crossed the Honduran border on March 15, 1988, to attack contra guerrilla bases. Although U.S. troops were sent merely as a show of military muscle, the stage was set for a wider regional conflict that neither Washington nor Managua wanted.

□ 9

Direct Military Intervention

Ted Galen Carpenter

Direct military intervention in the affairs of Third World countries has been a crucial component of U.S. foreign policy throughout the twentieth century.[1] The scope of such coercion is quite significant. Cambodia, Cuba, the Dominican Republic, Haiti, Iran, Korea, Lebanon, Libya, Mexico, and Nicaragua have all experienced the application of U.S. military might at various times. Certain characteristics of military intervention have remained surprisingly constant during the century, whereas others have changed in significant ways, especially since the end of World War II.

■ CONTINUITY AND CHANGE

The underlying motives for military intervention have remained fairly consistent. U.S. leaders typically employ force to prevent political instability in important client states and to install or preserve regimes considered friendly to perceived economic and security interests. It is somewhat ironic that the United States, a nation that once symbolized revolutionary republican values, now seems obsessed with maintaining "stability" in the world. Nevertheless, U.S. actions throughout this century, and especially since the onset of the cold war rivalry with the Soviet Union, have exemplified the objectives of a conservative status quo power. In virtually every case in which Washington has resorted to military force, it has done so to prop up clients—including several highly authoritarian ones—or to thwart radical insurgencies. The emphasis on the sanctity of stability has always been rather selective, however. U.S. leaders have rarely hesitated to foment coups d'état (as in Guatemala in 1954 and Chile in 1973) or, as Grenada demonstrated, to employ direct military action against incumbent governments deemed hostile to U.S. interests.[2]

The official justifications for various coercive episodes also exhibit fairly constant and predictable features. Frequently, those justifications bear little resemblance to the more plausible political, economic, or strategic motives for intervention. U.S. leaders habitually stress idealistic and emotionally laden objectives to mobilize and maintain public support for what otherwise might be divisive interventionist initiatives. The strategy contains two elements: an exaggeration of the importance of the conflict (usually describing the adversary as an unplacable menace to U.S. security) and an emphasis on the moral imperative of the U.S. reaction.

This approach was apparent as early as World War I. President Woodrow Wilson repeatedly described the conflict in millennial terms, insisting that it was a struggle to "make the world safe for democracy," while portraying Wilhelmine Germany as the blood-thirsty "Hun" bent on global domination. U.S. leaders have employed similar rhetoric to justify military intervention during the cold war era. For example, the complex Vietnam struggle was reduced to a simplistic conflict between the forces of freedom and democracy in South Vietnam and a monolithic communist aggressor threatening the security of the free world.[3]

A reliance on such justifications frequently produces an embarrassing chasm between rhetoric and reality. In the case of the Vietnam War, many Americans were properly skeptical of the arguments put forth by the administrations of Presidents John F. Kennedy, Lyndon B. Johnson, and Richard M. Nixon. They were unwilling to believe that if the United States did not fight communists in Southeast Asia it would eventually confront them in San Francisco. Similarly, a parade of corrupt, authoritarian regimes in Saigon thoroughly discredited the moral basis of U.S. policy.

Another consistent feature of U.S. military interventions in the twentieth century is the paucity of congressional control or influence. The various coercive missions undertaken against Latin American states have all been executive branch operations. There were no requests for declarations of war or even limited forms of explicit congressional authorization. Congress acquiesced in these repeated dilutions of its war-power prerogatives with only scattered murmurs of protest.

The pattern of executive dominance became even more apparent with the emergence of the imperial presidency during the cold war era.[4] President Harry S. Truman brazenly bypassed Congress when committing U.S. forces on a massive scale to assist South Korea in 1950. Similarly, President Johnson acted solely on his own authority when he sent troops ashore in the Dominican Republic in 1965. President Ronald Reagan did the same with regard to the 1983 Grenada "rescue mission," the air strikes against Libya in 1986, and the Persian Gulf naval operations in 1987.

On those rare occasions when Congress did provide some policy input, its influence was decidedly limited. President Dwight D. Eisenhower sent the U.S. Marines to Lebanon in 1958 at least arguably pursuant to the provisions of a congressional resolution approved the previous year. But that measure essentially gave the president a blank check to use U.S. forces to defend Middle Eastern nations from "communist-inspired" aggression. The more famous Gulf of Tonkin Resolution that Johnson used as a pretext to escalate U.S. involvement in the Vietnam conflict exhibited a similar vagueness, thereby enabling the chief executive to conduct the war in virtually any manner he chose. It is also pertinent to observe that U.S. military activity in Vietnam was quite substantial long before Congress approved the Gulf of Tonkin Resolution in August 1964. Executive initiative, therefore, has invariably been a salient feature of U.S. military intervention in the Third World.

Although the actual motives and official rationales for U.S. interventionist policy, as well as executive branch control of that policy, have remained rather constant throughout the twentieth century, other features have changed in important ways. One discernible change is a decline in the geographic selectivity of U.S. military intervention. During the early years of this century, the United States repeatedly coerced recalcitrant hemispheric neighbors and asserted its dominance in Central America and the Caribbean. Nicaragua experienced the most frequent and prolonged examples of U.S. intervention and was occupied on a nearly continuous basis between 1912 and 1933.[5]

This stifling paternalism in the Western Hemisphere contrasted with a general lack of U.S. military activity elsewhere in the world. Still heavily influenced by a potent isolationist heritage, the U.S. rarely employed its military power outside the hemisphere until World War II. The Spanish-American War in 1898, however, was an unpleasant omen of subsequent U.S. meddling throughout the Third World. Although the conflict itself was a brief, comic-opera affair, its consequences were not. At war's end the United States acquired its first overseas colonies, most notably the Philippines. Acquisition of colonies expanded U.S. geopolitical interests—especially in the Far East—and, equally significant, it helped create an imperial mentality among U.S. political leaders.[6]

Isolationist traditions acted as a brake on U.S. imperial impulses outside the Western Hemisphere until World War II, but the disappearance of such inhibitions at the end of that conflict greatly expanded the geographic scope of interventionism. During the cold war era, U.S. military might was employed in distant regions, with Korea, Lebanon, and Vietnam the most obvious cases. Although the United States remains especially prone to use its armed forces in the Caribbean Basin—as evidenced by the invasions of the Dominican Republic and Grenada—in the 1980s other regions also constitute arenas for the application of U.S. power.

But at the same time that the United States has become geographically less selective in employing military force, it has become more selective in adopting that tactic as the preferred option. Earlier in the century, U.S. leaders rarely hesitated to "send in the marines" to restore order or implement political and economic objectives. The frequency of intervention throughout the Caribbean prior to the mid-1930s was ample testimony to the popularity of that approach. Since

World War II, however, U.S. officials have preferred to rely on other policy tools whenever possible. More subtle techniques, such as the selective use of economic and military assistance programs and economic sanctions (see Chapters 5 and 6), have come into vogue to expand U.S. influence over foreign governments. When such methods are not sufficient, the CIA is frequently called in to conduct covert operations. As noted in Chapters 7 and 8, covert operations range from propaganda and psychological warfare to election intervention, coups d'état, assassination plots, and paramilitary intervention.

It is not so much that the use of military coercion is considered an option of last resort. The distinction is somewhat more subtle. There is undoubtedly a greater hesitation to employ military force now than there was prior to the advent of nuclear weapons. This reluctance is especially evident when both superpowers have stakes in a Third World situation, and military intervention by either party might escalate out of control. It is difficult to imagine, for example, the United States continuing to tolerate a communist regime in Cuba were it not for the restraint required in a thermonuclear context.

Despite this generalized danger, the United States has resorted to military force on occasion. In most instances, officials chose the military option not when other tactics proved insufficient but when rapidly changing events precluded the use of more subtle techniques. The decision to assist South Korea in 1950, the occupation of Lebanon in 1958, the occupation of the Dominican Republic in 1965, and the invasion of Grenada in 1983 all clearly fit this pattern. Even the decision to establish the multinational peacekeeping force in Lebanon in 1982 appears to reflect similar considerations, as the Israeli invasion forced Washington's hand. Only in Vietnam did the United States embrace the military option after other techniques had been tried for an extended period of time and were found wanting.

The unsatisfactory outcome of the Vietnam intervention produced an important change in the willingness of U.S. leaders to embrace the military option. It became clear in the aftermath of that episode that public support for prolonged interventionist campaigns involving substantial numbers of U.S. troops was problematical at best. Secretary of Defense Caspar Weinberger clearly recognized this reality in his 1984 National Press Club speech. Weinberger argued against sending U.S. forces into combat unless the stakes were "vital," and then the troops must be sent "with the clear intention of winning." Those forces should serve "clearly defined political and military objectives" and should be limited to the levels "needed to do just that." Finally, there must be "some reasonable assurance" of popular and congressional support, and "the commitment of U.S. forces to combat should be a last result."[7]

Weinberger's guidelines underscored the principal characteristics of most military interventions during the Reagan years. A premium was placed on achieving decisive results in a brief period of time with a minimum commitment of U.S. personnel. The invasion of Grenada and the bombing raids against Libya were the quintessential examples of how such a preference for low-intensity conflicts operated, and the administration was rewarded with widespread public acclaim. When U.S. leaders became more adventurous, principally in the Lebanon peacekeeping operation of 1982–1983, popular support eroded rapidly, graphically demonstrating that the American people remained wary of situations that harbored the potential to become Vietnam-style quagmires.

Perhaps the greatest change has occurred in the style of military intervention. Prior to World War II, U.S. military initiatives were typically undertaken on a unilateral basis. An isolationist heritage stressed the need to avoid alliances and other foreign entanglements. This tradition made unilateralism mandatory whenever the United States used its armed forces, especially in the Western Hemisphere, a region viewed as constituting a special U.S. sphere of influence.

Virtually the opposite strategy has prevailed since World War II. U.S. officials routinely have portrayed military operations as multilateral enterprises, often going to elaborate lengths to do so. In part, this stratagem is necessary to preserve the impression that military action against another country is consistent with provisions of the UN Charter, which explicitly recognizes both an individual and a collective right of self-defense. Although both provisions are inherently vague, the former seems to be narrower in scope, referring primarily to a nation's right to repel an assault on its territory or citizens. The collective right of self-defense, outlined in Article 51, has somewhat broader implications, authorizing nations to take joint action against a threat to the peace of their region. As one of the founders of the UN, the United States wishes to maintain at least the image of compliance with the principles of that organization—hence, the reliance on multilateral rather than unilateral interventions.

The vast U.S.-led alliance system that emerged during the first decade of the cold war relied heavily on the collective-defense provisions in Article 51. Beginning with the Rio Treaty in 1947 and NATO two years later, there was a proliferation of such regional mechanisms. Most U.S. military interventions also have been conducted on a multilateral basis—or, more accurately, with a plausible multilateral cover. In addition to paying official respects to UN requirements, this technique has the more practical benefit of diluting accusations of U.S. imperialism or aggression, even though at times the multilateral cover has been rather threadbare. For example, the Korean "police action"—ostensibly a collective peacekeeping operation conducted under the auspices of the UN—was patently a U.S. enterprise.

Most other U.S.-directed interventions have exhibited a similar or even greater degree of U.S. dominance. Yet, with the exceptions of the 1958 occupation of Lebanon and the April 1986 air strikes conducted against Libya, the United States has avoided acting on an explicitly unilateral basis when conducting major military operations. (Hostage rescue episodes and immediate, self-defense cases, such as the 1981 Gulf of Sidra incident in which U.S. and Libyan fighter planes clashed, have, of course, been handled unilaterally.) And significant mitigating circumstances accounted for the atypical unilateralism in the

Lebanese and Libyan cases. Specifically, in neither instance were nations in the region sufficiently strong that they could court domestic discontent by enlisting in the operation. Moreover, at least in the case of the Libyan raids, Washington's principal European allies were emphatically opposed to the strategy.

■ EPISODES OF INTERVENTION

Various episodes during the cold war illustrate the complex nature of U.S. military intervention in the Third World. The Korean conflict was especially representative of four features: the employment of military force in a rapidly evolving situation; executive branch dominance; the insistence on a multilateral cover; and the gilding of actual motives. It became evident within hours of the June 25 invasion that South Korea would not be able to stem the onslaught from the north. Truman immediately ordered U.S. air units to assist South Korea and then sought a UN Security Council resolution calling on member nations to help repel North Korean aggression. The United States was able to gain approval of the resolution because the Soviet Union was boycotting Security Council sessions at the time and was unable to exercise its veto power. Truman promptly invoked the UN measure to justify sending U.S. ground units into Korea. The president took all of these steps without once requesting congressional authorization—an omission that provoked vehement protests from critics such as Republican Senator Robert A. Taft.[8]

Truman's exclusion of Congress from any decisionmaking role was not accidental. He asserted that because the Korean intervention was a UN police action, he needed no congressional declaration of war; because the Senate had ratified the UN Charter, the president was supposedly empowered to act upon the call of the Security Council. Truman explicitly rejected the suggestion of some aides that he at least seek an authorizing resolution from Congress, fearing that such a step might trigger a divisive debate over Korean policy and lead to undesirable congressional interference.[9] This insistence on exclusive executive branch control over the Korean intervention persisted throughout the conflict, even after the PRC's involvement created a wider, bloodier, and considerably more dangerous war.

The multilateral facade for the operation was also continued. Truman insisted that the United States was acting as an agent of the UN—merely one member among many responding to the Security Council's call to repel aggression. Military units in Korea were carefully designated "UN forces," and the UN flag flew over their installations. Nevertheless, the assertion that Korea symbolized a truly multilateral peacekeeping enterprise lacked credibility. The commander of UN forces was always an American, and the United States provided approximately 90 percent of the troops and equipment. Crucial decisions, such as whether to cross the 38th parallel into North Korea, were made in the White House and the Pentagon, not at UN headquarters.[10] It is difficult to escape the conclusion that rhetoric about "collective security" was largely used to disguise a military operation that primarily served U.S. foreign policy objectives.

Just as the administration stressed the supposed multilateral nature of the Korean intervention, it insisted that the United States was helping to preserve freedom and democracy in South Korea, as well as resisting the initial stage of a possible global communist offensive. Although U.S. leaders may have sincerely believed the latter point, they were certainly aware that there was a dearth of South Korean freedom and democracy. President Syngman Rhee was a ruthless autocrat who routinely harassed and jailed political opponents and censored the press.[11] Yet, both the Truman and Eisenhower administrations conveniently overlooked that reality when justifying the Korean intervention to the American people.

The dispatch of U.S. Marines to Lebanon in July 1958 mirrored the Korean intervention in some respects but differed from it in others. Like the Korean episode, the United States responded to rapidly deteriorating events. Following a bloody coup d'état in Iraq staged by admirers of Egyptian President Gamal Abdel Nasser, U.S. officials feared for the survival of fragile pro-Western governments in Lebanon and Jordan. Lebanese leader Camille Chamoun had faced significant opposition for several months following his effort to gain an unprecedented second term as president, but opposition forces seemed to acquire added strength after the Iraqi revolution.

In a sense, Eisenhower's decision to send the marines to keep Chamoun in office was not an example of unfettered executive power. Several months earlier, Congress had passed a resolution expressing support if the president decided to use military force to "secure and protect the territorial integrity and political independence" of Middle East nations from "any nation controlled by International Communism." Yet, even Eisenhower conceded privately that the Lebanese situation did not really fit the criteria of this "Eisenhower Doctrine," as it involved an internal political struggle, not external aggression.[12] Nor was it at all clear that the rebel forces were procommunist, although some elements were emphatically anti-United States.

Eisenhower simply chose to ignore such inconvenient matters. In justifying the Lebanese intervention to Congress and the American people, he stressed the danger of a communist takeover of Lebanon.[13] Although the intervention was not on the same scale as Truman's presidential war in Korea (the U.S. occupation force consisted of a division-size unit), Eisenhower's action certainly stretched the intent of the congressional resolution. His explanation for the intervention also replicated the Truman administration's lack of candor. Moreover, the Lebanon incident represented an especially graphic example of U.S. willingness to use force to keep a compliant, pro-U.S. regime in power in a region that was considered strategically and economically important.

Lebanon also constituted an apparent exception to the post–World War II strategy of orchestrating ostensibly multilateral interventions, as all of the troops involved in the occupation were U.S. forces. But this atypical unilateralism occurred more from default than any conscious design. Indeed, there is evidence that Eisenhower originally wanted to pursue a joint operation with British forces but was dissuaded by John Foster Dulles and other advisers who reminded him of Britain's odious imperial reputation throughout the Middle East.[14]

Perhaps even more significant, no multinational mechanism for such a mission existed in that region. The embryonic Baghdad Pact had effectively disintegrated with the overthrow of the pro-Western monarchy in Iraq, and any UN endorsement was out of the question, especially given the Soviet Union's veto power on the Security Council. U.S. officials would face a similar obstacle in 1982 when they had to create a hasty, ad hoc multinational peacekeeping force for Lebanon. The absence of a regional peacekeeping organization comparable to NATO or the Organization of American States (OAS) has always posed a problem for U.S. military policy in the Middle East.

Even with the existence of the OAS, the Johnson administration found it difficult to portray the U.S. occupation of the Dominican Republic in 1965 as a truly multilateral enterprise. Part of the problem was that Mexico and other key OAS members were bitterly opposed to coercion of a Latin American nation by the "Collossus of the North." An equally important reason was that the Dominican crisis flared so rapidly it became impossible to recruit hemispheric clients for a joint operation.

The seeds of intervention had been sown two years earlier when conservative military forces in the Dominican Republic ousted the elected president, Juan Bosch, and installed Daniel Reid Cabral as a front man. As Bosch had angered U.S. sugar companies and other business interests with an assortment of left-leaning reform measures, Washington was not especially displeased with his ouster. In fact, the U.S. government sent Reid Cabral's regime more than $5 million in economic aid to help keep it in power. This effort proved in vain. On April 24, 1965, young pro-Bosch army officers launched a coup d'état that drove Reid Cabral from office. Disorder rapidly engulfed the capital of Santo Domingo as pro- and anti-Bosch military units—and armed civilian factions—vied for power.

Johnson reacted to these developments swiftly and decisively. On April 28, he sent in a contingent of marines, followed a few days later by the army's 82nd Airborne Division. By early May, the occupation force totaled approximately 22,000 personnel—slightly larger than the Lebanese operation seven years earlier. Johnson acted without soliciting OAS participation or even providing advance notification, both because of the perceived need for rapid action and the avoidance of embarrassing opposition. For essentially the same reasons, he excluded Congress from a decisionmaking role.

Once the situation stabilized, however, the administration sought to give the occupation a multilateral image. In his memoirs, Johnson stated that the United States wanted the other members of the OAS to "share responsibility" for the operation.[15] That goal proved elusive, as Chile, Mexico, Venezuela, and other major OAS members continued to oppose the intervention. Within a few weeks, Washington was able to obtain token military contingents from other nations, thus giving the ongoing occupation at least a plausible multilateral patina. But the political orientation of those partners—Brazil, Honduras, Nicaragua, and Paraguay—was revealing: These were Washington's most authoritarian clients in the Western Hemisphere.

The alleged multilateralism of the Dominican operation was largely an illusion, and U.S. explanations for the invasion were equally dubious. Johnson initially contended that action was necessary to protect Americans who were caught in a dangerously turbulent political situation—a rationale President Reagan would use with respect to Grenada two decades later. Almost immediately, however, he adopted a different argument, asserting that communists had been gaining control of the insurgency, thereby threatening to transform the Dominican Republic into another Cuba. The U.S. embassy in Santo Domingo subsequently issued a list of fifty-eight "prominent and documented Communist and Castroite leaders" in the rebel forces, a list, it was later revealed, that had been compiled by longtime Dominican dictator Rafael Trujillo in the late 1950s and bore little resemblance to reality.[16]

It is possible that the Johnson administration sincerely, albeit erroneously, believed the communist-takeover thesis. A more likely explanation, however, is that U.S. leaders desperately wanted to thwart the restoration of Bosch to power. They considered him soft on communism and were hostile because he had previously penalized U.S. business interests on the island. Whatever the reason, the United States had shown a willingness to use military force to keep the Dominican Republic in the pro-U.S. camp.[17]

The invasion of Grenada in October 1983 demonstrated that the United States was equally willing to use its armed forces to oust a regime considered inimical to U.S. interests. Since early 1979, Grenada had been ruled by a radical leftist regime led by Maurice Bishop, who came to power in a coup d'état that ousted the corrupt and erratic Prime Minister Eric Gairy. Although the Reagan administration repeatedly criticized the Bishop regime for its growing ties with Cuba and other members of the Soviet bloc, it was the massacre of Bishop and many of his followers by a rival faction in the ruling New Jewel Movement (NJM) on October 19, 1983, that triggered the U.S. invasion.

Even though events evolved almost as rapidly as they had in the Dominican Republic, the Reagan administration was able to create a multilateral facade for the Grenada operation. The official rationale for the invasion was that the United States was responding to a "request" from the previously obscure Organization of Eastern Caribbean States (OECS) for action against a threat to the peace of the region.[18] Most members of that group did provide token forces for the invasion and occupation, although their level of participation could scarcely disguise the fact that it was a U.S. operation.

The rapidity with which the United States organized this supposedly multilateral military campaign (less than six days passed between Bishop's assassination and the invasion) strongly suggests that the Reagan administration had prepared the diplomatic groundwork long before. The notion of a spontaneous OECS request is plausible but unlikely. Another portion of the official U.S. justification—that the invasion was primarily a "rescue mission" to protect some 700 American students at St. George's University Medical School—also strains credulity. Despite considerable pressure from U.S. government officials, many of the students insisted they had not been in danger. There was certainly no evidence that they were in greater peril on October 25 than during the turmoil immediately following the events of October 19.

Two other elements of the Grenada invasion typified U.S. military interventions in the cold war era. First, President Reagan completely excluded Congress from any role in the decisionmaking process. Much as Truman did in Korea and Johnson had done in the Dominican Republic, he merely informed congressional leaders of a policy that he had already adopted. Moreover, Reagan relayed that information barely hours before the first troops landed in Grenada. This move seemed calculated to neutralize any criticism or opposition—a motive that also may have contributed to the unprecedented decision to prevent the press from covering the invasion.

The other predictable element of the Grenada operation was the heavy emphasis placed by Reagan administration officials on an alleged communist threat to the East Caribbean region. They implied that the Soviet Union and Cuba were behind the hard-line Marxist faction that had ousted Bishop—an especially curious assertion as the Castro government vehemently condemned the coup d'état.[19] U.S. leaders also exaggerated the number of Cubans on the island and insisted these were professional soldiers when most were apparently construction workers employed on the Point Salines airport project. The airport itself was portrayed as a future base for Soviet bombers despite the longstanding contention of the Bishop government that it was needed for jumbo jets to bring tourists to the island. The plausibility of that benign explanation was underscored when the postinvasion, anticommunist Grenadian government also desired the airport to enhance tourism and successfully solicited U.S. aid to complete the project. In sum, the Reagan administration's contention that the invasion thwarted the creation of a new Soviet puppet in the Western Hemisphere was exaggerated at best and disingenuous at worst.

The largest and best-known interventionist episode in the cold war period—Vietnam—exhibited many of the same characteristics of other episodes, but also some subtle differences. The most significant difference was the prolonged, gradual evolution of the U.S. commitment, as opposed to the rapidly deteriorating political and military situations that virtually precluded the use of more subtle tactics in the previous case studies. The massive combat role that dominated the Johnson and Nixon years followed a sizable but relatively restrained program of military aid under Eisenhower and the fateful introduction of hundreds, ultimately several thousands, of combat "advisers" under

Kennedy. It was only after it became evident that such measures were insufficient to preserve a pro-U.S. government in Saigon that Washington made the disastrous decision to escalate the military stakes.

The scale of the Vietnam intervention likewise was unique. It substantially surpassed both in size and duration even the Korean episode and utterly dwarfed the operations in Lebanon, the Dominican Republic, and Grenada. At the peak of the conflict in 1968, more than 500,000 U.S. troops were involved. Equally important, the war generated far more domestic opposition than any previous or subsequent intervention.

In other respects, Vietnam corresponded to the pattern of U.S. cold war interventionism. The calculated exaggeration of an alleged North Vietnamese threat to U.S. security already has been noted. Manifestations of the imperial presidency were also present. Congress did play a minor role with the passage of the Gulf of Tonkin Resolution and the continued funding of a military presence in Southeast Asia, but the operation remained predominantly a presidential war. In fact, both Johnson and Nixon insisted that their inherent constitutional powers as commanders in chief authorized them to pursue that conflict even in the absence of the Gulf of Tonkin Resolution or any other congressional authorization.[20] Nixon even expanded military operations into Cambodia and Laos on that basis.

The United States also sought to portray the Vietnam War as a multilateral undertaking. Washington exerted diplomatic pressure to persuade various allies and clients—most notably Australia, New Zealand, and South Korea—to send combat units. Except for South Korea, however, these commitments never surpassed the level of tokenism. Those additional forces served little relevant military purpose, but they did help preserve the fiction that the Vietnam intervention was a collective regional peacekeeping enterprise rather than superpower meddling in the affairs of a small Third World nation. In this case, the attempt at a multilateral cover was even less credible than in the other interventionist campaigns.

The most recent use of U.S. military coercion—the massive naval buildup in the Persian Gulf and the subsequent attacks on Iranian targets—also generally fits the pattern of cold war interventionism. Washington predictably cajoled its Japanese and Western European allies as well as client states in the region to support U.S. strategy. That campaign to give the operation a multilateral image was only partially successful. Britain and France overcame their initial reluctance and ultimately dispatched modest naval contingents in response to intense U.S. diplomatic pressure, but Japan remained aloof and the Persian Gulf states seemed willing to provide only meager, covert support.

Disingenuous official explanations were prominent throughout the buildup. Despite official rhetoric about protecting U.S.-flag shipping in the Gulf, the Reagan administration's primary motive was to blunt growing Iranian power throughout the region. The naval operations symbolized a clear U.S. tilt toward Iraq in its war with Iran. An important secondary motive was to preempt any

Soviet move to become a major power in that portion of the Middle East. It is interesting, however, that in this instance, concern about Islamic fundamentalism seemed to overshadow the usual cold war obsession with Soviet designs.

■ PITFALLS AND LIMITATIONS OF MILITARY INTERVENTION

The results of decisions to employ direct U.S. military coercion have been decidedly mixed during the cold war era. Vietnam was an obvious failure. Despite a military commitment lasting longer than a decade at a cost of 58,000 American lives and more than $100 billion, communist forces triumphed throughout Indochina. Moreover, subsequent events in the rest of East Asia have demolished the original rationale for U.S. intervention. Contrary to alarmist predictions, the noncommunist nations bordering Indochina did not fall like so many dominoes. Quite the contrary—Malaysia, Singapore, Thailand, and other East Asian countries proceeded to enjoy an unprecedented degree of economic expansion, and (with the exception of the Philippines) are less vulnerable to external or internal pressure from communist elements in the 1980s than they were in the 1960s.

The other interventions appeared superficially to be successful—at least from the standpoint of advancing U.S. geopolitical objectives. A more comprehensive examination, though, casts some doubt on that sanguine conclusion. The United States did prevent a unification of the Korean peninsula on communist terms, but that effort required a considerable expenditure in lives and national treasure. The situation remains volatile, as heavily armed North and South Korean forces confront each other along a truce line that possesses scant legitimacy in the rival capitals. Moreover, although the recent political reforms under President Roe Tae Woo are gratifying, they are fragile and suggest that Washington's goal of nurturing freedom and democracy in that country is still not assured.

The results of the Lebanon intervention were ultimately far more disappointing. For several years, it appeared that the U.S. occupation had preserved a pro-Western government, thereby sustaining a useful client in the Middle East. But that illusion was dispelled in the mid-1970s when a chaotic civil war engulfed Lebanon. Eisenhower's intervention did not fundamentally alter the destiny of that unhappy country; it only delayed the inevitable.

Indeed, the "successful" Eisenhower intervention merely set the stage for a second U.S. effort to maintain a pro-Western Lebanese regime. Seizing an apparent opportunity to rectify unpalatable developments in Lebanon afforded by the Israeli invasion in the summer of 1982, the Reagan administration embarked on another occupation program—this time as the leader of a multinational peacekeeping force. The policy was ill conceived and ineptly executed. The "government" of Amin Gemayel, which the U.S. supported, enjoyed the allegiance of only one faction among many in the bitter internecine struggle and was unable to exert control over any sizable portion of the country. The U.S. attempt to restore Lebanon as a client collapsed ignominiously in the rubble of the U.S. Marine barracks when a suicide driver detonated a truck bomb killing 241 marines in 1983. Both the marines and U.S. policy became victims of political and religious forces Washington could not defeat with conventional military measures nor even comprehend.

The United States apparently has enjoyed somewhat greater success in the Dominican Republic and Grenada. Moreover, the professed commitment to freedom and democracy in those cases was followed by some constructive action, unlike the developments in Lebanon, Vietnam and—for many years—Korea. The United States presided over elections in the two Caribbean countries that were at least free of obvious fraud or intimidation (the more subtle influence resulting from the presence of U.S. occupation forces and the flow of financial assistance to pro-Western factions is another issue). Happily for U.S. policymakers, candidates acceptable to Washington won the elections. Even in these two countries, however, substantial economic and social problems remain, and the possibility of political instability is an ever-present danger.

The April 1986 air strikes against Libya produced more ambiguous results. The prediction of critics that such attacks would merely strengthen and radicalize the Libyan regime of Muammar Qaddafi, leading to increased acts of terrorism, have not yet been borne out. At the same time, the United States did not succeed in its larger policy objective—using the raids to pressure dissident military elements to overthrow the mercurial dictator. Moreover, as a response to state-sponsored terrorism, the Libyan raids are not a very useful model. Washington moved against Qaddafi because he was weak—the leader of a minor country with no powerful allies. (Soviet support for Libya has always remained quite limited and tenuous.) U.S. boldness with respect to Libya stands in sharp contrast to its passivity toward Syria, another country deeply involved in terrorist activities. The reason is readily apparent; Syria has a very close security relationship with the USSR.

U.S. intervention in the Persian Gulf may have temporarily diminished Iran's power and influence, although the Islamic fundamentalism symbolized by the Khomeini regime remains a potent force. More important, such a limited short-term gain may have been achieved at considerable cost. The U.S. tilt toward Iraq and the violent clashes with Iran, culminating in the tragic destruction of an Iranian airliner in July 1988, have almost certainly delayed an improvement in relations between the two countries. Moreover, the United States may have positioned itself to be the perfect scapegoat for the failure of Tehran's war effort, fostering renewed anti-U.S. sentiment among the Iranian people. The Reagan administration's use of gunboat diplomacy also has led to closer ties between Tehran and Moscow while enabling the USSR to foster its image as a restrained, "honest broker" in the Middle East—precisely what Washington hoped to prevent.[21] As in the case of most U.S. interventionist initiatives, the long-term consequences of the Persian Gulf episode are likely to be negative for U.S. interests.

The pattern of U.S. military intervention in the Third World during the cold war era suggests that it is a strategy possessing only marginal effectiveness. U.S. leaders understandably seem to prefer using more gradual and less blatant mechanisms, including economic and security assistance programs and the various covert activities of the CIA. Only when such measures fail or the pressure of rapidly evolving developments preclude those tactics, has the United States opted to use military force. When it has resorted to such force, the emphasis is upon quick and decisive solutions, in large part because the American people will not countenance costly, drawn-out crusades. Korea and Vietnam demonstrated that quick, decisive outcomes are not always possible, and Lebanon demonstrated that apparent gains can prove exceedingly ephemeral. Although no great power can eschew the use of military force in all circumstances, the history of U.S. post–World War II interventions illustrates the various pitfalls and limitations of that strategy.

Part 4

CONSTRAINTS ON INTERVENTION

10

The Domestic Environment

Jerel A. Rosati

Since the United States became a global power during World War II, the U.S. domestic environment has changed dramatically. Throughout the late 1940s and 1950s, a domestic consensus supported an active and globally interventionist U.S. foreign policy. Based on popular antifascist sentiment and later followed by strong anticommunist feelings, this consensus was reinforced by the growth of a national security state—that is, the growth of political and economic institutions oriented around the president and directed toward the promotion of U.S. global policy. Thus, the beliefs and institutions of U.S. society provided encouragement for the policy of intervening throughout the globe, most notably in the Third World, in order to contain the threat of communism.

The agonizing U.S. defeat in Vietnam shattered the U.S. domestic consensus and modified the national security state that supported the anticommunist impulse to intervene abroad. Americans subsequently disagreed over the external threats and the proper policy responses. More important, Congress, the media, and private interest groups no longer acquiesced to presidential leadership; they became increasingly critical of presidential goals and aspirations while simultaneously seeking independent policy roles. Whereas presidents were once given wide latitude to construct policies in the name of national security and the national interest, constraints on executive branch power multiplied substantially following Vietnam. These constraints have made it increasingly difficult for presidents to implement interventionist policies in the Third World and have led to such crises of leadership and legitimacy as Watergate, the Iran hostage crisis, and the Iran-contra scandal.

■ THE COLD WAR YEARS AND THE RISE OF ANTICOMMUNISM

Following the end of World War II, Americans gradually became more and more preoccupied with the potential threat posed by the Soviet Union and communism. Isolationist tendencies associated with the prewar period had been firmly discredited with the Japanese bombing of Pearl Harbor and U.S. entry into the conflict. Most Americans realized that the United States had become too powerful to minimize its global involvement following the war. Therefore, a great debate took place among leaders and intellectuals of U.S. society about the world around them, the nature of the Soviet Union, and the proper foreign policy of the United States.[1]

Some people, like Henry Wallace, Franklin Roosevelt's former vice president and presidential candidate in 1948 on the Progressive party ticket, argued it was important to maintain a cooperative relationship with the Soviet Union and prevent a new conflict from arising, through policies emphasizing spheres-of-influence and a type of détente. Others, like George Kennan, a Sovietologist and important policymaker in the administration of President Harry S. Truman, asserted that the major threat was Soviet expansion in Europe; therefore, the United States needed to contain the Soviet threat in Europe. Still others, like Paul Nitze, another important policymaker in the Truman administration, emphasized that the Soviet Union was a revolutionary state with designs to aggressively export communism throughout the world. Such a threat meant that the United States had no choice but to contain the Soviets militarily throughout the globe.

During the late 1940s, individuals representing the two more pessimistic schools of thought struggled for control of foreign policy within the Truman administration. Truman himself was initially undecided about the nature of the Soviet Union and the appropriate U.S. response. With time, however, he increasingly became skeptical of Soviet intentions. Problems over a divided Germany, the communist coup d'état in Czechoslovakia, the "fall" of China, and the North Korean attack of South Korea eventually convinced most members of the Truman administration, including the president, that the Soviet Union was indeed a revolutionary, communist state attempting to achieve world domination. Therefore, the United States had no choice but to assume the role of leader of the "free world" to stop communist aggression.

It is not surprising that Congress and the public were reluctant to support such an activist policy abroad so soon after the country had fought a world war. Nonetheless, there was an underlying anticommunist sentiment embedded in U.S. society that could be traced back to the policies of President Woodrow Wilson following the Bolshevik Revolution in 1917. Therefore, when the Truman administration responded to the post–World War II environment with proclamations like the Truman Doctrine, which committed the United States to assist Greece and Turkey in order to contain the communist threat, the result was growing and substantial public support for an overall policy of containment. The paramount lesson of World War II that was conveyed—that the "appeasement" of Adolf Hitler and fascism by England and France at Munich only produced more aggression—was transferred to the situation at hand: The United States must not appease Stalin and communist aggression. Instead, the United States would build up its military and contain communist aggression wherever it occurred.

These same events also propelled another segment of U.S. society to the forefront of politics—people who feared that the United States was losing the cold war because it was not doing enough to stop and defeat communism. Not only did they perceive that the United States was losing the war *abroad,* especially in Asia; they believed the United States was threatened by subversion from *within*. Therefore, they argued that containment was not enough; a policy of rollback was necessary to stop and defeat communist advances. People who shared this view gained control of Congress during the late 1940s and early 1950s and were prominent within the Republican party—most notable was Senator Joe McCarthy. They attacked the policy of containment, as well as the Truman administration and its supporters, for losing the cold war.[2]

McCarthyism was not successful in getting either the Truman or the Eisenhower administrations to reorient their foreign policies beyond containment. However, the challenge had two lasting effects. First, it reinforced perceptions held by U.S. policymakers and the public that communism was monolithic—controlled by the Soviet Union—and an ever-present threat. Second, liberals and those of the political left who were critical of the policy of containment and argued for a more cooperative policy (such as Wallace) lost all credibility and legitimacy during the cold war years.[3]

In short, a consensus had developed within the United States by the 1950s that the world was divided by two hostile forces: communism led by the Soviet Union and democracy led by the United States. Despite disagreements over tactics (how much force? and where?), most Americans agreed on the nature of the threat—communism—and the necessity to use force to forestall its expansion in the Third World. This consensual view fostered the development of certain U.S. institutions to fight communism, thus leading to the rise of the national security state.

■ THE RISE OF THE NATIONAL SECURITY STATE

Containment originally was applied to Europe and then to Asia by the Truman administration, then extended throughout the globe during the administrations of Presidents Dwight D. Eisenhower, John F. Kennedy, and Lyndon B. Johnson. The United States relied initially on economic assistance in the form of programs like the Marshall Plan to defeat the threat of communism. However, beginning with the Truman Doctrine, the threat and use of force became the basis of containment—by developing nuclear weapons, expanding and deploying the military throughout the world, creating alliances, providing military assistance, conducting covert operations, and overtly intervening abroad with armed troops. In other words, U.S. foreign policy increasingly became globalized and militarized. To promote and maintain such a policy direction, there was a corresponding growth in the national security apparatus of the United States.

Before World War II, few institutions within the government or throughout U.S. society were oriented toward foreign affairs and national security. The policymaking elite was extremely small and centered within the executive branch in the State Department. World War II changed this dramatically. Overnight, the U.S. government was redirected to devote itself to waging a global war; the military expanded enormously, and civilian agencies grew to assist the president in pursuing the conflict. This governmental effort, in turn, put the economy and the society on a war footing to provide the necessary personnel, equipment, and services to achieve U.S. victory. With time, the national security state was formed.

Unlike the situations after previous wars in U.S. history, however, the United States demobilized only for a short time following victory in World War II. With the rise of anticommunism, the United States once more expanded its resources in order to fight a global cold war. The national security state thus continued to operate and grow during the cold war years and became a permanent part of the U.S. landscape. The dominant elements of this apparatus consisted of the presidency, the national security bureaucracy, the foreign policy establishment, and a national security infrastructure throughout the economy and the society in general.

The president was the predominant policymaker in the making of foreign policy.[4] During times of national emergency, power has always tended to flow to the president, and, especially during war, the president is able to exert his considerable powers as commander in chief, head of state, chief diplomat, and chief administrator. The 1950s and 1960s were perceived to be such a time of national emergency, when the national security of the United States was directly threatened by communism. The United States was preparing to fight World War III directly with the Soviet Union in Europe, while it indirectly fought the Soviet regime for the "hearts and minds" of the people and the elites of the Third World by intervening throughout the globe.

The development of consensus in U.S. society behind the need to contain communism helped make the president dominant on questions of war and peace. Congress became increasingly acquiescent to presidential initiatives. The president committed troops to foreign lands with little or no input or consultation from Congress. The rise of a bipartisan consensus between Democrats and Republicans that developed by the mid-1950s resulted in the virtual abdication of the congressional constitutional right to declare war. These decisions now became presidential decisions.

Congressional passage of the National Security Act of 1947 provided the president with a national security bureaucracy to make foreign policy. The act created the National Security Council, reorganized the military into the Department of Defense, and developed an intelligence community under the Central Intelligence Agency.[5] The NSC was to provide policy advice to the president and be supported by a director and staff. Eventually, the NSC became responsive to presidential needs, serving as the mechanism by which presidents centralized and coordinated foreign policy in the executive branch. This was very important to the president's power in foreign affairs, particularly as the national security bureaucracy grew dramatically in size and scope during the cold war.

The repercussions of the National Security Act were felt in institutions beyond the White House as well. Prior to 1947, the military was made up of two separate departments—Navy and War. The act created the Department of Defense, which consisted of three branches—Army, Air Force, and Navy; the Joint Chiefs of Staff to promote military coordination; and the Office of the Secretary of Defense to provide civilian leadership and policy advice to the president. The Department of Defense soon became the largest bureaucracy in the U.S. government. With the globalization of containment, it grew to almost 3 million military personnel and 1 million civilians located in hundreds of military bases throughout the United States and the world. The primary mission of the department has been to develop and deploy the requisite military forces to provide nuclear deterrence and a conventional capability to defend Europe.

The National Security Act also produced a large intelligence community to collect and analyze information for policymakers. Numerous agencies were created and grew in importance, including the National Security Agency (NSA), the Defense Intelligence Agency (DIA), and the CIA. The CIA developed two additional functions. First, it coordinated the intelligence analyses of the various organizations; thus, the director of central intelligence (DCI) serves as the principal spokesman to the president. As noted in Chapters 7 and 8, the CIA also developed a covert operations capability—that is, the ability to conduct clandestine activities (such as propaganda campaigns, assassinations, and small paramilitary wars) in support of U.S. foreign policy objectives in the Third World.

Other executive branch organizations also have been involved in foreign affairs, including the State Department, the Agency for International Development, the Arms Control and Disarmament Agency, and the Peace Corps. In the area of international political economy, the Treasury Department, Commerce Department, and Department of Agriculture have been heavily involved, among others. In fact, almost every department of the executive branch has developed international divisions in response to the cold war and U.S. global activism. In sum, following World War II, foreign policy was no longer made principally in the State Department or with much congressional involvement; power moved away from Congress toward the executive branch and especially to the president through the use of the NSC.

The cold war years also saw the rise of a foreign policy establishment that produced much of the personnel and expertise that made up U.S. foreign policy.[6] The war effort forced the government to recruit personnel from all over U.S. society to staff the ever-expanding national security bureaucracy—especially, scientists, academics, lawyers, and businesspeople. For example, such people were brought together to work on the Manhattan Project in order to develop the atom bomb. Similar interactions in other foreign policy areas occurred throughout the government. Thus, as people began to meet each other and work together, a network of individuals from diverse walks of life developed who came to share the assumptions of the anticommunist consensus.

With the rise of the anticommunist consensus and the expansion of the national security bureaucracy following the war, many of the same people who had staffed the government during World War II became involved in the effort to fight the cold war. These same individuals, and many new recruits, constantly moved back and forth between the government and private world and usually became members of a few prominent groups, such as the Council on Foreign Relations. Thus, the foreign policy establishment was formed, providing a bridge between the government, the national security bureaucracy, and key institutions throughout U.S. society.

The development throughout the economy and the society in general of a support infrastructure—including U.S. industry, labor, academia, research institutes, and intellectuals—was the final element contributing to the rise of the national security state.[7] Much of U.S. industry was directly involved in expanding defense efforts in response to the cold war. This transformation began with the U.S. entry into World War II, when the production of materials and services for civilians changed to military production to defeat Germany and Japan. Many of the largest U.S. companies, such as General Motors, Chrysler, McDonnell Douglas, and Boeing, retooled their assembly lines to produce tanks and bombers rather than cars and airplanes. With the rise of the cold war, these same companies continued to work for the government and, especially, for the Defense Department. Thus was born the permanent cold war economy.

U.S. banks and companies increasingly became multinationalized following World War II, often locating in other countries where there was a strong U.S. governmental presence. U.S. businesses were routinely involved in other ways—such as through subcontracting the building of facilities at a local military base or by building a retail outlet near a base heavily patronized by military personnel. U.S. labor also supported the cold war effort. For example, the American Federation of Labor–Congress for Industrial Organization (AFL-CIO) became a major supporter of free trade and U.S. foreign policy throughout the world. Both organized and unorganized labor—that is, American employees—were bulwarks of the national security state and the anticommunist crusade.

Activity by business and labor was also reinforced by behavior in the scientific, research, and educational community. This class of individuals was important in communicating the need for containment, developing many of the national security ideas and plans (such as deterrence and nation-building), and often served as part of the foreign policy establishment and the government. Research institutes and "think tanks" devoted to national security concerns, such as the RAND Corporation, became a prominent part of the effort to contain communism. The same trend occurred throughout the entire educational system but was most visible at prominent universities such as Harvard, the Massachusetts Institute of Technology, and the University of California at Berkeley. Anticommunism, as well as the need for containment and intervention abroad, was further promoted by the supportive messages communicated to the public by the mass media. Finally, most intellectuals supported the rise of the anticommunist national security state.

Thus, the late 1940s and 1950s witnessed the rise of anticommunism and the national security state. Both developed at the same time and reinforced each other; the rise of anticommunism resulted in the growth of the national security state, and the development and expansion of the national security state reinforced the anticommunist fervor that permeated U.S. society. Rather than working as a constraint on U.S. intervention in the Third World, anticommunist beliefs and the national security state provided the foundation for—and, indeed, prompted—greater U.S. involvement and interventionism throughout the globe in order to contain communist aggression. This situation led directly to U.S. involvement in the Vietnam War.

■ VIETNAM: THE COLLAPSE OF CONSENSUS AND THE RISE OF FRAGMENTATION

The Vietnam War eventually became an agonizing experience for Americans. U.S. involvement, in support of the French effort to maintain its colonial empire in Indochina against Ho Chi Minh and the Vietnamese communists, began under the Truman administration and continued under Eisenhower. By 1954, the United States was paying 80 percent of the war's cost (about $1 billion a year). With the withdrawal of the French in 1954, following the battle of Dienbienphu and the signing of the Geneva Accords, the United States attempted unilaterally to support a stable and independent South Vietnam. However, under Presidents Kennedy and Johnson, the situation in the south deteriorated. The U.S. response was to Americanize the war—by 1967, over half a million U.S. soldiers were fighting a war in Vietnam at a cost of over $30 billion a year.

Throughout much of this period, the U.S. public—both elites and masses—tacitly supported increasing U.S. involvement in Southeast Asia. In reality, most Americans were unaware of where Vietnam was and what was happening there. They were not interested in foreign policy ventures so far from home. Moreover, this was still a time of consensus. If the president of the United States, supported by the national security state, contended that Vietnam was being threatened by communism and that all the region's nations would fall if the threat were not contained, the American people stood behind him. Most Americans did not question the assumptions that led to the nation's involvement in Vietnam. They believed that the containment policy was necessary to defend U.S. national security and promote democracy, liberty, and justice throughout the world. It took U.S. involvement in the Vietnam quagmire to get people to ask questions again about the nature of the world and the proper U.S. foreign policy response.

What made Vietnam so traumatic for many Americans and so significant for U.S. society was that it was the first war in its history that the United States had lost. Americans were used to winning; they expected to succeed. In addition, behind the anticommunism and containment policy of the consensus years was a common set of values that most Americans shared. As noted in Chapter 2, Americans were raised to believe that they were an innocent society, a benevolent society, an exceptional society.[8] Americans see themselves as a defensive people—not aggressive or imperialistic. Furthermore, when Americans do become involved in war, they become involved to help all people—"the war to end all wars." Americans typically see themselves in the forefront of civilization and progress in the modern world, a society that with "Yankee ingenuity" can accomplish anything it sets its mind to do.

The Vietnam War undermined many of these beliefs held by Americans. How could the most powerful country in the history of the world lose to a guerrilla insurgency? The war in Vietnam was a failure. Furthermore, Americans were dying for a lost cause—over 55,000 Americans died in Vietnam. For what? The tragic loss of American lives led people to doubt the appropriateness of a foreign policy based on the global containment of monolithic communism. But there was more than just a questioning of the policy of global containment. The conduct of the war effort in Vietnam, such as the use of napalm and the My Lai massacre, also led many to question such deeply held values as American innocence and benevolence. In other words, not only did most Americans question the practicality of a policy of global containment, Vietnam also forced many Americans to question the morality of U.S. foreign policy as well as that of its society. The result was that the consensus that had developed during the 1950s was shattered.

The events of the 1960s resulted in the rise of the political left in the United States and an alternative understanding of U.S. society.[9] Although the rise of anticommunism and, in particular, McCarthyism, had silenced most liberals and leftists during the early 1950s, the new left began to emerge on the political scene in the late 1950s with the rise of the civil rights movement and grew dramatically as the Vietnam War intensified. The hard-core political activists and members of the counterculture dissented and rebelled against mainstream society, the anticommunist consensus, and the national security state—all of which were perceived as being responsible for producing Vietnam. Members of the antiwar movement advocated U.S. withdrawal from the war. By the late 1960s, a substantial number of the American people had also turned against

U.S. involvement in Vietnam—some wanted out via withdrawal, others wanted out through escalation.

For a while, the polarization between the antiwar movement and the executive branch, the counterculture and mainstream society, verged on civil war. But polarization gave way to fragmentation. Whereas once a consensus had been the basis of U.S. society and U.S. foreign policy, disagreement became the norm—especially in the area of foreign policy. Since Vietnam, different schools of thought have competed for ascendancy within U.S. society.[10]

Some people, especially those on the political right, continue to believe that the major global threat to the United States is communism directed by the Soviet Union. Proponents of such a conservative position argue that U.S. foreign policy needs to contain, if not roll back, Soviet communism. It should be pointed out that disagreement exists among conservatives concerning the severity of the communist threat and the appropriate foreign policy strategy. Those who tend to see a more monolithic communism tend also to favor a strategy of massive rearmament at home and rollback abroad. Those who focus more on the threat of the Soviet brand of communism emphasize a defense buildup and a more modest containment strategy.

Other people, especially from the liberal left, see a much more complex and interdependent world, made up of many important countries and actors. Advocates of this liberal position argue that in such a complex global environment, the United States needs to deemphasize the role of force in addressing East-West issues (such as the U.S.-Soviet conflict), West-West issues (such as U.S.-Japanese trade), and North-South issues (such as Third World debt). Although there is no consensus among the liberal left, the emphasis is on downplaying the Soviet threat and relying on preventive diplomacy to promote global peace and prosperity throughout the world.

Proponents of the third most popular position, especially among the mass public, which traverses the political spectrum, recognize the increasing complexity of the world and the difficulty the United States has in affecting it. They argue that the United States needs to limit its involvement to those few areas where it really has vital interests—especially Western Europe and Japan. Although other points of view exist beyond these three, they are the most popular vying for control of U.S. foreign policy.

The fragmentation of public beliefs, especially at the pragmatic mass level, seems to have contradictory implications for U.S. foreign policy in the Third World. Most Americans continue to be fearful and skeptical of communism; yet they also want more cooperative and peaceful relations with communist countries, including the Soviet Union. Likewise, most Americans continue to believe in a strong defense; yet they are reluctant to use force that may result in American boys dying abroad in a war. In other words, as a result of the Vietnam War, the "Munich appeasement syndrome," which dominated the thinking of the 1950s, has now been joined by the "Vietnam syndrome." Most Americans do not want to appease communism, but they want to avoid another Vietnam.

The net result of the collapse of the anticommunist consensus for U.S. foreign policy is that U.S. interventionism in the Third World is more tentative and precarious. Short-term, small-scale interventions like Grenada are palatable; long-term, large-scale interventions, as in Lebanon and Central America, are looked upon more skeptically. Thus, there had been a fluctuation in support for the contras and President Reagan's aim to overthrow the Sandinistas without direct U.S. military intervention. Presidents gradually learn that, unlike the consensus years, they do not come to office with automatic majorities behind their policies. No matter what the president and his advisers believe, there is a substantial segment of U.S. society—among both elites and masses—that will disagree with presidential policy. This constraint is reinforced because much of the support that the president has initially, upon election, withers away over time.

The existence of fragmentation in public beliefs over U.S. foreign policy gives the president great opportunities but also great risks. Unlike the 1950s, presidents are no longer driven to pursue only an anticommunist policy of containment. Yet, it is increasingly unclear how far the president can go in pursuing a policy before losing majority support. Most Americans expect presidents to fulfill the expectations that they have generated in public, but the dissensus of the post-Vietnam years makes it much more difficult for presidents to deliver.

■ VIETNAM: THE NATIONAL SECURITY STATE AND THE RISE OF PLURALISM

The post-Vietnam domestic environment has also resulted in the collapse of the foreign policy establishment, the reassertion of Congress, a more critical media, and the rise of divergent interest groups. Thus, presidents are not only confronted with greater diversity of thought, they are increasingly constrained by the existence of competing domestic actors and institutions on the foreign policy scene. The domestic environment has become much more complex and pluralistic. Moreover, these developments have limited the power of the national security state, exacerbated the eclipse of presidential power, reinforced the constraints on Third World interventionism, and produced inconsistency in U.S. foreign policy with each change in administration.

The key to the U.S. foreign policy establishment's past ability to serve as the bridge between the different elements of the national security state was the existence of an informal network of like-minded individuals. But once the Vietnam War challenged the domestic consensus, members of the establishment differed over the war and proper U.S. foreign policy along the lines of the three different schools of thought previously discussed. So, as public beliefs fragmented, the consensus that held the foreign policy establishment together also dissolved, even more intensely given the establishment's level of individual interest and involvement in foreign policy.[11]

The Vietnam War also strained executive branch relations with the legislative branch. President Richard M. Nixon was elected in 1968 based on a secret plan to end the war. The secret plan consisted of a strategy simultaneously involving deescalation, escalation, and negotiations. Deescalation meant that the use of U.S. troops was slowly phased out through a process of "Vietnamization." Escalation entailed the stepped-up bombing of Indochina, as well as the invasion of guerrilla sanctuaries in Cambodia and Laos. Both deescalation and escalation were intended to produce a negotiated agreement with the North Vietnamese to end the war and buy South Vietnam a "decent interval" for survival. However, with escalation, the antiwar movement reached its height, calling for the immediate withdrawal of U.S. forces.

Much of the dissent reflected in the antiwar movement eventually surfaced in the U.S. Congress. The president was no longer seen to be doing what was necessary in the name of national security. Instead, more and more members of Congress saw an unresponsive and unaccountable "imperial presidency." Turnover in congressional membership—brought on as older, more conservative members retired or died—produced major battles between the legislative and executive branches over the conduct of foreign policy. Congress was clearly no longer willing to assume the acquiescent role it had played during the 1950s, when it rallied behind presidential policy. Many representatives and senators were now interested in directly affecting the conduct of foreign policy.

The president resisted congressional efforts to reassert its authority in foreign policy. Nevertheless, through its power to control appropriations, to investigate, and to pass legislation, Congress did reclaim some of its constitutional authority. For example, in 1973, it was able to regain part of its ability to be involved in decisions of war and peace by passing the War Powers Act. In 1975, it officially ended U.S. involvement in Vietnam by eliminating all funding. Congress also pressured the executive branch by exposing secret security commitments made by U.S. presidents to numerous countries throughout the world and publicizing CIA abuses abroad, including efforts to assassinate leaders and overthrow unfriendly regimes.[12]

Although Congress has become more interested and active in the making of U.S. foreign policy, the president continues to exercise considerable power. Three general patterns have emerged. For a few issues, such as human rights, Congress has often taken the lead in the making of foreign policy. For some other issues, like Central America, Congress has become a major participant and, in the mind of the president, a major obstacle to presidential management of U.S. foreign policy. For most issues, however, Congress continues to be on the sidelines, reacting to presidential initiatives. Therefore, the president remains powerful in foreign policy, with the knowledge that presidential power may be constrained by congressional participation if an issue becomes politicized. Thus, President Gerald R. Ford's covert intervention in Angola in 1975, President Jimmy Carter's efforts at SALT (Strategic Arms Limitation Talks) II ratification in 1979, and President Reagan's efforts to militarize Central American policy throughout the 1980s all met congressional opposition.

The turbulence of the 1960s, the Vietnam War, and the revelations of executive branch abuses in the name of national security shocked most Americans and made them very skeptical and critical of the presidency and the government. Whereas Americans once had great trust in their representatives and governmental institutions, lack of success in Vietnam and the revelations of Watergate prompted most of the public to lose faith in the honesty and integrity of the U.S. political system. This cynical attitude is clearly reflected in the mass media. Journalists during the 1950s and early 1960s played a major role in communicating the perils of communism and the need for a global, interventionist foreign policy to contain the threat—they operated within the consensus. The end of consensus, however, meant that journalists also became divided in thought and much more partisan. More important, Vietnam and Watergate taught many members of the media that they could no longer trust public officials to tell the truth, that they had to look below the surface for the real story. Thus, the media has become increasingly critical of government activities and public officials, including presidents.

This is consequential for presidential power, as most people are heavily dependent on the media for telling them what to think about (that is, the media sets the political agenda) and for being the source of most of their information. The media in the 1980s is a major force in both making and breaking public personalities. Thus, Presidents Carter and Reagan relied on media coverage in ascending to the presidency, and both were damaged politically by media coverage of the Iran hostage crisis and the Iran-contra affair, respectively.[13]

The breakdown of consensus also has broadened and diversified the larger societal environment within which the government must operate. U.S. industry, labor, academia, and the intellectual community no longer stand united behind a global, interventionist U.S. foreign policy. As U.S. economic might has declined relative to the growth of Japan, Western Europe, OPEC, and the newly industrializing countries, the paths of U.S. business and government no longer coincide as in the past. Some U.S. companies are more free-trade oriented, whereas others have become more protectionist. U.S. labor has become more protectionist over time. In academia and among intellectuals, the diversity of thought that exists in society is even more visible. In other words, beliefs have become less uniform and more divisive throughout the institutional fabric of U.S. society.

The rise of a pluralistic environment clearly can be seen when examining interest-group activity in the area of foreign policy. Beginning in the 1960s, new national security and public interest groups have arisen from a variety of different ideological perspectives, many of them involving people who were once part of the old-boy network referred to as the foreign policy establishment—conservative groups such as the Heritage Foundation and the American Enterprise Institute and liberal groups like the Institute for Policy Studies and the Brookings Institution. The large number of interest groups and the variety of their foreign policy activity reflects the diversity of thought that followed Vietnam. These groups have been active in influencing Congress, the media, and the public to promote their interests (whether the goal is overthrowing the Sandinistas or imposing sanctions against South Africa). All this foreign policy activity has made it that much more difficult for the president to control the agenda successfully and manage U.S. foreign policy.[14]

About the only patterns that did not change much are the national security bureaucracy and the military-industrial-scientific complex that developed throughout society during the cold war years, both oriented around a large defense and the threat of force. The NSC, Defense Department, intelligence community, industrial defense contractors, and defense-oriented research community, as well as the individual networks that tie them together, have continued to exist and even prosper. However, they exist in a domestic environment that is much less supportive and occasionally more hostile than during the consensus years.

■ CRISIS OF LEADERSHIP AND U.S. INTERVENTION

Understanding the continuities and changes in the domestic environment holds important implications for U.S. interventionist practices in the Third World. First, the national security bureaucracy, the military-industrial-scientific complex, and the segment of society that emphasizes the threat of Soviet communism all act as a powerful force in promoting U.S. foreign policy in the direction of a large defense and a reliance on the threat of force, including Third World interventionism. Second, the breakdown of consensus, the collapse of the foreign policy establishment, the rise of a reassertive Congress, a more critical media, and competing interest groups mean that no foreign policy orientation is able to maintain much public support over time.

In the past, given the rise of anticommunism and the national security state, the problem was that the president could lead the country, but only in the direction of fervent anticommunism, containment, and interventionism. In the 1980s, with the collapse of consensus and the changes in the national security state, the problem is that the president—and really, the political system—cannot generate leadership in any direction for a sustained period of time. All post-Vietnam presidents have failed. None have been able to generate a new consensus or sustain sufficient support behind their policies.

Presidents Nixon and Ford attempted to promote a more stable global order through a realpolitik policy based on détente with the Soviet Union. However, Nixon's legitimacy was devastated by Watergate, and he was forced to resign. Ford's lack of leadership resulted in his inability to win election to the presidency. President Carter tried to promote a global community in response to a complex world by emphasizing preventive diplomacy across a variety of issues.

Yet, Carter's stewardship was called into question by the Iran hostage crisis and the Soviet invasion of Afghanistan. President Reagan attempted to resurrect the containment policy of the past in order to deter and defeat Soviet communist expansion. Reagan's leadership, the most politically successful, was nonetheless also called into question by the Iran-contra affair.

The nature of the domestic environment has produced a crisis of leadership for the presidency and the country. The president, the only person capable of providing national leadership, is unable to lead the country. The fragmented nature of American beliefs, as well as competing domestic interests and institutions, have constrained presidential action. No matter what the president promises, domestically or in foreign policy, he is unable to fulfill expectations. The complexity of the domestic environment and the complexity of the global system no longer allow much leeway for presidential success. Presidents cannot lead and manage foreign policy for long, whether its direction is interventionist or not. This crisis of leadership means that U.S. foreign policy, as it changes with each new administration, will continue to be incoherent and inconsistent into the future.

11

Government and the Military Establishment

Stephen Daggett

Shortly after Ronald Reagan was reelected president in 1984, a noteworthy debate broke out between Secretary of Defense Caspar Weinberger and Secretary of State George Shultz. "If we ever decide to commit forces to combat," Weinberger told the National Press Club in November 1984, "we must support those forces to the fullest extent of our national will for as long as it takes to win. We must have in mind objectives that are clearly defined and understood and supported by the widest possible number of our citizens. And those objectives must be vital to our survival as a free nation and to the fulfillment of our responsibilities as a world power."[1] The secretary's cautionary statement was, by all accounts, extremely popular inside the Pentagon, reflecting the sentiments of a senior military leadership still scarred by its experience in Vietnam, a trauma revived in some measure by the loss of 241 U.S. Marines in Lebanon in 1983.[2]

The speech was not so well received, however, elsewhere in the government. Secretary of State George Shultz, who opposed the withdrawal of U.S. forces from Lebanon after the marine barracks attack, responded two weeks later with a speech that pointedly challenged Weinberger's timorousness. "There is no such thing," said Shultz, "as guaranteed public support in advance. . . . Americans will always be reluctant to use force. . . . But a great power cannot free itself so easily from the burden of choice. It must bear responsibility for the consequences of its inaction as well as for the consequences of its action." The use of force is legitimate, said Shultz, "when it can further the cause of freedom and enhance international security. . . . And on such occasions we will be able to count on the full support of the American people."[3]

Though events in Lebanon motivated Weinberger's speech, and the military's experience of Vietnam shaped its content, the Weinberger-Shultz debate reflects a pattern of bureaucratic interests and conflicts that has characterized U.S. decisionmaking throughout the post–World War II era. In this chapter I consider the governmental-bureaucratic forces that influence the U.S. ability and willingness to intervene militarily in the Third World. I suggest that significant barriers to the effective application of force persist in the U.S. government—especially within the military establishment—despite efforts in the 1980s by some elements of the political leadership and by parts of the military to prepare for armed responses to conflict in the Third World.

■ BUREAUCRACY AND IDEOLOGY

The Weinberger-Shultz debate illustrates the institutional barriers to interventionism within the U.S. military bureaucracy. In justifying the use of force, Shultz's argument was primarily ideological, evoking U.S. responsibility as a great power to preserve international security and stability and citing a democratic nation's moral duty to advance the cause of freedom. Weinberger's argument, in contrast, was shaped by the necessarily more practical point of view of the military services. Weinberger listed six conditions that should be fulfilled whenever U.S. military units are sent into action: (1) An engagement must be vital to U.S. national interests or those of its allies; (2) a commitment must be undertaken wholeheartedly, with the clear intent of winning; (3) objectives must be clearly defined; (4) the relationship between objectives and forces must be continually reassessed and adjusted if necessary; (5) there must be a reasonable assurance of public and congressional support; and (6) forces should be committed to combat only as a last resort.[4] Weinberger generally has been seen as one of the more intensely ideological officials in the Reagan administration, but in this instance the secretary of defense was clearly representing his agency; he had become, in bureaucratic jargon, a "captive" of the bureaucracy he led. Although there was a moral dimension to his analysis, the moral view was primarily that of senior officers in the military services, insisting that if assigned a task, they should be given the tools to carry out the job.

This contrast between the pragmatic caution of the U.S. military bureaucracy and the ideologically motivated activism of senior administration political officials outside the Pentagon has recurred throughout the post–World War II period. In most instances of direct U.S. military involvement in distant conflicts, the decision to intervene has been initiated by the top political leadership of a particular administration and acceded to with some reluctance by the armed forces. As Morton Halperin wrote in his 1974 study of the foreign policy bureaucracy:

> The attitude of the military services toward commitments and the use of force is surprising to observers who expect a bellicose outlook. . . . On the issue of American military intervention, the armed services have been in general quite cautious. At different times they have resisted proposals for intervention, remained neutral, or asked for authority to use all their existing forces to make the gamble of involvement less risky if taken at all. Professionally they prefer

> a conservative estimate of the readiness of forces, and they are sensitive to the danger of using forces where they might be defeated or where they would be drawn away from the primary theater of operations.[5]

Halperin cited several examples, going back to the earliest days of the cold war, to illustrate his point. During the Berlin Crisis of 1948, he noted, the JCS in Washington refused to endorse a proposal to confront the Soviets by sending an armed convoy down the road from the American zone to Berlin. The military, he said, did not recommend intervening at the outbreak of the Korean War in June 1950, nor were they the driving force in planning the Bay of Pigs invasion. The military opposed proposals to intervene in Laos in 1961 unless granted full authority to use all forces, including nuclear weapons. And the services did not ardently advocate U.S. involvement in Vietnam.[6]

The principles that Weinberger articulated in his Press Club speech, therefore, were not simply offspring of the post-Vietnam era. Rather, they reflect institutional interests and perspectives that are a persistent feature of the U.S. military establishment. In part, these interests are simply bureaucratic: Officials in bureaucracies typically are averse to risking the organizational damage that would result from failure. As such, military leaders prefer to avoid conflict except under conditions in which success is almost assured. But more fundamentally, the historical roots of the current U.S. military structure make preparation for small wars into a kind of organizational afterthought.

■ THE PRIORITY OF LARGE WAR PLANNING

The defining characteristic of the U.S. defense posture in the post–World War II era is that the U.S. military sees its primary job as deterrence of a major war with the Soviet Union and its allies in Europe. From the start of the U.S. military remobilization at the time of the Korean War, Europe has been the centerpiece of U.S. defense planning. Indeed, even in the midst of the Korean War, senior defense planners were preoccupied with the military situation in Europe, fearing that the North Korean attack on the South might be a diversion, presaging a Soviet offensive in Europe. As a result, once the initial buildup of forces for Korea was completed, the services substantially bolstered the strength of U.S. forces assigned to Europe.

After the Korean War and into the 1960s, the United States formally maintained a "two-and-a-half" war posture—that is, a requirement that it be able to carry on, simultaneously, two major wars, one in Europe and one in Asia, and a minor war somewhere else. But except during the administration of John F. Kennedy and the early years of the administration of Lyndon B. Johnson, planning for a major war in Asia and for Third World "half-wars" was a very low priority. During the administration of Richard Nixon, Secretary of Defense Melvin Laird explicitly renounced the two-and-a-half-war requirement, saying that the strategy was "overly ambitious" and that it had resulted in "an overdrawn military establishment." "Since then," Laird wrote later, "American ground forces have been postured according to the precept that forces sufficient for the defense of Europe are also capable of effectively responding to lesser threats elsewhere."[7] Even during the administration of Jimmy Carter, when the Persian Gulf became a preoccupation, and into the administration of Ronald Reagan, when officials laid out an expansive vision of the number of worldwide threats that might demand military responses, defense planning has, in fact, been based predominantly on the requirements of a major war in Europe.

Indeed, although the Reagan administration widely bruited a strategy of preparing to meet several contingencies around the globe simultaneously, forces never grew sufficiently to meet the planning requirements, and the shift in doctrine only exacerbated what came to be called the "strategy-resources mismatch." When the JCS estimated the size of the force that would be necessary to provide a "reasonable assurance" of accomplishing the missions assigned to U.S. troops—an exercise carried out annually as part of the Planning, Programming, and Budgeting System (PPBS)—the result was very far from the force structure available. In 1982, the Joint Chiefs' "reasonable assurance" force called for twenty-two aircraft-carrier battle groups, rather than the fifteen projected to be available by the end of the decade, and thirty-three active divisions in the U.S. Army and Marine Corps, compared to the twenty-one actually planned.[8]

As it has turned out, with defense budgets leveling off after 1985, the Reagan administration had been unable to sustain even the relatively modest increases in the size of the force that it undertook during the president's first term. For example, in 1983 the army announced plans to grow from sixteen active divisions to eighteen. The two new units, along with three others in the active and reserve force, were organized as Light Infantry Divisions (LIDs), designed to be smaller and much more easily transportable than a full armored or mechanized division. These five divisions were intended for smaller conflicts, primarily outside of Europe.

The army's growth however, was achieved not by adding personnel but by reorganizing to reduce the number of active-duty troops assigned to support functions. Thus, from the start, the growth to eighteen divisions was rather hollow. A full third of the army's forces intended for rapid deployment are in the reserves, and even the units that would be deployed first in a crisis depend heavily on the reserve component for critical support functions. Such forces would take a considerable amount of time to train and deploy, a posture that may be appropriate for European contingencies but not for crises that could develop rapidly and unexpectedly elsewhere.

Similarly, the expansion of the U.S. Navy toward 600 ships (with fifteen deployable aircraft-carrier battle groups and four battleships) is frequently taken as evidence of the Reagan administration's interest in adding forces for small wars in distant parts of the globe. But the main burden of the navy's argument for expanding to 600 ships was not to meet requirements for Third World contingencies. On the contrary, senior officials justified the navy's expansion on the basis of the contribution that the navy could make to winning a major war with the Soviet Union. The central principle underlying the navy's new "maritime strategy" was that naval forces could be used in the event of a global conflict to take the offensive and carry the war directly to the Soviet homeland. Secretary of the Navy John Lehman explicitly insisted that the naval buildup was not to be justified in terms of peacetime deployments in the Persian Gulf or the possibility of minor wars there or elsewhere. "Every dollar" he said, "has to be justified by what it can do to defeat the Soviet maritime threat in time of war, and that is it and it only."[9]

■ ORGANIZATIONAL PRIORITIES

The fact that the U.S. military is primarily organized to deter a major war with the Soviet Union and its allies in Europe does not, of course, mean that smaller-scale military action is ruled out. The commitment of a significant number of U.S. troops to a small war for any length of time would draw away forces that are earmarked for a full-scale conflict with the Soviets. But even if a large-scale Korea- or Vietnam-style war appears unlikely in light of bureaucratic priorities, limited military forces, the legacy of Vietnam, and continuing public skepticism about extended military adventures overseas, the United States may nonetheless be increasingly prepared to engage in limited military actions and to offer military support to beleaguered Third World regimes. As noted in Chapter 3, proponents of low-intensity warfare, a doctrine that the Reagan administration wholeheartedly embraced, have identified several kinds of operations short of a major war to which U.S. forces might conceivably be committed—including proinsurgency, counterinsurgency, terrorism counteraction, peacetime contingency operations, and peacekeeping.

However, the orientation of U.S. military forces toward a major war not only constrains the commitment of relatively large numbers of troops to a small war; it also makes it more difficult in important ways to prosecute even relatively limited military actions. Although sufficient forces will always be available for actions like the invasion of Grenada or the bombing of Libya, and though some forces have always been specifically organized, trained, and equipped for small-scale operations, the bureaucratic structure of the U.S. military establishment is biased against a major focus on such minor, secondary conflicts; the U.S. ability to carry on small wars is, therefore, limited in significant ways. The military's focus on a major European conflict means that forces are trained, weapons are procured, and combat units are configured primarily for a large war. "The most substantial constraints on America's ability to conduct small wars," wrote Eliot Cohen, an academic expert on military policy, "result from the resistance of the American defense establishment to the very notion of engaging in such conflicts, and from the unsuitability of that establishment for fighting such wars."[10]

As the major counterinsurgency effort in which the United States has been involved in the 1980s, the war in El Salvador forcefully illustrates how bureaucratic factors constrain prosecution of even a relatively limited intervention. Some of the constraints on U.S. military involvement in El Salvador are not per se bureaucratic and have been widely discussed. For example, rather than risk running afoul of the War Powers Act, which requires congressional approval to maintain the presence of U.S. troops in situations in which hostilities are imminent, the Reagan administration limited U.S. troop strength in El Salvador to 55 advisers and prohibited advisers from accompanying Salvadoran forces into the field. (In practice, the ceiling is stretched by the presence of temporary personnel, military attachés at the embassy, and other means, so that more than 150 U.S. military personnel are typically in El Salvador at a given time—but the ceiling nonetheless imposes a real constraint.)

In addition, in 1981 and 1982, as the Reagan administration was beginning to escalate its commitment to the government of El Salvador, the U.S. ambassador, Robert White, was often at odds with U.S. military officials in the region. Disputes involved how to deal with violations of human rights by the Salvadoran military and the extent of Salvadoran military involvement in civil administration. For their part, U.S. military officials have frequently expressed frustration with the extent of civilian control over U.S. policy in situations like that in El Salvador, where they perceived a military crisis. Even with a new, much more sympathetic ambassador in place, the military remained dissatisfied with legal requirements that separated administration of economic assistance from military aid and with a congressional prohibition on the training of foreign police agencies (though officials have found some ways around this restriction).

Apart from such environmental factors limiting military freedom of action, however, constraints *within* the U.S. defense establishment also profoundly affect the ability of the military to engage in effective counterinsurgency. The most basic constraint remains the low priority accorded minor conflicts in Pentagon planning. In the case of El Salvador, the secondary status of the conflict was reflected, first of all, in the failure of military officials to pursue consistent long-term funding for military aid and otherwise to give priority to requirements of the action.

Funding for the war in El Salvador was always a contentious issue in the U.S. Congress and remained so in 1988. Beginning in 1981, the Reagan White House lobbied vigorously but rather inconsistently for assistance, frequently arguing that a tenuous military situation required aid on an emergency basis as a means of overcoming congressional resistance. As a result, military planning on the ground in El Salvador was disrupted by a process that U.S. military advisers there characterized as "living from one supplemental [appropriation] to the next."[11] Despite the complaints of in-country advisers, senior officials in the Defense Department reacted rather passively, reflecting the fact that El Salvador was not at the top of their agenda. Four army officers who extensively interviewed U.S. military and nonmilitary officials involved with the conflict reported that the military advisers complained that officials in Washington did not take the war seriously. "In the eyes of those serving in the theater," the officials noted, "support was grudging and suggested that overall 'peacetime' priorities survived intact despite the existence of their war. . . . Some changes occurred on the margins, but real priorities were unaffected." In short, serious consideration was reserved for the traditional "peacetime concerns" and the "big-ticket" theaters such as NATO.[12]

A former commander in chief of the U.S. Southern Command, the senior U.S. military official in the region, reportedly "concluded after numerous trips to Washington to present his case, that the Department of Defense viewed Central America primarily as a potential 'distraction' that could derail the Reagan military build-up by irritating the Congress."[13] The low priority accorded El Salvador by senior defense officials is also reflected in the Pentagon's failure to pursue development of a coherent, integrated, government-wide policy that would unambiguously articulate U.S. goals and strategy.

The disinterest of senior Washington-based military leaders is not the only way in which the focus of U.S. military planning on big-ticket theaters affected conduct of the U.S. intervention in El Salvador. It also influenced the military equipment that the United States provided, the quality and skills of U.S. military personnel assigned to the war, and, most important, the military organization and strategy that U.S. advisers brought to the conflict.

□ Equipment

U.S. military equipment is designed for fighting a major war against a sophisticated enemy in Central Europe. Indeed, it is intended to be more sophisticated than anything the enemy can put into the field in order to overcome disadvantages in numbers with superiority in technology. It is also designed for intense conflict in which the ability to deliver massive firepower on selected targets is of decisive importance. Almost of necessity, such equipment, though sometimes offering advantages, is not optimal for counterinsurgency warfare. In El Salvador, the availability of large amounts of U.S. military assistance has encouraged the military to "heavy up" infantry units with artillery and other equipment that only serves to slow response time and extend logistics tails. Massive military assistance also has led to an overemphasis on airpower. The Salvador Air Force grew from about 20 aircraft to 135 by 1988, but this huge expansion only created a shortage of pilots and maintenance personnel.[14] It also built into the Salvadoran military budget a large, permanent requirement for funds to operate and maintain the new equipment. Now that the war has settled into a protracted, classic guerrilla action, with few large battles, the firepower that infantry and air force units acquired is of little real use but continues to cost a great deal. The natural U.S. reaction to a military confrontation, however, will always be to put in more sophisticated equipment—a "rich man's approach to war."[15]

□ Personnel

Perhaps the most dramatic way in which the U.S. focus on large wars manifests itself is in policies governing the assignment of military personnel to counterinsurgency conflicts. The peacetime U.S. defense establishment is a huge, bureaucratic structure designed not to fight small wars but to prepare for the big one. Promotion policies reflect this fact of life. The people who advance up to the general officer level are those with command experience in the major theaters of operation, with personal contact with senior officers in the Pentagon, and, in the 1980s, with experience in the weapons procurement system. Officers who serve in other areas for too long cannot develop the expertise that is most important to each of the military services and, just as important, do not develop ties with superiors willing to go to bat for smart young protegés. Indeed, each major arm within each of the services develops a subculture of its own and wants to promote its own in order to maintain its influence in inside decisionmaking; submariners, for example, compete with navy pilots for top slots, as the Strategic Air Command competes with the Tactical Air Command for predominance within the air force.

Dedicated low-intensity conflict forces are outside of the principal organizational structures of each of the services. Only within the army is there a very large special forces complement, and even there it is not of sufficient mass to significantly influence promotions, budgets, or weapons-system development. Indeed, within the army, special forces personnel are often rather derisively referred to as "snake-eaters," a term that reflects the fact that they remain alien to the professional values of the peacetime military.

In El Salvador, the priority of career paths other than special forces was acutely felt. Typically, the brightest, upwardly mobile officers in the army, which is the service principally responsible for counterinsurgency training, tried to avoid assignment to the war, preferring relatively short tours of duty in a number of slots that would advance their careers ("ticket punching," in the military vernacular). As a result, El Salvador received a group of military advisers that one army study group referred to as the "second team." The report noted that each of the services has a "first team," as determined by factors that make sense to that service. Yet, apart from the military group commander, the study group noted that "virtually none of the eligible Army officers assigned to El Salvador had commanded a battalion beforehand. Very few—only two by our count—went on to command subsequent to serving in El Salvador." Stressing that other indicators painted a similar picture, the report concluded that "the system has not exerted itself to supply the MILGROUP [military group] with only the best soldiers available. The personnel managers have not made winning in El Salvador a priority."[16]

□ Military Organization and Strategy

Because U.S. defense priorities are focused on a large, global war, U.S. command colleges train officers in strategy and tactics for a major conflict, and the organization of U.S. military forces is designed for a major conflict in Europe. Counterinsurgency is taught at places like the Army War College, but it receives a secondary priority in the curriculum. More important, in the event of a major war, the role of the military would be, in a sense, relatively limited—its job is simply to fight the war. In a guerrilla conflict, however, the central task eventually is to reconstruct a functioning social order capable of winning the loyalty of the civilian population. But this requires accomplishing a set of tasks that are alien to the U.S. military tradition. Counterinsurgency theory recognizes the need for nonmilitary action as well as for military tactics appropriate for a guerrilla conflict. But, in practice, the U.S. military finds it difficult to implement an effective, coherent, multidimensional counterinsurgency program. It is good at fighting large military actions but not so good at organizing to combat an insurgency.

U.S. skill in organizing for large-scale combat was actually useful in the initial period of U.S. involvement in the Salvadoran war, from 1980 to 1984, when the guerrilla movement (the Faribundo Martí Front for National Liberation, or FMLN) attempted a "final offensive" designed to achieve a military victory over the Salvadoran army. Between 1980 and 1984, with U.S. advice and funding, the Salvadoran military was transformed from essentially a constabulary into a much larger combat force organized into battalions with large numbers of trucks, helicopters, close air support aircraft, and artillery. When the FMLN was determined to battle the enemy directly, such large, firepower-reliant units were relatively effective, and the final offensive failed.[17]

Since 1984, however, FMLN tactics have changed, emphasizing hit-and-run attacks with small units, primarily directed against economic targets. But the Salvadoran military has not changed its organization or tactics accordingly. Instead, it has maintained its large-unit structure and adopted a primarily defensive posture to protect military garrisons, plantations, and the economic infrastructure. Efforts by U.S. advisers to wean the Salvadoran military away from the organization and strategy that originally proved successful (and that emulated the U.S. pattern) have led nowhere.[18] In large part, the failure of the Salvadoran military to adopt small-unit tactics and related counterinsurgency strategies—including psychological operations, organization of village civil defense units, and military civic action programs—is not the result of any lack of encouragement by U.S. advisers. On the contrary, U.S. special forces advisers detailed to El Salvador are heavily indoctrinated in counterinsurgency theory, which they, in turn, attempt to convey to their in-country students.

These efforts, however, appear to have foundered, in part because of resistance by a Salvadoran military establishment with its own institutional culture and in part because of the plain inadequacy of U.S. advice to the task at hand. The U.S. doctrinal contribution amounted to little more than very good instruction in small-unit operations—what one official termed a "band-aid approach" to fighting the "other war"[19]—together with solemn affirmations that the outcome of the war would be determined by the ability of the Salvadoran military to appeal to popular hearts and minds. In practice, the United States was unable to devise an adequate approach to winning the battle for popular support. To the extent that classical counterinsurgency was attempted, with a combination of psychological operations, formation of village defense units, and a targeted infusion of economic development projects, it ultimately foundered. As a result, the Salvadoran military grew frustrated with it, and Salvadoran officers fell back on techniques that at least did not fail dismally.

This problem is almost unavoidable in the U.S. military. To the extent that Americans in El Salvador were aware of the need for a radical reorganization of the entire society, the U.S. military was not fully capable of defining, let alone imposing, the necessary changes. A few U.S. Green Berets could not bring about a revolution in Salvadoran class relations.

■ THE STRUCTURE OF COMMAND

The big-war orientation of the U.S. military not only affects its ability to carry on counterinsurgency operations that are inherently challenging; it also can interfere with the conduct of short military actions with clear objectives—the kinds of operations that obviously fulfill Weinberger's criteria for the use of force. Interservice rivalries and simple bureaucratic rigidity have repeatedly undermined the effectiveness of relatively minor, if demanding, military operations in the 1980s.

The abortive April 1980 Iran hostage rescue mission, for example, was a case in which poor planning, caused in part by the organization of the U.S. military, contributed to a disastrous failure. Part of the problem was that each of the military services insisted on getting a piece of the action, to the detriment of the operation. Air force C-130 transport aircraft flew army assault troops to "Desert One" where they were to meet with navy helicopters flown from an aircraft carrier by navy and marine pilots. The mission was aborted because six helicopters were required to carry on the mission, but only six of the eight assigned to the operation arrived at the desert rendezvous site, and one of those broke down. The failure of the operation was compounded into tragedy when a helicopter crashed into a C-130 after the mission was aborted, and eight members of the team were killed.

Though the mission was difficult and could very well have failed at a later point, it is not too much to expect that forces at least could have flown to the destination. A Pentagon investigative panel chaired by Admiral James Holloway concluded that the key problem with the operation probably involved the selection of helicopter pilots. Navy and Marine Corps pilots had far less experience in flying long distances over land than available air force pilots—but navy and marine pilots were assigned nonetheless.[20] Any pilot would have had difficulty flying through the sand storms that the mission encountered, but pilots more experienced in similar operations might have had a better chance of getting to the rendezvous point.[21]

It has also been argued that the operation suffered from the lack of a single, overall commander. "There were," wrote one analyst, "no less than four commanders: the rescue force commander, the air group commander, the on-site commander, and the helicopter force commander," whereas the Joint Task Force commander was located aboard ship in the Persian Gulf. "The result," this writer claimed, "was an inability to improvise when things went wrong."[22]

Another case in which the lack of coordination among the services obviously interfered with the conduct of an operation occurred in the Grenada invasion of 1983. When the NSC, with the authority of the president, initially directed the military to prepare plans for evacuating U.S. citizens from the island, the task fell to the commander in chief of the U.S. Atlantic Command (CINCLANT), a navy admiral, as Grenada lies in his command's geographical area of responsibility. At first, the commander, Admiral Wesley McDonald, planned to employ a marine amphibious unit that was on its way to Lebanon but was still nearby. On reviewing the plan, the JCS concluded that army units should also be assigned to the operation. This has prompted speculation that the Joint Chiefs were merely ensuring, in classic fashion, that each service should have a piece of the action. But the JCS has unequivocally denied this. Instead, according to the JCS, the change was ordered because even McDonald had by then concluded that the mission exceeded the capability of a single marine battalion.[23]

Leaving aside the dispute over bureaucratic motives, it is clear that the operation suffered from a lack of coordination among the different service elements involved. It was decided that marine units would be responsible for taking the northern half of the island and army units the southern half, with overall command authority vested in Vice Admiral Joseph Metcalf, commander of the Second Fleet. But some army units initially could not communicate effectively with navy ships offshore to request and coordinate naval gunfire. Also, some messages failed to reach army forces on the ground, including one message concerning the existence of a second campus of the island's medical school where 224 American students were located.

The lack of communication was so serious that navy aircraft were initially prohibited from flying south of the marine sector without special permission. And even on the third and last day of heavy fighting, naval gunfire was not adequately coordinated with a major army assault. One underlying problem was that there was no unified commander on the ground—the army and Marine

Corps commanders each reported separately back to Admiral Metcalf, who was aboard his command ship, the *Guam,* at sea.[24] To be sure, these problems were not enough to prevent the success of an operation in which U.S. forces possessed overwhelming military superiority (although the failure to locate the second campus in a timely fashion could have been a disaster had the Grenadians decided to retaliate by assaulting the unprotected American students). But the flaws in the operation do raise serious questions about the bureaucratic forces that determine the command structure in low-intensity conflict situations. As military theorist Edward Luttwak has pointed out, command was vested in naval officers Metcalf and McDonald, even though every aspect of the operation involved land warfare. If experienced army officers had planned the entire operation, Luttwak argued, a very different and more effective approach might have been employed—what Luttwak called a *coup de main,* in which forces simultaneously assault all key military targets in overwhelming force. Instead, the naval commanders elected to establish beachheads, in the style of the Normandy invasion, with subsequent, relatively slow advances.

One can, of course, dispute Luttwak's armchair strategy, and it is true that the naval commanders had advice from experienced Marine Corps officers attached to the navy and from army officers assigned to the operation as deputies. Nonetheless, Luttwak has a point in complaining that authority over the operation devolved on navy officers who were "expert in supervising the stately rotation of aircraft carriers between the Atlantic and Mediterranean, and in the planning of antisubmarine warfare and convoy escort," hardly the skills needed in directing a small-scale, short-term military action such as the invasion of Grenada.[25]

The Iran rescue mission and the invasion of Grenada illustrate the damage caused to small-scale military actions by the historic lack of coordination among the services. Each of the military services feels entitled to play a role at every level of military combat, making it difficult to assign sole responsibility for any one operation to any one service.

The most significant lesson of the Iran rescue mission and the invasion of Grenada is not about interservice rivalry, however. Rather, the underlying lesson is that the U.S. military is organized primarily to perform the peacetime mission of preparing to fight an all-out global war in order to deter that war. This peacetime function defines what Halperin would call the "organizational essence" of the contemporary U.S. military.[26] And this organizational structure is not designed for carrying on small-scale military action. Instead the operational control of U.S. forces is vested in commanders in chief of "unified commands," organized geographically, with support from "specified commands" that perform functions such as strategic airlift. The primary function of the commanders in chief, with the possible exception of the Southern Command in Panama, is to prepare for a major conflict with the Soviet Union. Nonetheless, the commanders in chief receive responsibility for the conduct of any small operation within their areas of authority and, indeed, will combat any effort to remove their control over such operations. Planning of the Grenada invasion, for example, bypassed the Joint Deployment Agency (JDA) that was established in 1979 to coordinate rapid deployment forces. Logistics were handled on an ad hoc basis and suffered severely from disorganization and delay.[27] And operational control of the ground campaign, as Luttwak noted, was vested in a navy commander.

During the 1980s the Defense Department has been reorganized to establish an institutional base for low-intensity conflict. The department now has an assistant secretary of defense in charge of special operations, and a special operations command, headed by a four-star army general, has been set up at MacDill Air Force Base in Florida. It is instructive, however, that these organizational changes were imposed on the military by a few persistent members of Congress, over the opposition of an unhappy defense establishment. It took the Pentagon more than six months after Congress established the positions to appoint officials to the two new, senior special operations posts—and the appointment of an assistant secretary was tied up in haggling over the credentials of the administration's first choice. The navy's special operations forces have not been integrated into the new command—indeed, navy commanders have always viewed special operations as primarily a support function for larger-scale military action. Direct intervention by Defense Secretary Frank Carlucci was required to prevent the military services from cutting special-operations-related budgets substantially as part of their effort to trim the FY 1989 budget to meet spending targets. The resistance of senior military leaders to an elevated status for special operations forces speaks eloquently of the priority still accorded planning for a major war in the U.S. defense establishment.

■ GOVERNMENTAL-BUREAUCRATIC FORCES IN PERSPECTIVE

To point out that the big-war focus of U.S. military planning interferes with the U.S. ability to fight small wars is not to suggest that the United States should fundamentally reorder its military priorities, although some low-intensity warfare experts might wish as much. To the contrary, the fundamental principle of military planning is to be strong on the central front. Although a war in Europe is extremely unlikely, this old geopolitical axiom makes as much sense in the 1980s as ever.

Moreover, the institutional caution of the military in committing forces to low-intensity conflict may be useful to the extent that it helps to avoid future Vietnams or future Lebanons. Bureaucratic checks and balances are often of positive value. For example, the Iran-contra arms sales debacle would not have been possible if normal bureaucratic procedures had been followed. To list all the bureaucratic limitations on the inclination and ability of the U.S. military to intervene in low-intensity conflict situations, however, is not to say that a resurgence of U.S. military activism is inconceivable. Though Weinberger's conditions on U.S. military involvement in minor conflicts appear restrictive, it also seems that they are being honored largely in the breach. The U.S. decision to escort reflagged Kuwaiti oil tankers in the Persian Gulf, for example, grew into an open-ended commitment in which the relationship between ends and military means was unclear. Whether such conditions would prevent a major commitment of U.S. forces in the future is open to doubt. As former Senator William Fulbright commented, the Weinberger conditions "are so broad and subjective, so amenable to the widest variety of interpretation, that, had they been in place at the time, it is hardly likely they would have posed a serious obstacle to our involvement and escalation in Vietnam."[28] In the end, the decision to use military force is a political one—good choices, therefore, depend on the quality of elected leaders.

12

The Structure of the International System

Harry Piotrowski

When World War II came to an end, two "superpowers" emerged triumphant. The Soviet Union had pushed its frontiers, political influence, and military might into the center of Europe and the Far East. The United States, similarly, had advanced its own political, military, and economic power into the same regions. The former Europe-centric international system, which had been dominant since the sixteenth century and whose members had been devastated by war, had been replaced by an emerging bipolar system led by the two superpowers. In the process, military cooperation against Germany and Japan quickly gave way to a political deadlock (notably on the question of Poland's postwar government) and then to a confrontation that in 1947 became military in nature when President Harry S. Truman intervened in Greece to suppress the uprising by communist insurgents.

This "turning point in American foreign policy," as Truman called it, rested on two premises. The first premise drew upon the lessons of history that the West had learned in dealing with Adolf Hitler: The aggressive aspirations of all dictators must be thwarted at the earliest moment possible; failure to intervene leads only to a wider conflict. Truman's second premise—that ideological compromise with the USSR was impossible—divided the world into two hostile camps: communism versus capitalism, totalitarianism versus the free world.

Truman's justification for intervention across the globe, however, contained two serious flaws. First, he assumed that Joseph Stalin's foreign policy was a carbon copy of Hitler's, that all dictators were driven by the same expansionist logic. Stalin, Truman explained in his memoirs, was out to conquer the world. But Truman would not appease Stalin; he would, instead, halt all manifestation of communist aggression. Yet Truman applied this lesson to Stalin at a time when Stalin was consolidating his position by withdrawing his troops from a host of countries: Albania, China, Czechoslovakia, Denmark, Iran, North Korea, Norway, and Yugoslavia. Khrushchev later completed what Isaac

Deutscher called Stalin's policy of "self-containment" by withdrawing Soviet troops from Austria and Finland.[1]

The second flaw in Truman's argument consisted of his failure to recognize that communist movements often operated independently of Stalin, that the international stage contained actors other than those directed from Moscow and Washington. World War II had accelerated processes independent of Moscow. It had produced a civil war in Greece between the left and the right; in Vietnam, it had set into motion the resistance first against the Japanese and then against the French; it had revived anticolonial movements in Asia and Africa. In much of the world the war had produced a decisive shift to the left, a challenge to the status quo. Revolutionary movements tended to draw on Karl Marx's theory of historical inevitability and Vladimir Lenin's organizational program without, however, subordinating such movements to the will of Moscow. Much of the world was in flux at the time the United States set out to stem what the British premier Harold Macmillan later called "the winds of change."

The result was foreign policy that treated any and all revolutionary activity as evidence of Stalin's evil machinations, the work of an international communist conspiracy. With such a narrow focus, Washington found it difficult to comprehend that other factors within the international system were at work: resurgent nationalism and anticolonialism, indigenous applications of Marxism-Leninism, communist polycentrism, the proliferation of both conventional and nuclear weapons, the rise of regional powers, and the relative decline of U.S. economic and military power. The international system was changing, but as long as the United States continued to base its foreign policy on Truman's original premises, intervention in the Third World became increasingly more counterproductive, difficult, and costly in terms of political capital, money, and blood.

■ BIPOLAR VISION CONFRONTS NATIONALISM

Truman's division of the world into two camps rested on the assumption that nations all too readily were willing to subordinate their interests to the grand ideal of supranationalism. But the proposition that nations were either part of the free world or of the communist bloc ignored the elemental force of nationalism. World War II had revealed European vulnerability, particularly in Asia, when the Japanese appeared, if only for a brief time, as liberators and drove out the Americans, British, Dutch, and French.

When the French sought to reassert themselves in Vietnam, they faced an organized resistance. The Vietminh leadership consisted of communists, but their leader Ho Chi Minh explained that it had been "patriotism not Communism that originally inspired me." "The reason for my joining the French Socialist Party," Ho wrote, was that it expressed sympathy for "the struggle of oppressed people. But I understood [at the time] neither what was a party, a trade-union, nor what was Socialism or Communism."[2] Ho instead operated in the context of an ancient Vietnamese revolutionary tradition.[3] When the French, and later the Americans, focused on the communist content of the Vietnamese revolution, they ignored nationalism, the more potent element. In Vietnam, Ho grafted the national liberation movement onto communism, which gave him a vision of the future, the certainty of an historic process that promised victory, and an organizational blueprint.

During the early 1960s, the Vietnamese Buddhist monk Thich Nhat Hanh tried, without much success, to explain to U.S. readers that it was first and foremost Vietnamese nationalism that gave the National Liberation Front (NLF) its great popular support.[4] Communist ideology, the focus of U.S. obsession, scarcely played a role in motivating the resistance. The U.S. reporter, John Mecklin, wrote of a sixty-six-year-old headman of a village the communist-led Vietminh had controlled for thirteen years. This headman had never heard of the United States, the USSR, or even France. But he knew of "the big bird that spit fire [napalm] from the sky."[5] The Austrian reporter Bruno Knoebl described the interrogation of an NLF solider who had no understanding of communism and could not understand the questions, let alone answer them. Of Karl Marx he knew nothing; but at the mention of Ho Chi Minh's name his face lit up. He recognized the name of the man who had driven out the French. Knoebl cited a U.S. official who explained that many prisoners "first learn what Communism really is from us during interrogation, in prison camps, and in reeducation courses."[6]

Indeed, U.S. involvement in the Vietnam War demonstrates the ignorance of U.S. officials concerning the potent force of nationalism and their inability to accommodate themselves to alien Third World cultures. U.S. officials envisioned the unfolding of a U.S. myth, the carrying forth of its own revolutionary heritage into the frontiers of emerging nations in the expectation that a distinctly American story would unfold. Instead, the United States ran head on into the ferocity of the Vietnamese revolutionary tradition.[7] Cold war rhetoric and propaganda repeatedly masked the reality in that country. The U.S. media, notably Henry Luce's *Time* and *Life,* heaped voluminous praise on the dictator Ngo Dinh Diem, referring to him as the "Churchill of Southeast Asia,"[8] ignoring the fact that he had just received 605,025 votes from 450,000 registered voters in Saigon[9] and was consolidating his dictatorship.

Frances FitzGerald was the first U.S. journalist to make a serious effort to put the revolution in South Vietnam into the context of Vietnamese history. She divided her book into two equal parts, the first dealing with the Vietnamese themselves, their history, revolutionary tradition, and culture. In her analysis of the NLF, she focused on the indigenous aspects of that organization, rather than treating the organization as something created and manipulated from the outside. Only in the second half of the book did she turn to the United States and its creation, the Saigon government.[10] As it was, her book appeared only in 1972, when domestic political considerations had already produced an irrevocable commitment to withdrawal.

In Algeria, a process of nationalist resistance similar to that in Vietnam took place. The French colonialists spoke of assimilating the Arabs into French society and culture without, however, offering them the opportunity to do so. More important, few Arabs sought to become French. The Arab rebellion, which manifested in the May Day and the V-E Day parades of 1945, underscored the warning by the Muslim scholar Abdelhamid Ben Badis that "the Algerian people are not French, do not wish to be and could not be even if they did wish."[11] When the French replied that Algeria was an integral part of France (a province no less), they were merely deluding themselves. The French subsequently killed 1 million Algerians between 1954 and 1962, yet they were unable to suppress the rebellion.

The immediate postwar years saw the success of several anticolonial, nationalist movements: in China, in 1949, under the communist Mao Zedong; in the Dutch East Indies, in 1949, under Achmed Sukarno; during 1947–1948, the British quit Burma, Ceylon, and India; the French abandoned Indochina in 1954. In Africa, the process of decolonization proceeded a bit slower. In the Gold Coast (today's Ghana), Kwame Nkrumah organized an effective political campaign while in a British prison, and in 1957 Ghana became the first African colony to gain its independence. The year 1960 saw a large number of African states follow suit, with Kenya and Tanzania, the former in a bloody uprising, gaining their independence in 1963. The Portuguese, the first Europeans to colonize Africa, were the last to leave (not counting the Dutch in South Africa), after they were beaten and finally withdrew from Angola and Mozambique in 1975.

Nationalist pressures and Washington's apparent inability to accommodate its role in a changing international system continued well into the 1970s and 1980s. During the three decades immediately preceding the Iranian revolution, the United States repeatedly underestimated the power of the religious mullahs, believing until the very end that the pro-U.S. Shah Mohammad Reza Pahlavi could ride out the storm. As is more fully discussed in Chapter 14, there was no appreciable understanding in Washington of the religious revival taking place and its links to fervent nationalism. The administration of Jimmy Carter was taken by surprise by the massive anti-U.S. demonstrations after it granted the shah permission to enter the United States for treatment of cancer. Many Iranians had not forgotten that in 1953 the CIA had returned the shah from his first journey into exile, and they now feared a repetition of history. The result was the hostage crisis from which the Carter administration never recovered.

In the Middle East, the United States has long been involved as a champion of Israel. This has produced a tendency to ignore the historical claims of the Arabs. The Palestinians became invisible, marginal people without a history and who, at best, played only a negative role as they stood in the path of the reconstitution of the historic state of Israel. It was only after the Palestinians began to take matters into their own hands, when they began to use terror to publicize their cause, culminating in the massive uprisings in the Israeli-controlled West Bank and Gaza Strip beginning in late 1987, that the United States began to take notice of Palestinian nationalism. As is discussed in Chapter 18, the United States similarly has been reluctant to embrace and recognize the legitimacy of black nationalist movements in South Africa.

Third World nationalism has repeatedly asserted itself since 1945. The Western response to it has been either to combat it—particularly when it was linked to communism—or to preempt it, to weld it to ideas of liberal capitalism with a resultant continued dependency on the West. But the revolutionary movements demanded a complete break with the Western heritage, its colonial control, economic exploitation, and racism. They sought instead the reconstitution of a national identity and the radical reconstitution of society; in short, a distinct break with the past tied to a view of the future. Revolutionary communism—and later militant Islam—offered such a solution to colonial dependency and humiliation.

■ MONOLITHIC COMMUNISM OR POLYCENTRISM?

A large number of Third World revolutionary movements are officially communist, but they are not necessarily controlled from Moscow—despite the rhetoric of "international communist solidarity." A national brand of communism is nothing new. Stalin always understood that among communist states, national interests would always predominate. From the outset, he was interested in developing the strength of his own state and relegating the interests of other communist parties to those of the Soviet Union. In 1948, a scant three years after the establishment of communist states other than the Soviet Union, the split between Stalin and the Yugoslav communist Joseph Tito took place over the elemental question of whose interests Tito should serve, those of the Soviet Union or those of Yugoslavia. The Italian communist Palmiro Togliatti later spoke of "polycentrism," of the existence of many communist centers. Polycentrism, however, is a euphemism for no center at all.

When U.S. officials took the view that there existed a monolithic communist bloc (that is, that communist movements were acting on Moscow's behest), they never properly understood that they would have had a relatively easy time neutralizing such a bloc if it had existed. When, during the 1930s, Stalin demanded and received absolute subordination to his authority from foreign communist parties, he also dealt them a mortal blow. These parties were now seen as agents of another power, brutal and uncivilized, more interested in defending the interests of the schemers in the Kremlin than those of their own working classes. The damage Stalin inflicted on these parties, however, has never been properly appreciated in the West.

Third World nationalist and communist movements have never suffered from this handicap. For one, they were always primarily nationalist—namely, anticolonialist—and only secondarily communist. Moreover, they had relatively little contact with Moscow. The Chinese communist revolution was on its own after 1927, after Stalin had told the communists to cooperate with the Nationalists led by Chiang Kaishek, who then turned on them. When the U.S. journalist Edgar Snow established contact with Mao Zedong in the late 1930s, Mao went to pains to explain his independence of Moscow. During World War II, U.S. agents of the OSS were unanimous in confirming this state of affairs. In Vietnam, Stalin played no role; only in 1952 did he even acknowledge the revolution's existence.

Yet, even when U.S. officials showed a measure of understanding and sympathy for the indigenous roots of revolution and upheaval, they all too often ran afoul of the official line, and their positions became untenable. During the McCarthy era, for example, a number of old China hands were accused of treason by the "China lobby," as attempts were made to place blame for "losing China" to communism. In 1949, Truman's State Department issued its famous White Paper on China—meant to stop criticism by the China lobby—to explain that it had done everything possible to save China from communism, that it had not lost China but that Chiang Kaishek had lost the support of his people. Truman's secretary of state, Dean Acheson, who had thought that the charges "flowed from ignorance of the facts" and believed "that the human mind could be moved by facts and reason,"[12] found out that facts and reason were irrelevant. The China lobby established a new set of facts: The Christian Chiang and his "democratic" government had been betrayed in Washington,[13] and woe to the administration that made another such mistake and suggested that a communist revolution enjoyed a measure of popular support.

The White Paper proved to be a disaster for the State Department. The critics reaffirmed the deeply ingrained view that what had transpired in China had not been a Chinese affair but had been orchestrated behind the walls of the Kremlin. They prevented an independent analysis of a world that was moving away from the official bipolar model toward a more multipolar international system (one with several political and military powers of varying strength). Not the least, they prevented a scholarly and independent analysis of events unfolding in Vietnam during the 1950s. The Democrats themselves quickly fell into line and began to repeat the arguments of the critics of the White Paper. Ignorance became an officially mandated policy, and the Truman administration made no use of individuals of differing views. George F. Kennan, who in 1947 had made his reputation by his analysis of Soviet behavior, was shortly eased out of the State Department.

After Stalin's death in 1953, the Communist Party of the Soviet Union (CPSU), at its 20th Congress in February 1956, sanctioned the legitimacy of Titoism when it acknowledged each party's right to an independent path to communism. Theoretically, polycentrism should have worked to the advantage of the United States, as it pointed to a fragmented communist camp. Instead, the

United States now faced powerful independent nationalist movements whose communist content proved to be no handicap in organizing rebellions.

The fragmentation of the communist world was but one side of the coin. The Western camp witnessed a similar process. For one, Western hegemony came to an end in many parts of the world where a Third World political movement was emerging. Leaders of newly independent nations, notably Jawaharlal Nehru of India and Gamal Abdel Nasser of Egypt, joined by Tito, took a third, neutral road and refused to become pawns in the great game of ideological conflict between Moscow and Washington. The Brahmin Hindu Nehru, the Muslim Arab Nasser, and the atheist communist Tito insisted on the superpowers' recognition of their national independence and dignity. They represented the bulk of the world's population as a counterweight to the imperial ambitions of politicians in Moscow and Washington.

Second, since the end of World War II, the Western European nations had experienced their own movement toward polycentrism. In the 1960s, Charles de Gaulle insisted that France carve out a diplomatic and military posture independent of Washington. France remained a member of NATO but decided to rely first and foremost on its own independent nuclear deterrent, the *force de frappe*. Since the 1960s, the partners of the United States have shown an increased tendency toward independence. Over the years, they have questioned the wisdom of a number of U.S. policies. Britain and France, for example, established diplomatic relations with Beijing at a time when U.S. politicians, such as Nixon, were feverishly opposed to it. None of the NATO members drew the same dire conclusion from the Vietnamese insurrection (that is, that nations would fall like dominoes throughout Southeast Asia) as did the policymakers in Washington. When in April 1986, President Reagan sought to punish Libya's Muammar Qaddafi, France and Spain, both members of NATO, refused to cooperate. U.S. F-111 tactical fighter bombers stationed in Britain were forced to take a circuitous route around the Iberian peninsula that required midair refueling.[14] Finally, U.S. attempts to overthrow the Sandinista government in Nicaragua and the reluctance of Washington to deal effectively with the Palestinian question in the Middle East have not been supported by the majority of Washington's NATO allies.

■ THE RISE OF REGIONAL POWERS

The ferment in the international arena after 1945 produced several regional powers and continues to erode the bipolar structure World War II had created. The earliest and best example is the People's Republic of China. Shortly after its successful revolution in 1949, the PRC held the United States to a bloody draw in Korea when the United States sought to unite all of Korea under the aegis of the anticommunist Syngman Rhee. Mao Zedong gave notice that the PRC would not permit U.S. hegemony (nor that of the USSR, as it later turned out) along its borders. U.S. policymakers initially scoffed at the notion of Chinese military intervention against U.S. firepower only to suffer a rude awakening when the People's Liberation Army (PLA) drove U.S. forces back into South Korea. The PRC became the protector of North Korea and a regional force to be reckoned with. Subsequent talk in Washington of unleashing the Nationalist Chiang Kaishek of Taiwan proved to be at best political hot air, at worst dangerous nonsense. The Korean War showed that neither the United States nor Chiang could solve the problem of Red China.

More important, Mao cast China's long shadow into Vietnam. President Lyndon B. Johnson and his advisers repeatedly blamed Mao for the war in Vietnam, but the U.S. Joint Chiefs of Staff took seriously Mao's threats, as they had not during the Korean War, to intervene once the United States crossed the 17th parallel into North Vietnam. In the wake of the 1968 Tet offensive by the NLF and the North Vietnamese, it became clear that the United States did not have sufficient troops to win in Vietnam, let alone to take on the giant to the north with its unlimited human resources. Too many American boys were already dying without directly taking on the PLA. The United States had reached a dead end in Vietnam.

Among earlier attempts to establish a regional presence, Egypt's Gamal Abdel Nasser sought to lead the Arab world from the beginning of the 1950s until his death in 1970. In short order, he freed himself from Western control, accepted Soviet military and economic aid, denied French and British control over the Suez Canal, and twice took the lead in failed wars to destroy the state of Israel. Nasser was unable to unite the fractious Arab world, but he gave notice that nations need not remain pawns in the great bipolar power struggle between East and West.

Iran emerged as a regional power in 1979. The shah had always dreamed of reconstituting the glories of ancient Persia, but in the arena of foreign affairs he proved to be quite cautious. He leaned toward the West, bought weapons largely from the United States, but was careful to maintain good relations with the USSR, which looked the other way as he chased down the Marxist Tudeh party. It was the shah's successor, however, the Ayatollah Ruhollah Khomeini, who sought to spread his revolution's influence far beyond Iran's borders. Khomeini, as the titular head of the Shiite wing of Islam, began to attract followers throughout the Middle East. The Shiites are, for the most part, the politically and economically dispossessed, who share a grievance against the status quo. They find their inspiration in the Prophet Mohammed's revolutionary activity in Mecca on behalf of the downtrodden. Their challenges to entrenched political power (Islamic or otherwise) have elevated political disobedience to a religious duty. They find comfort in Allah's will "to favor those who were oppressed . . . and give them power in the land."[15] When the United States intervened in the Lebanese civil war in 1983 on the side of the Maronite Christians, the U.S. Marines became the target of the full fury of a Shiite suicide mission. Reagan quickly realized the limits of U.S. intervention, declared the mission a success, and then pulled out.

Khomeini's influence in the Middle East has been limited for the same reasons that have stayed the hand of the United States in other parts of the world—namely, the overbearing power of nationalism. Apart from the Shiites in Iran, nearly all Shiites in the Middle East are Arabs, and Khomeini proved incapable of bridging the ancient breach between Persians and Arabs. After Saddam Hussein of Iraq launched his invasion of Iran in 1980, Khomeini appealed to Iraq's majority Shiite population, which, however, did not rally to his cause. They remained, their Shiite affiliation notwithstanding, first and foremost Arabs. Still, Khomeini's revolution remained a force to be reckoned with. Despite U.S. military might, Iran humiliated the "Great Satan" during the hostage crisis of 1979–1981; its influence spread to Lebanon; it supported the mujahedin in Afghanistan who were fighting the lesser Satan, the officially atheistic Soviet state; and it appealed to the resurrection of Islam in an open challenge to the Western presence in the Middle East.

In Latin America, several nations have sought to play regional roles. The first was Fidel Castro's Cuba, which declared its economic and political independence from the United States in 1959. The United States initially responded with economic pressure by denying Castro the lucrative U.S. market and, when that did not prevent Castro from turning to the Soviet Union, by organizing the ill-fated attempt to invade Cuba at the Bay of Pigs in April 1961. In the summer of 1962, Adlai Stevenson, the U.S. envoy to the United Nations, categorically rejected any acceptance of a communist government in the Western Hemisphere. But the Cuban missile crisis of October 1962 was resolved only after the United States acknowledged the sovereignty of Cuba and that the Monroe Doctrine (by which it reserved the unilateral right of intervention in Latin America) no longer applied to that nation. At first Cuba's influence remained restricted to the ideological sphere, as it was the first Latin American nation to have successfully repudiated its unequal relationship with the Colossus of the North. But in 1965, Ché Guevara, Castro's former comrade-in-arms in the struggle against Fulgencio Batista, launched his unsuccessful attempt to rouse the poverty-stricken peasants of Bolivia. And in 1975, Castro successfully intervened, with Soviet help, in the Angolan civil war by providing 50,000 troops to sustain that nation's Marxist government against rebel forces backed by the strange coalition of the PRC, South Africa, and the United States.

Mexico, despite its economic and political difficulties, has also sought to play a larger role to stay Washington's hand in Central America. The Reagan administration was stymied by a Central American consensus against U.S. intervention, despite Washington's persistent argument that the Sandinistas posed a common danger to the entire region. The last thing even the conservative government of Mexico wanted was to give the United States another opportunity to implement its self-appointed right to intervene. In many parts of Central

America—Cuba, the Dominican Republic, Guatemala, Mexico, Nicaragua, Panama—the memory of U.S. intervention has been kept alive in histories, films, museums, and popular folklore. The leaders of these nations showed little desire to be seen as supporters of Yankee imperialism.

The Latin American nations understand that individually there is little they can do to oppose the United States but that there is power in unity. The Contadora Group (Colombia, Mexico, Panama, and Venezuela) called in 1983 for the withdrawal of all foreign advisers from Central America—U.S., Soviet, and Cuban—in short, for the political neutralization of the region. The president of Costa Rica, Oscar Arias, later proposed a similar solution, which earned him the prestigious Nobel Peace Prize in 1987. These proposals left the United States and its creation, the contras, diplomatically isolated. U.S. intervention in Nicaragua, à la Vietnam, would have to be in direct contravention of the wishes of Latin American nations, particularly after Cuba, Nicaragua, and the Soviet Union accepted Arias's plan.

In November 1987, the presidents of the Group of Eight—Argentina, Brazil, Colombia, Mexico, Peru, Panama, Uruguay, and Venezuela—met for the first time independently of the United States. In June 1988, seven of their foreign ministers met in Oaxaca, Mexico, where they issued a communiqué rejecting the frequent U.S. criticism of Latin America. Instead, they took the United States to task for doing little about the drug trade at home and rejected the notion that Latin America was solely responsible for the U.S. drug problem. They criticized the heavy-handed U.S. approach toward Nicaragua and Panama, while at the same time expressing little sympathy for Panamanian dictator Manuel Noriega (whose representative was not invited) and the Sandinista regime of Nicaragua. In the communiqué, they also complained about Latin America's economic dependence on the United States and urged, instead, closer economic ties with the Western European Community and Southeast Asia.[16]

Vietnam has become another regional power. It did so by virtue of its victory over the United States, the willing support of the Soviet Union, the inheritance of massive U.S.-weapons supplies, its political control of Laos, and its occupation of Cambodia. In 1979, Vietnam beat back the PLA when Beijing attempted to teach it a lesson in response to Vietnam's invasion of Cambodia in 1978. Beijing had no more luck than the United States, as Southeast Asia, a region the United States had once deemed vital to its security, remained in control of a communist regime loyal to the Soviet Union.

The exercise of U.S. political, military, and economic power in the Third World has become an increasingly difficult task. China has long been outside the U.S. sphere of influence, and the current Chinese leadership bristles at the thought of the United States playing the "China hand" against the Soviet Union. In Southeast Asia, the United States has played an extremely limited role since 1975, with the exception of diplomatic support of the murderous Pol Pot regime in Kampuchea. Its pervasive influence in Iran came to an end in 1979. Similarly, the Nicaraguan revolution served notice that U.S. influence has come to an end in that country.

The trend toward regionalism has also made it increasingly difficult for the United States to control its clients. West Germany, the post–World War II creation of the United States, has long ceased to be a ward of its creator. In the wake of the fatalities at the U.S.-sponsored air show in Ramstein, West Germany, in 1988, U.S. authorities were reminded that such displays—and the dangerous training exercises—could only continue at the pleasure of the host. The United States, after all, is but one member of NATO, an alliance of sovereign nations. Israel has long rejected U.S. advice on how to deal with the West Bank, and, in order to free itself of overbearing dependence on the United States, it has developed not only its own nuclear arsenal but, in September 1988, launched its first reconnaissance satellite. The United States has to recognize the new reality of increasingly powerful regional powers or continue to swim upstream against currents it cannot control.

■ RELATIVE DECLINE OF U.S. POWER

The flip side of the rise of regional powers has been the relative decline of the economic and military power of the United States vis-à-vis the rest of the world. Four aspects of this relative decline—nuclear proliferation, spread of conventional weapons, alternative sources of external support, and rising economic costs of overseas commitments—pose additional constraints on the ability of the United States to bring its economic and military might to bear in the Third World.

Following the dismantling of U.S. conventional forces at the end of World War II, the United States was left in Europe with a nuclear deterrent but without enough troops to engage the Soviet Union in a land war. Although possessing the means to destroy the Soviet Union, the United States lacked the means to occupy that vast land and impose its political will.

If war, as Karl von Clausewitz said, is the continuation of politics and diplomacy by other means, nuclear weapons, although capable of destroying the enemy, cannot resolve the political issues. Moreover, in 1949 the Soviet Union broke the West's nuclear monopoly and by 1955 had built the long-range bombers that gave it the means to annihilate the United States. As early as 1950, during the Korean War, President Truman understood the risk of using nuclear weapons to obtain his political aim—the unification of Korea under U.S. auspices. A nuclear attack on the PRC could have put into motion the Soviet war machine, which at the time had the capability of overrunning Western Europe and delivering nuclear weapons against U.S. allies' installations in Europe and Asia.

During the Cuban missile crisis in 1962, the United States possessed a large advantage in nuclear warheads. But the crisis was resolved only after the United

States granted the Soviet Union what it had been unwilling to concede earlier. It removed permanently its nuclear missiles from Turkey and offered a public pledge to respect the sovereignty of communist Cuba. The extraordinary nuclear power of the United States proved to be useless in resolving the political question of Cuba. In short order, the United States went from a rejection of diplomacy (namely, its refusal to recognize the Cuban revolution) to a consideration of military intervention (which would have meant war with the Soviet Union) to a diplomatic compromise (which removed the Soviet missiles from Cuba and those of the United States from Turkey and also eliminated the direct U.S. threat to Cuba). The Cuban missile crisis pointed to Khrushchev's proclivity toward "hare-brained schemes" (as his own party later charged), but it also underscored the limits of the U.S. ability to pursue the interventionist impulse to its logical and deadly conclusion in a world marked by increasing nuclear proliferation.

The missile crisis was resolved by the superpowers without Castro, who to his chagrin found out that he did not figure in the equation. In the late 1980s, however, the world stands on the threshold of a nuclear proliferation whereby smaller nations will soon acquire nuclear capabilities. It is generally assumed that Israel and South Africa already have nuclear weapons. Both Iraq—long a vocal foe of Israel—and Pakistan—since its creation in 1947, on a war footing with India (a nuclear power since 1974)—seek to build the first "Islamic" bomb. The long slumbering territorial disputes among the lesser powers have the potential of escalating into nuclear confrontations the great powers will be unable to control.

The world also has become increasingly awash in conventional weapons. Wars have traditionally ended with the belligerents drained of their capacity to continue the war. The productivity of the industrial nations, however, has put an end to this pattern. At the end of World War II, Germany and the Allies produced more war materiel than at the outset of the war. By the end of the conflict in Indochina, the NLF and the North Vietnamese army possessed a much greater store of weapons than at the beginning. Their chief supplier was the Soviet Union, but they also used Chinese and captured U.S. weapons.

One of the most notable trends of the post–World War II period is the increasing share of weapons acquisition by Third World countries and the growing proliferation of weapons producers. Whereas the chief arms exporters traditionally have been the United States, the Soviet Union, France, Britain, West Germany, and Italy, there has been a steady growth of second-tier producers in the Third World—most notably Brazil, the PRC, Egypt, India, Israel, Singapore, North Korea, and South Korea.[17]

According to Michael T. Klare, this has resulted in two major developments: First, Third World recipients have been able to diversify their sources of arms and subsequently weaken strong patron-client relationships with either of the two superpowers. "In many cases," Klare noted, "this has resulted in a greater degree of political autonomy on the part of Third World countries—often at the expense of the two superpowers, which have suffered dramatic political reversals in recent years." Second, diversification "has also made it easier for belligerents to obtain the arms and equipment needed to sustain high levels of combat—even in the face of an embargo imposed by the major suppliers." Klare concluded that this "is perhaps the outstanding lesson of the Iran-Iraq conflict, which has continued for seven grueling years despite the nominal efforts of both superpowers to limit arms transfers to the protagonists."[18] In a case of guerrilla warfare, the Algerian National Liberation Front received its arms mainly from West Germany but also from Argentina, Belgium, Czechoslovakia, Egypt, Ghana, Lebanon, Morocco, and the PRC.[19] With occasional exceptions, arms producers are willing to sell to anyone. The determinant is the bottom line of the ledger sheet.

The notable trend of U.S. decline is demonstrated by these alternative sources of military and economic support that both Third World governments and guerrilla movements can count on in the post–World War II period. When the United States intervened in Greece, it did so on the assumption that the world was organized around two poles. Had that in fact been the case, the United States would have had a much more difficult time in Greece. The world's communists would have stood solidly behind their comrades to deny a victory to the United States, the bastion of counterrevolutionary capitalism. But Stalin refused to enter the contest for Greece. He wrote Greece off in his meeting with the British Prime Minister Winston Churchill in October 1944; it now belonged to the Western sphere. Stalin wanted no part of the Greek communist revolution; he wanted it instead to "fold up . . . as quickly as possible," as he feared the projection of U.S. naval power into the eastern Mediterranean.[20] Moreover, Tito continued to support the Greek communists until his break with Stalin in 1948; then he too turned his back on the Greek communists, shut down the Yugoslav-Greek border, and denied them a place of refuge. In Greece, Truman had a free hand.

In short, between 1947 and 1955, the United States intervened in areas where the Soviet Union scarcely played a role. Stalin dug in behind his iron curtain and did not become involved in adventurous escapades abroad. After Stalin's death in March 1953, the CIA acknowledged that Stalin "did not allow his ambitions to lead him to reckless courses of action in his foreign policy." The CIA warned, however, that his successor might not be as cautious.[21] In 1955, Khrushchev overcame the opposition of the Stalinists, led by Foreign Minister Viacheslav Molotov, and began to commit the Soviet Union to a role outside Stalin's satellite empire. He would not tolerate Washington's policy of containment, which, he charged, was meant to encircle and strangle the Soviet Union. The first recipient of Soviet weapons and military advisers was Egypt's Nasser. The list of Soviet clients quickly grew: Angola, Cuba, Ethiopia, India, Indonesia, Iraq, Libya, Mozambique, Nicaragua, Peru, Syria. U.S. intervention henceforth would mean facing opponents who could count on a steady flow of weapons.[22] The days of 1954, when the United States was able to interdict the shipment of Czechoslovak weapons to Jacobo Arbenz of Guatemala, or when communist insurgents such as those in Greece were on their own, are long past.

Finally, the relative decline of U.S. power has an economic side. In the thirty years between 1950 and 1980, the U.S. share of the world's GNP declined from approximately 40 percent to 20 percent. Between 1960 and 1980, U.S. military expenditures in relationship to the rest of the world dropped from 51 to 28 percent.[23] This economic slide has continued. The self-imposed burden of empire has become increasingly expensive. Allies often have to be bought at a high price. The Camp David agreement between Israel and Egypt was largely purchased with U.S. money.

The presidents of the 1970s—Richard Nixon, Gerald Ford, and Jimmy Carter—adjusted their foreign policies in response to the relative decline of U.S. power. Nixon grudgingly ended the U.S. involvement in Vietnam and made peace with the PRC, in full contradiction of the original premise of U.S. involvement—namely, to halt Chinese communist expansion. Ford, who inherited Nixon's secretary of state, Henry Kissinger, offered no major departures and oversaw the helicopter evacuation of the U.S. Embassy in Saigon. Carter understood that there was little he could do as the Nicaraguan revolution unfolded in favor of the Sandinistas, who toppled the Somoza dynasty, long a loyal ally of the United States in the struggle against radicalism in Central America. Carter also made clear to the shah of Iran that the United States could not save his throne. All three presidents realized that the United States could not win an open-ended nuclear arms race with the Soviet Union and that the national interest demanded an agreement with the Kremlin to limit strategic weapons.

The Reagan administration, however, initially perceived these adjustments as the cause and not the consequence of the decline. The result was an ambitious and expensive armaments program to restore the strength and prestige of the United States. But this program came at an extraordinary price; U.S. society had to borrow against the future and, in the process, more than doubled the national debt. In the end, Reagan returned in part to the policies of the 1970s.[24] Indeed, negotiations over the settlement of regional conflicts and the conclusion of the INF Treaty (destroying an entire class of nuclear weapons) in the last year of Reagan's term in office harkened back to the détente era of the Nixon administration.

■ THE SYSTEM AND U.S. INTERVENTION IN PERSPECTIVE

In 1947, President Harry Truman designated the United States as the guardian at the gates of the free world. In practice, this meant that the United States would become the world's policeman against the revolutionary ferment World War II had put into motion. The moment of truth came when the United States had to decide whether or not to accommodate itself to a new order—to accept resurgent nationalism, the struggles against colonialism, the rise of regional powers, the proliferation of conventional and nuclear weapons, and the relative decline of U.S. power. In the U.S. political lexicon, however, accommodation with revolutionary movements smacked of appeasement. In the process, the interventionist impulse became one of the dominant factors in U.S. post–World War II foreign policy.

The cold war has always been driven by the simplest of arguments, but these no longer suffice. Ho Chi Minh was never Hitler, and Nikita Khrushchev was not Lenin, let alone the firebrand Leon Trotsky. The greatest triumph of the presidency of the anticommunist Richard Nixon came when he took advantage of the Sino-Soviet split and sent his national security adviser, Henry Kissinger, to Beijing to sound out the PRC leadership. In a rare display of statesmanship, a U.S. president abandoned the official fiction that the PRC was but a puppet of Moscow. Nixon, a politician who had always seen the world in stark black-and-white colors, recognized that the world had become increasingly more complex since his red-baiting days as a young congressman and that the time had come to acknowledge a new reality. But Nixon's act was but a single step on a longer journey. The United States has not been able to shake itself of the impulse toward unilateralism and interventionism.

Conditions in the late 1980s are more favorable for a reevaluation of U.S. foreign policy than at any time since World War II. President Reagan's dealings with Soviet leader Gorbachev constituted a significant positive step, as such meetings breathed life into the UN, which has begun the slow and painful process of resolving regional conflicts in Angola and in the Persian Gulf. Perhaps for the first time since the creation of the UN in 1945, there exists a basic accord among the five members of the Security Council that makes possible the utilization of that international agency for its original purpose—to resolve the world's conflicts. Indeed, negotiations within the framework of the UN have made it possible for the Soviet Union to end its bloody occupation of Afghanistan. In Angola, the U.S.-brokered Namibia and Angola Accords signify an important step in the process of negotiating the end to a long conflict. Most significant, perhaps, is recognition by Washington and Moscow—through negotiation of the INF Treaty—that it is pointless to pursue the quest of nuclear superiority.

Over the years, the United States has frittered away much moral capital that it may readily restore by learning to live in a complex and changing world, by abiding by the rules of international law, and by consulting with its allies rather than going it alone and against their wishes. Mikhail Gorbachev's "new thinking" in foreign affairs has not only put the United States on the defensive, but it also has forced the United States to reevaluate its cold war policies. The United States has to free itself of many of the lessons learned in the past, lessons of dubious value for the future.

□ 13

International Law

Christopher C. Joyner

Save for very select, special circumstances, not all of which are universally accepted by international legal experts, intervention by one state into the affairs of another state for the express purpose of changing the latter's policies or conditions is flatly prohibited by international law. Despite this general prohibition, the United States has often intervened in the affairs of Third World countries, most notably in Central and South America. The primary legal justification for U.S. intervention in the post–World War II period has been "self-defense" against the intrusion of the Soviet Union's ideological influence within a particular region. In Latin America, for example, this rationale has been cited for paramilitary aid given by the United States since 1981 to the anti-Sandinista contras in Nicaragua and has been invoked to legitimize U.S. interventions in Guatemala (1954), Cuba (1962), the Dominican Republic (1965), Chile (1973), and Grenada (1983). Although this anticommunist ambition may appear clearly advantageous and laudable for U.S. national interests, it nevertheless skirts the fundamental issue of legal propriety: To what extent does such intervention, irrespective of its high-minded purposes, properly comport with the recognized tenets of international law governing the use of force between states? My fundamental aim in this chapter is to foster a better appreciation for international law's role as a constraint on every state's conduct of foreign policy. It becomes apparent that national governments—in this case, the government of the United States—sometimes adopt convenient legal license to interpret international law such that it serves their own interests as a supportive foreign policy instrument rather than as a force of restraint conducive to greater public world order.

■ THE NORM OF NONINTERVENTION

One of the oldest duties of states under international law is to refrain from intervention in the internal or external affairs of any other state or, for that matter, the relations between other states. During the twentieth century and, notably, in the post–World War II age of superpower bloc politics and regional spheres of influence, this duty has been all too frequently ignored. As a result, the international law pertaining to intervention—particularly the universally recognized cardinal norm of nonintervention—has been clouded in the public mind and laid open to question.[1]

As a coercive act, intervention involves a conflict between two fundamental principles of international law: the right of self-defense by the intervening state and the right of independence on the part of the target state. International law does not furnish unrestricted license to any state to undertake a unilateral right of intervention that contravenes the right of another state's independence.[2]

The norm of nonintervention has been expressly set out and codified since World War I in several international instruments. The first modern international treaty designed to regulate state conduct in the use of force was the League of Nations Covenant. Article 10 of the Covenant declared that the "Members of the League undertake to respect and preserve as against external aggression the territorial integrity and existing political independence of all Members of the League."[3] Although the Covenant is no longer in force, its promulgation unmistakably indicated the direction in which international law was heading. The Covenant supplied an institutional framework for nonintervention, as it unequivocally advocated the protection of a state's territorial integrity and political independence. These two fundamental principles of international law represent the twin pillars upon which the very foundation of the contemporary legal concept of nonintervention rests.

With respect to the Americas, two regional treaties made early contributions to explicating the norm of nonintervention. In 1928, the Convention on the Duties and Rights of States in the Event of Civil Strife was signed in Havana, Cuba.[4] This treaty not only contained a general prohibition against intervention but also established a specific duty for governments to forbid intervention by their nationals into the affairs of other states. Likewise, in 1933 the Convention on Rights and Duties of States was signed in Montevideo, Uruguay. This multilateral accord tersely asserted in Article 8 that "[no] State has the right to intervene in the internal or external affairs of another." This rule was grounded in customary international law and articulated in Article 3, which maintained that "the State has the right to defend its integrity and independence . . . to organize as it sees fit, to legislate its interests [and to] administer its services."[5]

To complement these regional efforts exposing the impermissibility of intervention, an Additional Protocol Relative to Non-Intervention was concluded to the Convention on Rights and Duties in 1936 in Buenos Aires. Article 1 of the Protocol plainly affirms that the "High Contracting parties declare inadmissible the intervention of any one of them, directly or indirectly, and for whatever reason, in the internal or external affairs of any of the contracting parties."[6] In 1937 the emerging principle of nonintervention was again reinforced with the entry into force of the Convention on the Fulfillment of the Existing Treaties between the American States.[7] In reaffirming the Treaty of Non-Aggression and Conciliation concluded at Rio de Janiero in 1933,[8] the Americas Treaty Convention noted the prohibition against resorting to diplomatic or armed intervention, even in cases in which states are found to be in non-compliance with a treaty. Consequently, even if some state were to breach a treaty, other states party to the agreement would be bound to refrain from undertaking punitive intervention against the treaty violator.

The thrust of the contemporary norm of nonintervention is contained in Article 2, paragraph 4, of the United Nations Charter, which provides that "[all] Members shall refrain in their foreign relations from the threat or use of force against the territorial integrity or political independence of any State, or in any other manner inconsistent with the Purposes of the United Nations."[9] This statement entails a minimum condition for public order and has come to be regarded as the core provision of the Charter with respect to the use of force. The mandate clearly resides in contemporary international law that a state's violation of Article 2(4) through an act of intervention would constitute an act of aggression, unless legitimizing circumstances could be otherwise convincingly demonstrated.

The 1947 Inter-American Treaty of Reciprocal Assistance (Rio Treaty) reiterates the obligation of nonintervention set down in Article 2(4). Article 1 of the Rio Treaty mandates that states should not "resort to the threat or use of force in any manner inconsistent with the provisions of the Charter of the United Nations or of this Treaty."[10] Subsequent provisions reaffirm the inviolability of states' territoriality and political independence.

The Charter of the Organization of American States established a binding international legal regime particularly for those states in the Western Hemisphere. As such, it holds preeminent importance for any state's policy in the region that is thought to support or entail an act of intervention. The prohibition against intervention is clearly enunciated in Article 18:

> No State or group of States has the right to intervene, directly or indirectly, for any reason whatsoever, in the internal or external affairs of any other State. The foregoing principle prohibits not only armed force but also any other form of interference or attempted threat against the personality of the State or against its political, economic, and cultural elements.[11]

Article 20 of the OAS Charter serves specifically to substantiate this fiat. It tersely asserts that:

> The territory of a State is inviolable; it may not be the object, even temporarily, of military occupation or of other measures of force taken by another State, directly or indirectly, on any grounds whatsoever. No territorial acquisitions or special advantages obtained either by force or by other means of coercion shall be recognized.[12]

Other international legal documents underscore the unlawfulness of intervention. Foremost among them is the Declaration on the Inadmissibility of Intervention in the Domestic Affairs of States and the Protection of Their Independence and Sovereignty, adopted by the UN in 1965. This General Assembly statement unmistakably confirms the impermissibility of intervention in the modern international situation, and its first two provisions capture the essence of nonintervention in international law today:

> 1. No State has the right to intervene, directly or indirectly, for any reason whatever, in the affairs of any other State. Consequently, armed intervention and all other forms of interference or attempted threats against the personality of the State or against its political, economic and cultural elements, are condemned.
> 2. No State may encourage the use of economic, political or any other type of measures to coerce another State in order to obtain from it the subordination of the exercise of its sovereign rights or to secure from it advantages of any kind. Also, no State shall organize, assist, foment, finance, incite or tolerate subversive, terrorist or armed activities directed towards the violent overthrow of the regime of another State, or interfere in civil strife in another State.[13]

Thus, it is plainly prohibited for one state to intervene into the affairs of other states, irrespective of the reason and circumstance. Under contemporary international law, considerations affecting regional politics, spheres of influence, or bloc cohesion remain insufficient for legitimizing acts of intervention by one state against another. This cardinal rule of international law was reiterated by the UN General Assembly in 1970 in its Declaration on Principles of International Law Concerning Friendly Relations and Co-Operation Among States. The Declaration of Principles actually incorporated verbatim the two paragraphs cited from the Declaration on the Inadmissibility of Intervention in order to affirm the "principle concerning the duty not to intervene in matters within the domestic jurisdiction of any State, in accordance with the Charter [of the UN]."[14] Although these General Assembly resolutions do not carry the full weight of legally binding international commitments, they nevertheless do carry considerable moral suasion and evidence a consensus of international legal thought condemning the illicit use of intervention.

As with most rules, the historical experience of dealing with intervention in international law has prompted occasion for certain exceptions to be acknowledged. These exceptions, sometimes designated as "intervention by right," are actually intended to be applied toward constructive ends, in very selective circumstances, by being very restrictive in application. Under international law, these exceptions are not intended to supply unbridled licenses for intervention that governments may seize for their legal advantage when it is politically convenient to do so. In evaluating the contemporary legal attitude of the United States in its policy toward intervention, it remains important to consider whether U.S. actions fall within the scope of any or some of these exceptions to the nonintervention norm.

■ THE PERMISSIBILITY OF INTERVENTION

International law in this century has come to accept in varying degrees situations in which armed intervention may be permitted to occur. These include: (1) in certain circumstances, during civil conflict; (2) in cases involving humanitarian considerations; (3) in the exercise of rights of individual self-defense; (4) in instances of collective self-defense; (5) in response to an explicit, willful invitation by the legitimate government of a state; (6) in situations in which an existing treaty permits such intervention; and (7) in rare circumstances of abatement. In seeking to extract guidelines for regulating interventionist policies in international law, and to appreciate the relevance of U.S. policies in practice, it will be useful to examine each of these exceptions in more detail.

□ Civil Conflict

The legal norms governing civil conflict are complicated and contentious. The contemporary legal status of guerrillas, insurgents, and national liberation groups remains open to polemical debate. Even so, some rules involving intervention are plainly evident. First, the fundamental international legal principles of political independence and territorial integrity forbid states from operating to overthrow foreign governments. Indeed, international law supports the basic right of states to create their own government, constitution, and domestic laws without external coercion or suasion of any kind. It is, therefore, unlawful for any foreign government to assist civilians, either at home or abroad, in waging an internal war in some other state. Similarly, a general prohibition exists against states supplying aid to insurgent movements in other states. Unless explicitly invited by the legitimate government, outside states are legally obligated to remain estranged from internal conflict in other states. Yet, international law unquestionably upholds the right to give aid to a government when there exists little or no organized movement in that state. International law, moreover, generally sanctions recognized governments to receive assistance from other states during periods of internal conflict. The lawfulness of aid to the threatened government may be embellished further if foreign assistance is being rendered to insurgents by some outside power. Nonetheless, curbs must be placed on the level of assistance given.[15]

□ Humanitarian Intervention

Situations with widespread atrocities or acute deprivation might present justifiable exceptions to the norm of nonintervention. Justification for armed intervention in these circumstances would rest upon the overwhelming need to act in the preeminent interest of humanitarian concerns. In the 1980s, the practice of states has revealed two major instances in which humanitarian intervention might be permissible: (1) for the protection of nationals abroad; and (2) for the protection of human rights.

Traditionally, in international law, the right of a state to intervene may be permitted when another government mistreats the nationals of that state. A cardinal restriction on this right mandates that the intervening power must act solely to protect its nationals; no other interference is allowed. In addition, the risk to the threatened nationals must be genuine, imminent, and substantial. The military operation should be a limited-purpose rescue mission, not a formidable attack against the authority structure of a state.

Similar arguments have been marshaled to justify the use of intervention against a government committing large-scale atrocities against its own nationals. In order to safeguard the fundamental human rights of those citizens, the argument runs, a moral imperative exists that justifies intervention by another state or by a group of states. Although this reasoning may be morally attractive, it fails in political practice. The liability inherent in humanitarian intervention is that it might be used as a legal facade or policy rationale to disguise ideological, hegemonial, or aggressive motives. Another obvious problem is that selectivity often occurs in applying human-rights standards to various national situations. Governments whose foreign policies are generally compatible with some other state are not very likely to be condemned by the latter for their domestic human-rights conditions, much less invaded. Such political realities depreciate the legal vitality and significance of humanitarian intervention and have called into question its legitimacy as an instrument of international law.[16]

□ Individual Self-Defense

A fundamental principle of international law gives states the legal right to use force in self-defense against an armed attack by another state. This principle is highlighted by Article 51 of the UN Charter, which provides in relevant part that "[n]othing in the present Charter shall impair the inherent right of self-defense if an armed attack occurs against a Member of the United Nations, until the Security Council has taken measures necessary to maintain international peace and security." However, this inherent right of self-defense does not automatically permit armed intervention into the territory or affairs of other states, as there are limitations and qualifications on the application of force in self-defense. Outstanding among these restrictions are, first, that the force used in self-defense must be actually necessary to defend the interest threatened and, second, that it must be reasonably proportionate to the danger to be averted.[17]

The notion of preemptive, or anticipatory, self-defense has been accorded legitimacy by some commentators but only in the event that a clear and present danger exists—that some armed attack is imminent and unavoidable. The situation involving a far-range anticipatory attack—that is, in which some perceived threat is foreseeable and conceivable but still remains a distant possibility that is more hypothetical than real—seems fraught with temptations for abuse. The interventionist practice of states in this century suggests that legalizing such a broad interpretation of anticipatory self-defense would be more likely to encourage acts of aggression than to deter them.[18]

□ Intervention as Collective Self-Defense

International law permits collective intervention by member states of an international organization if done on behalf of the world community to maintain peace and to enforce rules and principles of international law. This type of intervention is meant to include both preventive and remedial measures undertaken by such bodies as the UN. To wit, Article 51 of the UN Charter codifies "the inherent right of individual or *collective* self-defense" (emphasis added) should an armed attack occur. Collective self-defense is actually military assistance given in concert to another state. What is important is that collective self-defense is still restricted in its application by the same bounds that limit states in their individual response to threats or use of force. That is, actions taken in collective self-defense must be necessary, immediate, and governed by the bounds of reasonableness and proportionality.[19]

□ Intervention by Invitation

Intervention is permissible in international law when it comes at the genuine and explicit invitation of the legitimate government of a state. The legal merits of such invitational interventions will hinge on the particular circumstances of each individual situation. In this respect, the motives of the intervening state in taking the action, as well as the legitimacy of that government requesting the assistance, are critical for ascertaining the lawfulness of the case. To substantiate these criteria objectively remains difficult, and perceived permissibility may come down to political realities rather than neatly defined legal sureties.

Genuine invitations for outside intervention often have been made during civil conflicts, especially when the government in power wants to receive external assistance for quelling the insurrection. So long as the foreign aid and/or troops have been requested voluntarily by the host state's government, their interventionist status is sanctioned as permissible under international law.[20]

□ Intervention by Treaty

Under certain conditions, acts of intervention may be granted through treaty arrangements made by one state with another state. Some states have, in fact, concluded special bilateral treaties of "friendship and cooperation" specifying the possibility of intervention by the protector state in certain discretionary circumstances. Under these special, bilaterally negotiated conditions, the acceptability of treaty rights clearly is viewed in international law as a legitimate exception to the norm of nonintervention. The precondition here, of course, is that the treaty must still be in force and duly respected by both governments at the time an intervention occurs.[21]

□ Intervention for Abatement

International law recognizes the lawfulness of certain interventionist actions taken to abate an intolerable regional nuisance. Suppose that conditions in the territory of some state approach anarchy, and the constituted municipal authorities of that state are unable to restore domestic order. The abatement theory holds that neighboring states threatened by the chaotic situation may assume a legal duty to intervene, by armed force if necessary, in order to put down the disturbance. By that action, a neighboring state is entrusted with the responsibility to ensure that disruptive conditions do not spill over and upset its internal stability. As one recognized legal scholar has observed, "If no selfish aims are involved in the intervention in question, if no territorial aggrandizement or other gain is contemplated or realized, then it is difficult, in many instances, to deny a right, based on self-defense or self-preservation, to violate the ban on intervention for the sake of abating the nuisance at one's doorstep."[22]

In the case of intervention on grounds of abatement, the severity and magnitude of the turmoil in the afflicted state stand as critical determinants. External intervention is not permitted merely on the pretext of putting down insurrections next door. The turmoil in the affected state must be genuinely severe and sufficiently chaotic to pose a real threat to the territorial integrity and self-preservation of a neighboring state. Otherwise, the permissibility for intervention will be depreciated into an act of unlawful aggression.

■ INTERVENTION AND U.S. PRACTICE

The legal logic employed by the United States to support its use of intervention historically has been couched in the articulation of presidential doctrines. Accordingly, these dicta have significantly shaped the U.S. legal attitude toward the permissibility of intervention.

The foundation of U.S. interventionist policy in the Third World rests in the Monroe Doctrine and its Roosevelt Corollary. Enunciated on December 2, 1823, the doctrine asserted that: (1) no further European colonization should occur in the New World; (2) the United States should abstain from involvement in European affairs; and (3) European states must refrain from intervening in the affairs of governments in the Western Hemisphere.[23] Intended as a unilateral pronouncement of U.S. policy in dealing with the incursion or threat of incursion by European powers into the Western Hemisphere, the Monroe Doctrine came to be regarded as a defense doctrine, or what one commentator dubbed the "American doctrine of self-preservation."[24] Moreover, the Roosevelt Corollary, articulated by President Theodore Roosevelt in his Annual Message to Congress on December 6, 1904, expanded the scope of the doctrine by making the United States a self-appointed international policeman, providing a unilateral justification for increased intervention into the affairs of Latin American countries.

Important to realize is that neither doctrine drew its validity from any legislative pronouncement, nor from any international treaty instrument. Nor was the ambit of jurisdiction or application of either doctrine ever precisely defined by specific law or fiat. Indeed, both doctrines were applied historically on an ad hoc basis, in circumstances determined by the perception of U.S. policymakers, to explain the government's rationale for taking certain interventionist actions. In short, from the mid-nineteenth century through the early portion of the twentieth century, both doctrines were held out as pillars of U.S. foreign policy and, accordingly, were invoked periodically to justify unilateral interventions taken in the name of defending the Americas from European intrusions. For example, in the first three decades of the twentieth century, the United States intervened militarily on some sixty occasions in several smaller Caribbean and Central American states.[25] In all of these cases, little diplomatic consideration or formal concern was expressed by the United States about the international legal implications of these interventions or the critical attitude of other states.

Since World War II, the U.S. perception of aggression (that is, legally impermissible intervention) has been couched largely in terms of evaluating and containing communist intentions, capabilities, and strategies throughout the Third World in general and the Western Hemisphere in particular. Communist influence upon the domestic politics or governmental structure of a state may occur by friendly or hostile means. In either circumstance, an unstable situation in the region may intimate that a state is the victim of indirect communist aggression. Such a conclusion may be viewed as threatening to the U.S. security zone. This perception has historically produced reactions by the United States to provide military supplies to a receptive government (or political faction) in order to redress the communist threat. The temptation to engage in military intervention of one form or another has been more likely to rise as the perceived threat to U.S. security interests escalated. Important is that many of the fundamental principles embodied in the Monroe Doctrine have continued to influence U.S. interventionist policy in the Western Hemisphere. Indeed, the fundamental policy motive contained in the doctrine—intervention for self-defense—was resurrected and reactivated in post–World War II foreign policy doctrines.

The Johnson Doctrine derived from the episode in late April 1965 when the United States sent 21,000 troops to restore civil order in the Dominican Republic. The principal legal rationale for the action came to be self-defense—more accurately, anticipated national security considerations—against the perceived threat of communism being established in the Dominican Republic. The scope of the doctrine—the Western Hemisphere—was expanded in 1958 by the Eisenhower Doctrine and U.S. intervention in Lebanon to foster stability in that country. The Eisenhower Doctrine in effect authorized U.S. military action to prevent a communist takeover of Middle Eastern countries. As a consequence, both doctrines during the 1960s came to designate U.S. efforts to counter perceived communist threats in regions considered to be of significant foreign policy interest to the United States.[26]

During the 1980s, the administration of President Ronald Reagan articulated its own policy dictum to reinforce and expand this central theme of stifling communist intrusion into the Americas in particular and the Third World in general. Under the Reagan Doctrine, the United States indicated that it would aid and support paramilitary "freedom fighters" engaged in armed struggle against repressive totalitarian regimes of the left, including guerrilla movements in Angola, Afghanistan, Cambodia, and Nicaragua. Citing the legal rationale for the doctrine, President Reagan noted in his February 6, 1985 State of the Union Address:

> The Sandinista dictatorship of Nicaragua, with full Cuban Soviet-bloc support, not only persecutes its people, the church and denies a free press but arms and provides bases for communist terrorists attacking neighboring states. Support for freedom fighters is *self-defense and totally consistent with the OAS and U.N. Charters* [emphasis added].[27]

As Marxist encroachment is presumed in globalist fashion to be instigated by the Soviets in concert with its allies (such as Cuba in southern Africa and Nicaragua in Central America), the legal edict of self-defense is perceived by Washington policymakers as applicable. In the case of U.S. aid to the anti-Sandinista contras in Nicaragua, for example, the Reagan administration has gone to some lengths to justify its interventionist actions on legal grounds of self-defense, noting that Soviet-led communist intrusion is real, ongoing, illegal, and threatening to regional interests in general and U.S. interests in particular.[28]

The evolution of U.S. foreign policy doctrines—from the region-centric Monroe Doctrine to the seemingly worldwide edict of the Reagan Doctrine—underscores a progression of U.S. legal logic justifying U.S. interventionist practices in the Third World. The common factors linking these various doctrines are several: First, each doctrine was issued unilaterally, leaving the United States as their only interpreter. Second, the United States insisted upon retaining the sole, exclusive right of interpretation for activating these doctrines—for determining when they were necessary, the dimensions of that need, and where they should be applied—as conceived in terms of U.S. diplomatic and security interests. Third, the unilateral character of these doctrines points up the guiding concept of the "free hand." This refers to the notion that although the United States might be willing to act in concert with other states in the world, it reserves for itself the right to make the decision if, when, and under what circumstances any action would be undertaken. Finally, these doctrines explicitly have worked to fix a pervasive conviction in U.S. foreign policy during the twentieth century—namely, that the continued independence of states in the Third World from communist control is a diplomatic vital interest of the

United States, a vital interest that the U.S. government should be prepared to protect with force and by military intervention if necessary.

Accordingly, these foreign policy doctrines have largely shaped the U.S. legal attitude toward the permissibility of intervention. Yet, the legal dimension of these doctrines is grounded in notions that are drawn neither from U.S. domestic law nor from international law. In fact, the U.S. public's historical view of presidential doctrines has been that they are special legal edicts bestowing upon the United States the singular right to take certain interventionist actions throughout the Third World. Such an attitude, however much it appears appropriate for U.S. national interests, falls short of keeping up with the international legal norm of nonintervention. These doctrines are not real tenets of international law; they are merely political instruments of self-defense, to be applied exclusively by the United States as that government alone defines and construes each case in the Third World.[29]

The most important common factor underpinning these presidential doctrines is that they are all couched in international realpolitik rather than in consensual international law. That is, although stated in terms of the legal justification of self-defense, these doctrines cannot per force convey unilateral legal license to the United States to impinge upon the national sovereignty, territorial integrity, or political independence of any state in the Third World. To argue otherwise is to suggest the right of the United States to supersede the limits of self-defense and thereby mutate these doctrines into potential instruments for legitimizing the use of U.S. force throughout the Third World. The explicit view of international law clearly rejects the propriety of any such self-serving legal precepts. Yet, the lack of an overarching international enforcement mechanism (that is, reliance on voluntary adherence by individual states to international law) has ensured that states sometimes adopt legal license to interpret international law such that it serves their own interests.

The key legal facet of the Reagan Doctrine as implemented in Nicaragua, for example, centers around the rationale of U.S. self-defense and the related need to preempt Nicaraguan-sponsored armed aggression against El Salvador. However, serious questions surface over the applicability of Article 51 of the UN Charter to justify the U.S. interventionist role. In short, the legal notion of self-defense does not include the unilateral right of an outside power to intervene against the territory of an aggressor state. Even if it were proven that the Sandinista government was transporting significant amounts of aid to rebels in El Salvador—patently illegal under international law—any responsive action by the United States nevertheless should neither be taken against the Sandinista government nor conducted in Nicaraguan territory. According to international law, the United States should instead limit its actions to assisting the government of El Salvador in putting down the insurgency in its own state. Though this limitation may seem inherently unjust, providing opportunities for the instigating culprit, international law sanctions neither the notion that "might makes right" nor that "two wrongs make a right."

Moreover, an implicit justification of U.S. intervention into Nicaraguan affairs has been the necessity to preserve for Nicaraguans their inherent democratic right under international law to choose their own form of government. As a result of the absence of an international legal enforcement mechanism, states have developed a practice of violating Article 2(4) of the UN Charter, often with impunity. This justification for intervention, however, presumes that the principle of self-determination (the right of individuals in a country to choose their own form of government) carries more weight than the principle of nonintervention. That the principle of self-determination outweighs the principle of nonintervention is difficult to prove, particularly because UN Charter law is silent on the matter, and neither scholars nor governments have embraced such a position. As one author has noted, such a view "would introduce a new normative basis for recourse to war that would give powerful states an almost unlimited right to overthrow governments alleged to be unresponsive to the popular will or to the goal of self-preservation."[30] When one realizes that the Reagan administration's main foreign policy goal in Central America was to limit the hegemonial and ideological influence of the Soviet Union—while concomitantly projecting U.S. political values—it becomes quite evident that antithetical governments will disagree over the meanings of "popular" determination and "democratic" rule. The end result seems to be that spheres-of-interest politics are seriously impinging upon the ability of international law to maintain world order in general and regional order in Central America more specifically. Although this result is not new, it underscores the clear departure of the international system of the 1980s from that envisioned in the UN Charter.

Indeed, the case of Nicaragua underscores how U.S. policymakers, when U.S. doctrines clash with international legal edicts handed down by international bodies, have been able to ignore these edicts with relative impunity. On April 9, 1984, Nicaragua submitted a formal application—charging illicit intervention by Washington in Nicaraguan affairs—before the International Court of Justice (ICJ), which instituted proceedings against the United States. The application alleged that U.S. support of anti-Sandinista rebels and its mining of Nicaraguan harbors violated applicable norms of international law. On May 10, 1984, the ICJ issued an interim ruling, holding that the United States should respect the sovereign independence of Nicaragua and that it should refrain from supporting any further anti-Nicaraguan paramilitary activity. The Reagan administration agreed with the ICJ's decision regarding the prohibition against mining Nicaraguan harbors and stated that such practices had been terminated in late March and would not be resumed. The administration maintained, however, that the ICJ actually lacked proper jurisdiction to render a ruling because "the United States had suspended its agreement giving the Court the right to rule concerning Central America, and that Nicaragua itself had no right to plead because it never filed the instruments of ratification required to officially accept the Court's judgement."[31] The United States, therefore, did not consider itself legally bound to the ICJ's second ruling regarding cessation of paramilitary support for the contras.

Although the ICJ ruled that it did have proper jurisdiction over the U.S.-Nicaragua dispute and that Nicaragua had the legal right to plead its case, the Reagan administration announced on January 18, 1985, that it would boycott further proceedings dealing with the subject as presented in the court. The State Department, supporting the boycott, argued that the "conflict in Central America . . . is not a narrow legal dispute; it is an inherently political problem that is not appropriate for judicial resolution. The conflict will be solved only by political and diplomatic means—not through a judicial tribunal."[32] Irrespective of how unenforceable the ICJ's decision may be, it nevertheless constituted a significant statement about armed intervention and other international legal issues. In challenging the ICJ's jurisdiction and subsequently abandoning its proceedings, the United States called into question the sincerity of its commitment to a public international order under the rule of law.

When seen retrospectively in light of the Iranian hostage case, and the attempts at that time by the United States to uphold the ICJ as a crucible of international justice, it becomes clear that by turning away from the court, the United States lost legal credibility, appeared diplomatically disingenuous, and allowed Nicaragua to gain a propaganda advantage in view of its lawful appeal to the international legal forum. By refusing to appear before the ICJ and make public evidence that could substantiate the real aggressor in Central America to be Nicaragua, the Reagan administration effectively fostered the inescapable conclusion that it had a weak case. This generated a pervasive impression that the United States had something to hide and, accordingly, that it may have been guilty of some wrongdoing. In sum, the course of action chosen by the Reagan administration suggested that the Central American situation was assessed predominantly in terms of strategic interest and national security implications, with scant attention to international legal considerations.

■ THE BALANCE SHEET

Largely in reaction to U.S. interventionist policies between 1900 and 1930, the post-World War II attitude condemning the unlawfulness of intervention has become steadfast and staunch. Even so, the United States has persisted in legitimizing its interventionist policies on de facto grounds of preserving national security through self-proclaimed presidential doctrines. Throughout the 1980s, an upgraded effort has been made to fashion support for U.S. interventionist actions in international law, especially by suggesting that these actions fall within the context of permissible exceptions to the norm of nonintervention. The fact is, however, that U.S. interventionist policy remains motivated more by perceived national necessity and political expedition than by international responsibility and legal rectitude.

This observation does not mean that international law fails in its purposes, nor that U.S. interventionist practices are profound aberrations in contemporary international politics. Neither conclusion is accurate. What the historical attitude of the United States toward intervention in the Third World does signify is simply that governments tend to obey international law when it serves their national interests. For nearly all dealings in foreign relations, this remains the objective case. Yet, the reality is that in certain circumstances a state's respect for international law may be diminished when that government perceives its immediate interests to be better served by ignoring, circumventing, or violating specific international norms. This realization underscores the fact that states make international law, states apply international law, states enforce international law, and states break international law. The law is not wanting in its content or its practice or its enforcement; the governments of states are wanting in their willingness to respect the law on certain occasions.[33]

It is easy to make arguments based on absolutes at the cost of overlooking critical facts in an interventionist episode. It is also true that reliance upon absolutes for evaluating and appraising international events may be ill advised. Arriving at black-and-white legal answers rarely portrays the full accuracy of a situation in world politics. This realization is particularly apt with respect to intervention. International law is created by governments as they seek solutions for old problems and new crises. The history of regional and international efforts at cooperation is a record of pragmatic adjustments fashioned to reach objectives promoting general agreement. Acts of intervention tend to disrupt the entire international pattern of cooperation.

There is also the need to view international law from a practical vantage point and to realize that international law, as it is conceived, may take the form of practical idealism. Thus, the reality of interventionist practices suggests that international law should be seen as the deliberate, rational attempt to set order in the international community. To the extent that a state's policy comports with the norm of nonintervention, this attempt has succeeded. However, in cases in which a government opts to pursue its own policy priorities at the expense of intruding into the domestic affairs of some other state, serious questions must be raised about the propriety of such actions. Failure to do so not only shirks international responsibility; it also invites less respect for and greater abuse of the law. In this age of increasing political, economic, and sociocultural interdependence, such a disturbing trend hardly would be in the long-term interest of promoting world public order through legal recourse.

■ Part 5

CASE STUDIES

14

Iran

Eric Hooglund

U.S. foreign policy toward Iran since the end of World War II has been dominated by the globalist perspective. Washington's preoccupation with keeping Iran free of Soviet influence has been reinforced by a perception that the country has a vital strategic significance: Iran shares a 1,200-mile border with the Soviet Union in the north; its southern border is along the Persian Gulf; and it has been a major source of oil for the international market since the outbreak of World War I. The tendency to view Iran as a valuable pawn that could be won or lost in the game of international politics between the United States and the Soviet Union impeded official understanding of the strength of Iranian nationalism. This misunderstanding inevitably led to the formulation of U.S. policies that offended those Iranian political leaders popularly identified as patriots. The most spectacular of these policies was the covert intervention in 1953 to overthrow a popular prime minister and reinstate the power of a king perceived to be more amenable to Western interests. For the next twenty-five years, Iran, under the rule of Shah Mohammad Reza Pahlavi, remained a close ally of the United States.

Many Iranian nationalists never forgave the shah for using the support of the United States to create a royal dictatorship, and they resented the U.S. role in their country. The failure of the shah to achieve popular legitimacy and the widespread perception that he was subservient to the United States were important factors in the revolutionary turmoil of 1978–1979. That major political development, laden with anti-U.S. rhetoric and emotions, brought to power a new regime fearful of a repetition of the events of 1953 and determined to end the prospects for U.S. intervention in Iran's internal affairs. The protracted hostage crisis that bedeviled the last fourteen months of the administration of President Jimmy Carter dramatically symbolized Iran's assertion of independence from U.S. influence. Yet, U.S. policymakers seemed unwilling to accept that the altered relationship was permanent. Thus, efforts were initiated during the administration of President Ronald Reagan to woo Iran back into an anti-Soviet alliance. The clandestine arms sales to Iran during 1985–1986 represented striking evidence of the importance attached to Iran by those who viewed the country solely as a strategic asset or liability in the U.S. political rivalry with the Soviet Union.

■ WORLD WAR II AND THE 1953 COUP D'ÉTAT

U.S. involvement with Iran began during World War II when some 30,000 U.S. troops were sent there to join the allied British-Soviet forces that had occupied the then neutral country in 1941, ostensibly to purge it of German agents but, more practically, to utilize the railway from the Persian Gulf to the Soviet border for transporting military and other supplies to the Red Army. Cooperation between the United States and the Soviet Union did not long survive the war and as their alliance degenerated into a postwar competition for global influence, Iran emerged in early 1946 as a focus of their incipient cold war confrontation. The United States supported Iran's protests before the new UN Security Council that Soviet troops, still in occupation of the northern provinces of Iran, had not withdrawn from the country in accordance with the 1942 Tripartite Agreement, which provided for the withdrawal of all foreign forces from Iran within six months of the end of hostilities in all theaters of the war. Although the Soviet forces eventually did withdraw, the crisis helped to shape official thinking in Washington that the Soviet Union wanted to occupy Iran in order to have access to the oil resources of the Persian Gulf.[1]

As the administration of President Harry S. Truman developed a multifaceted containment policy toward the Soviet Union, Iran became an important element in the strategic concept of the Northern Tier, the string of nations along the Soviet Union's southern border that were to serve as a first line of defense against Soviet penetration into the Middle East. Accordingly, Iran was provided with modest amounts of military assistance intended to strengthen its defense forces. This assistance helped to develop the interest of Iran's king, or shah, in U.S. arms, an interest that would characterize the shah's relationship with successive U.S. administrations until he was overthrown in the 1978–1979 revolution.[2]

Economic and technical assistance programs also were used as part of an overall policy of keeping Iran a member of the U.S.-led bloc of anti-Soviet nations. In the early 1950s, these programs were popularly known as Point Four because President Truman had proposed economic aid initiatives for "less-developed countries" as the fourth point of his January 1949 inaugural address. Under the Point Four program, Iran received some $48 million for technical and developmental projects.[3]

Despite Washington's wooing of Iran, its full incorporation into an anti-Soviet defense alliance was delayed by the emergence of a strong nationalist movement that decried Iran's involvement in superpower rivalries and argued that true national independence meant neutralism in foreign policy and total sovereignty over all natural resources, especially oil (which, since 1908, had been controlled by the British). In 1949, the nationalists formed a National Front under the leadership of Mohammad Mosaddeq (1882–1967). The principal demand of the National Front was the nationalization of the British-owned Anglo-Iranian Oil Company (AIOC), which produced all of Iran's oil for domestic consumption and foreign export. When the National Front did come to power in 1951, it nationalized AIOC and thereby provoked a major crisis between Iran and Great Britain.[4]

The Truman administration was divided over how to deal with the nationalist challenge in Iran. Although Secretary of State Dean Acheson, Henry Grady, the U.S. ambassador to Iran, and other leading officials were fearful that the nationalist cause could be exploited by the Iranian Marxist party, the Tudeh, to bring Iran into the Soviet orbit, they believed that the nationalist demand for control over Iran's oil resources was basically a legitimate one. Consequently, they were reluctant to support the British, who were trying to get U.S. assistance for some form of military intervention, including even a coup d'état against Mosaddeq and the National Front.[5]

While Washington was trying to reach a consensus on a policy to keep Tehran from switching its allegiance from the Western superpower bloc to the Soviet-dominated Eastern bloc, political leaders within Iran were preoccupied with very different issues, such as the continuation of foreign influence on government, popular participation, and the distribution of power among competing interest groups. It was during this period that an irrevocable split occurred between the nationalists, who wanted a constitutional monarch or even a republic, and the royalists, who supported the concept of a strong monarchy for Iran. The shah (1919–1980) had acceded to the throne in 1941 after the British and Soviets had forced the abdication and exile of his father. Throughout the 1940s, the youthful shah generally had been unsuccessful in asserting his own authority over the parliament, or *majlis*. By 1951, when the shah was compelled to accept Mosaddeq as the prime minister chosen by the *majlis,* he had come to perceive the nationalists as the major threat to his own rule. In order to safeguard his position, the shah generally allied himself with those interests that were opposed to the National Front. Among the most powerful opponents of the National Front were foreign interests, in particular the AIOC and the British government.[6]

The stage for a coup d'état against the Mosaddeq government was set when the administration of President Dwight D. Eisenhower came to power in January 1953. Key officials, such as Director of Central Intelligence Allen Dulles and Secretary of State John Foster Dulles and the new U.S. ambassador to Tehran, Loy Henderson, perceived that the political situation in Iran made the country ripe to fall to the communists and uncritically embraced the British view that the nationalists were potential collaborators in turning Iran into a

Soviet satellite. The United States consequently began to cooperate covertly with the British and royalist elements in Iran in planning and executing a coup d'état to remove Mosaddeq from office and to restore the authority of the shah.[7]

Although the U.S.-assisted military coup d'état of August 1953 was successful, it also ensured that Mosaddeq became a nationalist hero and left the shah's popular image as that of a traitor, an image he never was able to shake during the next twenty-five years of his reign. Even more significant, in terms of U.S. interests, the coup made Iranian nationalists deeply suspicious of the United States. The memory of the 1953 coup remained forceful and played a significant role in the anti-U.S. sentiment that surfaced periodically and in particular during the revolution of 1978–1979.[8]

But in 1953, officials in Washington regarded the coup against Mosaddeq as a major triumph of covert action. In terms of U.S. strategic interests, they perceived the results of the coup as positive: Iran became unambiguously a client ally of the United States; in addition, the coup d'état not only restored the power of a pro-Western shah but, more significant, restored control over Iran's oil production to the West. Within one year of the coup, a new consortium of Western oil interests was created to manage Iranian oil. Although the fiction of Iranian ownership was maintained, actual production, pricing, and export of oil was given contractually to this consortium. Iran was required to compensate the AIOC—renamed British Petroleum—for the loss of its concession, but the British also were pressured into ceding 60 percent of the share of the consortium to a group of major U.S. and European petroleum companies. This agreement marked the beginning of U.S. economic interests in Iran, interests that would intensify during the next twenty-five years.[9]

■ STRENGTHENING OF THE U.S.-IRAN SECURITY RELATIONSHIP

After the 1953 coup, Iran was brought fully into the U.S. defense alliance system against the Soviet Union. The Northern Tier concept was finally realized through the creation in 1955 of the Baghdad Pact, a U.S.-sponsored collective security arrangement that allied Iran with Great Britain, Iraq, Pakistan, and Turkey. When a republican revolution toppled the pro-Western monarchy in Iraq in 1958, the Baghdad Pact was transformed into the Central Treaty Organization (CENTO). Although the United States never became a formal member of CENTO, it played an active role in coordinating meetings and providing military assistance and advice. Also, in order to counter the perceived threat of internal subversion, the United States helped the shah in 1957 to create a secret police force, known by the Persian acronym SAVAK (from its offical name of Sazman-e Attelaat va Amniyat-e Keshvar, National Security and Information Organization). Although intended to search out those who advocated a violent overthrow of the government, SAVAK was used primarily to silence those who criticized the regime or the person of the shah. It acquired an unsavory reputation and was one more factor that helped to tarnish the U.S. image.[10]

Iran also became one of the largest recipients of U.S. economic and military aid programs in the decade following 1953. The infusion of this assistance did not alleviate Iranian economic problems, however, which continued to be aggravated by widespread corruption at the highest echelons of the government. By 1960, there was a widespread feeling in Washington that the country was politically unstable. The administration of President John F. Kennedy, which shared the anticommunist views of its predecessors, believed that the principal threat to Iran (as well as to many other Third World countries) came not so much from external or internal subversion as from government incompetence and abuses that undermined its authority. The officials of the New Frontier were unimpressed with the shah's record and were determined to pursuade him and leading Iranian officials that basic reforms were essential to keep the country from falling to Soviet influence. Thus, the Kennedy administration pushed ideas such as land reform, which it saw as a panacea to Iran's problems. In order to convince the shah that the United States meant business, Washington cut military grants and expanded economic assistance programs.[11]

The prodding from the United States fortuitously came just as oil revenues were increasing as a result of new production quota agreements and the establishment of OPEC. This combination of diplomatic pressure and larger budgets induced the shah to support numerous economic reforms that eventually ushered in a period of sustained economic growth. These reforms primarily benefited the industrial sector, as the state became the main promoter and protector of capitalist development. A limited land reform program redistributed approximately one-half of the arable land—then owned by large-scale, absentee owners—to about one-half of the peasants. Even though "the best and the brightest" of the Kennedy-era policymakers had assumed that the types of reforms instituted by the shah would lead eventually to broader political participation and thus to political stability, this did not happen. On the contrary, governmental control of opposition groups actually intensified after 1962. Nevertheless, the overall performance of Iran's economy and the positive perception of the shah's reforms created a surface impression of political stability that gradually became entrenched in Washington.[12]

Political discontent, which had been repressed since 1953, exploded in major urban demonstrations and riots in June 1963. The catalyst for the protests was the arrest of Ayatollah Ruhollah Khomeini, a senior clergyman who in 1962 had begun preaching sermons increasingly critical of the shah's foreign policy, especially his dependence upon the United States. The nationalist forces, however, were not unified at the time, an important factor that helped the U.S.-equipped security forces to suppress the demonstrators. Khomeini himself eventually was deported, and less prominent members of the clergy were sentenced to internal exile in remote towns. These events further tarnished the image of the United States, an image that was still blemished on account of the

1953 coup. The shah, meanwhile, argued inaccurately (but persuasively) that the turmoil had been instigated by elements opposed to his reforms. Leading Kennedy administration officials, who initially had urged reforms out of concern for Iran's stability, embraced the shah's explanation and interpreted the successful suppression of the "antireform" demonstrations as evidence of new political stability.[13]

After 1963, the nature of the relationship between Iran and the United States began to change, in part because of the increasing preoccupation of U.S. policymakers with the war in Vietnam. But equally important was the rise in Iran's oil revenues as a result of increased oil production. The newfound wealth freed Iran from dependence upon U.S. economic and military aid and enabled the shah to pay cash for the military hardware he desired. As early as 1965, an attitude began to emerge in Washington that the shah should not be discouraged from purchasing military equipment (as long as he was willing to pay) even if particular systems seemed extravagant in terms of Iran's defense needs. This attitude was reinforced by the 1967 decision to end all economic and military assistance programs to Iran because it was no longer perceived to be a less-developed country. The cessation of assistance symbolized the end of Iran's economic dependence on the United States. By the late 1960s, policymakers in Washington were interpreting Iran's prosperity, induced by oil revenues, as evidence of political stability and were perceiving the shah as a valuable ally in the Middle East region.[14]

In 1969, when President Richard M. Nixon proclaimed his doctrine that the United States would provide the means—weapons, not personnel—for friendly regimes to assume responsibility for the security of their own countries and regions, Iran under the shah was ready to take on its role as Washington's policeman in the Persian Gulf. The shah's longtime fascination with military equipment, especially aircraft, now had the opportunity to blossom fully. Indeed, during the administrations of Presidents Nixon and Gerald R. Ford, U.S.-Iran relations were dominated by extensive sales of U.S. weapons. Iran's emergence as a major arms purchaser was legitimized by Nixon's instructions to the U.S. bureaucracy in 1972 to approve the sale of any weapons system requested by the shah no matter how sophisticated the system, with the notable exception of nuclear warheads. The shah's appetite for weapons proved almost insatiable as, beginning in 1974 as a result of the quadrupling of oil revenues, he had virtually limitless financial means with which to indulge his fancy. So important did the arms sales become for the U.S.-Iran relationship that the Department of Defense sent a special sales representative to Iran to advise the government on what systems to purchase. Between 1970 and 1978, the shah ordered over $20 billion worth of U.S.-manufactured arms, making Iran the single largest foreign customer for U.S. military hardware (a striking transformation of the relationship that had existed only twenty years earlier).[15]

Under the mantle of the Nixon Doctrine, the shah actively sought to curb what both he and the United States perceived to be radical regimes and movements. Chief among these was the republican government in neighboring Iraq, which was viewed as a subversive threat to the conservative Arab monarchies of the Arabian Peninsula and as a client of the Soviet Union. As early as 1971, the shah sought to destabilize Iraq by providing covert support to various leaders of that country's disaffected Kurdish minority, concentrated in the mountainous area along the Iran-Iraq border. Iran's assistance intensified in 1974 after the major Kurdish leader rose up in open rebellion against Baghdad. Iran served as a conduit for the clandestine delivery of U.S. and Israeli military supplies to the Kurds and also provided logistical support and air cover for Kurdish military operations. Iran's increasingly overt intervention and the lack of effective support from the Soviet Union pressured the government of Iraq to seek a political accommodation with the shah. Known as the Algiers Agreement, this March 1975 accord essentially was an acknowledgement of Iran's preponderant influence in the Persian Gulf region.[16]

The shah also opposed the Marxist government of South Yemen, which had come to power following the former British colony's independence in 1967. He shared the U.S. view that Aden actively was supporting various guerrilla groups attempting to overthrow the Arabian Peninsula governments. Four of these countries (Bahrain, Oman, Qatar, and the United Arab Emirates) were small states that only became fully independent of Great Britain in 1971. Consequently, there was concern in both Tehran and Washington about the long-term stability of these pro-Western, hereditary-rule regimes. The shah was especially uneasy about Oman, where a long-simmering revolt against the sultan had succeeded in "liberating" considerable territory near the border with South Yemen. In 1973, he decided to dispatch a contingent of Iranian troops to Oman in order to help put down the rebellion. The intervention, which had the support of the United States, eventually achieved its objectives, although Iranian military advisers remained in Oman right up to the revolution.[17]

The massive arms sales to Iran had become controversial by 1976. A critical U.S. Senate report on the issue concluded that the arms sales program was "out of control" and warned of the possibility that the large numbers of Americans hired to maintain the weapons could be endangered if there were to be a change in regime in Iran.[18] Presidential candidate Jimmy Carter made arms sales in general one of his election campaign issues and specifically criticized the Ford administration for the sales to Iran. Nevertheless, when the Carter administration assumed power in early 1977, it was reluctant to reverse the arrangement with Iran. In fact, during the first year of the Carter administration, arms sales continued on the same scale as in previous years.[19]

Carter also had made human rights one of his campaign issues and, during the election debates, had singled out Iran as an example of a country in which human-rights abuses were widespread. Thus, the Carter administration came to office committed to a policy of promoting human rights in those dictatorships that were allied to the United States. In the case of Iran, however, administration policymakers concluded early that continuing the strategic relationship was more important than trying to pressure the shah to improve his government's human-rights record. In practice, this meant that officials would reassure the shah of the U.S. commitment while (sometimes) privately encouraging him to proceed toward his 1976 objective of liberalizing Iran's political system.[20]

■ THE REVOLUTION AND U.S. POLICY TOWARD THE ISLAMIC REPUBLIC

The revolution of 1978–1979 caught the Carter administration—and the shah—by surprise. The (mis)perception that the regime of the shah was stable was deeply engrained in official Washington. Nevertheless, the revolution against the shah was based on a broad coalition of secular and religious nationalists who shared similar views about the shah and his relations with the United States. The provisional government that initially replaced the shah in February 1979 was dominated by politicians who had opposed the shah since the early 1950s, and who remembered with bitterness the role of the United States in the coup against their hero, Mosaddeq. Both they and the religious leaders of the secretive Revolutionary Council had spent years in prison for opposition. Thus, they tended to be deeply suspicious of the United States and feared that Washington would try to reinstate the shah, whom they perceived as a U.S. puppet and as a traitor to his country. Their immediate foreign policy goals included the termination of the special relationship with the United States. Consequently, billions of dollars of ordered but not-yet-delivered arms were canceled, Iran's membership in CENTO was terminated, and Tehran announced that it would no longer serve as the policeman of the Persian Gulf region. In addition, relations with Israel and South Africa were broken in the belief that these had served U.S. and not Iranian interests.[21]

Although the leaders who comprised the provisional government tended to suspect Washington's intentions toward their revolution, they believed Iran and the United States could maintain a relatively normal relationship once the former patron accepted the new political realities. More extreme revolutionaries, however, wanted to eradicate thoroughly U.S. influence from Iran. They viewed both the United States and the Soviet Union as equally malevolent powers in terms of their relations with the Third World but saw the United States as the greatest danger to Iran, underscoring the nature of the relationship between the two countries since the 1940s. These more extreme forces exploited the October 1979 admission of the shah into the United States for medical treatment to force a complete break in diplomatic relations. Their vehicle was the hostage crisis, which developed in November 1979 after students invaded the U.S. embassy compound in downtown Tehran and captured its personnel to hold as hostages for the extradition of the shah.[22]

The hostage crisis continued for 444 days, and during this time it preoccupied the Carter administration to such an extent that attention to other issues was adversely affected. After initial efforts to resolve the crisis through diplomacy and economic pressures proved unsuccessful, the president authorized a covert operation in April 1980 to forcibly rescue the more than fifty hostages. This first major instance of clandestine intervention in Iran since 1953 failed in the Iranian desert, and the circumstances surrounding the failure added to the sense of humiliation that the protracted hostage crisis engendered in the United States. Although covert planning for a second rescue attempt continued, the dispersal of the U.S. hostages to numerous secret locations throughout Iran made another attempt unfeasible. The hostage crisis was not finally settled—through an Algeria-mediated agreement (the Algiers Accord)—until the very day that Carter left office as president.[23]

The administration of President Ronald Reagan took office in 1981 with an ideological view of the Soviet Union that had not evolved from that of the mid-1950s. That is, the ideologues believed that the Soviet Union was an "evil empire" bent on aggression against the interests of the West, and they were convinced that the Soviet invasion of Afghanistan in December 1979 demonstrated the hostile intentions of the USSR. Furthermore, Soviet aims in Afghanistan were perceived as part of a broader scheme to extend Moscow's influence into the Persian Gulf. Inevitably, this perception of a Soviet threat to the Persian Gulf region conditioned views of Iran. Nevertheless, the emotional impact of the protracted hostage crisis made the development of a coherent policy toward Iran difficult. Consequently, the Reagan administration's Iran policy evolved through three phases: (1) covert support for antiregime groups while overtly ignoring the country; (2) secret efforts to woo Iran through clandestine arms sales; and (3) a military containment policy that began in 1987.[24]

From the beginning, the Reagan administration faced a paradox with respect to Iran. The Islamic Republic was a government that was avowedly anticommunist; it had boldly and repeatedly condemned the Soviet Union's invasion of Afghanistan; it had criticized the USSR for behaving like an imperialist power; and Tehran generally had poor relations with its big neighbor to the north. At the same time, however, Iran was even more hostile toward the United States. The war between Iran and Iraq further complicated the situation. This war had begun in September 1980 when Iraq invaded Iran and subsequently occupied its oil-producing southwestern province for twenty months. Some Reagan administration officials were alarmed by the conflict because they were convinced it was potentially destabilizing for U.S. allies in the Persian Gulf. They also had believed for many years that Iraq, which had a treaty of friendship with the Soviet Union, was one of Moscow's client states and argued that the anti-Soviet fervor of the regime in Tehran served overall U.S. interests. Other officials took the position that Iran's advocacy of exporting revolution was subversive of friendly regimes. Overlaying these contradictory political perceptions was a deep resentment of Iran because of the hostage crisis, an event that both conservatives and liberals believed had humiliated the United States.[25]

The different perspectives prevented the Reagan administration from formulating a coherent policy toward Iran. Throughout 1981, there did not appear to be any urgency to devise a specific policy, as Iraq seemed to have the upper hand in the Iran-Iraq war. In short, Iran was ignored. During the summer of 1982, however, the combined impact of Iran's successful offensives leading to an invasion of Iraq, the Israeli invasion of Lebanon, and the obvious worsening of relations between Iran and the Soviet Union compelled the administration to rethink its strategy. Achieving consensus was still not easy: Some officials began to fear "Islamic fundamentalism" nearly as much as communism, and advocated the containment of Iran; in contrast, other officials viewed Islamic fundamentalism as a potentially powerful ideological tool that could be used against the Soviet Union. The former group blamed Iran for a variety of Middle Eastern political developments that adversely affected U.S. interests in the region, in particular the incidents of terrorism in Lebanon. The latter group was less convinced of Iran's ability to direct anti-U.S. and anti-Western events in Lebanon and elsewhere and tended to believe in the possibility of reaching an understanding with Tehran based upon a shared interest in containing Soviet influence in the region.[26]

The lack of official consensus inevitably led to contradictory policies both within individual bureaucracies and between them. The CIA, for example, provided covert financial and material support as early as 1980 to various monarchist groups in exile that were advocating the overthrow of the regime in Tehran and the reestablishment of a pro-U.S. government. Yet, there was widespread disillusionment with these exile groups by 1984, and officials, such as CIA director William Casey, were ready to consider new approaches for regaining Iran. When some intelligence and national security officials became convinced that there were pro- and anti-Soviet factions within the Iranian government, the stage was set for devising a plan to cultivate the latter, who came to be referred to as the "moderates." The U.S. officials hoped to exploit the Iranian need for weapons in the war with Iraq to begin a process of assisting those Iranian factions who they believed were more sympathetic to the United States. The policy objective was to lay the groundwork for a new relationship with Iran, a relationship that could be developed after Khomeini died and an expected power struggle hopefully was won by the moderates. This rationale was used to justify arms sales to Iran; in return, the moderates were expected to use their presumed influence among the Arab groups holding U.S. hostages in Lebanon to seek the hostage's release.[27]

These views tended to dominate in the NSC and CIA during 1985 and 1986. They were not shared by officials in the State and Defense Departments who continued to perceive Iran as the principal threat to U.S. interests not only in the Persian Gulf but also in Lebanon. The inevitable result was contradictory policies toward Iran: Simultaneous with the covert policy of selling arms, the State Department was vigorously pursuing an overt policy—dubbed "Operation Staunch"—of trying to stop international arms sales to Iran. Operation Staunch was part of an undeclared but obvious U.S. tilt toward Iraq, a tilt prompted by a belief that Iraq could not win the war and a fear of the regional consequences if Iran were to win. The November 1986 revelations that former National Security Adviser Robert McFarlane had traveled secretly to Tehran for talks, and that arms sales agreements between the United States and Iran had been transacted even while Operation Staunch was in effect, demonstrated the deep divisions within the Reagan administration concerning the appropriate policy for dealing with Iran.[28]

The persistent fear of Soviet influence in the Persian Gulf served as the catalyst for the Reagan administration to unify around a consistent policy and extricate itself from the diplomatic scandal caused by the exposure of its secret arms deals with Iran. Soon after the initial revelations, the government of Kuwait renewed a request to both the United States and the USSR for protection of its oil tankers, frequently attacked by Iran in retaliation for Iraqi attacks upon Iranian shipping. When the Soviet Union agreed in February 1987 to lease three of its own tankers to Kuwait, the United States decided to respond by reflagging and escorting eleven Kuwaiti oil tankers while they transited the Persian Gulf. Although the United States proclaimed that its new policy of military intervention was to protect neutral international shipping, the bulk of commercial traffic in the waterway consisted of neutral ships carrying goods to or from Iran. Not only were these ships excluded from U.S. protection, but Iraq intensified its attacks upon them. The real aim, thus, was to protect from Iranian retaliatory strikes the shipping of the Arab states traditionally allied with the United States in order to discourage these countries from seeking Soviet protection for their commerce. The practical effect of the intervention was de facto support of Iraq against Iran.[29]

Though support of Iran inevitably had the result of actually prolonging the war, Washington maintained that its true objective was to help end the conflict. In tandem with the military policy, the United States pursued diplomatic efforts through the UN to achieve a cease-fire. These initiatives, too, had the appearance of being pro-Iraqi and anti-Iranian. In particular, the United States cooperated with Baghdad to revise a draft cease-fire resolution that had Iran's support so that it favored the Iraqi position and included provisions for an international arms embargo against the party that rejected it. Under U.S. prodding, the Security Council in July 1987 reluctantly passed Resolution 598, calling for an immediate cease-fire in the war. Iran, however, frustrated the U.S. expectation of a subsequent UN vote on impositions of an embargo by neither accepting nor rejecting the resolution, and the United States ultimately failed to win support for further UN sanctions.[30]

The Iran-Iraq war continued for a full year beyond the passage of Resolution 598. It was the worst year to date in terms of the number of civilian casualties, the majority of whom were victims of Iraq's intensified use of chemical weapons and missiles against Iranian cities and towns. Tehran accused the United States of shielding Iraq and perceived the deployment of twenty-seven U.S. naval ships to the Persian Gulf as a direct provocation. Over time, a series of military confrontations occurred between U.S. and Iranian forces, such as the April 1988 retaliatory strike in which the United States destroyed two Iranian oil platforms and sunk six ships (half of Iran's naval fleet), and the heightened tensions seemed to make a greater disaster inevitable. Such a disaster happened in early July, when the U.S.S. *Vincennes*, mistaking an Iranian civilian passenger airbus en route to Dubai in the United Arab Emirates for an attacking jet, shot it down over the Strait of Hormuz; all 290 aboard were killed.[31]

Even before the Iranian plane was shot down, the United States was concerned about the possibility that continued conflict with Iran would spiral out of control and lead to a general U.S.-Iran war. The international revulsion over Iraq's massive use of chemical weapons also made Washington uncomfortable with its policy of tilting toward Baghdad. Thus, when the airplane downing brought the United States and Iran to the brink of open war, the administration decided it was time to try to defuse the situation. The United States admitted that the shootdown was a "mistake" and offered to pay compensation to the families of the victims. Iran recognized the gesture as a signal and reciprocated by announcing its long-delayed acceptance of Resolution 598. In August, a cease-fire in the Iran-Iraq war was declared by the UN, which then dispatched observers to the area to monitor the front lines. The United States subsequently began to withdraw some of its vessels from the Persian Gulf. Obstensibly this was because neutral ships no longer needed military protection, but during the year the U.S. naval armada was in the Persian Gulf, more neutral ships had been attacked than in any previous year since the war began. The real aim of U.S. policy—to contain Iran and its revolution—could not be done simply by a show of force; the actual use of force to achieve this goal seemed too costly. Thus, it appeared by the end of 1988 that the United States was prepared to accept Iran, although officials in Washington were no closer to understanding the nature of Iranian—or Third World—nationalism than they had been before 1987.

■ LESSONS OF INTERVENTION

The history of the U.S.-Iran relationship demonstrates the problems for overall U.S. national interests of allying with a regime that does not have the popular support of its own people. For twenty-five years, the U.S. policy of unconditional support for the shah of Iran seemed to be paying off in terms of promoting U.S. interests in the Persian Gulf region. To policymakers in successive administrations between 1953 and 1978, Iran under the shah seemed like an excellent example of a country where Soviet influence had successfully been contained. The sudden and wholly unanticipated transformation of Iran from a dependable ally to an implacable foe during 1979 baffled Washington. More than nine years after the revolution, policymakers were still confused about how and why the relationship with Iran had collapsed, were generally unreconciled to accepting the new order, and were unable to formulate creative policies for dealing with Khomeini.

The post-1979 problems between Washington and Tehran were the direct consequence of the nature of U.S. intervention in Iran during the regime of the last shah. By 1953, there had crystallized in Washington widespread concern that Iran might become part of the Soviet bloc. This concern had arisen out of the collective inability of officials to appreciate the significance of political developments in Iran. For example, during the late 1940s and early 1950s, when Iranian nationalists were trying to end the British government's control of Iran's oil industry and also were attempting to curtail the autocratic powers of the shah, U.S. policymakers erroneously perceived Iran's internal political conflicts as instability provoked by communist subversion. This perception led the United States to collaborate with Britain in carrying out the 1953 coup d'état against the popular, but neutralist, government of Prime Minister Mosaddeq. The reinstallation in power of the pro-Western, anti-Soviet shah proved to be a boon for U.S. interests. By 1970, Iran was perceived as a model of stability, and its ruler, the shah, as the U.S. policeman of the Persian Gulf.

The shah imposed short-term stability on Iran by repressing political dissent. It is ironic that the more dictatorial his regime became, the closer the U.S.-Iran relationship became. Thus, U.S. intervention in Iran after 1953 took the form of supporting the shah, initially through economic and military assistance (up to 1967) and then through massive transfers of sophisticated arms for which the shah paid cash. As the United States progressively became identified with the unpopular political and military policies of the shah, the Iranian perception of the United States as a country of positive, democratic values was seriously undermined. By the 1970s, the image of the United States that had taken hold among those Iranians disaffected with the royal dictatorship was that of a superpower exploiting Iran's resources and strategic position for its own benefit. The shah's diverse religious and secular opponents accused him of being little more than a U.S. puppet, a leader serving the interests of U.S. economic and military interests to the detriment of Iran.

U.S. policy toward Iran during this period was flawed by pervasive insensitivity to the nationalist feelings of the population. The preoccupation with having in Tehran a government that shared the U.S. aim of keeping Soviet influence checked in the Persian Gulf blinded successive administrations to the inherent contradictions of supporting a pro-U.S. leader who was perceived as unpatriotic by his own subjects. In essence, the thrust of U.S. policy was not Iran but rather the containment of the Soviet Union. This anti-Soviet objective helped to create an official mind-set whereby internal Iranian political challenges to the shah tended to be perceived as having been fomented by local communists at the instigation of the USSR.

Inevitably, the hated shah was toppled in a popular revolution. Because the shah had been widely perceived in Iran as a puppet of the United States, anti-U.S. sentiment tended to be closely intertwined with the anti-shah feelings. Officials in Washington, however, were no more ready to acknowledge a legitimate basis for this animosity—a crucial first step in reaching a diplomatic reconciliation—after the revolution than they had been to recognize it before the fall of the shah. During the nine-month tenure of the provisional government that replaced the monarchy, the United States refused to authorize any U.S. official to meet with Khomeini, the leader of the revolution. This aloofness tended to reinforce the worst fears of many Iranians: that the United States opposed the revolution and was planning to intervene to restore the shah to power. Although no evidence exists that this was Washington's intention in 1979, the admission of the shah into the United States for medical treatment confirmed in the minds of some revolutionaries that the United States was plotting a coup. The response to this episode—the seizure of the U.S. embassy in Tehran and the holding of hostages—ruptured completely what remained of a relationship that, prior to 1979, had been important to both countries.

The hostage crisis demonstrated the extremes to which Iranians were willing to resort to thwart any possible U.S. intervention. Policymakers in Washington, however, perceived this crisis as evidence of the fanaticism of the revolutionaries, a perception that persisted during the last year of the Carter administration and throughout the Reagan administration. Indeed, anti-Iranian sentiment in Washington probably has become as strong as anti-U.S. sentiment in Tehran. The United States has provided covert support to groups opposed to the government in Tehran, but the focus of its intervention policies has been to contain, rather than to overthrow, the revolution. Although the NSC's secret initiative in 1985–1986 may seem to be an effort to adopt a more flexible policy toward Iran, it also was premised in part on a belief in the need to contain the revolution. In this case, the expectation was that arms sales would help pro-West moderates within the Iranian government eventually gain influence and adopt policies that would be less hostile to U.S. interests in the region.

In 1987, the United States undertook a more activist policy of trying to contain Iran with the threat of military force in the form of a naval armada in the waters off Iran's Persian Gulf coast. Washington assumed that a show of force would intimidate Iran into halting its retaliatory strikes against the shipping of Iraq and its Arab allies. This more strident containment policy not only failed to lessen Iran's attacks but actually brought Iran and the United States to the very brink of war. It also demonstrated how poorly policymakers had learned the primary lesson of U.S. intervention in Iran: that Iranian patriots, whether secular or religious, were determined that their country not be dependent on any foreign power and not be aligned with either the United States or the USSR in their superpower competition. The confrontations with Iran in the Persian Gulf exposed the limitations of military policies to achieve political objectives. The United States realized these limitations after the accidental downing of an Iranian civilian plane and began to find ways to defuse the tension between itself and Iran. Nevertheless, as long as the nature of Iranian nationalism remains misunderstood, it will not be easy for the United States to reach a mutually satisfactory accommodation with Iran.

15

The Philippines

Richard J. Kessler

The United States historically has been involved extensively in Philippine affairs, ranging from the colonization of that country in 1898 at the end of the Spanish-American War, through the patron-client relationship with Philippine President Ferdinand Marcos that spanned five U.S. administrations during the post–World War II period, to the ongoing close relationship between Washington and Philippine President Corazon Aquino. Yet, despite the intimacy of this relationship, U.S. policymakers have consistently been unclear or mistaken about the extent and character of U.S. leverage over the Philippine government, the utility of using it, and the ethical issue of intervening in internal Philippine affairs.

Some of the policy ambivalence was captured in a gaming exercise on the Philippines sponsored by the Pentagon in late 1984. One participating former State Department official, noting past U.S. experience with former client states such as Ethiopia, Iran, and Libya, asserted that the U.S. "capacity to manipulate the outcome of a political process in the state of disintegration, is very, very limited." The primary failing of U.S. foreign policy, which he noted was open to considerable debate, was that "we have failed quickly enough . . . to make clear our readiness to look at alternatives." More precisely, "we have failed to make clear our detachment from the sinking ship, and therefore have gone down with it."[1] As another member of the exercise stated, "there are points where we can misuse the tremendous leverage we have, and I think it would be a mistake to underestimate how much leverage we have."[2] Indeed, as the Philippines case will illustrate, the implementation of an interventionist foreign policy in the Third World is easier to discuss in theory than in practice.

■ EVOLUTION OF THE RELATIONSHIP

In 1898 President William McKinley prayed for God's guidance as to whether or not to colonize the Philippines after the Spanish forces in Manila had surrendered to U.S. Admiral George Dewey. According to McKinley, God approved and directed him "to educate the Filipinos, and uplift and Christianize them,"[3] conveniently ignoring three hundred years of the Catholic Church's impact under the Spaniards. Little did McKinley know of the quagmire he was getting into. Others would soon learn.

Philippine independence fighters who had struggled against Spain now turned their cudgels on the Americans attempting to occupy their country in the aftermath of the Spanish-American War. The three-year U.S.-Philippine war cost at least 4,234 U.S. lives and the lives of more than 16,000 Filipinos. In one of the most famous encounters, thirty-six men of Company C of the U.S. Ninth Infantry were killed in Balangiga, Samar, on a Sunday morning in September 1901. A group of insurgents had infiltrated the village disguised as women, concealing their bolo knives in the coffins of supposed cholera victims. After the raid, the head of Company C's captain was found roasting over a fire. In revenge, General Jacob H. Smith, a veteran of the U.S. Civil War and Indian campaigns, ordered Samar Island to be pacified, telling his men to "kill and to burn! The more you kill and burn, the better you will please me."[4] Samar was to be transformed into a "howling wilderness" with no one older than ten alive. Thus, the Philippines was conquered once again.

McKinley promoted a policy of "benevolent assimilation," asserting that U.S. policy was to give Filipinos "good government and security in their personal rights."[5] He established a context for U.S. policy that has remained constant, a mixture of idealism and self-interest. At critical moments self-interest has won over idealism. The present U.S. involvement is rooted in the inability to escape this historical legacy.

The United States ruled the Philippines for almost half a century, finally granting it independence on July 4, 1946. In the aftermath of World War II, the United States provided $620 million in rehabilitation relief and compensation for war damage (after Dresden, Manila was the most devastated city), conditional upon the new Philippine government acceding to U.S. demands for special trade benefits and military bases. The aid had little impact on the country's economic and political dislocation from the war, and a communist-led but peasant-based insurgency known as the Hukbalahaps (Huks) grew in strength during the late 1940s and early 1950s. CIA agents intervened in the 1953 presidential campaign to promote the candidacy of populist Ramón Magsaysay, then defense secretary. After Magsaysay's election, U.S. military and economic advisers became more deeply involved in formulating social reforms and developing a counterinsurgency program to fight the Huks. Success in defeating the Huks in the early 1950s became a model for later U.S. support to the South Vietnamese government.

The Philippine Council on U.S. Aid (PHILCUSA) was formed to administer a new aid program that emphasized agricultural and rural development, including land reform, as well as technical training and education. The program did not produce all the changes hoped for, mainly because "attitudes and institutional rigidities inherited from the past . . . prevented more effective use of larger amounts of aid."[6] The U.S. problem was that aid given directly to individuals did not help economic restructuring and aid given to the government ended up in the hands of individuals. This situation only worsened under the leadership of President Ferdinand E. Marcos. Marcos's strategy was to gain as much U.S. unconditional aid as possible by using access to Philippine bases as leverage. Over time, this approach proved to be very successful.

Although Marcos was elected president in 1965 partly on the nationalist promise to keep the Philippines out of the Vietnam War, he almost immediately reversed himself after President Lyndon B. Johnson promised large amounts of U.S. aid. In 1969 Marcos won reelection to a second four-year term and, on September 21, 1972, he declared martial law when his foes were massing to gain control of the presidency at the end of his constitutionally mandated limit of two terms. As part of this declaration, Marcos suspended the constitution and imprisoned thousands of his opponents, including Senator Benigno Aquino.

The martial-law period was ambivalently perceived both in the Philippines and in the United States. Despite the arrests, many Filipinos welcomed the respite from the factionalized politics that seemed to impede Philippine progress: Weapons were confiscated as private armies and economic empires were broken up. The economy, too, grew as a result of improved commodity prices and heavy borrowing after the first oil price shock of 1973–1974, which forced the international banks to recycle large amounts of new petrodollars to the Third World. Although deeply suspicious of Marcos, the United States continued to supply substantial aid; renegotiating compensation for the U.S. bases in 1979 and 1983 led to even more assistance. Yet, even by 1978, as the second world oil price shock hit the Philippine economy, it had become apparent that Marcos's hold on the nation was slipping.

In response, Marcos made tentative efforts at appearing to democratize the country—allowing local elections in 1980, lifting martial law in 1981, and permitting elections to the National Assembly in 1984—but he still maintained firm control, ruling by executive decree. The assassination of his principal opponent, Senator Benigno Aquino, on August 21, 1983, just as Aquino returned from exile, provided the match that lit the smoldering fire of popular discontent.

Under increasing domestic and U.S. pressure, Marcos announced "snap" presidential elections for February 7, 1986. The opposition parties hurriedly organized behind the candidacy of Senator Aquino's widow, Corazon Cojuangco Aquino. The turnout in support of Aquino overwhelmed Marcos's efforts to cheat. Still, Marcos clung to power even as the nation took to the streets to protest his proclamation of victory. It is ironic that the coup de grace was accomplished by the Philippine military, which revolted against him, backed by a stunning display of people power (demonstrators formed a human wall around rebelling troops to protect them from those still loyal to Marcos). Marcos was ushered out of the country aboard a U.S. Air Force jet to exile in Honolulu as

Corazon Aquino triumphantly took up residence at Malacañang Palace.

U.S. interest in aiding the transition to the post-Marcos era is considerable. The U.S. bases in the Philippines include Subic Bay Naval Base, which covers 62,000 acres (25,000 hectares) and contains an air station, naval magazine, and repair facilities. U.S. Air Force facilities at Clark Air Base in Tarlac and Pampanga provinces cover an enormous 130,000 acres. Both bases employ a total of 46,000 full-time Filipino workers. In addition, smaller communications, recreation, and air bases are spread throughout the archipelago, including the San Miguel Naval Communications Station, John Hay Air Station, Wallace Air Station, and a station in Mindanao that monitors Soviet atomic tests. Substantial, too, are U.S. economic interests in the country: Direct U.S. foreign investment is over $1 billion (nearly 50 percent of total foreign investment in the country); U.S. trade accounts for about one-third of the Philippines' total imports; and U.S. banks are owed about 60 percent of the Philippines' foreign commercial bank debt. Moreover, Filipino immigrants to the United States since 1972 have created a new bond between the two countries. By the year 2000, Filipinos will be the largest Asian ethnic group in the United States, according to the 1980 U.S. census figures.

■ THE MARCOS ERA AND LOST OPPORTUNITIES TO INFLUENCE POLICY

During the twenty years that Marcos held onto power, U.S. policymakers consistently reiterated U.S. support for the Filipino people and democracy. In reality, the United States became concerned about Philippine democracy only when democracy became a security issue. Indeed, U.S. policymakers from Johnson to Reagan turned a blind eye toward corruption and the destruction of democracy under Marcos as long as U.S. access to the highly valued military bases was assured. As was the case in Iran and Nicaragua (see Chapters 14 and 16), the United States largely ignored the domestic nature of the regime until social instability began to threaten perceived U.S. interests. Although the outcome in the Philippines is a far cry from the anti-U.S. revolutionary regimes that took power in Iran and Nicaragua, serious problems remain, the most significant being the strong guerrilla insurgency active in all provinces of the nation.

U.S. policymakers, rather than accept the destruction of democracy in the Philippines and the subsequent risks this destruction entailed, had numerous opportunities to prevent this occurrence or, failing that, to distance the United States from the corrupt nature of the Marcos regime. The first incident, which set the tone of the U.S.-Marcos relationship, took place early in Marcos's first term, when President Johnson courted him to gain Philippine military participation in the Vietnam War. Although as a senator Marcos had opposed Philippine President Diosdado Macapagal's request to send units to Vietnam, once he became president he introduced legislation in February 1966 to send an engineer construction battalion. The United States paid for the unit, providing all allowances and equipment, although the Philippines paid salaries. U.S. funds were distributed in quarterly payments directly to Marcos with no accountability as to their use.[7] In a visit to the Philippines in October of that same year, Johnson expressed his appreciation by referring to Marcos as his "right arm in Asia."[8]

The troop agreement established a pattern to U.S.-Philippine relations under Marcos. Marcos used the agreement to obtain considerable increases in aid and placed President Johnson in a debt of gratitude, referred to in Filipino as *utang na loob*. Yet, the Philippines itself contributed little to the cause (the troops were not even combat soldiers). As one U.S. official commented, "The history of our relations was determined by our *utang na loob* to them."[9] In short, Marcos had Johnson at a disadvantage—and both knew it: Marcos was able to obtain more than what normally would be possible, whereas the United States was limited in what it could expect in return. Thus, when Johnson in late 1966 tried to get increases in Philippine troop commitments, he was turned down.

A second key incident involved the 1969 Philippine election, in which Marcos was fighting a tough reelection campaign with the Liberal party candidate, Senator Sergio Osmena, Jr. Prior to martial law, weak party lines in the Philippine Congress meant that the president was frequently attacked by members of his own party. Some critics could be partly muffled by the appearance of a U.S. blessing of the president's leadership. In this regard, Marcos sought to improve his election chances by successfully receiving the personal blessing of President Richard M. Nixon, the impact of which cannot be overestimated. On July 26, President Nixon stopped briefly in Manila for an official visit. Moreover, Marcos pressed for and received the appearance of the U.S. ambassador, Henry Byroade, at his side while campaigning. In the heat of the campaign, Marcos requested an official Washington envoy and, in a compromise move, received Ronald Reagan, then governor of California, for a visit in September.[10] Vice President Spiro Agnew also came to Manila, although after the election in December. (The United States may have also deliberately aided Marcos's campaign by covertly injecting several million dollars into the government banking system after Marcos threatened to search every U.S. naval vessel for contraband.[11])

A third incident occurred in the period leading up to Marcos's declaration of martial law on September 21, 1972. Marcos initially hesitated to declare martial law because he was uncertain of the U.S. reaction and was by nature risk-averse. The U.S. uncertainty posed a dilemma for him. Strong U.S. disapproval could force him to reverse the decision. It was a moment, at least from Marcos's perspective, of great vulnerability to external factors. However, even tacit U.S. approval of his move would reverse the poles of dependence. Once the United States had sanctioned Marcos's dictatorship, it would be almost impossible to rescind approval.

Marcos thus worked to gain a U.S. endorsement. As it turned out, U.S. concern over involvement in another Southeast Asian crisis, the Vietnam War, and the U.S. policy of lowering the profile of the U.S.-Philippine special relationship both worked in Marcos's favor. Martial law was perceived by the United States as an internal Philippine problem. It is surprising, too, that when Marcos met secretly with Ambassador Byroade in order to find out how the United States would respond if he had to take "stronger measures," Byroade obtained from the State Department a confidential message that "in the event of serious insurgency problems the United States would support the Office of the President." In essence the United States was expressing its support for Marcos.[12]

The immediate U.S. response to Philippine martial law was cautious. In fact, Byroade asked Washington to minimize its response, thus perhaps echoing Secretary of State Henry Kissinger's view that martial law was something U.S. policy could transcend. Neither Byroade nor any other prominent U.S. policymaker believed that Marcos would keep martial law in effect for as long as he did—until 1981. By not denouncing it, the United States gave it tacit approval.

This sequence of events taught Marcos another important lesson in his relations with the United States: When put to the test, the United States would forsake its principles or, at least, wash its hands of involvement. As long as Marcos played the game by not threatening U.S. interests, and as long as the internal situation did not get out of his control and threaten those interests, Washington would be happy to ignore his actions.

Yet, Marcos was still afraid of a diminished U.S. role in the Philippines. A great fear among Philippine policymakers was that the United States would withdraw from Clark and Subic. After 1972, U.S. aid became more vital if Marcos was going to have the means to expand his coercive power in the military and enforce his one-man rule while promoting economic growth; indeed, one of the things Marcos most feared was that the United States would favor another Philippine leader. Thus, Marcos's policy was to use any means short of provoking a rupture in relations to secure his flank from potential U.S. efforts to replace him while also always pursuing greater U.S. aid commitments.

The reopening of the base negotiations was another instance in which the United States could have distanced itself from Marcos. Talks that had been suspended in July 1974 until the U.S. political situation, then immured in the Watergate investigation, was "clarified"[13] were reopened after President Gerald R. Ford's visit in 1976. Marcos really did not want a new base agreement; he wanted more money, as Ambassador William Sullivan then recognized[14] and was simply using the threat of negotiations to attain his goal. That Marcos was concerned about U.S. intentions was indicated by reports from the Philippine embassy in Washington: "Provisions should now be made in anticipation of a possible phasing out or minimization of U.S. aid to the [Philippines] . . . both for military aid and non-military items, considering the evolving temper of the American Congress."[15] This prospect scared Marcos, and he proceeded to provoke U.S. attention by raising any number of objections, including doubts about the bases' military value and suggestions that the bases were a threat to regional peace and security.[16]

His tactic of holding the bases hostage for greater aid had some impact, especially on the local base commanders and the U.S. Pacific Command in Hawaii. In their view, Marcos had leverage, although the Pentagon, which had never been eager to reopen the subject, believed differently. Marcos impeded base operations by putting pressure on the base labor force, turning demonstrations on and off, and suggesting that he might use even more dramatic measures, such as blockading Subic Harbor or disrupting the fuel line to Clark. The local commander's first responsibility was to assure base operability, and U.S. field commanders could imagine any number of scenarios for disruption.

Perhaps Pentagon concerns drove the Carter administration to continue base negotiations after they broke down in the last weeks of the Ford administration. Moreover, completing the negotiations gave the clearest signal yet of U.S. support for the martial-law regime that Marcos would receive until the Reagan administration invited him to Washington for a state visit in 1982. There was no intrinsic reason for changing the terms of the agreement other than Marcos's demand for more aid: The 1947 Military Bases Agreement (MBA) was not to expire until 1991. If Philippine nationalist sentiments needed to be assuaged, this could have been done unilaterally by permitting the Philippine flag to fly over the bases, reducing the bases' boundaries, or even appointing titular Filipino base commanders; a comprehensive new agreement was not needed. In addition, these actions would have signaled a willingness to put the Filipino people's interests above those of the United States and would not have been viewed as an endorsement of Marcos. Most important, nothing was gained by the base negotiations, but something was lost: an opportunity for the United States to distance itself from Marcos. The longer negotiations dragged on, the more important they became to Marcos. Failure to conclude the talks would have indicated a loss of U.S. support.

That Marcos tested the United States continually and found U.S. policy amenable is important, for he did it a fifth time in the dying days of his regime when General Fabian Ver was acquitted of conspiracy in Senator Aquino's assassination. Marcos chose to reinstate Ver as chief of staff despite numerous public and private U.S. statements to Marcos that such an action would trigger a "firestorm" of congressional protest and threaten U.S.-Philippine relations. When the firestorm did not occur in either Congress or the executive branch, this contributed to Marcos's decision to hold a snap presidential election in 1986 and use every available fraudulent method to win.

In the end, Marcos misjudged the United States, but not without cause. He had a sound basis for making his assessment of the U.S. character and U.S. policy interests in the Philippines. From 1972 to 1985, he had dealt with four U.S. presidents and found in all of them an essential unwillingness to rupture the U.S.-Philippine relationship even if basic U.S. values, such as respect for human life and freedom of speech, were at stake.

Perhaps this lack of attention to the Philippines was one of the additional costs of U.S. involvement in Vietnam. During their years in office following the U.S. withdrawal from Vietnam, Secretary of State Henry Kissinger and President Ford focused on shoring up U.S. Pacific allies through enhanced security assistance. Kissinger, emphasizing a point made by President Ford after his December 1975 trip to Asia, stated in July 1976 that "the linchpin of our Asian security effort must be a strong and balanced U.S. military posture in Asia."[17]

■ THE REAGAN ADMINISTRATION AND ATTEMPTS AT CHANGE

In the last year of Marcos's rule, U.S. policymakers tried to promote economic, political, and military reforms—acknowledging that it was unlikely that Marcos would agree to U.S. demands—all the while recognizing that if Marcos acceded to these changes, they would destroy his political power base. This decision to intervene more directly into Philippine affairs was only arrived at after a long internal debate. Some U.S. policymakers argued that the United States lacked the ability to influence Philippine affairs. Others argued that the United States had leverage but that using it would only worsen the situation. Finally, some believed that the United States should not intervene if U.S.-Philippine relations were to step beyond the confines established by the colonial experience. "This was a problem for Filipinos to resolve, not Americans," according to a senior State Department official.[18]

Senior U.S. policymakers finally had become convinced—in part, because of reports of Marcos's bad health—that his days were numbered and began focusing on protecting U.S. interests in a post-Marcos period. Thus, alternatives to Marcos's leadership became more important than retaining a close working relationship with him. In the 1984 National Assembly elections, the United States continually emphasized the importance of fair elections for restoring investor confidence and worked with the opposition to attempt to ensure a fair vote.[19] But even those policymakers who recognized that Marcos's term was ending hesitated to take forceful action, largely because of their belief that Marcos would hang on to power until his death. This explains the frustration expressed over the 1986 snap elections.

Early elections were not something the State Department desired, fearing that a disorganized opposition would be trounced easily by Marcos. Instead, the United States hoped that the basis for a democratic transition could be laid in the previously scheduled 1986 local elections and built upon with the then anticipated 1987 presidential elections. As one U.S. policymaker told me in November 1985, holding early elections had thrown off course the U.S. timetable, as this was the moment to be focusing on economic reforms.

With early presidential elections, U.S. policymakers tried to frame events in the best possible light, assuming Marcos would remain in power. With his reelection, the United States hoped that (1) there would be a vice president capable of taking over should Marcos become incapacitated; (2) Marcos would be in a position to undertake some difficult reforms, such as moving against his cronies (something he had previously feared doing); and (3) if his reelection was viewed as a "genuine mandate," then Filipinos would "feel better" and get on with addressing their social problems.[20] Yet, these desires depended on a scenario that was fundamentally at odds with Philippine realities; it presumed that Marcos retained majority support, that his political machine was intact, and that his coercive power was such that he could impose any settlement on the Filipino and U.S. peoples.

Through it all, Marcos was cognizant of the parameters of the U.S. relationship. He constantly sought to expand the boundaries of the relationship by pressing his policy objectives at multiple levels, pushing and prodding the United States to achieve his goals, using the back door to influence U.S. policy, always bargaining and manipulating. But his aims also knew limits. He was aware that the United States could change the Philippine policy environment almost overnight, although the Philippines could have no similar impact on the United States.

Marcos was particularly shrewd at exploiting U.S. security and economic interests in the Philipines, suggesting he could be trusted to safeguard U.S. interests while alternately issuing strong nationalist appeals and declaring that the Philippines could survive without U.S. support. As the rest of Asia stabilized and the Philippine domestic situation deteriorated, however, Marcos gradually began to enjoy less success in his endeavors. Only when the United States saw how crucial democracy in the Philippines was to U.S. security interests did the Marcos threat to break ties with the United States lose legitimacy. Much of the United States' problems in the Philippines may be traced to a lack of U.S. understanding and appreciation for the Philippine situation. Marcos understood the U.S. system; the United States did not understand his. Thus, the use of leverage by U.S. policymakers would have required more detailed knowledge of the dynamics of Philippine politics. Unfortunately, U.S. foreign policy tends to be driven by short-term pragmatism in four-year (or less) periods, with little strategic vision. As long as Marcos remained in control and the situation did not degenerate into crisis, there was little impetus to change policy.

What is striking about the 1977–1985 period was the slowness with which policymakers reacted to the gathering crisis and the failure of political appointees through successive administrations to pay attention to the concerns expressed by the professionals and then act accordingly. Low- and mid-level officials began documenting the problems long before Senator Aquino's assassination in August 1983. But even after Aquino's death, the reaction of policymakers at the highest level was minimal. As a senior NSC official observed in 1986, "The Philippines was going to be a crisis and we recognized it over two years ago." He further noted that "those of us involved in this policy who are Asianists, not politicos or pundits *knew* what we were doing."[21] Once a crisis was recognized, discussions focused on gaining agreement within the government as to the nature of the crisis and on developing a consensus on what actions the United States could and should take. A National Security Study Directive (NSSD) entitled "U.S. Policy Towards the Philippines," leaked in draft in early March 1985, concluded that Marcos was "part of the problem" but still "part of the solution" and suggested a range of actions the United States could take to encourage political, economic, and military reform, stating that "U.S. policies must be linked to progress" in all areas.[22] Yet, events overtook this carefully staged carrot-and-stick approach.

According to some views—that U.S. leverage is limited—it may be argued that the "people's-power revolution" in February 1986 could not have occurred in any other way or at any other time. U.S. policy could help influence the direction of change in the Philippines but not direct its course or determine the outcome and, thus, could not be anything else but ad hoc—that is, reactive rather than anticipatory to events.[23]

The timing of policy initiatives and the use of leverage were also affected by factors in Washington. Washington's political climate, with a conservative president, made it difficult to obtain approval for forceful policy initiatives against authoritarian allies. As Senator Paul Laxalt noted, Reagan had a "soft spot" for Marcos.[24] A prominent Reagan appointee to the State Department explained in November 1985 that Reagan had "a very profound distaste for the treatment meted out to the Shah."[25] Reagan's attitude slowed further the already laborious process of developing a policy consensus among government agencies.

In short, the path of least resistance was followed. Only when the Philippines became a crisis were people willing to change policy direction and, in President Reagan's case, only at the last possible moment. The war of words could have begun much earlier. The need for economic, military, and political reforms could have been just as forcefully argued in the 1970s or in Reagan's first term as they were in 1986. Change might have occurred sooner. Yet, policymakers were driven by memories of the downfall of U.S. clients in South Vietnam and Iran, just as a previous generation of policymakers had been affected by the loss of China to Mao Zedong and the need to stop communist aggression in South Korea when they formulated policy toward Indochina. The failure to anticipate the need for change and to understand the Philippines' structural problems made more difficult the process of a democratic transition under President Corazon Aquino and, in addition, reduced U.S. leverage on the new government.

■ AQUINO AND THE U.S.-PHILIPPINE SPECIAL RELATIONSHIP IN PERSPECTIVE

The events of February 1986 that ushered Corazon Aquino into power opened a new act in the U.S.-Philippine "special relationship." However, U.S. policymakers will continue to have to make difficult choices, affecting U.S. interests and involving U.S. values. Aquino came to power with little direct U.S. support and with considerable international fanfare. The people-power revolution increased the Philippines' international stature and, in turn, limited U.S. influence when the political situation in Manila once again began to deteriorate.

Soon after President Aquino's accession to power, this reduced U.S. influence became apparent over the issue of how to handle an increasingly widespread communist-led guerrilla insurgency. Early on, U.S. policymakers became concerned about the Aquino government's failure to articulate and implement a comprehensive civilian-military counterinsurgency approach to reducing the threat of the 24,000-strong New People's Army (NPA). During Marcos's rule, the Communist Party of the Philippines (CPP) had grown from a handful of cadres in 1968 to a political presence in almost all of the country's seventy-three provinces. By 1988, it controlled an estimated 20 percent of the nation's *barangays* (districts) and had a mass base of several million supporters. It is ironic that although Marcos used the insurgency as his excuse for declaring martial law in 1972, it was then very limited in scope and personnel.

Upon coming to office, Aquino enunciated a policy of "national reconciliation," releasing political prisoners from jails, including the Communist party's founder, José Maria Sison, and the NPA's first chief, Bernabe Buscayno. A truce was even signed with the CPP in late 1986. Aquino believed that only by bringing the left into the established political process could a long-lasting resolution of the guerrilla insurgency be found. Yet, both the Philippine military and the U.S. government—most notably the Pentagon—were opposed to any deal that led to power-sharing with communists, and they therefore worked to undermine the truce that eventually broke down in early 1987. The key to the breakdown of the accord and the continuing guerrilla insurgency, however, is that Aquino's administration has failed to address the root social causes of the rebellion, such as income inequalities and the lack of rural justice. The U.S. government had itself similarly failed to understand these problems and to design a program compatible with U.S. economic and military aid levels.

Land reform was the classic example. Although promising land reform during her presidential campaign, Aquino appeared to be interested less in developing and implementing a program upon becoming president. She did not want to rule by executive decree, as had her predecessor, desiring instead to leave major issues, such as land reform, to be resolved by a democratically elected congress. But the congress was not elected until May 1987 and did not take office until midsummer of the same year. By that time, it was evident that any land reform program would be half-hearted, given opposition by landowners who had begun organizing both politically and militarily, forming private armies, against any but the weakest initiative.

Although the United States recognized the importance of land reform as a means of reducing peasant grievances and improving incomes in rural areas, it too had done little to understand the dimensions of such a program. In fact, no one knew how much land was available for redistribution. No land surveys had been undertaken. The World Bank completed a land reform study by the summer of 1987, advocating redistribution of all farms above 7 hectares (approximately 17 acres). By the time that proposal was on the table, however, the political impetus for land reform had disappeared.

Another example of the limits of U.S. influence was the issue of military reform. Under both Marcos and Aquino, the United States advocated the need to "reprofessionalize" the Philippine military, providing it with better training, equipment, benefits, and leaders. Yet, although the military's revolt had been instrumental in bringing Aquino to power, she and many of her advisers remained suspicious of the military's intentions. Indeed, Defense Minister Juan Ponce Enrile—who had played an important role in the efforts that toppled Marcos—had presidential aspirations of his own and resisted Aquino's authority until he was fired in November 1987. Primarily because of the immediately perceived need to stem further dissension within the ranks, Aquino pursued a policy, not of reform, but of promoting officers who were loyal to her to key commands—a tactic that Marcos also had practiced, which eventually resulted in undermining his support among junior officers. Most important, Aquino's policy of national reconciliation—strongly resisted by the armed forces—in turn only made the military suspicious of her real intentions toward the communists. Only after an attempted military coup on August 28, 1987, did Aquino appear to recognize the need to win the military's support if she was to remain in office. Yet, when the United States pushed the importance of military reform and formulating a counterinsurgency campaign, it was accused by Philippine leaders of trying to undermine Aquino.

The difficulty of formulating a supportive but constructive policy limited U.S. influence. The desire to make clear complete U.S. support for President Aquino in order to dissuade potential usurpers from attacking her, to dispel the resentment of U.S. support for the Marcos regime, and to encourage foreign investment placed major constraints on U.S. policymakers. The "cobwebs of lingering doubt" about U.S. support for Aquino, as noted by her vice president Salvador Laurel in early 1986, were exploited by the Philippine government whenever the United States attempted to press issues such as economic and military reform.

U.S. influence was further limited by U.S. domestic budgetary constraints. Aid could not be increased to the levels necessary for the Philippine government to buy off the elites whose power base would be undermined if the government undertook the essential social reforms necessary to defeat the communist insurgency. But even more aid would not necessarily guarantee more effective programs if the government itself was not committed to reform. Indeed, Aquino's international stature had gained the Philippines major new commitments of bilateral and multilateral aid in her first two years in office, but efforts to use these funds were stymied by internal political disputes and her cabinet's inexperience at governing. By the end of 1987, aid amounting to $1.9 billion had backed up in the donor pipeline, leading many major donors to reduce their aid commitments for subsequent years.

In truth, many of the problems faced by the Aquino government were the creation of Ferdinand Marcos, but it would be false to blame Marcos for all the problems of the Philippines. With his absence, for example, communist rebels did not immediately come down from the hills, nor was corruption instantaneously eliminated from the society, nor did the military become at once professional and apolitical. The Marcos years had exacerbated existing social ills in the Philippines, but, despite his exile, the oligarchy-dominated political and economic system remained.

These were problems long apparent to U.S. observers of the Philippines. Yet, U.S. policy did little to anticipate their impact on Philippine stability. Nor did U.S. policymakers attempt to assess the consequences of these enduring problems on the stability of a successor government. Indeed, even after Marcos was replaced by Aquino, U.S. policymakers still did not reassess their economic and security aid programs in light of Philippine problems to make them more effective. Two years after Aquino came to power, the U.S. Agency for International Development mission in Manila was still supporting essentially the same types of projects it had supported during the Marcos years, with little thought given to how these projects contributed to Philippine development. Rather than being prepared for change once Marcos was gone, U.S. policymakers continued along the lines previously prescribed, and policy continued to be reactive. No thought was given to long-range planning with the objective of sustaining Philippine democracy. Policy instead focused, as it had in the past, on demonstrating strong support for the government in power.

The Reagan administration's need to show its support for Aquino was understandable, given the considerable doubts raised about President Reagan's personal feelings toward the new Philippine leader. But, in so doing, the United States again fell into the traditional trap of tying U.S. policy to the legitimacy of a particular leader rather than to the people of the country. What is ironic is that this approach—as it restricted the flexibility of U.S. policy—suited the Aquino government just as well as it had suited the Marcos regime. Secretary of State George Shultz aggravated these constraints by stating publicly that the United States would have preferred to give the Aquino government more financial aid but was unable to do so because of domestic budgetary cutbacks. In response, the Aquino government demanded more demonstrations of U.S. personal support for Aquino. Thus, even as the Aquino government initiated policies that the United States privately raised doubts about—for example, support for anticommunist vigilante groups, demands for more helicopters to fight the insurgency, or failure to proceed with a land reform program—the United States, as in the past, was not in a position to criticize openly or to influence privately the direction of internal Philippine affairs.

Like the government under Marcos, the Aquino government had maneuvered the United States into a position in which U.S. policy was hostage to U.S. security interests. In 1988, negotiations were reopened over the amount of aid the United States would provide for access to military facilities over the three-year period remaining in the 1947 Military Bases Agreement. Soon, as both Filipinos and Americans well recognized, general negotiations would begin over renewal of the MBA due to expire in 1991. U.S. policymakers felt constrained to keep any disagreement with the Aquino government as low-key as possible. Philippine policymakers recognized this constraint and exploited it almost as soon as the base negotiations began. By the fall of 1988, talks were briefly stalemated once again over the issue of money, with the Philippines requesting more than twice the amount the United States was willing to offer. The final agreement resulted in $481 million per year in economic and military assistance for the two years remaining in the MBA, which was substantially less than the over $1 billion the Philippine government was requesting. But the protracted and often bitter negotiations also impeded progress on other issues, as rising nationalist sentiment in the Philippines became hostile to any sign of U.S. intervention. These issues included economic reforms and a deteriorating human-rights situation, as vigilante groups supported by the Philippine military carried out their own private war against the peasants. Thus, during a period of difficult democratic transition, U.S. influence was ironically at its lowest point, perhaps, in the history of the U.S.-Philippine special relationship, with the future of Philippine democracy in doubt.

☐ 16

Nicaragua

Peter Kornbluh

For over 130 years, U.S. policymakers have considered Nicaragua a test case of their power to dictate events in Central America and beyond. The long and tragic legacy of U.S. intervention in Nicaraguan affairs began in 1856 when a soldier of fortune named William Walker overthrew the Nicaraguan government, elected himself president, and sought to transform Nicaragua into a slave state. This legacy continues in 1989 after eight years of the Reagan administration's multifaceted low-intensity warfare strategy to sponsor a counterrevolution against the Sandinista government.

Over the decades, the instruments of intervention have evolved from sending the U.S. Marines to sending the CIA. But the underlying foreign policy premises of such actions remain remarkably constant. Presidents from Theodore Roosevelt to Ronald Reagan have shared a hegemonic presumption about the role of the United States in the Western Hemisphere—the belief that the United States has both the right and the might to control internal events in Latin America regardless of international law and national sovereignty. "We do control the destinies of Central America and we do so for the simple reason that the national interest absolutely dictates such a course," as Under Secretary of State Robert Olds summed up this attitude in a January 1927 memorandum on Nicaragua; "it is difficult to see how we can afford to be defeated."[1] As international and domestic realities have changed, however, this policy of permanent engagement has become increasingly costly and counterproductive to the national interests U.S. policymakers claim to defend. And nowhere is this more dramatically demonstrated than in the past and current history of U.S. intervention in Nicaragua.

■ THE ERA OF HEGEMONY

Although Nicaragua gained its independence from Spain in 1821, due to geography it remained an object of empire. Situated in the middle of the Central American isthmus, the small nation of lakes, rivers, and volcanos was one of two potential sites for an interoceanic canal (the other, of course, was Panama). Hoping to reap the lucrative strategic and economic rewards of controlling a transisthmus waterway, the United States engaged in intense commercial and military competition with Great Britain for influence and control in Nicaragua in the mid-1800s. By the turn of the century, Nicaragua had become the principal staging ground for gunboat diplomacy, with U.S. Marines storming the shores in 1894, 1896, 1898, and 1910, occupying the country almost continuously between 1912 and 1933. U.S. officials handpicked Nicaragua's presidents, drafted electoral laws, trained the police, and authorized the national budget; and U.S. business interests—including lumber, mining, coffee, banana, shipping, and banking corporations—established virtually total domination over the Nicaraguan economy.

Pervasive U.S. control over all aspects of Nicaraguan society constituted nothing less than a U.S. version of colonialism. By 1927, as the noted columnist Walter Lippmann observed, it was clear that Nicaragua was "not an independent republic, that its government is the creature of the State Department, [and] that management of its finances and the direction of its domestic and foreign affairs are determined not in Nicaragua but on Wall Street."[2]

The national humiliation of total U.S. dominion over Nicaragua's affairs gave rise to what historians have called the United States' "first Vietnam"—a bloody five-year counterinsurgency war against the nationalist forces of Augusto Sandino. A diminutive-looking man who spent his early adulthood wandering through Central America, Sandino emerged from obscurity in the spring of 1927 when U.S. Marines once again intervened to impose political order in Nicaragua. Believing that bullets were the only defense of Nicaragua's sovereignty, Sandino and his motley army of miners and peasants vowed to take up arms until U.S. military forces withdrew from Nicaraguan territory. Although U.S. officials denounced him as a "common outlaw" and a "bandit," the *Washington Post* described Sandino as a "crude Bolivar of the Nicaraguan hills." His guerrilla campaign represented the first significant challenge to the exercise of U.S. hegemony in the Western Hemisphere.[3]

Between 1927 and 1933, the United States fought a running war of attrition with the first Sandinistas. At the height of the intervention, over 5,000 U.S. Marines were deployed in Nicaragua—a considerable show of force in an era when one U.S. warship on the horizon usually was sufficient to obtain Washington's foreign policy objectives in Central America and the Caribbean. The fighting was fierce. During the first year of combat with Sandino and his rag-tag Army for the Defense of Nicaraguan National Sovereignty, the U.S. Navy reported eighty-five confrontations and sixty-six troop casualties. "The

Naval forces ashore have encountered the most serious sustained guerrilla warfare that Central America records," the secretary of the navy reported to Congress in February 1928.[4]

Indeed, even in the heyday of gunboat diplomacy, the limits and costs of U.S. intervention were apparent. The U.S. Marines, with vastly superior firepower and numbers, found themselves confronting an enigmatic enemy whom they could neither physically eliminate nor politically contain. The continued military occupation and the inability of U.S. troops to quell Sandino's rebellion fostered extensive U.S. public dissent over the wisdom of the policy and sharp criticism from abroad about Washington's credibility. "We are being charged from one corner of the world to another with being the great threat to the peace . . . to have embarked upon an imperialistic program," U.S. Representative George Huddleston argued on behalf of a congressional resolution to withdraw the U.S. Marines from Nicaragua.[5] In a confidential memorandum to the U.S. military commander in Managua in March 1928, Secretary of State Frank Kellogg complained that "there is a great deal of criticism in the country about the way in which these operations are being dragged out, constant sacrifice of American lives, and without any concrete results. So far as anyone here can see what is now taking place can and will go on indefinitely."[6]

Unable to defeat Sandino, and under intense public pressure, President Herbert F. Hoover withdrew the marines in 1933. Before they departed, however, the United States implemented a policy of "Nicaraguanization"—creating and training a National Guard through which the United States would maintain preeminence in Nicaraguan affairs. Ostensibly, the Guardia was meant to be a nonpartisan police force that could enforce democratic stability and counter the expanding influence of Sandino. To be its commander, U.S. officials handpicked Anastacio Somoza, an English-speaking former latrine inspector. "I look upon him as the best man in the country for the position," U.S. diplomat Matthew Hanna stated in October 1932. "I know of no one who will labor as intelligently and conscientiously to maintain the non-partisan character of the Guardia."[7]

Instead of remaining nonpartisan, however, the National Guard became Somoza's vehicle to dictatorial rule. On his orders, guardsmen assassinated Sandino in February 1934, eliminating the only man who had the military or political capacity to challenge Somoza's accession to power. In 1936, he overthrew President Juan Sacasa, the long-standing leader of Nicaragua's Liberal party (and Somoza's uncle by marriage), and had himself installed in the presidency.

From the start, the corrupt nature of the regime the United States had created was well known in Washington. Even before the marines departed, reports of widespread opposition to the Guardia's repression began to filter back to the State Department. Intelligence assessments of Somoza's rule were sharply worded. In one "strictly confidential" cable dated December 2, 1939, the U.S. Chargé Laverne Baldwin reported that Somoza's was a "purely military dictatorship" that was "ridden from top to bottom with graft, wasting the substance of a State which needs every centavo in the face of existing world conditions and the ever present extreme poverty of its lowest classes."[8] Somoza's excessive greed and his regime's endemic corruption had serious policy ramifications for the United States, Baldwin concluded:

> It seems that there are two possibilities for future action by the United States in the face of this trend of corruption which, if continued, must lead to the man's hanging himself by a noose placed by his own hands. We might let the man fall by lack of support from us. Such course . . . would necessarily mean an upheaval in the country and a period of revolutionary destruction. Presumably no serious thought will therefore be given it.

An alternative policy option, Baldwin wrote, would be "to assist the existing administration financially."[9]

With an extraordinary degree of prescience, Baldwin urged the administration of President Franklin D. Roosevelt to develop a long-range policy toward Nicaragua, noting that continuation of the military state and corruption under Somoza would "inevitably create strong and growing resistance to and criticism of the Government and its officers." Depending on what steps the United States took, Baldwin predicted "armed outbreaks" against Somoza's rule and noted that, because of Somoza's close ties to Washington, the government that succeeded him would prove much less hospitable to U.S. interests.[10]

■ CARTER AND NICARAGUA: CONTAINING THE REVOLUTION

Four decades later, the administration of President Jimmy Carter confronted the Sandinista revolution. In the interim, Nicaragua had become the most important anticommunist client state in the Central American/Caribbean region, providing a staging ground for U.S. intervention in Guatemala (1954) and Cuba (1961). In return for his cooperation, one U.S. administration after another had looked the other way as Somoza created a family dynasty, passing power first to his oldest son, Luis, in 1959, and then to Anastacio, Jr., in 1967. U.S. military and economic assistance to Nicaragua increased steadily between 1945 and 1975, even as Somoza's sons refined and expanded the repression and corruption that had characterized their father's rule. The elder Somoza's cruel joke—"Bucks for my friends, bullets for my enemies"—epitomized the nature of the dictatorship.[11] By 1978, when a spontaneous uprising led by the Frente Sandinista de Liberación Nacional (FSLN—Sandinista National Liberation Front) began, the Somoza regime was internationally renowned, and repudiated, for its boundless greed and vicious human-rights violations.

Forty years of Somoza family rule left Nicaragua a corrupt, impoverished, and divided state. The dynasty's foundation of power finally began to crumble in the aftermath of a devastating earthquake that destroyed much of Managua in

December 1972. For Nicaragua it was a disaster of major socioeconomic consequences; for Somoza it was a grand opportunity for self-aggrandizement. Taking advantage of his compatriots' suffering, he channeled millions of dollars of international relief assistance into his own coffers and those of his cronies. His greed not only undermined Nicaragua's economic redevelopment, it alienated the entrepreneurial and propertied classes, leaving the Somoza regime politically isolated and wholly reliant on National Guard force to stay in power. Somoza's escalating repression, however, only served to radicalize the situation, empowering the opposition to organize and unify and contributing to the growing popularity of the Sandinista guerrilla movement. In 1979, the broad dissatisfaction with Somoza's rule gave way to the revolutionary insurrection that Baldwin had foreseen almost forty years before.[12]

Although Jimmy Carter takes credit for a reformist interlude in U.S. interventionist history, his policy toward the Nicaraguan insurrection was based on the same presumptions of hegemony that dominated the approaches of his predecessors. Uncontrolled change in Central America remained anathema to U.S. officials wedded to the notion that Washington had a historical imperative to dictate events in its traditional sphere of influence. In language reminiscent of Under Secretary of State Robert Olds's imperial justification for U.S. intervention in 1927, Carter's NSC adviser, Zbigniew Brzezinski, argued that what was at stake in 1979 was "not just the formula for Nicaragua but a more basic matter, namely whether in the wake of our own decision not to intervene in Latin America politics, there will not develop a vacuum, which would be filled by Castro and others." "In other words," Brzezinski told Carter, "we have to demonstrate that we are still the decisive force in determining the political outcomes in Central America and that we will not permit others to intervene."[13]

The Carter administration's policy objectives during the Nicaraguan revolution were unambiguous: to prevent a Sandinista victory. Trapped by its own rhetoric on human rights and Somoza's unconcealed brutality, unilaterally sending the marines was not an option for the White House. Nevertheless, U.S. policymakers exercised every conceivable option of persuasion, short of brute force, to manipulate the course of Nicaragua's future.

Through diplomatic coercion, Washington applied its traditional influence over the Nicaraguan government. Having placed the first Somoza in power in 1933, in June of 1979 the United States informed his son that it was time to go. Carter officials recognized that Somoza had become a catalyst for radicalization and instability; the sooner he left, they reasoned, the easier it would be to block the ascendency of "radical" forces led by the heirs of Sandino—the FSLN—to power. Thus, on June 28, U.S. Ambassador Lawrence Pezzullo cabled Washington that he had met with Somoza and "suggested that we design a scenario for his resignation."[14]

The Carter administration's scenario for a transition of power in Nicaragua called for creating a provisional government of moderates that excluded the FSLN and preserving the National Guard, as Assistant Secretary of State Viron

Vaky instructed Pezzullo "to avoid leaving the FSLN as the only organized military force."[15] Although the administration ruled out unilateral intervention to implement this strategy, it considered a U.S.-led multilateral military force to be a policy option. On June 15, Assistant Secretary of State Vaky sent a telex to all Latin American diplomatic posts stating that the United States wished "to explore selectively reactions and ideas regarding possible formation of an inter-American peace force to guarantee the transition process and facilitate pacification"—to halt the Sandinistas' push for power. U.S. embassies were told to inform their host governments that the United States feared the "potential for a Castroist takeover in Nicaragua" and sought a political solution involving the "preservation of existing institutions, *especially the National Guard*" (emphasis added).[16] Ten days later Secretary of State Cyrus Vance formally proposed this initiative to the Organization of American States. Representatives of the Latin American nations overwhelmingly rejected the initiative as a multilateral smokescreen for overt U.S. intervention.

During the final weeks of Somoza's rule, the Carter administration frantically attempted to alter the course of history in Nicaragua. The U.S. ambassador arranged for Somoza to step down, name an interim president who would call for a cease-fire, and appoint a new commander for the National Guard. The United States then delayed Somoza's departure, first allowing him to bomb civilian townships in order to halt the advance of FSLN troops and then using the date of his resignation as a bargaining chip to influence the membership of the transitional government selected by the Sandinistas.[17] In the end, however, these diplomatic schemes failed. On July 17, the day Somoza left for Miami, Florida, the National Guard disintegrated. Within forty-eight hours Washington's plan of succession collapsed, as Sandinista troops marched, unopposed, into Managua in triumph.

In the aftermath of the Carter administration's failure to deter the Sandinista's accession to power, U.S. officials shifted from a policy of hostility to cautious accommodation. Nevertheless, U.S. policymakers did not abandon hope of moderating the course of the new Nicaraguan government. "The real issue facing American foreign policy," Assistant Secretary of State Vaky stated, "is not how to preserve stability in the face of revolution, but how to create stability out of revolution."[18] Using the carrot of economic assistance, the White House advanced $15 million in emergency reconstruction aid to Nicaragua and pushed a $75-million assistance package through Congress. At the same time, however, President Carter authorized the CIA to covertly pass funds to anti-Sandinista labor, press, and political organizations—an operation resembling the CIA's destabilization campaign against the Chilean government of Salvador Allende a decade earlier.[19] Thus, when Ronald Reagan took office on January 20, 1981, he inherited a CIA covert operation against the Sandinistas already under way.

■ REAGAN AND NICARAGUA: LOW-INTENSITY WARFARE

The Reagan administration came into office predisposed to escalate U.S. intervention in Nicaragua. For the president and the conservative ideologues around him, Central America represented a symbol of Washington's loss of global preeminence in the aftermath of the Vietnam War. Yet, the new administration viewed Nicaragua more as a test of Reagan's campaign pledge to "project American power throughout the world" than as a serious threat to U.S. national security. Noting the long history of U.S. influence in Central America, former NSC adviser Robert McFarlane later explained to Congress that the failure to intervene in Nicaragua would have jeopardized Washington's ability to dictate events elsewhere in the Third World. "If we could not muster an effective counter to the Cuban-Sandinista strategy in our own backyard, it was far less likely that we could do so in the years ahead in more distant locations. *We had to win this one*" (emphasis added).[20]

But, even an administration as committed to the use of force as Reagan's faced strict parameters on its instruments of intervention. Unlike the earlier era of gunboat diplomacy, in the 1980s a U.S. president could not cavalierly dispatch the marines to Central America. The Vietnam syndrome—a widespread public reluctance to see U.S. troops once again engaged in a distant Third World conflict—constrained Reagan's national security managers as they plotted U.S. strategy in Nicaragua. Ultimately, U.S. officials turned to an emerging doctrine known as low-intensity conflict (LIC) for post-Vietnam intervention in the Third World in general and Nicaragua in particular. In fact, reversing the Nicaraguan revolution became a test case for the Reagan Doctrine of supporting anticommunist insurgencies in an effort to roll back pro-Soviet regimes around the globe.

In "Covert Action Proposal for Central America," dated February 27, 1981, one of the earliest documents concerning the Reagan administration's plans to undermine the Nicaraguan government, McFarlane presented the case for a multifront assault short of direct military intervention: "The key point to be made now is that while we must move promptly, we must assure that our political, economic, diplomatic, propaganda, military, and covert actions are well coordinated." This approach reflected a new reliance on the LIC doctrine, which, according to Pentagon manuals, called for the "synergistic application of comprehensive political, social, economic and psychological efforts."[21] By combining various methods of pressure short of overt military deployment, the United States could engage in what one LIC proponent called "total war at the grassroots level," without the domestic and international political backlash that a conventional war would provoke.[22]

In Nicaragua, this "total-war" strategy called for four main fronts: (1) a paramilitary war; (2) a campaign of economic destabilization; (3) military pyschological operations; and (4) a propaganda war directed not only at Nicaragua and Western allies, but also at the U.S. public.

☐ The Paramilitary War

The Reagan administration's low-intensity warfare strategy depended on the creation of a proxy force of exiles such as the CIA had used to overthrow the Arbenz government in Guatemala in 1954 and in its failed effort against Fidel Castro at the Bay of Pigs in 1961. Thus, in 1981 a new generation of CIA-backed counterrevolutionaries emerged. The CIA organized disparate bands of former Nicaraguan National Guard officers and disaffected civilians into one group—the Nicaraguan Democratic Force (FDN). Although the contras, as they came to be known, subsequently went through several organizational reincarnations—the United Nicaraguan Opposition (UNO) and the Nicaraguan Resistance (RN)—the FDN remained the core of the anti-Sandinista forces.

The Reagan administration initially depicted the contras as an "interdiction force" meant to halt arms allegedly flowing from Nicaragua to guerrilla insurgents in El Salvador. When that justification for CIA paramilitary operations became politically untenable, Reagan officials presented the contras to the public as freedom fighters deserving of U.S. support. Privately, however, the administration was well aware of the character of its surrogates. Robert Owen, a key NSC liaison with the FDN, reported to Lieutenant Colonel Oliver North in March 1986 that the contra leaders were "liars and greed and power motivated" and that "this war has become a business for them." Owen concluded that the contras "are not the people to rebuild a new Nicaragua."[23]

For those in the Reagan administration wishing to "bleed" the Sandinista regime, nevertheless, the contras were perceived as the perfect instrument for a policy of punishment, enabling the United States to directly undercut Nicaragua's fragile postrevolutionary economic and social reconstruction. What U.S. officials depicted as a campaign to harass and pressure the Sandinistas into halting their alleged export of revolution into neighboring El Salvador, in practice translated into vicious attacks on small villages, state-owned agricultural cooperatives, rural health clinics, bridges, electrical generators, and, finally, civilian noncombatants. Indeed, CIA training manuals explicitly advised the contras on how to "neutralize carefully selected and planned targets," such as court judges, magistrates, police, and state security officials.[24]

Even with these ongoing attacks, senior U.S. policymakers demanded ever more dramatic and devastating paramilitary operations. "What [more] can we do about the economy to make these bastards sweat?" CIA director Casey repeatedly inquired of his subordinates running the Nicaragua project.[25] In response, the CIA launched its own direct attacks on Nicaraguan installations. In September 1983, CIA commandos launched a series of sabotage raids on Nicaraguan port facilities. In October, CIA operatives set ablaze Nicaragua's largest oil storage facility, destroying 3.4 million gallons of fuel and forcing the city of Corinto to be evacuated for two days.

This campaign of economic sabotage culminated in the first three months of 1984, when CIA "Unilaterally Controlled Latino Assets" (UCLAs)—the CIA term for their Latin American contract agents—mined Nicaragua's major harbors. "Our intention is to severely disrupt the flow of shipping essential to Nicaraguan trade during the peak export period," NSC officials Oliver North and Constantine Menges informed Robert McFarlane in a top secret memorandum on the minings. To advance "our overall goal of applying stringent economic pressure," North and Menges recommended expanding this program to include sinking a Mexican oil tanker in Nicaragua's port. Asserting that "our objective is to further impair the already critical fuel capacity in Nicaragua" and to increase Nicaraguan dependency on the Eastern bloc, North and Menges concluded: "It is entirely likely that once a ship has been sunk no insurers will cover ships calling in Nicaraguan ports. This will effectively limit their seaborne trade to that which can be carried on Cuban, Soviet Bloc, or their own [ships]."[26]

Although this plan never came to fruition, the United States continued direct paramilitary assaults on Nicaragua even after Congress terminated direct and indirect assistance to the contras in October 1984. In December of that year, for example, Oliver North contracted with a former member of the British Special Air Service, David Walker, to engage in "special operations" inside Nicaragua. Walker's saboteurs undertook a number of covert demolition activities in and around Managua—among them the March 6, 1985, bombing of a military complex that included a hospital.[27] Such "special operations attacks against highly visible military targets in Nicaragua," Oliver North indicated in a March 20, 1985, memorandum to NSC adviser Robert McFarlane, were "timed to influence the vote" in Congress to restore CIA assistance to the contras.[28]

□ Economic Destabilization

CIA/contra attacks on economic targets inside Nicaragua complemented the Reagan administration's efforts to destabilize the Nicaraguan economy from abroad. Much as the administration of President Richard M. Nixon had done against the socialist government of Salvador Allende in Chile, the Reagan White House successfully employed economic aid and sanctions as tools of intervention.

Whereas the Carter administration had used bilateral assistance as a carrot, the Reagan administration used it as a stick. Within weeks of taking office, the president terminated all U.S. economic aid programs to Nicaragua. Trade was similarly curtailed. A 1983 top secret CIA National Intelligence Estimate noted that "Nicaragua remains highly dependent on trade with the United States."[29] In May of that year, the White House cut Nicaragua's quota of sugar exports to the

United States. Two years later, President Reagan invoked the International Emergency Economic Powers Act to declare a full trade embargo with Nicaragua.

By necessity, the administration's economic war policy against the Sandinistas had international dimensions. To isolate Nicaragua economically, the United States pressured its allies in Latin America and Western Europe to curtail their own trade and aid to the Sandinistas. In 1983, according to an NSC action plan, Secretary of State Shultz was mandated to "press Western European governments at the highest level to cease financial support for the Sandinistas."[30] Mexico, Nicaragua's most important trading partner in Latin America, came under a concerted U.S. campaign of pressure to cut off Nicaragua. In National Security Decision Directive 124 (NSDD 124), signed in February 1984, the president authorized U.S. agencies to "intensify [their] diplomatic efforts with the Mexican government to reduce its . . . economic and diplomatic support for the Nicaraguan government."[31]

Moreover, the administration took its economic destabilization campaign into the boardrooms of the multilateral financial institutions, particularly the World Bank and the Inter-American Development Bank. There, U.S. representatives worked behind the scenes to build voting blocs against loans to Nicaragua, orchestrate negative project evaluations, or, if all else failed, block Nicaraguan grants from coming before the executive boards for final approval. Although the Sandinista government received rave reviews from internal bank assessments of the development projects they completed, Nicaragua received no loans from the World Bank after 1982 and no loans from the Inter-American Development Bank after 1983.

□ Military Psychological Warfare

The third component of the Reagan administration's low-intensity war on Nicaragua was an unprecedented military buildup in Central America and continual joint U.S.-Honduran military war games in the region—part of an extensive psychological operation program to instill uncertainty in the Nicaraguan government about U.S. intentions. As one U.S. official noted, "One of the central purposes is to create fear of an invasion, to push very close to the border, deliberately, to set off all the alarms."[32] These operations also had an economic imperative. With government coffers already drained from the fight against the contras and the economic blockade, the constant threat of a direct U.S. military assault forced Nicaragua's leaders to divert personnel and resources from social programs into planning for the worst-case war scenario.

What LIC proponent Robert Kupperman called "the threat of force to achieve political objectives without the full-scale commitment of resources" proved an effective method of destabilizing the Sandinistas.[33] More than once, highly publicized U.S. military maneuvers with such names as Big Pine I and II, Grenadero 1, Ocean Venture, and Solid Shield provoked major war scares inside Nicaragua. Scores of citizens were sent home from work to dig air-raid shelters; thousands of Nicaraguans prepared for an invasion by taking militia training. In the meantime, economic production halted, cash crops went unharvested, and exports sat on docks. Without firing a shot, the Reagan administration managed to severely disrupt the normal political, economic, and social functions of an entire nation.

□ The Propaganda War

In the parlance of the Pentagon, these military psychological operations (psyops) against Nicaragua were called "perception management" programs. But the Reagan administration also conducted similar operations at home, against the U.S. public. This component of U.S. policy, known by the Orwellian term "public diplomacy," reflected the administration's understanding that the battle for the "hearts and minds" of the U.S. public was critical to its ability to wage even an unconventional war in Central America. "We continue to have serious difficulties with U.S. public and Congressional opinion which jeopardizes our ability to stay the course," one NSC Planning Group report on Central America noted as early as April 1982.[34]

The administration's obsession with shaping public opinion was manifested in President Reagan's January 1983 National Security Decision Directive 77 (NSDD 77), entitled "Management of Public Diplomacy Relative to National Security." NSDD 77 determined that "it is necessary to strengthen the organization, planning and coordination of the various aspects of public diplomacy of the United States Government."[35] This directive authorized the creation of a "public diplomacy" bureaucracy within the executive branch to facilitate propaganda on Central America. In a July 1, 1983, memorandum, NSC adviser William Clark advised other administration officials that "the President has underscored his concern that we must increase our efforts in the public diplomacy field to deepen the understanding of and support for our policies in Central America."[36] Clark authorized the creation of an Office of Public Diplomacy for Latin America and the Caribbean (S/LPD), to be housed in the State Department but run out of the NSC.

On the surface, the Office of Public Diplomacy operated as a ministry of information, producing and distributing vituperative anti-Sandinista and pro-contra White Papers, pamphlets, and briefing books for Congress, the press, and the public. Behind the scenes, however, the Office of Public Diplomacy conducted what one official called a "huge psychological operation, the kind the military conduct to influence the population in . . . enemy territory."[37] Indeed, the office drew on intelligence specialists for its staff, and the director of S/LPD, Ambassador Otto Reich, recruited psyops officials from the Department of Defense to assist the public diplomacy activities. "Current S/LPD projects of a priority nature require the expertise available from personnel of the 4th Psychological Operations Group, Fort Bragg, North Carolina," Reich wrote in a March 5, 1985, request to the Pentagon that resulted in the transfer of five military officials to Washington.[38]

The priority projects of the Office of Public Diplomacy included overt and covert propaganda, pressure on the media, and illegal lobbying tactics to manipulate public opinion against the Sandinista government and garner congressional votes for the contras. These operations went on until December 1987, when Congress closed the office pursuant to a General Accounting Office (GAO) investigation that revealed that the administration had engaged in "White Propaganda" operations—planting articles in the U.S. press. According to the GAO, the Office of Public Diplomacy "arranged for the publication of articles which purportedly had been prepared by, and reflected the views of, persons not associated with the government but which, in fact, had been prepared at the request of government officials and partially or wholly paid for with government funds." GAO investigators concluded that administration officials had "engaged in prohibited, covert propaganda activities designed to influence the media and the public to support the Administration's Latin American policies."[39]

The Reagan administration's public diplomacy operations played a significant role in achieving the president's preeminent foreign policy objective in 1986—restoration of official assistance to the contras. Whereas Congress had terminated monies for the contra program in October 1984, in August 1986 U.S. legislators approved $100 million in lethal and nonlethal assistance for the contras and lifted all restrictions concerning CIA and Department of Defense participation in the paramilitary war. The Office of Public Diplomacy "played a key role in setting out the parameters and defining the terms of the public discussion on Central America policy," Ambassador Reich noted in one May 1986 report to his superiors. "Despite the efforts of the formidable and well-established Soviet/Cuban/Nicaraguan propaganda apparatus, the achievements of U.S. public diplomacy are clearly visible."[40]

Indeed, through the end of 1986, the architects of the administration's Nicaragua policy—CIA director William Casey, Robert McFarlane, John Poindexter, Oliver North, and Elliott Abrams—could count a number of successes. The public diplomacy apparatus had succeeded politically in "gluing black hats on the Sandinistas and the White Hats on the contras," as one secret NSC memorandum described the propaganda objective.[41] The contras had been secretly supplied for more than two years with arms and ammunition through a network of private intermediaries run out of the White House, enabling them to sustain their war of attrition until the U.S. Congress restored official funding. Moreover, that war had taken a heavy toll on human life and economic development in Nicaragua. In legal briefs filed at the International Court of Justice, the Sandinista government counted 2,961 military and 3,799 civilian deaths and over 10,900 persons wounded in the seven years of war. Material damage to property, according to Nicaraguan estimates, totaled $275,400,000, with production losses from contra and CIA sabotage valued at $1,280,700,000. Finally,

Nicaraguan economists estimated losses to the gross domestic product (GDP) from contra violence, the mining of the harbors, and the trade embargo at $2,546,400,000, while asserting that the dire social consequences of the damage caused to Nicaragua's development potential "cannot be valued technically in monetary terms."[42]

■ IRAN-CONTRA AND THE PRICE OF INTERVENTION

If a cargo plane from the NSC's illicit contra enterprise had not been shot down over southern Nicaragua on October 5, 1986, and a Lebanese journal had not published a month later an account of Robert McFarlane's secret trip to Iran, the Reagan administration might have successfully carried its policy of punishment against the Sandinistas to fruition. But former Attorney General Edwin Meese's November 25, 1986, admission that Reagan administration officials had diverted funds from covert arms sales to Iran to the covert war in Nicaragua intervened in U.S. politics. The revelations created what *Newsweek* called "instantly the worst scandal" in the Reagan presidency, paralyzing the executive branch, and prompting a massive congressional inquiry into the covert policies of the national security state.[43]

The investigations of the House and Senate Select Committees on the Iran-contra operations revealed the intricate, and often ugly, history of how the policy of rollback in Nicaragua was made and implemented. Thousands of pages of top secret NSC, CIA, Pentagon, and State Department memoranda released by the committees detailed U.S. blackmail of Central American officials to support U.S. intervention in Nicaragua, diplomatic efforts to sabotage the Contadora peace process, and Washington's orchestration of almost every facet of the contras' political and military operations.

Even more important, the Iran-contra investigations revealed the extent to which the U.S. capacity to intervene in a small Third World nation like Nicaragua had been unleashed upon the very democratic institutions of the United States that such policies are ostensibly designed to protect. U.S. national security managers perceived Congress and the American people much the same way as they viewed the Sandinistas—as targets to be manipulated and coerced. The Iran-contra affair "was characterized by pervasive dishonesty and inordinate secrecy" as well as "a disdain for the law" that challenged the basic checks and balances of the U.S. Constitution, the Select Committees concluded in their final report.[44] The ability to circumvent legislative accountability and run "off-the-shelf," independently financed covert operations, represented a bald attempt to undermine the United States' very system of governance. "That," according to the *Report of the Congressional Committees Investigating the Iran-Contra Affair,* "is the path to dictatorship."[45]

In essence, the Iran-contra scandal represented the ultimate price to be paid for U.S. intervention in Nicaragua. By the last year of the administration, U.S. influence in the region was at an all-time low; U.S. credibility had collapsed.[46] Moreover, it was self-evident that the administration's policy of rolling back Third World revolutions in the name of democracy had become subversive to the very ends it was meant to serve. The crisis highlighted the damage done to U.S. national interests and the U.S. political system by the Reagan administration's effort to reimpose an imperial design on a postimperial world.

The lessons of the scandal appeared obvious: Even a low-intensity war in Nicaragua carried high costs for U.S. policy objectives abroad and the sanctity of U.S. democracy at home. Nevertheless, the administration refused to explore an alternative foreign policy of employing the force of example, rather than the example of force, in U.S. relations with Nicaragua. Instead, in the waning months of his tenure, Reagan continued on his interventionist course in Central America. U.S. officials sought to undermine the prestige of Costa Rican president and 1987 Nobel Prize winner, Oscar Arias, whose regional peace plan threatened to undermine the administration's efforts to sustain the war.[47] In June 1988, the State Department once again sought to pressure the Central American nations into an alliance against Nicaragua—this time without success.[48] And the administration continued to press Congress for more lethal and nonlethal assistance to the contras.

In so doing, U.S. policymakers failed to address the underlying cause of the Iran-contra scandal: the historical presumption that the United States may unilaterally impose its will on the smaller countries around the globe. Indeed, the origins of the administration's self-defeating policy in Nicaragua derive directly from the imperial legacy of U.S. intervention in the Third World. The same arrogance of power responsible for gunboat diplomacy against Sandino earlier in the century served as the foundation for the abuses of power that produced the Iran-contra operations.

Set in its historical context, the scandal produced one inescapable conclusion: As long as the United States fails to come to grips with the necessity of coexisting in a world of increasing diversity, there will always be men like William Casey and Oliver North and institutions like the NSC and CIA—ready to murder, lie, and bribe in the name of the American way. Until U.S. policymakers understand that revolutions in countries like Nicaragua represent a test, not of Washington's ability to successfully intervene abroad, but of the United States' ability to coexist with its smaller neighbors, the specter of U.S. intervention will continue to haunt the American people, in whose name such ill-advised policies are conducted.

17

Grenada

Tony Thorndike

"Grenada, we were told, was a friendly island paradise for tourism. Well it wasn't. It was a Soviet-Cuban colony being readied as a major military bastion to export terror and undermine democracy. We got there just in time."[1] Such was President Ronald Reagan's justification for what he termed the "rescue mission," the rapidly organized and executed U.S.-led intervention in Grenada on October 25, 1983, to overthrow the deeply unpopular revolutionary military government of General Hudson Austin. Hudson had seized power six days earlier, after the execution by army firing squad of the charismatic and widely popular Prime Minister Maurice Bishop, three cabinet ministers (including Education Minister Jacqueline Creft, who was carrying Bishop's unborn child), two trade-union leaders, and some other civilians who had accidentally been in the wrong place. In addition, some sixty others, mainly young people, had been shot down by People's Revolutionary Army (PRA) soldiers. Altogether it was a bloody and violent climax to an internal struggle within the ruling left-wing New Jewel Movement (NJM), which had led a popular insurrection on March 13, 1979, against the corrupt and authoritarian rule of Sir Eric Gairy. As the NJM imploded in an orgy of self-destruction, it was not surprising that the 90,000 Grenadians were shocked and traumatized.

Reagan, however, was off target in his justification for intervention, for evidence of a "Soviet-Cuban military colony" was sparse indeed. He should have argued the moral case for the intervention—invasion, to those who disagreed—as evidenced by the widespread welcome given the U.S. Marines and the 82nd Airborne combat troops. After the bloodshed committed by Austin's forces and an unprecedented ninety-six-hour curfew—a dreadful experience for the majority of the population whose homes had few amenities and who depended on the land for a living—this welcome was not surprising. To socialists in the region and elsewhere, and to nationalists, this enthusiastic reception was highly embarrassing. There were questions, too, for international lawyers. The illegality of the action was beyond doubt: Grenada's sovereignty was violated; no U.S. citizens were held hostage or were otherwise in danger despite repeated allegations to the contrary; and there was no attempt at negotiation with the revolutionary military government that had usurped power. But law and morality do not always coincide, and the variance is exploitable. As a U.S. military officer put it, the president "in his decision to use force in Grenada balanced morality, legality and reality [and] secured the real and moral high ground for America."[2] It is clear that the Grenada intervention will be a source of controversy for some time to come.

■ THE CARIBBEAN AS A U.S. LAKE

Up to the time of the March 1979 insurrection, few Americans had heard of Grenada, and their numbers had not greatly increased by the time of the revolution's collapse. Part of the Commonwealth Windward Islands, Grenada's historical relationship was with Britain. Britain's first colonial empire was established in the Caribbean between 1624 and 1815, and its West Indian territories were prized possessions in the era of high sugar prices and slavery. Although British imperial attention later turned to India and then Africa as the economic and political worth of the British Caribbean waned, there remained close trading and constitutional links between the mostly small territories and London. U.S. interest in Grenada must, therefore, be seen as part and parcel of a developing and ultimately extensive U.S. concern with the entire Caribbean.

Although the United States willingly acknowledged Britain's traditional role and did not interfere with British colonial policy in the region, Britain had in truth long conceded to the U.S. position in the Caribbean. As early as 1850, agreement—the Clayton-Bulmer Treaty—was reached between Britain and the United States restricting the former's influence in Central America. In 1895, British warships withdrew in favor of the U.S. Navy in an incident off the Essequibo coast, a disputed area claimed by both Venezuela and what was then British Guiana. The implicit understanding was cemented in the Destroyers for Bases deal in 1940 when, in return for fifty old but desperately needed warships, Britain granted leases on several of its islands and territories for U.S. Air Force bases. After World War II, many of these became international gateways through which ever-greater numbers of U.S. tourists flowed. U.S. investment, particularly in oil and bauxite, also became predominant. The Grenada intervention and the subsequent U.S.-sponsored militarization of the Eastern Caribbean marked the finale of a historical process.

This process was driven by a geopolitical logic—that of the unity of the Caribbean Basin, the islands as well as the Central American rimland. This concept of a basin was not formulated until the Reagan era. Until then, not only were Central American and Caribbean issues handled separately by Washington—an acknowledgement of their different historical experiences and social, ethnic, and political environments—but also the territories with which France and the Netherlands had historical and constitutional links were, like their British counterparts, of intermittent and only indirect interest to the United States. The new cartographic definition of the region as a whole gave final expression to what had become a political reality, the vision of the Caribbean Basin as a "U.S. lake," where U.S. influence was, and would remain, predominant, despite the glaring exception of Cuba and an unenthusiastic acknowledgment of the status of the French *départements* of Guadeloupe, Guyane, and Martinique as integral parts of metropolitan France. Expressed colloquially, the Caribbean was the U.S. backyard.

As the basin concept made clear, the central U.S. concern in the region had long been, and remains, strategic. Of all U.S. borders, the southern is perceived as the most vulnerable. This perception has provided U.S. strategic decisionmakers with a luxuriant array of geopolitical theories, foremost being the notion of "stepping-stones"—that each island offers a potential beachhead for projecting power, presumably hostile, toward the United States. Rich in myth, this perception is backed by an impressive historical pedigree that reinforces both official and popular apprehensions and prejudices. The Monroe Doctrine of 1823 set the scene and was complemented in 1904 by President Theodore Roosevelt's infamous corollary. The Roosevelt Corollary permitted and rationalized direct military intervention in a number of Caribbean and Central American states until its repeal in 1934, but U.S. pressure in economic and commercial terms continued to be exerted effectively when deemed necessary.

There was also the direct experience of war. Between 1940 and 1944, the Caribbean and its approaches became the focus of considerable Nazi submarine activity, which undoubtedly threatened U.S. lifelines. The U.S. Air Force bases on the British islands were critical in resisting German U-boats. Thereafter, the Cuban Revolution of 1959 and the searing memory of the 1962 missile crisis ensured that the strategic importance of the Caribbean would remain high on any administration's agenda. Neither could the Cuba factor be neutralized or even removed, for within the agreement between President John F. Kennedy and Soviet First Secretary Nikita Khrushchev was a U.S. assurance that the United States would not militarily invade Cuba as long as the island was not used by the Soviet Union as a forward operational military base. The agreement stated that the number and type of Soviet forces would be strictly limited. The loss of Cuba had to be accepted, but there would never be a repetition, as the U.S. intervention in the Dominican Republic in 1965 to oust the leftist government of Juan Bosch sought to demonstrate. Thereafter, and until Grenada, indirect methods of economic destabilization were favored, such as those directed at Michael Manley's democratic socialist but pro-Cuban regime in Jamaica between 1974 and 1980.

The aim to stabilize the Caribbean Basin in a pro-U.S. equilibrium was further justified by the region's role in U.S. commerce. Nearly a quarter of U.S. oil imports either originate in, or pass through, the area, and it is the most important source to the United States of bauxite and alumina. Caribbean sea-lanes carry traffic to and from the Panama Canal, and 37 percent of U.S. waterborne commerce is handled by Gulf of Mexico ports. Illicit narcotics shipments from Latin America transit the area, and the region is an important drug producer in its own right. Finally, the Caribbean countries are major tourist destinations and, together with Mexico and Central America, are the source of massive, often illegal, immigration.

Private U.S. business interest in the region is questionable, however, as adverse trading conditions since the mid-1970s have led to considerable divestment and capital flight by U.S. corporations. Although this has had a disruptive effect on the region's vulnerable economies, there has been no widespread public reaction, largely because of a broad readiness among Caribbean peoples and their generally conservative governments to maintain good relations with the United States. One might expect that poor, dependent states adjacent to a superpower would harbor deep resentments and embrace highly nationalistic policies. But, to the contrary, there is a great deal of Caribbean support for the United States for a wide variety of reasons—material, political, historical, cultural, social, and ideological. Those Caribbean states that have mounted challenges—foremost, Cuba—are as much exceptions to the rule as the anticapitalist and antiimperialist pressure groups in the region are firmly in the minority.

In sum, multifaceted U.S. interests in the Caribbean endow the area with a psychological significance for Americans unequaled anywhere else beyond U.S. shores. The region's sensitivity to the popular American psyche is such that any erosion of U.S. prestige within the Caribbean Basin would be perceived as tantamount to failure and even as undermining its position in the world.

■ REVOLUTION AND THE NEW JEWEL MOVEMENT

Grenada may be described as a small and poorly developed country with an essentially conservative society, where social values and political institutions inherited from nearly two centuries of British colonialism were accepted virtually without question. The experience of slavery largely supplanted indigenous African culture with the culture of Western Europe, and this was gradually reinforced with the culture of North America through personal contact, travel, tourism, and the media. Emancipation from slavery in 1834 and the collapse in world sugar prices saw the near demise of the country's plantation system and the development of peasant farming.

The New Jewel Movement was formed in 1973 out of a number of small radical groups, both urban and rural. Headed by lawyer Maurice Bishop, it consisted largely of young professionals who had returned from overseas study, where they had been politicized by Vietnam protests, socialism, and "black power" philosophy. There was also a Rastafarian element that stressed self-sufficiency. Yet the Grenadian environment was not propitious for revolution. Despite the precarious existence of many on the island, land title had enormous symbolic importance, representing independence, freedom, and status. Imported values and religious sentiments were deeply imbedded. Trade unions existed not to promote socialism—the capitalist ethic was embraced at all levels of society—but to improve the worker's lot within the existing system. Structural inequalities, informal class and race barriers, and a variety of injustices were rarely addressed, but Grenada was not unique in the British Caribbean in that respect.

The reason why the NJM grew and eventually was able to seize and retain power in 1979 was that, unlike the other English-speaking territories, Grenada had spawned a corrupt dictatorship under Sir Eric Gairy. Once a very popular trade-union leader and a mystic versed in the occult, Gairy had taken the island by political storm in 1951 after leading a highly successful strike. Soon the darling of the peasantry and of the working classes in general, he went on to become premier (although deposed for a period by the British for alleged corruption and "squandermania") and, on independence in February 1974, Grenada's first prime minister. Opponents were victimized or suffered violence at the hands of "police aides"—variously the "Mongoose Gang" and the "Night Ambush Squad." NJM activists were prime targets.

The NJM took an active role in the widespread demonstrations that accompanied independence (Bishop's father Rupert was killed by the police aides) and gained working-class recruits. It headed an alliance of opposition parties in the 1976 election and with them won six seats (out of fifteen), enabling Bishop to become leader of the opposition. The NJM had by then privately resolved to be Marxist-Leninist and an elite party based on Leninist principles; it also had been joined by former university lecturer Bernard Coard, an uncompromising apostle of scientific socialism. Having developed a clandestine armed wing, the nucleus of the PRA, the NJM found its opportunity to seize power when Gairy left for the United Nations to propose the establishment of an international agency to investigate extraterrestrial phenomena. To general acclaim, the People's Revolutionary Government (PRG) was established after a nearly bloodless insurrection spearheaded by the PRA.

The NJM dominated the PRG and became progressively more elitist and restricted in membership. In late 1979, it modeled its structure on that of the Communist party of the Soviet Union,[3] developing various party-directed mass organizations as its link with the masses and as a means of popular mobilization and education. This was supplemented by a form of "people's power." Under the name of "participatory democracy," this largely consisted of meetings at the local village level—the zonal councils—to discuss local issues (the councils had no real power) and infrequent nationwide meetings of delegates from the councils and the mass organizations (especially the National Women's Organization and the National Youth Organization) to discuss and approve specific policy, most notably the annual budget. As the country's constitution had been suspended, a series of "People's Laws" was promulgated and often announced by Bishop at rallies. Elections were postponed indefinitely pending agreement on a new constitution incorporating socialist principles and "people's power," with the NJM firmly in the vanguard. The inherent contradictions of "people's power" and a vanguard Leninist party were to be firmly resolved in favor of the latter.

The confidence of the NJM, boosted by the ease at which power was seized and by clear public support—especially for the highly charismatic Bishop—doubtless affected dealings with the United States. The revolutionary regime was convinced that economic dependency was the root cause of Caribbean underdevelopment and that Caribbean peoples were slaves to a colonial mentality that incorporated subservience and deference to bourgeois capitalist values. Grenada had the legal and inalienable right as an independent state to conduct a foreign policy based on "principled positions," which had at their core the struggle against injustice, dependency, and imperialist superpower hegemony. It was argued that solidarity with "progressive" Third World states, especially through the Non-Aligned Movement (NAM), would create a security shield behind which the U.S. colossus could be challenged. But this shield had to be backed up by militarization and firm alliances with states the PRG saw as sharing its principles—namely, the Soviet bloc and, most particularly, Cuba—to ensure material as well as moral assistance.

Although there had been contacts between the NJM and Cuban leadership before the March 1979 insurrection, they were not significant. As soon as power was secured, however, the new government assiduously wooed Cuba. Cuba proved willing to respond. Anxious to bypass the continuing U.S. economic embargo and the ever-constant threat to its security, Castro saw in Grenada an opportunity to show the world what Cuban aid could do. An added advantage to Grenada was that Castro was to assume the chair of the NAM at the forthcoming September 1979 summit in Havana. When Castro took the highly unpopular stand within the NAM of support for the 1979 Soviet invasion of Afghanistan, Grenada became an even more important ally—and showcase for what Cuban aid could accomplish.

Aware from the start of the PRG's wish to develop relations with Cuba and suspecting (rightly) that Cuban arms had been sent to supplement those dispatched by Guyana, the administration of President Jimmy Carter sent a warning through Ambassador Frank Ortiz that the United States would "view with displeasure any tendency on the part of Grenada to develop closer ties with Cuba."[4] A small amount ($5,000) of aid was offered, the limit available from funds under direct ambassadorial control. Although some controversy remains as to the degree of clumsiness on Ortiz's part, the Carter administration appeared neither to want a confrontation nor to deny further consideration of assistance to the PRG, at least during the course of the first year of the regime. To that extent, the PRG was fortunate, for the Carter administration was the first in

U.S. history to focus upon the Caribbean in terms of economic development and the promotion of human rights through democracy rather than on the basis of a perceived security threat. Underpinned by a variety of bilateral aid and regional development initiatives, the emphasis on human rights, democracy, and development rested upon the premise that security from external aggression was assured by the hemispheric collective security provisions of the OAS, whereas internal stability would be promoted by development programs aimed at challenging and tackling the political consequences of structural inequalities. In other words, "the United States could not guarantee a regime against political instability; all it could do was provide resources and suggest a strategy."[5]

Far from working this outlook to its advantage, the PRG leadership was determined as Castro had been over twenty years earlier to make clear its anger and resentment at the United States and its commitment to follow its own path. Bishop made this crystal clear:

> Sisters and brothers . . . we are a small country . . . we are a poor country, with a population of largely African descent . . . we are part of the exploited Third World . . . but [a] proud people who are fighting for democracy, dignity and self-respect based on real and independent economic development. . . . No country has the right to tell us what to do or how to run our country or who to be friendly with . . . we are not in anybody's backyard, and we are definitely not for sale.[6]

Unfortunately, this sentiment served only to add to a growing concern in Washington during 1980 that U.S. global interests were being undermined and that firm responses were needed. In the Caribbean, political stability appeared threatened by a rapid military buildup by the Sandinista government in Nicaragua and developing Cuban influence in Grenada, Jamaica, and Suriname, all taking place against a backdrop of economic decline.

Despite this concern, the Carter administration chose to treat Grenada as a regional rather than a global issue, preferring to follow the lead of Grenada's Commonwealth partners in their regional organization, the Caribbean Community (CARICOM). However, as PRG denunciations of the United States intensified and it became clear that Bishop would not call elections, despite earlier assurances, U.S.-Grenadian relations cooled. Washington's displeasure and concern for democracy was shown by an increase in aid to Grenada's Caribbean neighbors and diplomatic obstructions and delays directed toward the PRG.

■ THE REAGAN ADMINISTRATION'S "GET-TOUGH" POLICY

The Reagan administration, entering office after the United States had been humiliated in Iran and determined to counter national defeatism epitomized by the so-called Vietnam syndrome, was under no illusions about the need for a dynamic "get-tough" policy in the Caribbean Basin. The new president perceived his predecessor's policy—promotion of human rights and attempts at détente with Cuba—as alienating several of Washington's traditional allies. The benefits to be gained by this approach had been, in his view, far outweighed by the new assertion of Soviet and Cuban influence in Africa and Central America. In the Caribbean, it was clear that Cuba was the culprit behind insurrection. Policymakers feared a worst-case scenario in which "a chain reaction of leftist revolutions would turn the once subservient tropical basin into a rim of hostile Marxist states taking their cues from Castro's Cuba."[7]

In the single-minded pursuit of anticommunism, a firm Cuba containment policy became a clear priority. Convinced that Cuba was but a Soviet surrogate,[8] Reagan renamed the "backyard" the "frontyard," to make clear that the Caribbean was the new front line against world communism. It was the Caribbean where communism was to be rolled back, the central tenet of what was baptized the Reagan Doctrine. Moreover, there were clear advantages both domestically and internationally in stressing the region. As one observer noted,

> The Basin is an excellent low-risk place . . . because an anti-leftist campaign there is less likely to produce a serious confrontation with the U.S.S.R. than might be the case in, for example, the Middle East. This is attractive to Reagan not only from a tactical viewpoint, but also because it minimizes his vulnerability to charges that he is irresponsibly "shooting from the hip," thus putting him in a good position to neutralize his critics and to mobilize public support.[9]

The Reagan administration's ideological aversion to the left in general and to Castro in particular, coupled with the NJM's revolutionary anti-U.S. rhetoric and fervent support of Cuba, ensured that a fog of mutual incomprehensibility enveloped U.S.-Grenadian relations from which neither could escape. Cuban aid to Grenada was generous, to the point at which it is doubtful the PRG could have survived without it, for most traditional sources of aid to the island had fallen away in protest over PRG policies or, in some cases, following U.S. pressure. U.S. concern centered on the huge $71-million international airport project at Point Salines, largely funded and constructed by Cuba. Although British and Finnish companies were also involved, and despite the fact that there were no installations suitable for military use, the United States claimed that the airport was to be a Cuban-Soviet base from which to strike Venezuela and northern South America.

The U.S. response to Grenada from 1980 took on a variety of forms. A new U.S. ambassador to the Eastern Caribbean pointedly refused to present her credentials in Grenada, and the nomination by Grenada of an ambassador to the United States was turned down, thus placing diplomatic recognition in doubt. U.S. economic aid programs were suspended, and pressure was exerted on allies to do likewise. The United States succeeded in ending International Monetary Fund and British aid, but it encountered more difficulties with the European Community and the regional Caribbean Development Bank (CDB). Whereas Brussels did respond to U.S. pressure by reducing potential aid, especially for the airport project,[10] a U.S. $4-million aid package for the subregional forum, the Organization of Eastern Caribbean States (OECS), to be administered by the CDB, was refused when the United States made it clear that Grenada, an OECS member, was to be excluded. (Although Grenada's fellow members were careful not to associate this move with any approval of the revolutionary regime.[11]) There was also a sustained U.S. propaganda barrage, which, besides making Grenada's traditional allies more wary of dealing with the PRG, had the effect of greatly reducing Grenada's tourist trade, particularly from the United States itself. The most dramatic message from Washington, however, was in a series of military maneuvers in the region. In August 1981, in Operation Ocean Venture 1981, off the Puerto Rican coast—involving more ships than were used in the 1944 Allied landings in Normandy—the U.S. Navy staged a mock invasion of a Caribbean island; "Amber and the Amberines" (Grenada and the Grenadines) were invaded to depose its unfriendly government and maintain an occupation until elections were called. Another operation, Ocean Venture 1983, occurred much nearer to Grenada: Using Barbados as a base, a large number of U.S. and allied warships sailed to within six miles of the Grenadian coast in March 1983.

For its part, the PRG became more strident in its opposition and pressured Cuba to use its influence in Moscow and elsewhere to involve the socialist community in Grenada's development. Bishop developed a particularly close friendship with Castro and made visits to the USSR, Eastern Europe, and North Korea. Coard, on the other hand, was considerably closer to the Soviet Union and had less to do with Cuba. Whatever their subsequent differences, the two men and their party fell into a trap they were trying to avoid: a dependency upon imported values and norms. In this case, however, the values and norms were by no means traditional. According to captured documents from the U.S. invasion, the NJM was desperate to be seen as a trustworthy communist party, whose orthodoxy and faithfulness to the Soviet model was without question and who would be Moscow's "eyes and ears" in the Eastern Caribbean.[12] There was, however, very little sign in the economy and everyday life that the PRG was leading Grenada toward scientific socialism. Loyalty was strictly limited to the realm of foreign policy.

It is debatable whether and to what extent U.S. pressure was responsible for the slow deterioration of the Grenadian economy. Aid denial certainly played a part, but there was no restriction on remittances from Grenadians working in the United States to their families on the island. Commercial letters of credit were hard to obtain and undoubtedly slowed trade, but the United States was never an important market for Grenadian exports. The reduction in U.S. tourist arrivals, from 9,081 in 1979 to 5,031 in 1982 (out of a total of 32,303 and 23,270 tourists, respectively),[13] was more of a blow, as their high-spending profile could not be replaced. By and large, economic decline in the world market economies, falling commodity prices, and the devaluation of the pound sterling, the value of which determined the profitability of much of Grenada's exports, were more to blame. There was also the problem of sheer overwork by the small band of activists in the government. Policymakers felt that the masses did not know "the science" and could not be trusted. The Soviet Union, moreover, was very cautious in its relations with the PRG and would commit few resources. Above all, the social and economic environment of Grenada itself was far from conducive to the application of socialist policies.

Cocooned within their tightly sealed shell, the NJM members vented their frustration. A greater commitment to Marxism-Leninism was deemed essential. Blame eventually focused on the "undisciplined" Bishop. But no one could dispute his extraordinary oratory power and hold on the people, to whom he was "we leader." The solution proposed by the radical majority in the Central Committee was joint leadership. Coard would be responsible for party organization and tactics, whereas Bishop would concentrate on leadership and mobilization of the masses. Bishop reluctantly agreed but changed his mind during a visit to Eastern Europe. Placed under house arrest on his return, he was rescued six days later by some four to five thousand people and taken to Fort Rupert, the old slave fortress, which overlooks the harbor of the capital. The PRA stormed the fortress and, under instructions from the Central Committee (now allegedly under Coard's leadership), executed Bishop and most of his associates. The power struggle within the NJM provided the Reagan administration with the perfect opportunity to operationalize its rollback policy and consign the Vietnam syndrome to history. Yet, the U.S. intervention was not required to end the 1979 Grenadian revolution; that had already ended with Bishop's house arrest and, certainly, with his death.

■ OPERATION URGENT FURY

The U.S.-led invasion of Grenada, codenamed Operation Urgent Fury, lasted for a week. There were clear intelligence shortcomings and some operational communications failures verging on the criminally negligent. Initial resistance by the nearly 2,000-strong PRA and militia, assisted at the airport site by some of the 636 Cuban construction workers, was greater than expected and necessitated reinforcements. Over 6,000 U.S. combat troops initially were involved, the bulk leaving very soon afterwards to resume their journey to Lebanon from where they had been diverted. Some 1,500 soldiers remained until December 1983, and by June 1984 almost all of them had been pulled out. This left only a small force to continue training the postintervention Special Service Unit, the paramilitary police force similar to others being developed simultaneously on several of Grenada's small island neighbors. The U.S. forces were not alone, for once the main military objectives were secured, troops from Jamaica and Barbados arrived and were supplemented by police contingents from Antigua, Dominica, St. Kitts-Nevis, St. Lucia, and St. Vincent. Together with the U.S. military, they constituted the Caribbean Peace-Keeping Forces. The force would not be withdrawn until September 1985.

The intervention was surprisingly low in casualities. Of those killed in action, eighteen were Americans (but over half the deaths were caused by accidents), twenty-four were Cuban construction workers, and sixteen were PRA troops.[14] Another eighteen Grenadians were killed, all of them mental patients, when their hospital was accidentally bombed. Following the lessons of Vietnam, where the televising of war into U.S. living rooms had strongly influenced public opinion, comprehensive restrictions were imposed upon the world's media, to be lifted only when "psychological warfare" teams had flown in from Central America and Defense and State Department spokespersons were in place. Not that there was great need; the U.S. public was on the whole delighted with the quick victory, particularly as it came after the large and tragic loss of Marine Corps lives a few days before in Beirut. Grenadian civilian enthusiasm was similarly shared by most of the other nations of CARICOM, the smaller OECS members, and their respective publics. In short, it was the OECS that had *invited* the United States to intervene in the affairs of a fellow Caribbean country.

Five of the seven OECS members (Antigua and Barbuda, Dominica, St. Kitts-Nevis, St. Lucia, and St. Vincent) resolved on October 21 in Grenada's absence to invoke Article 8 of the 1981 OECS Treaty. Article 8, which concerned security matters, allowed for the establishment of a Defense and Security Committee (consisting of the relevant ministers) to advise and make arrangements for collective security measures against external aggression. The committee's recommendation was "to seek the assistance of friendly countries to stabilize the situation and to establish a peacekeeping force."[15]

This OECS invitation for intervention, however, was surrounded by legal confusion and controversy. First, although the treaty required the unanimity of all those members legally competent to act in such circumstances, Grenada (such a member) deliberately had not been invited. Second, the treaty lacked a provision that would allow for action to be taken against a member state (as was the purpose of the invasion). Finally, there was manifestly no external aggression.[16]

A more legally exploitable agreement was the October 29, 1982, *Memorandum of Understanding Relating to Security and Military Cooperation* concluded between Antigua, Barbados, Dominica, St. Lucia, and St. Vincent. The signatories had the seizure of power by the NJM and their own domestic vulnerability at the time of signature clearly in mind. The agreement permitted them to request external assistance if the security of any of their number was threatened. It was argued by Prime Ministers Vere Bird (Antigua and Barbuda), Eugenia Charles (Dominica), and John Compton (St. Lucia), in particular, that the military regime in Grenada constituted such a threat to all the signatories. They supported secret meetings held by Prime Ministers Edward Seaga of Jamaica and Tom Adams of Barbados with U.S. diplomatic representatives, making clear that U.S. military involvement was much preferred by them to the alternative CARICOM peacekeeping force strongly urged by Trinidad and Tobago's Prime Minister George Chambers.[17]

U.S. military involvement was finally decided upon on October 22 after the State Department, which favored negotiation, had been outflanked by the hawks in the NSC, notably Admiral John Poindexter, Colonel Oliver North, and Constantine Menges. Menges, formerly of the CIA, painted a particularly dismal scenario of a massive Cuban airlift and establishment by the Soviet Union of a nuclear base if no military action was undertaken.[18] Thus, the NSC was willing to act on the oral request of the OECS chairperson, Prime Minister Charles, for U.S. military assistance. The positive response was confirmed in writing on October 23.

This request by Charles greatly strengthened the U.S. legal case for intervening. Until that time, the rationale rested only upon the need to "rescue" some 500 mainly U.S. students enrolled at St. George's University, an offshore U.S. medical school. Although Austin himself assured the students' safety, and allegations that they were hostages and that their lives were in danger were denied by the head of the school, parallels with the 444-day-long ordeal of the 132 U.S. embassy hostages in Iran during 1979–1981 were nonetheless highlighted. Much was made in the U.S. media of the emotional return to the United States of some of the students after the invasion.

It is, of course, inconceivable that such a dramatic course of action would have taken place in isolation. Although the bloody events of Austin's seizure of power on October 19 constituted the trigger, there was an underlying disposition by all involved to move against the NJM-dominated People's Revolutionary Government of Grenada. Of course, Grenada's CARICOM and OECS partners had different concerns from those of the United States. Whereas Washington fretted about the PRG's close links with the Soviet bloc in general and Cuba in particular, the Anglophone Caribbean was angered by the abject refusal by the PRG to hold elections and by its cavalier attitude toward human and civil rights. Symbolizing U.S. apprehension was Grenada's diplomatic support in the United Nations for the Soviet intervention in Afghanistan; the Grenadian import of considerable (and often old) Soviet, Cuban, and North Korean weaponry and military equipment; widescale Cuban aid to Grenada (notably for the airport project); and Grenada's links with Libya, radical Arab states, and other nontraditional partners. In the eyes of CARICOM members, Grenada's press censorship, provisions for imprisonment without trial ("preventive detention"), general militarization, and an often bellicose attitude expressed by PRG leaders and spokespersons toward those "Uncle Tom" and "bourgeois" regimes who dared to voice criticism proved to be the more worrisome developments.[19]

Prior to October 19, however, most CARICOM members had committed themselves to accepting the principle of ideological pluralism that the Grenadian revolution had put firmly onto the regional agenda. As the November 1982 CARICOM Heads of Government Summit Conference in Ocho Rios, Jamaica, resolved:

> . . . the emergence of ideological pluralism in the Community responds to internal processes and is an irreversible trend within the international system. . . . The right of self-determination [includes] the right to choose their own path of social, practical and economic development and insist[s] that there can be no justification for any external interference with the exercise of that right.[20]

In other words, Grenada's CARICOM associates were prepared to tolerate the PRG regime and not to overthrow it. They could not deny clear evidence of popular support for the regime, and some admired the PRG's advanced social, educational, and welfare programs, struggle to instill a sense of national dignity, and attempts at weaning the people away from values inherited from slavery and impressed by colonialism.

Yet, the monstrous events of October 19 created common ground between the United States and most of the Commonwealth Caribbean: The U.S. could rid itself of a "communist canker" in the midst of an area of high strategic concern, and the Caribbean nations could remove a possible regional threat, however far-fetched the possibility. Countervailing British influence was noticeably absent, but it is doubtful whether it would have made any difference, given the shared objective. In any event, Britain's first empire was, in 1983, fully incorporated into the U.S. sphere of influence. As Barbados Prime Minister Adams made clear in London in 1984, "In hemispheric terms, 1983 is bound to be seen as the watershed year in which the influence of the United States, willy-nilly, came observably to replace that of Great Britain in the old British colonies."[21] Not that this development was entirely Britain's fault. Although the Margaret Thatcher government disapproved of the intervention, a position resented by most of Britain's Caribbean partners in the Commonwealth, the British did not condemn it, recognizing that it removed a pro-Soviet regime.[22] However, Thatcher was greatly angered that Reagan, her closest ally, had failed to consult her.

■ INTERVENTION IN PERSPECTIVE

What may be concluded from the intervention in Grenada? First and foremost, the intervention was wholly expressive of deeply held perceptions by the U.S. body politic of the vulnerability of the U.S. backyard, a perception and apprehension nourished by the Reagan administration. The boost this event gave to Reagan's popularity at home served him well in the 1984 elections and beyond. The intervention was politically acceptable because it was low in casualties, short in duration, relatively cheap, and—above all—successful. But the invasion did not overcome the Vietnam syndrome, as Reagan had hoped; the majority of Americans continued to be opposed to the use of U.S. armed forces in a long war and particularly in one in which prolonged resistance would virtually be guaranteed, as would be the case in Central America.

The short-term military success notwithstanding, there was little strategic gain in overthrowing the small leftist regime, except that the intervention reduced Cuba's influence in the region for the time being. Although much was made of the weaponry and the contents of 25,000 documents captured by the CIA in the aftermath of the invasion, the former were qualitatively unimpressive and the latter provided sparse evidence of a Soviet-Cuban plot, as insisted by Reagan and other administration officials. More significant, the invasion confirmed the deeply held suspicions of Central and South American countries that the United States remained interventionist, thereby increasing long-term anti-U.S. feelings and further damaging an already suffering image. As for the Soviet Union, its image in the region underwent little change as its political, economic, and military profile outside Cuba and, to a far lesser extent, Nicaragua was minimal. The Soviets were to reap benefits later: Latin American resentment at U.S. interventionism in the Western Hemisphere aided the diplomatic thrust made by Moscow in Latin America in late 1987, the scale of which surprised many observers.[23]

An important distinction surrounding U.S. success is that the historical circumstances surrounding the action were highly and uniquely favorable to Washington—what one author has described as a "contingent in history."[24] This aura of favorability was only made possible by the violent collapse of a government perceived as offensive but not dangerous to the United States, against which denial policies and sabre-rattling were hitherto deemed appropriate, and by the remarkably extensive political and military support of a large majority of Commonwealth Caribbean states. The situation was also unique because a regime without popular support had seized power. Had the United States intervened earlier, when Bishop was "we leader," possibly using the March 1983 maneuvers as cover, military victory would still have been secured but at a much higher military and political price. There would have been little of the welcome accorded the incoming troops by common Grenadians, as there genuinely was after Bishop's execution, and regional support would, on the whole, have been noticeably lacking; indeed, the contrary would have been the case. Although the intervention prevented yet another "second Cuba," it cannot be seen as a warning to other aspirants to relief—if not independence—from U.S. hegemony. U.S. policymakers would be seriously misleading themselves if the lesson they drew from success in Grenada was that intervention in the Caribbean Basin and beyond was an easy option and that the United States had the capacity to control events using military means. Grenada was small, vulnerable, and had very few friends—a situation most unlikely to be repeated.

The military invasion also obviously could not affect the numerous developmental problems that remained once U.S. troops withdrew. The structural inequalities and economic dependency of Grenada that the PRG had tried to tackle remained as firmly entrenched as ever. Indeed, the U.S. invasion deepened the reality of dependence, as Washington faced the task of creating a government out of quarrelsome factions, united, it seemed, only by their eagerness for foreign aid. The alliance that eventually was formed won the December

1984 election by a handsome margin, but the economy was in deep crisis once the United States refused more blank checks. Considerable amounts of the over $80 million worth of U.S. aid granted between 1983 and 1986 had been squandered, and the newly created Special Service Unit had been used too many times for comfort against any hint of leftist opposition. Moreover the alliance was by late 1987 in serious disarray and six members, including three ministers, formed an opposition party. Neither was Gairyism dead, for Gairy continued to exert considerable influence in the rural areas.

Psychological dependency also flowered in Grenada in the wake of the U.S. military and aid agencies, expressed as a popular eagerness to go beyond compliance with U.S. orders to the enthusiastic adoption of North American values and mores, political, economic, and social. Even without pressure from the United States, socialism went into limbo—and not only in Grenada—for it was now linked in the popular mind with militarism and killing, an association constantly refreshed by the long legal process surrounding the trial during 1984–1988 of many of the radicals of the NJM Central Committee and some PRA personnel. Although by 1988 a sense of national consciousness had begun to reemerge in Grenada, there remained an unwillingness to begin to consider alternative approaches to the development problem other than through U.S. aid. Forms of socialism are beginning once again to find some popular expression in the English-speaking Caribbean, and Grenada will potentially follow in time, albeit under Washington's suspicious eye.

With insignificant exceptions, these formulations are democratic rather than revolutionary socialist, but not because to do otherwise would attract U.S. antagonism in the defense of its self-declared sphere of interest. It did not take an invasion of a small tropical West Indian island to force a realization by socialists, and others from all points of the ideological spectrum with an interest in Caribbean political development, that a Marxist-Leninist and pro-Soviet orientation as embraced by the New Jewel Movement is inappropriate to small open economies and to the objective circumstances of West Indian culture and tradition. Even the radicals of the NJM Central Committee would have come to that conclusion in time.

□ 18

South Africa

R. Hunt Davis, Jr., and Gwendolen M. Carter

The challenge presented to U.S. foreign policy by the situation in South Africa is a deep and difficult one. South Africa is unique in that, unlike most other Third World countries, it is self-sufficient in food production; has a strong industrially based economy; boasts a highly developed infrastructure in terms of transportation, energy, education, and social services; and was a founding member of both the League of Nations and the United Nations. Yet, these attributes of development are illusory, as access to the country's economic wealth and political system is highly skewed along racial lines under a system commonly known as apartheid. Whereas many black South Africans, especially those in the rural areas, suffer from acute poverty and malnutrition, nearly all whites are, at a minimum, relatively affluent in this racially segregated society. Parliamentary elections held in May 1987 in which black Africans had no vote underscore the political side of the exclusionary equation.

The Afrikaner government's systematic exclusion of the majority black population from reaping the economic and political benefits of South Africa has led to increasing domestic instability and the regime's estrangement both regionally and within the international system. The majority of sub-Saharan African countries since independence have consistently condemned the South African state for its treatment of the majority of the population and have contributed toward making apartheid a major issue in the international arena. The United States, reacting to heightened polarization and instability within South Africa and the region as a whole, pressures from African countries, and a highly vocal domestic antiapartheid movement, increasingly has been forced to reassess its relationship with the South African regime.

■ EVOLUTION OF U.S. POLICY

U.S. policy in southern Africa historically has been relatively inert and passive. One scholar, for example, has stated that "until the Carter administration, the United States took virtually no initiative in southern Africa, content at first to rely on the European imperial powers to maintain Western supremacy there."[1] Of course it should be kept in mind that much of the United States was still segregated into the 1960s (for example, the Selma, Alabama, march took place in 1965), so that a racially stratified South Africa did not seem all that much out of step to U.S. foreign policymakers. Furthermore, Washington's principal ally, Great Britain, had an enormous economic stake in South Africa, which was a much more important concern to the United States than was apartheid.

On March 21, 1960, a large crowd of Africans (estimates of its size range from 3,000 to 20,000) gathered before the police station at Sharpeville to demonstrate against the pass laws. Nervous white police opened fire, killing 69 and wounding 180. A chain reaction of events spread throughout South Africa, ending with a declaration of a state of emergency and the outlawing of African political organizations.[2] The Sharpeville incident drew U.S. attention to the problems of apartheid in a dramatic manner and led to a gradual hardening of policy toward South Africa. In 1963, for example, President John F. Kennedy declared his administration's intention to end the sale of military equipment to South Africa. In 1965, President Lyndon B. Johnson ended the practice of U.S. warships calling at South African ports. Overall, though, the United States continued to adhere to a low-profile approach on South African issues—as well as for Africa as a whole—except when crises such as the Sharpeville incident brought African issues to the attention of the U.S. foreign-policy-making elite.

The administration of President Richard M. Nixon initiated a shift in policy toward South Africa, a shift that backed off from the cautious limits that previously had been placed on relations with that country. This change in policy was embodied in National Security Study Memorandum 39 (NSSM 39), one of eighty-five reviews ordered by the new administration in 1969. NSSM 39 set forth five options for a future U.S. foreign policy toward the southern African region: (1) closer association with the white regimes of the region; (2) broader ties with both white-ruled and black-ruled countries in order to foster moderation; (3) lessening ties with the white states and strengthening those with black states; (4) severing ties with the white states and establishing closer relations with the black states; and (5) withdrawal from the entire southern African region. The administration opted for the second option—dubbed "tar baby" by the option's opponents in the Department of State who felt that closer relations with the whites would become a quagmire for the United States—which in turn led to a relaxation of the political isolation and economic restrictions that had been placed on South Africa and the other white-ruled states in the region (Angola, Mozambique, and Rhodesia). The basic premise of the new policy was that "the whites are here to stay" and that constructive change can only come through them; blacks cannot hope to gain political rights through violence—this only serves to open up opportunities to communists. The new policy thus sought to increase communications with the white minority governments of the region in order to induce them to modify their racial and colonial policies. It also provided more substantial economic assistance to the independent black states of the region in order to increase U.S. influence with them.[3] The mind-set behind this new policy was clearly a globalist one, for the real key to the situation in southern Africa, as far as Secretary of State Henry Kissinger and other U.S. policymakers were concerned, was the communist threat posed by guerrilla insurgencies supported by Moscow.

Events soon overtook the vital assumption of NSSM 39 that white rule would continue as a permanent feature of southern Africa. On April 25, 1974, a military coup d'état against the Marcello Caetano government in Portugal led to the demise of Portuguese colonial rule in Angola and Mozambique, facilitating the rise of black nationalist movements to power in both countries by 1975. Rather than accommodating the new political forces, however, Kissinger's fixation on the Soviet threat in the region resulted in U.S. covert intervention in Angola's 1975–1976 civil war, an action described by one author as one of "Washington's worst policy debacles" in Africa.[4] The result was just the opposite of what had been intended; rather than stemming Soviet influence, the action led instead to stepped-up Soviet aid to the self-proclaimed Marxist government in Angola and, ultimately, to the massive Cuban military presence that has continually bedeviled Washington since then. In turn, U.S. intervention also led to a congressional break with the administration in 1976 with the passage of the Clark Amendment to the Defense Appropriations Bill, which prohibited all covert aid to any of the parties in Angola. It was not until April 1976 that Kissinger finally ventured into southern Africa and, in a speech in Lusaka, Zambia, promised a thorough reevaluation and basic revision of U.S. policy toward the region. Though giving a clear recognition that the situation had changed (some two years after the Portuguese coup, it might be added), the new policy varied little "beyond making the absolute minimum of concessions to African states (and critical Americans) who had to be kept in good humor."[5]

The election of Jimmy Carter to the presidency in 1976 seemed to herald a considerable change in U.S. policy toward Africa in general and a hardening of opposition to apartheid in particular. Gone was the low-profile approach toward South Africa. The issue of apartheid quickly moved into the foreign policy spotlight with the appointment of civil rights activist Andrew Young as ambassador to the United Nations and the heavy stress the new administration placed on human rights. One of the first steps was to secure congressional support for repealing the Byrd Amendment, legislation that had permitted the United States to import essential minerals from minority-ruled Rhodesia (Zimbabwe since 1980). Repeal put the United States back in compliance with UN sanctions on Rhodesia. Carter also moved well beyond his two predecessors and called for majority rule not only for Rhodesia and Namibia but also for South Africa itself.

In a May 1977 meeting with Prime Minister John Vorster of South Africa, Vice President Walter F. Mondale reiterated the administration's position on majority rule.

What on first appearance seemed to be a new direction in U.S. policy was revealed upon closer examination, however, to be a continuation of two of the mainstays of the Nixon-Ford years—opposition to the liberation movements and a search for moderate solutions. For example, although in the end refusing to recognize the April 20, 1979, elections in Rhodesia—which led to Bishop Abel Muzorewa becoming prime minister of a "new" Rhodesia-Zimbabwe—the Carter administration had been indecisive and ambiguous about the elections in the first place. Furthermore, in the previous year, the administration had strengthened the legitimacy of the Rhodesian government when it had acquiesced to the demand of twenty-seven U.S. senators that Prime Minister Ian Smith, Bishop Muzorewa, and several other leading white Rhodesians receive visas to visit the United States in order to generate support for their cause. What appeared to turn the administration away from looking at southern Africa on its own terms was the perceived increase of Soviet influence on the continent. In particular, the Angolan-based invasions of the Shaba province of Zaire in 1977 and 1978 and the massive Soviet and Cuban support of Ethiopia in its war with Somalia in late 1977 were critical events in this shift. As elsewhere on the continent, then, the seeming initial "success of the pro-Africa policy . . . was merely apparent, never real, and it was soon eclipsed by the contrary influences of National Security Adviser Zbigniew Brzezinski and his globalist approach over the regionalist approach of Young."[6] Yet, critical as one may be of the failure of the Carter administration to move more aggressively on the question of South Africa, nonetheless the administration had abandoned the pro-white tilt of its predecessors.

The pro-white tilt of Washington returned in full and renewed force with the election of Ronald Reagan in 1980 and his appointment of Chester Crocker as assistant secretary of state for African affairs. Crocker was the theoretician behind the Reagan administration's policy of "constructive engagement." The central argument of this policy was that "purposeful, evolutionary change toward a nonracial system" was a genuine possibility in South Africa and that U.S. interests lay in fostering such change. Pressure clearly would be necessary, but there also should be "a clear Western readiness to recognize and support positive movement, and to engage credibly in addressing a complex agenda of change."[7] The policy made reaching an accommodation with the white rulers of South Africa the key for securing U.S. economic and security interests in the area. Within South Africa, the Reagan administration pointed to the 1984 constitution, which extended a limited franchise to Colored and Indian voters, as proof that its policy was working; outside South Africa, it viewed the 1984 Nkomati Accord between South Africa and Mozambique, which committed the two countries to ending support of covert activities against each other, in a similar manner.

The true focus of the constructive engagement policy, however, was not the southern African region but the global arena. The key to policies directed by Crocker and his deputy, Frank Wisner, was their belief that Soviet military aggression in southern Africa would increase and, less convincingly, that Cuban forces in Angola would be its focal point.[8] As a result of its globalist orientation, the Reagan administration reverted to the military option in two respects: (1) by engineering revocation of the 1976 Clark Amendment; and (2) by securing congressional backing under the auspices of the Reagan Doctrine for arming guerrilla forces led by Jonas Savimbi—the National Union for the Total Independence of Angola (UNITA)—that were attempting to overthrow the pro-Soviet Angolan regime headed by the Popular Movement for the Liberation of Angola (MPLA). It is significant that, in spite of these efforts, the MPLA government remains in power and continues to enjoy the backing of a large contingent of Cuban soldiers.[9]

In a development parallel to events of the mid-1970s, events of the mid-1980s overtook U.S. policy toward southern Africa and compelled a reevaluation and a new direction. Widespread unrest among black townships, beginning in 1984 and intensifying through 1986, coupled with the South African government's attempts to control this unrest and eliminate organized political opposition (most notably underscored by the imposition of a state of emergency in 1986), ensured that U.S. foreign policy toward South Africa faced both a challenge and a crisis. Although the Reagan administration was slow to size up the situation, Congress acted by passing the Comprehensive Anti-Apartheid Act of 1986 (overriding the president's veto), which imposed a package of economic sanctions stronger than any hitherto adopted. The sanctions served to discourage U.S. business involvement in South Africa by ending the tax treaty that had allowed U.S. companies to claim a tax credit in the United States for taxes paid in South Africa; passing a limited ban on new investment; and prohibiting bank loans to both the public and the private sector. It also banned imports of certain goods (agricultural products, coal, food, iron, steel, sugar, textiles, and uranium), continued the earlier ban on the sale of Krugerrands in the United States and exports of computers to government agencies, and terminated South African landing rights and banned all direct flights between the two countries.

The Anti-Apartheid Act thus represents a major change in the thrust of U.S. foreign policy in southern Africa. Abandoned is the central assumption of the constructive engagement policy—that of friendly pursuasion. Pushed even further into the past is the central tenet of the Kissinger policy that the main actor and thus U.S. partner in southern Africa was South Africa. And gone altogether was the basic premise of NSSM 39 that the "whites are here to stay" and that "constructive change" can only come through them. Although U.S. policy at the end of 1988 still sought to avert violent change and, even more unpalatable to Washington, a communist successor regime, Congress at least recognized that whites are no longer the only actors that count, nor are they even the main actors.

Of further importance and significance is the shift from a passive U.S. foreign policy supportive of continued white minority rule to an active and interventionist policy aimed at establishing a democratically elected majority government. An essential component of this change is the recognition that it is no longer possible to maintain the status quo or to mollify the opponents of apartheid with condemnatory rhetoric.

■ A CHANGED ENVIRONMENT AND DIRECTION FOR U.S. POLICY

At the heart of the policy challenge confronting the United States—as is pointed out by the U.S. government's 1987 analysis of that situation, *A U.S. Policy Toward South Africa: The Report of the Secretary of State's Advisory Committee on South Africa*—is "the clash between the legitimate demands for justice and economic opportunities of a long disenfranchised black majority and the fears of the ruling white minority that major concessions could be suicidal."[10] Confronting the likelihood that, in this situation, the South African government would fail to institute the fundamental changes so urgently needed and thereby precipitate a human tragedy that might endanger the viability of all of southern Africa, the United States has been increasingly, if somewhat reluctantly, searching for policies and a strategy that would lead to the abolition of apartheid and the establishment of a democratic and nonracial system in South Africa.

It is apparent, and was acknowledged even implicitly by the Reagan admininstration, that constructive engagement failed to achieve its primary objective of promoting change through "support for evolutionary change [which] implies sensitivity to the concerns of local actors."[11] The shift in policy was initiated by Congress with its passage in 1986 of the Comprehensive Anti-Apartheid Act. The Secretary of State's Advisory Committee on South Africa sought to continue this momentum for changes in policy, stating in its report that "U.S. policymakers now face a situation markedly different from that which existed in 1981" and concluding that "a new policy is now urgently required."[12]

The advisory committee correctly noted that positive features exist in the South African situation on which a new policy could be built. Blacks already make up over 40 percent of the professional work force, and there are more than one hundred registered trade unions with over a million members, 600,000 of them connected with the Congress of South African Trade Unions (COSATU). Furthermore, blacks and whites participate jointly in religious practices. An important change took place in October 1986 when the General Synod of the Dutch Reformed Church, to which the great majority of Afrikaners belong, withdrew its previous theological support of apartheid. Long before that action, however, Archbishops Desmond Tutu and Denis Hurley and the Reverends Beyers Naude and Alan Boesek had been leading evangelical efforts to build understanding and increase interaction across racial lines.

Even more effective in bridging racial differences have been the United Democratic Front (UDF) and the African National Congress (ANC). The UDF is an umbrella body for several hundred smaller organizations that advocates a nonracial socialist democracy and is closely linked with the principal African political organization, the ANC, which was founded in 1912. Despite having been banned since 1960, the ANC's popularity has grown significantly in the 1980s. In the U.S. advisory committee's policy report a white industrialist was quoted as saying that "lasting peace and stability will never be created without it."[13] Moreover, in considering the potential role of the ANC in South Africa's future, the report dealt with the issue of communist influence in the organization. Rather than giving credence to the charge that the ANC's supposed communist ties were the issue, it was argued that by banning the group and blocking peaceful political opposition to apartheid, the South African government contributed significantly to the strength of the South African Communist party. Furthermore, "the longer the delay before blacks obtain their rightful role in the governance of South Africa, the greater will become the appeal of communism to future generations of blacks."[14]

The role of whites in a postapartheid South Africa has been a major concern for U.S. policymakers. The policy report dealt with this issue by highlighting the ANC's Freedom Charter declaration that "South Africa belongs to all who live in it, black and white" and the affirmation of this principle by the current generation of black leaders. It is clear, in any case, that South Africa's nearly 5 million whites form a powerful group through their own resources, military power, and skills. If, from their side, they would accept the principle of individual human rights, they would probably find allies among many other minority groups.

Though the advisory committee stated in its report that the basis for multiracial accommodation exists, it also concluded that that basis is fast eroding. This erosion stems from (1) the absence of any reference to political rights for Africans in the 1983 constitution, which provided separate representation in Parliament for Coloreds (8.7 percent of the total population) and Indians (2.7 percent of the population); (2) the lack of any noticeable effort on the part of the South African government to repeal the key elements of the apartheid system; and (3) the escalating spiral of violence and repression that first erupted in 1984. The committee concluded that bitterness is intensifying in black circles, which in turn poses the threat of even more widespread and violent outbursts. Thus, the "first and foremost priority" of the United States, according to the report, should be to facilitate the beginning of "good faith" negotiations between the South African government and "representative leaders of the black majority," with the objective of shaping "a nonracial democratic political system and a nonracial economic system." Furthermore, the United States, in conjunction with its major allies, should begin a diplomatic effort to achieve this objective.[15]

The advisory committee recognized that, for any diplomatic effort to succeed, it was necessary to satisfy both "the disenfranchised black majority's legitimate demands for political justice and economic opportunity" and the white majority's concerns about its future. Thus, the South African government was called upon to take a series of steps in order to create the necessary conditions to initiate "open-ended negotiations with genuine black leaders": (1) repealing key restraining measures (such as the Group Areas Act, which divided the country into areas in which only those of a designated racial group could live and work); (2) establishing a legal system that fully recognizes basic civil liberties; (3) restoring full citizenship to all Africans; (4) making the so-called homelands—the ten ethnically based territorial entities for Africans that contain 13 percent of the country's surface area—an integral part of South Africa; (5) launching efforts to break down barriers between blacks and whites; and (6) facilitating communication between blacks and whites on the political future of South Africa.[16]

To start the process, several bold steps were proposed. First, the South African government should release ANC President Nelson Mandela, in prison since 1962, and all other political prisoners. Second, it was recommended that the ban on the ANC and all other political organizations be lifted and the free and full expression of political opinions, formation of political parties, and participation in the political processes allowed. Finally, the committee called for terminating the state of emergency, under which the government has ruled with extraordinary police powers since mid-1985, and releasing all detainees held under its provisions.

Recognizing the far-reaching consequences of its proposals, the advisory committee saw the "most urgent challenge" facing the United States and other members of the international community to be convincing South African President Pieter W. Botha and his supporters that it is in their interest to negotiate now rather than later.[17] Aware, however, that they were unlikely to do so, the committee also looked to high-ranking contacts between the two governments as offering the most effective routes for influence. Such efforts would require strong U.S. presidential leadership.

In addition to contact with the government, it was recommended that contacts be expanded with opposition groups through both public and private channels. The objectives of the contacts and various assistance projects, particularly in education, should not only be to end apartheid but also to promote the reconciliation and healing necessary for avoiding a "bitterly fractured society."[18]

As part of its concern with the shape of postapartheid South Africa, the advisory committee voiced some alarm with "growing black hostility to capitalism and free enterprise." A remedy it proposed was for U.S. companies to take steps to ensure that the existing system overcame past failures to "provide sufficient economic opportunities for blacks." Among these was adherence to the Sullivan Principles, a code of practices for U.S. corporations operating in South Africa designed to promote fair employment and to combat segregation in the workplace, which the Comprehensive Anti-Apartheid Act had now given the force of law. Furthermore, in recognition of the disinvestment process that was already under way, the committee called for companies that did pull out to "make every effort to have black employees and investors participate in the purchase of the business."[19]

Although much of the new policy directions recommended in its report consisted of persuasion and dialogue, the committee departed sharply from the policy of constructive engagement in its call for effective external pressure: "Concerted international pressure must be an integral part of any effort to bring the South African Government to the bargaining table." The 1986 Comprehensive Anti-Apartheid Act constituted the strongest signals yet of U.S. rejection of apartheid. The next step was for the United States to enlist the support of its allies for a multilateral program of sanctions. "We believe," it was stated in the report, "that the urgency of the situation demands that such a multilateral program of sanctions should be put in place unless the South African Government releases all political prisoners, unbans the ANC and other political parties, and terminates the State of Emergency."[20]

Although multilateral sanctions along the lines of the Comprehensive Anti-Apartheid Act represented the first stage of external pressure, the advisory committee urged that continued intransigence from Pretoria should lead to additional diplomatic and economic steps. These "might include a comprehensive multilateral trade embargo and consideration of ways to establish effective international sanctions on newly mined South African gold." Along with mounting internal pressures, the effect would be to press home upon the white regime "the reality that economic growth and political stability are unlikely unless and until apartheid is ended and a . . . government based on the consent of the governed is initiated."[21]

Finally, the committee unreservedly recognized the existing linkages between U.S. policy toward South Africa and that for the region as a whole. Indeed, it asserted, "it is impossible to develop an effective policy toward South Africa without taking into account the broader regional context."[22] Specifically, the United States should reinvigorate international efforts to achieve a Namibian settlement, reevaluate military support for Savimbi in Angola, and take steps to minimize the human and economic toll that a prolonged struggle for majority rule in South Africa is likely to exact upon its neighboring states.

In a concrete sense the goals for U.S. policy articulated in the report of the Advisory Committee on South Africa did not differ from what had long been the rhetoric of U.S. policy statements: an end to apartheid and the establishment of a government based on the consent of the governed. Nor was the core of the tactics it proposed all that different from tactics of past administrations: Attempt to work with "moderate" and "reasonable" elements in and out of the government to bring about reforms in order to stave off the type of upheaval that would end in a radical, revolutionary regime coming to power. The specific proposals, though, are another matter, for the committee suggested much tougher actions than had ever before been attempted. Thus, given the essentially conservative nature of the Reagan administration and its reluctance to take any punitive measures against Pretoria, it should not be surprising that the administration did not pick up on any of the report's proposals other than the Namibian negotiations in 1988. And, the discussions on Namibia took place only in the context of the administration's globalist approach to international relations, as they were directly linked to the Soviet withdrawal from Afghanistan.

■ PARLIAMENTARY ELECTIONS, PROTEST, AND NATIONALISM

In the midst of the violent turmoil gripping their country, white South Africans went to the polls on May 6, 1987, to elect a new parliament. The election results dimmed the already fragile hopes within South Africa and abroad, and within the Reagan administration, that there might be a sufficient swing to the liberal- (that is, reform-) minded Progressive Federal party (PFP) to cause the government to change its policies in a significant manner.[23] Instead, the PFP and its ally, the New Republic party (NRP), were the big losers. The PFP lost 7 seats, leaving it 19 seats in all, and the NRP held on to only 1 of its 4 seats. In sharp contrast to the decline of the moderate and liberal elements of the white electorate stood the rise of the extreme right-wing Conservative party who increased their number of seats from 17 to 26 and, in the process, became the official opposition. The ruling National party entrenched even further their governing majority by gaining 7 seats for a total of 123 seats in the new National Assembly. Furthermore, if the 26 percent of the vote won by the Conservatives is added to the 56 percent garnered by the Nationalists (for a total of 82 percent), it becomes even clearer how much these two parties of the right dominated the election in which 68 percent of the white electorate voted. The March 1988 election for two parliamentary seats further underscored the 1987 results, as the Conservative party won both races. In the October 1988 local elections, the Conservatives continued their electoral momentum, wresting control of a number of town councils in the Transvaal from the Nationalists, who, in turn, ousted the PFP from control of the Johannesburg City Council and retained control of the Pretoria City Council.

Routed on the electoral front, the increasingly likely trend for liberal whites will probably be to follow the lead of former PFP leader Frederick van Zyl Slabbert to abandon the electoral process and to find other means "to keep the voice of moderates alive in a polarizing situation and to keep a white-black dialogue going as far as possible."[24] One such means was the much publicized July 1987 meeting in Dakar, Senegal, between a group of mostly Afrikaner whites, headed by van Zyl Slabbert, and the ANC. Such meetings, however, seem only to antagonize the Botha government and, presumably, the majority of the white electorate.

While the whites were preparing to go to the polls, black workers provided a powerful demonstration to publicize their bitterness over their exclusion from the franchise. Staging a stay-at-home during the week in which the whites were voting, more than 1.5 million workers and a million students participated in the demonstration, which was called by COSATU, UDF, and the National Education Crisis Committee.

What may be expected from the strike and also from the Nationalist victory? Rather than discouraging black labor-union militancy, the white electoral results seem to have had the opposite effect. For example, COSATU president Elijah Barayi told 1,500 cheering delegates at his organization's July convention that "I'm here to bury P. W. Botha, not to praise him."[25] President Botha, for his part, viewed the election results as a mandate for tougher security measures and gradual reform: "The outside world must now have a clear picture that they cannot dictate to South Africa. The outside world must accept that the white electorate is here to stay and have a special role to play. We will follow our conviction in this regard."[26] To back up his supposed dual mandate, Botha renewed the state of emergency for another year in July 1987 and made a widely publicized trip to Soweto to carry on discussions about reform with those he described as black leaders.

These reform efforts seemed doomed to failure. None have yet met with general Afrikaner approval and, particularly in light of the substantial Conservative vote and the narrow margins by which many National party parliamentarians won over Conservatives, it seems unlikely they will do so. More important, Botha's talk of reform has failed to elicit a positive response from politically active Africans. Nor will it, unless the president unbans the ANC and other political organizations, releases Mandela and other imprisoned leaders, ends the state of emergency, and moves to abolish the foundation pieces of apartheid legislation such as the Population Registration Act (passed in 1950, it requires the classification and registration of all South Africans according to race); the Group Areas Act (also passed in 1950, set forth guidelines for demarcating the entire country into distinct areas for one or another racial group); the Urban Areas Consolidation Act (legislation passed in 1945 and subsequently amended on several occasions, which sharply restricts the right of Africans to live in South Africa's cities and towns); and the Bantu Education Act (enacted in 1953, it established a separate and inferior system of education for Africans). These are the very measures called for in the U.S. secretary of state's advisory committee report; but the May election has meant that President Botha is even further from taking steps in this direction.

The formulation of an effective U.S. policy has been made especially complex by the strong forces of nationalism that prevail in South Africa. The country is the home of one of the most successful nationalist movements on the continent, that of the Afrikaners, which culminated in the 1948 electoral victory that gave the National party control over the government, which it has held ever since. During the Carter years, and since 1985 under the prodding of Congress, the United States has attempted to apply pressure on the National party leadership (that is, the South African government) to accept the inevitability of major change. The results of the May 1987 election are indicative of the difficulties involved in attempting to redirect Afrikaner nationalism. One of President Botha's chief campaign planks, for example, was defiance of "outside interference."

Although according full legitimacy to Afrikaner nationalism, U.S. policymakers have not been willing to do so for African nationalism. True, since the 1960s the United States has opposed apartheid on the grounds that it represses the black majority. At the same time, however, the U.S. view has been that the initiative for change was supposed to come from the white rulers and not the black challengers. For example, Chester Crocker, in the *Foreign Affairs* article that led to his appointment as assistant secretary of state for African affairs, stated: "Basic to any . . . deeper analysis [of the South African reality] is . . . the importance of Afrikaner nationalism . . . as a distinctive and determining feature in the political equation."[27] He stresses the ethnic mobilization that led to ultimate political control, which in turn holds major implications for political change. Crocker finds no such sense of nationalism among Africans; although "a new level of political awareness and ferment" has pervaded the black communities of South Africa, "black politics are fragmented on tactical and leadership issues," with the result that "the black political arena is an increasingly complex puzzle." Recognizing that the ANC "possesses significant assets as the oldest nationalist movement," Crocker at the same time saw many other challengers for power among blacks and many potential issues that "could splinter nationalist unity."[28]

There are several problems with Crocker's analysis. First, it places too much emphasis on Afrikaner unity, assuming that having once been achieved (and, in fact, never as completely as he suggests), it will continue more or less as is. Second, he assumes, on the basis of insufficient information, that fragmentation is an essential feature of black politics. Although it would be erroneous to dismiss the political divisions within the black community, the fact is that the ANC has clearly gained in strength in the intervening years since his article appeared in 1980. Finally, he believes that whites "continue to hold effective power and cannot be forced to share or transfer it."[29] As Pauline Baker has noted, however, the open revolt that began in fall 1984 and has continued in one form or another through 1988, has demonstrated that "blacks have achieved a momentum that the government appears increasingly desperate to stop."[30] The secretary of state's advisory committee's report sought to rectify the errors of past policy by according appropriate recognition to the forces of African nationalism. Yet, the advisory committee also hoped to channel these forces in directions congruent with perceived U.S. interests.

■ NEW DIRECTIONS

From the perspective of the ongoing crisis within South Africa, what insights may be gained into U.S. foreign policy toward South Africa and its neighboring states? First, the course of U.S. policy in the region offers clear evidence of the inadequacy of the globalist foreign policy approach to the Third World. Twice in little more than a decade events within the region have caused major political crises. The first crisis came with the overthrow of Portuguese colonialism in Angola and Mozambique in 1975. Rather than accommodating the new political forces, U.S. covert intervention in Angola prompted a massive Soviet/Cuban response that provided the Soviets and Cubans with a major foothold and ally on the African continent. Although the Carter administration initially abandoned a globalist approach in southern Africa, this approach soon crept back into policy formulations, again fully blossoming with the election of the Reagan administration. Once more, in the mid-1980s, events in the region, this time mostly within South Africa itself, have overtaken and laid bare the fundamental problems with the U.S. policy of constructive engagement.

By taking the view that the Soviet/Cuban presence and supposed threat constitute the paramount foreign policy issue for southern Africa, as Crocker and Wisner have, the United States has tolerated South Africa's military intervention in neighboring states, especially Angola, and did not push on the issue of independence for Namibia until 1988. Only after the Reagan-Gorbachev meetings in 1987 and 1988 and the lessening of U.S.-Soviet tensions around the globe, beginning with the Soviet withdrawal from Afghanistan, did Crocker become actively involved in brokering an agreement among Angola, Cuba, and South Africa for the mutual withdrawal of foreign troops from Angola and for South African acquiescence to implementing the UN plan for the independence of Namibia. The Reagan administration remained adverse to applying extensive pressure on South Africa to dismantle its sociopolitical order based on white supremacy, as it continued to view that country as an ally in the effort to stem the spread of Soviet influence, even if the tensions between the United States and the Soviet Union have somewhat lessened. The primary flaw with this globalist logic is that the United States and South Africa fundamentally do not have shared interests, as Washington has believed, for Pretoria's paramount foreign policy objective has been to protect its system of white supremacy. Thus, regional instability and a modest Soviet/Cuban presence in the region have served South African interests, for these factors have deterred the West from acting more energetically on the issue of apartheid.[31] This stance has had the effect of increasing instability and intervention in the region and has plunged it into the crisis that the secretary of state's advisory committee fully detailed in its report.

The flip side of overemphasis on globalist foreign policy concerns is the need for greater attention to regionalist factors and concerns. The dramatic failures of U.S. policy in southern Africa are in themselves convincing arguments for adopting a regionalist perspective. For example, if the United States had recognized Angola as an independent country from the date of Angolan independence, it is a plausible hypothesis that a significant Cuban military presence never would have been established there. The reverse hypothesis also seems true—by shaping its policy toward Angola on the basis of external factors (that is, a globalist approach), the United States has pushed Angola into the Soviet camp. A regionalist perspective toward South Africa would make the internal dynamics paramount; issues such as access to the Cape sea route and strategic minerals would be secondary, rather than the other way around, as in the policy of constructive engagement. A regionalist perspective would also place the primary emphasis on South Africa as an *African* country ruled by a *white minority* and containing other minorities, instead of on the view that it is a white-ruled country where the main issue is the future of the white minority. Finally, such a perspective would terminate efforts to utilize South African economic, political, and military power to support U.S. policy objectives in the region. Thus, U.S. military involvement with South Africa, whereby the United States and South Africa back Savimbi and his UNITA forces in Angola, would end, and the United States would cease endorsing future Nkomati-type accords between South Africa and its weaker neighbors.

The biggest stakes involve South Africa's well-developed capitalist economy. One of the most popular arguments in defense of South Africa in certain political quarters in the United States is its alleged status as a bulwark against communism. South Africa's leaders long have recognized the value of this theme and, beginning with passage of the Suppression of Communism Act in 1950, have played it for all it is worth. Defense of the capitalist order is another gauge of U.S. concern that a socialist economy might ultimately emerge. Thus, an argument particularly favored by the Reagan administration was that U.S. investment represents a progressive force for change in South Africa. According to this proposition, capitalism is inherently hostile to apartheid. In fact, though, capitalism in South Africa has continually grown and prospered alongside the intensification of apartheid. Even the generally progressive U.S. advisory committee report avoided coming to grips with the increasing possibility that the social change that it purports to support might ultimately occur under the auspices of a socialist and openly anticapitalist regime. Rather, the committee sought reform of the existing economic system. It is, thus, one thing to tolerate a socialist regime in Mozambique, where U.S. economic interests have been minimal, but something quite different for South Africa, where the West has a major economic stake.

The United States needs to recognize the legitimacy of African nationalism in South Africa and, thus, to tolerate the social change that will accompany its ultimate success, rather than seeking to block it on the grounds of ideology. As relations with other countries in the region have demonstrated, an official socialist or Marxist ideology does not prevent fruitful relations. For example,

U.S. policy during the winter of 1987-1988 firmly supported the Marxist government of Mozambique in its efforts to rebuild its economy and stamp out South African–backed guerrillas. Although U.S. relations with Zimbabwe have often been difficult—heightened at times by tensions deriving from a globalist approach to foreign policy—nonetheless, that country has steadily strengthened its economic ties with the West despite its Marxist rhetoric. Even in Angola, despite the lack of U.S. diplomatic relations and U.S. backing of antigovernment guerrillas, U.S. oil companies have been engaged in successful ventures since that country's independence in 1975. But the size of the U.S. economic stake in South Africa is far greater than elsewhere in the region. An ANC government (the most likely majority government to emerge under current circumstances), with its commitment to the broad and general socialist principles set forth in the 1955 Freedom Charter (which remains a basic ANC document), would not at present constitute a clear and unambiguous danger to this economic stake. Yet, as one writer has noted, "there is a growing anti-capitalist sentiment, growing interest in socialism, a great disappointment with the United States and antagonism toward it, and in particular a deep anger toward President Reagan."[32] If U.S. policy continues on its current course and, thus, further fuels this discontent, then the prospects for overall U.S. relations with an eventual majority government will be much dimmer than is the case in 1989.

Finally, there is the matter of sanctions. It is clear that the United States cannot induce change in South Africa through a policy of friendly intercourse with its government, as was tried under both the Nixon-Ford and Reagan administrations. Nor will a policy of external pressure cause the South African government to disengage and retreat in upon itself. Rather, this so-called *laager* mentality of disengagement has long been a feature of Afrikaner nationalism, especially when it has been under pressure, and, as events within South Africa have unfolded in the past few years, this inward-looking posture has reemerged in full force. The one policy weapon that remains for the United States is that of sanctions.

There are essentially two approaches to sanctions. One is to adopt a policy either explicitly or tacitly aimed at toppling the government of the state in question. The other is to attempt to move events in a different direction than they are currently taking. It is clear that, for the present at least, the former approach is out. The white regime in South Africa still enjoys strong political support from a varied set of powerful interests in the United States and elsewhere in the Western world. These interests are clearly strong enough to prevent actions that are aimed at overthrowing the South African government. Yet, the South African government's use of force to quell even the mildest dissent and opposition to its internal policies has, in turn, created a constituency for those who advocate that the United States must act and take the lead in getting its Western allies also to act to disassociate the Western democracies from the Afrikaner regime. U.S. leadership in pushing for mandatory international sanctions would produce sanctions that give clear force to the often-stated disapproval of apartheid that has for many years run through U.S. policy statements on the subject of South Africa.

It would also leave the door open to support those forces for change that remain in South Africa. Oppressive as the South African government has been, it has been unable to stamp out either the aboveground or the underground opposition. Indeed, just the opposite has happened, for the opposition seems to have diversified and grown in strength. Sanctions of disapproval would thus lend support to the opposition forces and, at the same time, lessen U.S. complicity in the apartheid regime.

Yet, even though no one can accurately forecast the course of events in South Africa, given their complexity, in the long run the situation in South Africa may well deteriorate to the point at which the United States and its allies may feel compelled to implement the type of sanctions that aim at toppling the South African government. Under such circumstances, the intent would no doubt be to forestall out-and-out revolution. Rather than stand by and allow conditions to reach such a point, however, the Western powers should enact and enforce stringent sanctions against South Africa in an effort to forestall a scenario that would lead to more direct intervention and to the multitude of policy and political dilemmas that such a step would produce. Yet, whatever policy decisions the United States and its allies do make, the interlocking dimensions of the crisis that continue to assert themselves are such that the process of charting an effective U.S. policy toward South Africa will be, at best, an extremely difficult one.

■ Part 6

CONCLUSION

19

U.S. Intervention in Perspective

Peter J. Schraeder

The geographical realm of U.S. intervention in the Third World has evolved from the relatively constrained Western Hemisphere focus of the Monroe Doctrine during the nineteenth century to the worldwide embrace of the Reagan Doctrine as the twentieth century draws to a close. Whereas an intrusionary Europe was the target of President James Monroe, containment of the Soviet Union and communism—albeit in varying degrees—became the cornerstone of post–World War II administrations from Presidents Harry S. Truman to Ronald Reagan.[1]

Similarly, the intensity of U.S. intervention increased substantially in the aftermath of World War II as Washington's foreign-policy-making elite brought numerous instruments to bear on the cold war struggle with the Soviet Union. Foreign economic and military aid, for example, has totaled nearly $825 billion (in 1988 dollars) during the last four decades. At the other end of the coercive spectrum, direct U.S. military intervention, after a lull in the early post-Vietnam period, has witnessed a resurgence under the guise of the doctrine of low-intensity conflict. Moreover, during the 1980s there has been a significant expansion of covert action led by a rejuvenated CIA, the formalization of a coherent strategy of paramilitary intervention known as the Reagan Doctrine, and the continuation or initiation of thirty-one cases of economic sanctions (out of a total of fifty-two for the entire post–World War II period).

Despite this trend toward greater interventionism, two parallel trends—one domestic and one international—have placed more constraints on the successful application of U.S. power in the Third World. In the domestic realm, a fragmented U.S. political culture is no longer content, as it was during the 1950s and the 1960s, to follow the lead of the executive branch in support of an interventionist cold war policy. Similarly, growing pluralism within the international arena, as the bipolar system of the 1950s evolves toward an emerging multipolar system, has unleashed new forces that question Washington's simple dichotomies of capitalism versus communism, freedom versus totalitarianism.

The net result of these trends, as Harry Piotrowski eloquently stated in Chapter 12, is that U.S. intervention in the Third World, resting as it has on the faulty premises of the cold war, has become "increasingly more counterproductive, difficult, and costly in terms of political capital, money, and blood." Whether one looks at the failures of U.S. intervention, such as direct military involvement in the Vietnam War, or the possible successes, such as the contributing role of paramilitary aid in securing a Soviet withdrawal from Afghanistan, one cannot deny that there has been a price paid by U.S. society.

My purpose in this chapter is to offer an alternative set of guidelines for U.S. foreign policy that builds upon both past successes and past failures. These guidelines are not intended to be steadfast rules applicable regardless of history or context, but rather to serve as the basis for reassessing over forty years of U.S. interventionist practices. In this sense, my primary purpose in this chapter is to contribute to the ongoing debate over what should constitute a proper U.S. foreign policy, recognizing that there will forever be differences of opinion and interpretation among individuals of intellectual integrity. It is only by presenting these points for subsequent discussion, however, that a policy consensus—the basis for an effective foreign policy in a democracy—can be achieved.

■ FOREIGN POLICY GUIDELINES FOR DEALING EFFECTIVELY WITH A CHANGING THIRD WORLD

One of the most significant dilemmas in the post–World War II period, especially in the wake of Vietnam, has been the balancing of perceived national security interests with the need for openness and public debate required by democracy in the formulation of foreign policy. As noted in several chapters, inherent in this balancing act is the growing conflict between the executive branch and Congress over the role that each should play in the foreign-policy-making process. In the words of one observer, there exists a "chronic tension" between the U.S. democratic domestic political system and its nondemocratic national security system.[2]

In the wake of perceived executive branch excesses concerning the foreign conduct of the Vietnam War, the domestic abuses of Watergate, and illegal covert activities in the Third World, Congress attempted during the 1970s to strengthen its oversight capabilities by adopting the War Powers Act and creating intelligence oversight committees. The explicit goal of these initiatives was to avoid future Vietnams by requiring that proposed interventions be submitted to reasoned debate apart from that within the limited circle of the president and his immediate staff. The implicit goal, however, was to check what was perceived to be overly powerful national security bureaucracy elites—headed by an imperial president—who "circumvented the authority of Congress and the courts, viewed themselves above the law, particularly in foreign policy matters, and used secrecy and distortion to deceive Congress and the public in order to accomplish their policy objectives."[3]

Indeed, the executive branch steadfastly has resisted congressional attempts at enhanced oversight, sometimes with tragic results. Refusing to recognize the constitutionality of the War Powers Act, for example, and subsequently failing to submit policy to the scrutiny of public debate, President Ronald Reagan unilaterally acted to send the U.S. Marines to Lebanon as part of a "peacekeeping" force, changing course only after their tragic deaths. The Reagan administration similarly refused to submit to congressional scrutiny its Persian Gulf policy of escorting neutral ships, which inevitably led to hostile confrontations with Iran. Yet, it could be argued that, even with congressional consultation at the outset, both policies would have continued exactly as desired by the executive branch.

More significant is when questionable executive branch actions have impinged directly upon the domestic democratic rights of the U.S. population. In the case of the administration of President Richard M. Nixon, the Federal Bureau of Investigation (FBI) employed wiretaps and informants to monitor, harass, and suppress political dissent against the growing war in Indochina, eventually applying these covert activities against the Democratic party. An April 1976 Senate select committee report noted that these tactics were "unworthy of a democracy and occasionally reminiscent of the tactics of totalitarian regimes."[4]

As discussed in Chapter 16, the Reagan administration resorted to similar illegal tactics against the U.S. public to further its paramilitary goals in Nicaragua. These various tactics, declared illegal by a GAO investigation, included pressure on the U.S. media not to print stories; lobbying tactics to manipulate U.S. public opinion against the Sandinistas and, therefore, to achieve congressional support for the contras; and "white propaganda" operations—the planting of false articles in the U.S. press. Yet, the most damaging aspect of the administration's secret war was the Iran arms-for-hostages deal and the subsequent illegal diversion of profits from these sales to the contras in violation of the Boland Amendment. As Harry Howe Ransom perceptively concluded in Chapter 7, the Iran-contra episode revealed "the corruptive impact of secrecy, which invites serious violations of law and moral standards. . . . Invisible government, based upon a doctrine of ends justifying means, had become a reality."

The question remains how to restore accountability and relegitimize the foreign-policy-making process. Noting the damaging effects of past policies, it is hard to accept the view espoused by proponents of the national security bureaucracy that "saving constitutional democracy may require partially sacrificing it."[5] Taking a completely different view, Morton A. Halperin has convincingly argued that a successful national security policy, especially as it pertains to major episodes of military and covert intervention, requires public and congressional approval.[6]

Halperin's solution for restoring accountability and fostering a foreign policy partnership revolves around amending the War Powers Act in three aspects and making it inclusive of both military and covert intervention. The first amendment would delete the "60–90" statute that requires the president to withdraw U.S. forces from the combat zone within ninety days if, after sixty days, the action has not been approved by Congress. Not only has the executive branch considered the statute unconstitutional (citing it as its reason for not complying with the reporting and consultative provisions of the War Powers Act), but reformers have viewed it as unnecessarily tying the hands of the president.[7]

A second amendment would create a "permanent consultative body" comprising the majority and minority leaders of both houses, the speaker of the house, and the president pro tempore of the Senate, with whom the president would have to consult before initiating any military or covert actions. An expanded consultative body—including the individuals already mentioned as well as the chairperson and ranking minority members of the House and Senate Armed Services, Foreign Affairs, and Intelligence Committees—"would join in consultation with the president and discuss among themselves an appropriate legislative response to the situation at hand." Finally, a third amendment would require advance congressional approval of any military or covert action save for three specific exceptions: to repel attacks against U.S. armed forces located outside U.S. territory; to repel direct attacks against U.S. territory; and to rescue American hostages.[8]

Halperin has argued that these amendments ensure a balance between the war-power prerogative of Congress and the necessity for the president to be able to take "immediate action to defend the United States and its citizens" when time is of the essence. Moreover, the proposed policy partnership ensures that (1) questionable or otherwise risky policy would receive a much-needed "second opinion," as the "potential for making mistakes or abusing power increases when the number of alternative views declines"; (2) advance congressional approval would legitimize U.S. intervention once initiated, fostering bipartisanship and a united front to both allies and adversaries; and (3) prior approval would aid in preventing "the backlash from Congress that inevitably follows a foreign policy failure."[9] In short, these reforms would contribute to relieving the "chronic tension" between justified national security concerns and the requirements of democratic society, as well as helping to resolve what Jerel A. Rosati referred to in Chapter 10 as the "crisis of leadership" of the executive branch. With policies built upon the solid foundations of congressional and public support, the president could lead with confidence, charting a consistent and coherent foreign policy in the Third World.

The most important guideline of any future foreign policy is that U.S. policymakers must discard the ill-conceived notion that Third World countries are mere pawns in the greater East-West struggle and that the primary source of conflict in these countries is external Soviet interference. As Piotrowski noted in Chapter 11, one of the primary flaws of the administration of President Truman was the failure to recognize that communist movements often acted independently of the wishes of Soviet leader Joseph Stalin. Indeed, the past four decades have witnessed the growing polycentrism of communism in the Third World and the growth of actors independent of both Washington and Moscow. Yet, official tunnel vision, whereby social change is viewed through East-West glasses, has ensured a reactive policy that is constrained by the blinders of anticommunism.

In a manifestation of this tunnel vision, the United States assumed the right to overthrow even democratically elected leftist regimes in Iran (1953) and Guatemala (1954) in the name of anticommunism and subsequently contributed to long-term results that have been quite sobering: Iran now boasts a radically anti-U.S. regime, and Guatemala continues to suffer from a legacy of military dictatorships and guerrilla insurgencies. The crisis generated by U.S. intervention in Iran and the potential for future U.S. foreign policy crises in Guatemala suggest that perhaps the United States would have been better off (or at the least no worse off) siding with each country's democratic, albeit leftist, regime.[10]

Another significant outcome of U.S. success in these two initial attempts at overthrowing leftist regimes was that it gave subsequent administrations a false sense of power and ability to control the nature of other Third World regimes. As Ransom noted in Chapter 7 concerning U.S. intervention in Iran, "the political leadership in Washington drew more about the efficacy of covert action than was warranted from this example. The heady wine of success led them to believe that this was a foreign policy tool that could be applied with equal success in other problem areas of the world." Yet, both regimes represented fragile democratic coalitions with powerful domestic enemies—most notably, disenchanted militaries—that were all too happy to take control in exchange for U.S. economic and military support. As discussed later, Washington was soon to learn that unstable democratic regimes are much easier to destabilize than regimes governed by revolutionary nationalist movements.

A further guideline for U.S. foreign policy is that although it is important to recognize, as the globalists do, the contributing role that the Soviet Union plays in a regional conflict, policymakers should place greater emphasis on the regional economic, cultural, political, and historical causes for a particular conflict. In this fashion, the conflict becomes legitimate in its own right and lends itself to resolution based on internal reform.

The administrations of Presidents John F. Kennedy and Jimmy Carter were somewhat representative of this regionalist emphasis. Both deviated from the dominant viewpoint that revolutions are caused primarily by external communist aggression by centering on the internal causes of upheaval and the need for structural reform to alleviate them. Despite these reformist interludes, both administrations' attempts at resolving the internal conditions that breed insurgency failed because, like their predecessors and contemporaries, Kennedy and Carter still favored excluding leftist groups from political participation. Genuine structural reform, and hence any defusing of the guerrilla threat, "is highly unlikely as long as the left is automatically to be excluded from political participation."[11]

The case of El Salvador may be instructive. A reform-minded junta took power there in October 1979, aspiring to initiate reformist changes that had the potential of alleviating the country's growing guerrilla insurgency.[12] The junta accepted leaders from the centrist opposition and was willing to carry out a dialogue with the radical left with the idea of including them in a future reconciliation government, but they were soon stymied by rightist elements within the military. Although politically willing to move against the rightist elements (a group whose power had to be broken before genuine reform could take place), the junta hesitated for lack of support from the Carter administration. Despite its advocacy of social reform, Washington "balked at the October junta's willingness to bring the popular organizations into the government and to seek an accord with the guerrillas," inevitably leading to a continuing stalemate in the guerrilla war.[13] When successor governments in the 1980s attempted to initiate agrarian reform—one of the key problems fueling the conflict—the net result was failure: A still powerful right resisted, and the left, still disenfranchised politically, responded with increasing guerrilla attacks. Although favoring social reform, Carter's reliance on the cold war precept of limiting leftist participation mitigated its potential benefits. This trend was exacerbated by the Reagan administration's overwhelming commitment to a military, as opposed to a negotiated, settlement of the conflict.

As noted in Chapter 1, one case stands out as the exception to the traditional U.S. reflex to limit leftist participation: the transition from white minority to black majority rule in Zimbabwe (formerly Rhodesia), even though this ensured a regime dominated by the Marxist Patriotic Front (PF). The case is significant for three reasons: (1) A more ideological approach would have eschewed supporting the PF because of its obvious communist links and outspoken preference of its leaders for Marxism; (2) the United States recognized the legitimacy of the guerrilla struggle and that its resolution depended on internal political and economic reforms; and (3) the United States recognized the positive role to be played by the radical left in the reform equation. Indeed, despite the Marxist rhetoric of Zimbabwe's Prime Minister Robert Mugabe, he clearly has followed a pragmatic policy of socioeconomic reform and maintenance of ties with the West—underscoring that ideology should not be the yardstick by which the United States determines enemies or allies in the Third World. Most important, U.S. willingness to involve the left in meaningful political participation where it previously had been denied a role demonstrated that such participation could be the key to alleviating long-term guerrilla insurgency.

These lessons provide the basis for reassessing traditional U.S. responses to left-wing guerrilla insurgencies. In the case of El Salvador, it would require recognition by policymakers that the revolution is driven by lack of social reform and not by the Soviet-Cuban bloc—the guerrilla struggle is caused by legitimate, unfulfilled popular needs. Although reliance on massive military aid may be able to prevent short-term victory by the guerrillas, in the long run it merely strengthens those forces opposed to reform, promotes a temporary military stalemate, and almost ensures the future intensification of the guerrilla insurgency. The proper U.S. approach should be to emphasize its belief in the negotiated resolution of the conflict between the Salvadoran government and the guerrillas, based on national reconciliation and socioeconomic reform.

Traditional U.S. mistrust of democratically elected leftist regimes and consistent efforts to suppress leftist insurgencies, however, are part of a greater problem: Washington's inability to formulate an effective policy that deals constructively with revolutionary nationalism. In this regard, U.S. policy has been excessively driven by ideology: Whereas leftist insurgencies are perceived negatively and are to be suppressed, antileftist insurgencies fighting revolutionary nationalist regimes are perceived positively and are to be supported. The Reagan Doctrine and its commitment to aiding anticommunist guerrilla insurgencies fighting pro-Soviet Third World regimes is a manifestation of this point of view. The primary fault with this ideological focus, which provides a further guideline for U.S. foreign policy, is that opposing ideologies do not in and of themselves preclude a mutually beneficial relationship. Indeed, the Reagan administration's firm economic and military support for the Marxist government of Mozambique, despite conservative demands that guerrilla forces opposing the government be aided under the umbrella of the Reagan Doctrine, provides an excellent case in point.

Rather than emulate the example of Mozambique, the United States generally has sought a confrontational policy with revolutionary nationalist regimes, especially when they have overthrown former pro-U.S. regimes. Often the relationship between the United States and the revolutionary regime in this context is at first strained. In the case of Nicaragua, the Sandinista leadership was suspicious of U.S. attitudes toward the revolution, primarily because of past U.S. support for a string of Somoza dictatorships and previous intervention in Latin America, whereas the United States feared that the Sandinista regime would become "another Cuba," providing forward bases for Soviet forces and attempting to expand its revolution throughout Central America by force. Yet, fears should not become the basis for foreign policy; when they do, they create a self-fulfilling prophecy.

The parallels between the counterproductive U.S. efforts to overthrow both the Cuban and Nicaraguan revolutions are especially instructive. As was noted in several chapters, the United States, fearful that the revolutionary leaders of both countries would become the tools of Soviet intervention in the Western Hemisphere, employed various instruments of coercion—ranging from diplomatic isolation, to the adoption of economic sanctions, to the support of paramilitary guerrillas—in an effort to derail their revolutions. In the case of

Nicaragua, the primary problem with the interventionist approach was that it underestimated the popular support of the Sandinista regime and the legitimacy of the 1979 revolution. The same mistake was made with Castro's Cuba, and nearly thirty years of confrontation with that regime has achieved little if any benefit for U.S. foreign policy. Most important, continued U.S. intervention, coupled with the very real fear of a direct U.S. invasion, provided both regimes with little recourse other than to seek a closer security relationship with the Soviet Union—the exact opposite of what Washington said it was trying to achieve. In the Cuban case, for example, Soviet Premier Nikita Khrushchev ridiculed as "stupid" U.S. efforts to "drive Castro to the wall," nonetheless relishing the expected results: "Castro will have to gravitate to us like iron filing to a magnet."[14]

The paradox of U.S. intervention against radical revolutionary regimes, according to Anthony Lake, former director of policy planning in the U.S. State Department, is that "polls have generally shown that while the [U.S.] public wants success (the defeat of these regimes), it must come at little cost to the United States (that is, involve no great losses through intervention, grain embargoes, or other actions)."[15] Thus, although the U.S. public supported the swift, low-casualty Grenada invasion, it undoubtedly would not support the likely protracted guerrilla war and thousands of casualties that a similar operation against the Sandinista regime would entail. Cognizant of this fact, the Reagan administration resorted to the lower-cost strategy of paramilitary intervention. Yet, as discussed in Chapter 8, although this type of intervention has exhibited the ability to disrupt severely the target country's economic and political system, it is inadequate if the goal is to overthrow the revolutionary regime or force the leadership to dismantle its chosen system of governance. Rather than folding in the face of external pressure, both Cuba and Nicaragua were able to exploit the tension to whip up popular support. Moreover, U.S. intervention allowed both revolutionary regimes to more easily silence domestic opponents, concentrate power, and blame Washington for failed domestic economic policies.

The increasingly evident failure of intervention to achieve the goal of overthrowing revolutionary regimes in Cuba and Nicaragua, short of a direct U.S. invasion, is indicative of what should constitute another guideline in U.S. foreign policy: a deemphasis on the role of military force when pursuing long-term goals in the Third World. This should not be taken to the other extreme, however, to mean that the United States must adopt a strict policy of nonintervention. As Ted Galen Carpenter correctly concluded in Chapter 9, "no great power can eschew the use of military force in all circumstances." Rather, the challenge lies in establishing those circumstances in which the use of force is both a legitimate and useful tool of intervention. A brief comparison of U.S. efforts in Afghanistan and Nicaragua provides several tentative guidelines:

1. *Majority support within the target country.* The popular or unpopular

nature of the target Third World regime is especially crucial to successful U.S. intervention. In Afghanistan, popular feelings are almost unanimous in desiring a Soviet withdrawal from their country, and traditional Afghani nationalism has ensured a steady stream of recruits to carry out a jihad (holy war) against the atheistic invaders. In Nicaragua, however, the Sandinistas were ushered into power on the back of popular revolutionary nationalism, which, although waning, still remains strong, whereas the contras, primarily because of the great number of Somoza sympathizers among their ranks, are rejected by the majority of the population as an artificial creation of Washington.

2. *Majority regional and international support.* A second gauge of the legitimacy and the probable success of an interventionist policy is its level of regional and international support. In Afghanistan, the mujahedin enjoy overwhelming regional and international support. U.S. efforts not only have been supported by traditional regional allies, such as Pakistan and Saudi Arabia, but also by communist China and revolutionary Iran. A 1987 vote in the UN General Assembly that overwhelmingly called for a Soviet withdrawal (123 voted in favor, 19 were opposed, and 11 abstained) indicates the substantial level of support enjoyed by the mujahedin.[16] U.S. efforts in Nicaragua, to the contrary, are opposed by the majority of nations within the region as well as within the international system, most notably U.S. allies in Europe.[17] Most significant are Latin American denunciations of U.S. military efforts to overthrow the Sandinistas. Rather, the Contadora nations, led by Mexico, and the Central American nations, led by President Oscar Arias of Costa Rica, have preferred to pursue a nonmilitary solution to reaching an accommodation with Nicaragua.

3. *International law.* Although international law prohibiting intervention may be ignored with relative impunity by nations pursuing self-interested policies, as Christopher C. Joyner underscored in Chapter 13, there is no denying its importance as a legitimizing factor (as to what goals and actions are acceptable within the consensual framework of law). In the case of Afghanistan, accepted precepts of international law clearly brand as illegal the Soviet invasion and occupation of that country, legitimizing aid to insurgents seeking to force a Soviet withdrawal. But the International Court of Justice has ruled that U.S. support of the contras violated international legal norms and that the United States should immediately terminate such activities. By refusing to accept the judgment of the World Court, Joyner concluded, "the United States lost legal credibility, appeared diplomatically disingenuous, and allowed Nicaragua to gain a propaganda advantage in view of its lawful appeal to the international legal forum."

Although the combination of these three guidelines cannot, of course, guarantee a successful interventionist episode—indeed, success depends on a host of factors, including the goal pursued—they at least enhance the *possibility* for success and most certainly ensure that U.S. policies foster a legitimacy that will allow it to lead both regionally and within the international system. The key to this type of policy is that the United States act in a multilateral framework in coordination with other nations and not according to some self-prescribed ideological litmus test.

The type of goal pursued is very important. In the case of Afghanistan, for example, U.S. military aid should be limited to achieving the withdrawal of foreign occupation forces. As analyst Jonathan Kwitny perceptively noted, "the arms we supply, and our contact with Afghans, must be governed by the knowledge that when the issue of Soviet occupation is resolved, other local issues will continue to divide the Afghans, both within the country and in their relations with their neighbors." Kwitny concluded that the United States "must not be lured into a continuing dispute that would ally us against new and so far undreamed-of-enemies."[18] As was discussed in Chapter 8, U.S. policymakers failed to resist the urge to intervene in Angola's civil war in 1975 and suffered the consequences of a hostile, anti-U.S. regime when its faction lost in the ensuing power struggle. In short, rather than attempting to control revolutionary nationalism in Afghanistan—as was attempted in Angola, Cuba, Nicaragua, and elsewhere (with highly negative results)—Washington should instead build upon its faithful support of mujahedin aims and foster a positive relationship with the government that eventually comes to power. Concrete actions, rather than the ideological makeup of the regime, whether monarchist, socialist, Marxist, democratic, or some variant therein, should be the basis for any future relationship with Washington. Positive steps taken by any future regime should be met by equal enthusiasm on the U.S. side.

Just as ideology often has led U.S. policymakers to oppose leftist regimes blindly, so too has it led these same individuals to support blindly or to place in power right-wing dictatorships who joined the United States in its anticommunist crusade. Examples include Fulgencio Batista of Cuba, Ferdinand Marcos of the Philippines, Mobutu Sese Seko of Zaire, Jean-Claude Duvalier of Haiti, and the Somoza family dynasty in Nicaragua. The often disregarded long-term problem with this anticommunist strategy is that the elites who become the "bastions for democracy" and, therefore, staunch U.S. allies have usually been traditional dictators who lack popular support, concern themselves primarily with personal aggrandizement, and therefore demonstrate a general disregard for social reform or broadly shared development policies. The core of the problem is that these dictators (whether of the right or the left) seek legitimacy in the form of external economic and military aid in the international arena rather than attempt to build a popular basis for support among their own people. When the United States has been willing to fill the role of patron by dispensing generous amounts of aid, the dictator's need to foster popular domestic legitimacy is sorely circumscribed. Likewise, as dissent against the regime grows, the tendency is toward greater repression than reform.

The negative result of backing authoritarian rulers more willing to repress than reform has been a long string of revolutions that have vented an accompanying anti-U.S. rage, including the case studies of Iran and Nicaragua, as described in Chapters 14 and 16. This result should not be surprising, as the United States has generally been perceived by the disaffected portion of the population in such countries as both the midwife and primary prop of the hated regime. Although the United States may be able to buy stability in the short term, such successful actions as defeating the nationalists in Iran in 1953 or suppressing Sandino's forces in Nicaragua during the 1930s often bode ill for stability and U.S. interests in the long term.

Distinguished experts on Central America have formulated a set of straightforward, yet stringent, guidelines for stemming the cycle of repression and resultant anti-U.S. revolutions in that region that are similarly applicable to the entire Third World.[19] First, apart from humanitarian assistance, which should be distributed "strictly on the basis of need," economic aid should be withheld from regimes "determined to maintain deep social inequality or that are gross and consistent violators of internationally recognized human rights." The authors have warned that when dealing with such regimes, the United States "must guard against the temptation to reward minimum changes that are no more than cosmetic efforts to influence U.S. aid policy." Yet, when countries show a genuine commitment to broadly shared development programs that attack the root causes of social inequality—such as land reform, literacy, and rural health care—the United States should be willing to lend a helping hand.[20]

The guidelines for military assistance are even more stringent. This type of aid, according to the Central America experts, "should be limited to governments that enjoy some popular basis of legitimacy so that U.S. aid will not be used for the repression of popular dissent—a more restrictive criterion than the simple absence of gross and consistent human rights violations." In this regard, the authors noted only two legitimate needs for military equipment that the United States should be willing to meet: "the need for adequate forces to defend a nation against external aggression, and the need to defend democratic institutions against internal violence by a small, well-armed minority."[21] The necessity for a popular basis of legitimacy (not necessarily a multiparty, democratic system) is extremely important. In instances in which this attribute is missing, U.S. military support becomes the basis for internal repression and control, again working counter to long-term U.S. interests in the Third World.

The key to this restructured foreign aid program, which inevitably would require the reduction of special relationships currently held with authoritarian governments, does not mean that the United States should adopt an isolationist foreign policy. Rather, it underscores the necessity of committing valuable resources only to those nations sharing an interest in promoting and maintaining societies built on popular consent and broadly shared development. In this sense, the United States actively should cultivate close relationships with regimes carrying out these programs, assisting financially when the need arises. Yet, as the authors of these guidelines have warned, regimes that pursue none of these goals "but try to curry favor merely by aligning themselves with the United States against the Soviet Union, do not deserve our assistance."[22] In sum, a regime committed to the principles of broadly shared development and respectful of the human rights of its people inevitably enhances its domestic support and represents a positive, long-term investment for the United States.

U.S. policymakers will inevitably find themselves confronted by a situation in which a close ally's democratic institutions and processes are subverted by a leader or faction desirous of assuming personal control and power. Richard J. Kessler, in Chapter 15, has described in detail how this occurred from 1965 to 1986 in the Philippines under the administration of President Ferdinand Marcos. In cases like this, the United States should utilize its economic and military influence (gradually curtailing both types of aid, beginning with military) with the country in question to foster a return to democratic practices. Kessler noted that the United States lost several opportunities to influence policy, the most notable being when Marcos broached the possibility of declaring martial law and suspending the constitution to illegally remain in office. As Kessler concluded, strong U.S. disapproval could have forced him to reverse the decision. "It was a moment, at least from Marcos's perspective, of great vulnerability to external factors."

The most important aspect of the Philippine case study is that five U.S. administrations ignored the dismantling of Philippine democracy because of strategic concerns over continued U.S. access to bases in the country; as Kessler noted, the United States became concerned about democracy in the Philippines "only when democracy became a security issue." Even the Carter administration's human-rights program, which questioned the utility of identifying the United States with inherently unstable dictatorships, was compromised by strategic exceptions; when the pursuit of human rights clashed with perceived national security interests, especially in proven allies of strategic importance (such as Iran, the Philippines, South Korea, and Zaire), national security interests won out.[23] Putting aside the debate over whether or not the United States actually requires bases in the Philippines or elsewhere in the Third World, long-term U.S. interests logically demand that the United States not turn a blind eye while democracy is destroyed in order to maintain these security interests. As the United States learned the hard way in Ethiopia, Iran, and Nicaragua (that is, in other nations of so-called strategic concern, past or present), ignoring the repressive nature of regimes that lack popular support is a surefire way to lose these strategic assets in the long run, as well as to foster the eventual creation of a government hostile to the United States.

A further reality of the international system is that there exists a whole host of authoritarian governments of both the right and the left that systematically abuse the rights of their people, but which are not reliant upon the United States for either economic and military aid. As the United States cannot and should not be the guardian of all the countries of the world, it should maintain no more and no less than proper relations with these countries, withhold any type of military and economic aid, and make its abhorrence of their human-rights transgressions known within the international system. In extreme cases, however, when the international system is confronted with a regime that grossly violates accepted international standards of human rights, the United States should join other nations in adopting multilateral sanctions to change the nature of that regime. As the United States should not casually be in the business of dictating the structure of Third World regimes, sanctions should adhere to the same rigorous formula of legitimacy as was earlier applied to the use of military force: (1) The action should comport with internationally accepted standards of international law; (2) the sanctions should be supported by the majority of the target nation's population; and (3) the sanctions should be supported overwhelmingly both regionally and within the international system. Again, the key to this type of policy is that the United States act in a multilateral framework in coordination with other nations and not according to some self-prescribed ideological litmus test. One case study that fits these requirements is South Africa.

Sanctions in the case of South Africa would fall within the bounds of the international legal tenet of humanitarian intervention (see Chapter 13), are supported by the majority of South Africa's black population as well as regionally within southern Africa, and enjoy a large degree of support that transcends ideological lines in the international arena. Yet, as was noted in Chapter 18, South Africa is clearly strong enough such that even comprehensive, well-enforced sanctions in the short term will not force the dismantling of apartheid by its current leaders. Indeed, critics of sanctions underscore that, in the similar case of UN-imposed sanctions against Zimbabwe-Rhodesia from 1966 to 1980, sanctions in the short term did not affect the minority white regime, as the economy expanded and became increasingly self-reliant. Yet, as William Minter has noted, "In the long run, however, sanctions exacted major economic costs and represented a constant drain on the white regime—especially after the rise of oil prices and the escalation of guerrilla warfare in the 1970s." He concluded that "without sanctions, the war would probably have continued for many more years. With stronger enforcement of sanctions, Zimbabwe could have been independent much sooner."[24]

This conclusion, it seems, is most relevant to the South African situation and to sanctions in general. Several authors have concluded that strongly enforced international sanctions could bring greater pressure to bear on the South African regime.[25] Furthermore, nobody, including opponents of sanctions, discounts that majority rule is inevitable. The purpose of sanctions is not to achieve that goal immediately but to hasten the process along and avoid the unnecessary deaths and radicalization of the opposition that a more protracted guerrilla struggle would entail.

A final guideline for U.S. foreign policy is to take advantage of the consensus-building role to be played by multilateral negotiations within the context of the UN or regional organizations. The ultimate goal of any intervention should never be simply to "bleed" the Soviet Union, anti-U.S. revolutionary regimes, or pariah regimes such as South Africa, but rather to achieve a just and negotiated diplomatic settlement. Efforts within a UN framework clearly contributed to the 1988 Geneva Accords concerning Soviet withdrawal from Afghanistan and the truce in the Iran-Iraq war achieved during the same year, as well as provided an important forum for resolving ongoing conflicts in Angola, Cambodia, and the Western Sahara.[26] As was stated in 1988 by Richard Williamson, assistant secretary of state for international organization affairs, indicating a substantial shift in the Reagan administration's stance, "The UN has a tremendously valuable role to play as a facilitator in ending regional disputes."[27]

Yet, whereas the Reagan administration obviously was willing to compromise in Afghanistan (as well as in Angola and Cambodia) to achieve a settlement of the conflict, such was not the case in its Central American backyard. The policy of the administration was to make a test case out of reversing the Sandinista revolution, subsequently scuttling any regional attempts at negotiating Nicaragua's peaceful existence that would have left the Sandinistas in power. The inadequacy of this short-sighted strategy is clear in that eight years of military intervention only made the Sandinistas more intransigent and anti-American. If the nations of the region, led by the six signatories of the Arias proposal and the Contadora Group, are satisfied with allowing a socialist neighbor to coexist along their borders—albeit one that does not interfere in their domestic affairs—the United States should respect their wishes. Rather than seek to overthrow the Sandinistas, the administration of President George Bush should wholeheartedly support the major tenets of the Arias plan in an attempt to bring lasting peace to the region. Indeed, just as U.S. economic and military power has been able to impede the prospects for peace on terms undesirable to Washington, so too could the enormous weight of that influence be brought to bear as a means for fostering compliance with the Arias peace plan.

■ LEADING WITH CONFIDENCE

The last forty years of U.S. interventionist practices in the Third World literally have guaranteed the extension of U.S. power to virtually all corners of the globe. For better or for worse, the United States rose out of the ashes of World War II to become the most powerful nation the world had ever seen. U.S. economic and military power reached its height in the decade immediately following the war, but the twin trends of the fragmentation of U.S. political culture and the rising pluralism within the international system have since seriously changed the parameters within which U.S. policies must be formulated. Yet, as Joseph S. Nye, Jr., perceptively noted, "Although the United States must adjust to a new era of multipolarity and interdependence in world politics, Americans should not underestimate U.S. strength." Indeed, "with more than one-fifth of world military and economic product, the U.S. remains the most powerful state in the world and will very likely remain that way far into the future."[28]

For the United States to lead with confidence well into the twenty-first century requires the basic redesigning of U.S. interventionist practices, as outlined here. In the domestic realm, the president should establish a greater partnership with Congress, formulating policies built upon the strong foundations of congressional and public support. Secure in this support, the president could lead with confidence, charting a consistent and coherent foreign policy in the Third World. In the international realm, interventionist practices should attempt to build upon both a multilateral regional and international consensus, with the United States taking the lead in utilizing the forum of the UN and accepted precepts of international law in garnering support. Although adherence to the guidelines put forth in this chapter may not always guarantee the success of U.S. foreign policy in the Third World, they raise the possibility for success substantially and most certainly ensure the legitimacy that is necessary for leadership both regionally and within the international system.

Notes

■ CHAPTER 1

1. Tim Shorrock, "The Struggle for Democracy in South Korea in the Rise of Anti-Americanism," *Third World Quarterly* 8, 4 (October 1986): 1203–4.

2. Third World countries have also been referred to as "undeveloped," "underdeveloped," "developing," "less-developed," and "nondeveloped." For an examination of the nonaligned movement and the NIEO, see Richard L. Jackson, *The Non-Aligned, the U.N. and the Superpowers* (New York: Praeger, 1986).

3. For a more in-depth discussion of these characteristics, see Joseph Weatherby, Jr., et al., eds., *The Other World: Issues and Politics in the Third World* (New York: Macmillan, 1987), esp. ch. 1.

4. For further discussion, see Peter Worsley, *Three Worlds: Culture and World Development* (Chicago: University of Chicago Press, 1984), esp. pp. 306–44.

5. The statistics in this section are derived from U.S. Department of Commerce, Bureau of the Census, *Statistical Abstract of the United States 1987* (Washington, D.C.: Department of Commerce, 1986), pp. 782–86, 837.

6. Quoted in Michael T. Klare and Peter Kornbluh, "The New Interventionism: Low-Intensity Warfare in the 1980s and Beyond," in Klare and Kornbluh, eds., *Low-Intensity Warfare: Counterinsurgency, Proinsurgency, and Antiterrorism in the Eighties* (New York: Pantheon, 1988), p. 4.

7. See Russell Watson (with John Barry), "The Military Choices Will Not Be Easy," *Newsweek*, February 22, 1988, pp. 54–55.

8. For a discussion on the foreign policy impact of the Committee on the Present Danger, see Jerry W. Sanders, *Peddlers of Crisis: The Committee on the Present Danger* (Boston: South End, 1983). For Cato Institute analyses, see Sheldon L. Richman, "The United States and the Persian Gulf," Cato Institute Policy Analysis no. 46, January 10, 1985; and Ted G. Carpenter, "U.S. Aid to Anti-Communist Rebels: The 'Reagan Doctrine' and Its Pitfalls," Cato Institute Policy Analysis no. 74, June 24, 1986. For a detailed discussion of how U.S. stakes and threats have been exaggerated in the Third World, see Robert H. Johnson, "Exaggerating America's Stakes in Third World Conflicts," *International Security* 10, 3 (Winter 1985-86): 32–68.

9. William Shawcross, *Sideshow: Kissinger, Nixon and the Destruction of Cambodia* (New York: Pocket, 1979), esp. pp. 19–35.

10. Figures are derived from *The World Almanac and Book of Facts 1988* (New York: Pharos, 1987), pp. 338–39.

11. See, for example, Luigi Sensi, "Superpower Interventions in Civil Wars, 1945–1987," paper prepared for the 29th Annual Meeting of the International Studies Association, St. Louis, Mo., March 30–April 2, 1988.

12. Quoted in Arthur Schlesinger, Jr., "Foreign Policy and the American Character," *Foreign Affairs* 62, 1 (Fall 1983): 5.

13. Richard J. Barnet, *Intervention and Revolution: America's Confrontation with Insurgent Movements Around the World* (New York: World Publishing, 1968), p. 56.

14. William M. Leogrande, "Cuba," in Morris J. Blachman, William M. Leogrande, and Kenneth E. Sharpe, eds., *Confronting Revolution: Security Through Diplomacy in Central America* (New York: Pantheon, 1986), pp. 232–33.

15. Morris J. Blachman et al., "The Failure of the Hegemonic Strategic Vision," in Blachman, Leogrande, and Sharpe, *Confronting Revolution*, p. 391.

16. For a good discussion of these factors, see Barry Rubin, *Modern Dictators, Third World Coup Makers, Strongmen, and Populist Tyrants* (New York: McGraw-Hill, 1987), esp. pp. 76–108.

17. This does not mean, however, that the United States always supported such a program nor that U.S. influence was the key in determining the process. For instructive accounts, see Anthony Lake, *The "Tar Baby" Option: American Policy Toward Southern Rhodesia* (New York: Columbia University Press, 1976); and Henry F. Jackson, *From the Congo to Soweto: U.S. Foreign Policy Toward Africa Since 1960* (New York: Quill, 1984).

18. See Blachman, Leogrande, and Sharpe, *Confronting Revolution*, chs. 3, 12–14.

19. Gary L. Guertner, "Global Strategy and Regional Pragmatism in U.S. Foreign Policy," *International Studies Notes* 12, 1 (Fall 1985): 17.

20. Robert O. Keohane and Joseph S. Nye, *Power and Interdependence: World Politics in Transition* (Boston: Little, Brown, 1977), pp. 27–28.

21. Richard E. Feinberg, *The Intemperate Zone: The Third World Challenge to U.S. Foreign Policy* (New York: W. W. Norton, 1983), p. 34.

22. For a discussion of conflicting lessons, see Richard A. Melanson, *Writing History and Making Policy: The Cold War, Vietnam, and Revisionism* (Lanham: University Press of America, 1983).

23. Melvin Gurtov and Ray Maghroori, *Roots of Failure: United States Foreign Policy in the Third World* (Westport, Conn.: Greenwood, 1984), p. 173.

24. See Charles F. Doran, George Modelski, and Cal Clark, eds., *North/South Relations: Studies in Dependency Reversal* (New York: Praeger, 1983).

25. Rubin, *Modern Dictators*, p. 315.

26. Walter LaFeber, *Inevitable Revolutions: The United States in Central America* (New York: W. W. Norton, 1983), p. 15.

27. See Benjamin Hart, "Rhetoric vs. Reality: How the State Department Betrays the Reagan Vision," Heritage Foundation Backgrounder no. 484, 1986. For a brief discussion of the conflict between U.S. conservatives who favor support and State Department rejection of those demands, see James Brooke, "Visiting U.S. Aide Condemns Mozambique Rebels," *New York Times*, April 27, 1988, p. A6.

■ CHAPTER 2

1. See Albert Weinberg, *Manifest Destiny: A Study of Nationalist Expansionism in American History* (Baltimore: Johns Hopkins Press, 1935).

2. "Memorandum of a Conversation, July 6, 1945," in U.S. Department of State,

Foreign Relations of the United States: The Conference at Berlin, vol. 1 (Washington, D.C.: Government Printing Office), pp. 997–98.

3. "Secretary's Exposition of American History at the Kraft Dinner, November 13, 1952" (by an unknown notetaker), *The Papers of Dean Acheson,* Harry S. Truman Library, Independence, Mo.

4. Quoted in Lloyd C. Gardner and William L. O'Neill, *Looking Backward: A Reintroduction to American History* (New York: McGraw-Hill, 1974), p. 54.

5. The complicated process by which social tensions, especially in the major port cities, combined with the aspirations of colonial elites to produce the American Revolution (then turned outward against external enemies) is discussed in Gary B. Nash, *The Urban Crucible: Social Change, Political Consciousness, and the Origins of the American Revolution* (Cambridge: Harvard University Press, 1979). The roots of James Madison's famous prescription for preserving republicanism by enlarging the sphere, as outlined in *Federalist Papers* no. 10 and no. 51, so as to diversify and separate factions, may be seen clearly in the prerevolution decade.

6. Francis Wharton, ed., *The Revolutionary Correspondence of the United States,* vol. 6 (Washington, D.C.: Government Printing Office, 1889), p. 132.

7. William Appleman Williams, *The Contours of American History* (New York: World Publishing, 1961), p. 179.

8. Jefferson to James Madison, August 16, 1807, in Paul Leicester Ford, ed., *The Writings of Thomas Jefferson,* vol. 9 (New York: G. P. Putnam's, 1896), pp. 124–25.

9. Patricia Nelson Limerick, *The Legacy of Conquest: The Unbroken Past of the American West* (New York: W. W. Norton, 1987), pp. 18–19.

10. The Big Three met at the Potsdam Conference in 1945 to begin discussion of postwar problems. Frustrated by the delays and the wrangling, President Truman exclaimed to an aide: "Jimmy, do you realize that we have been here seventeen whole days? Why, in seventeen days you can decide anything!" Robert Murphy, *Diplomat Among Warriors* (New York: Pyramid, 1965), pp. 278–79.

11. Limerick, *Legacy of Conquest,* p. 324.

12. Quoted in Richard W. Van Alstyne, "Empire in Midpassage, 1845–1867," in William Appleman Williams, ed., *From Colony to Empire: Essays in the History of American Foreign Relations* (New York: Wiley, 1972), p. 111.

13. See Walter LaFeber, "The 'Lion in the Path': The U.S. Emergence as a World Power," *Political Science Quarterly* 101, 5 (1986): 705–18.

14. Ibid.

15. Frederic Bancroft, *The Life of William H. Seward,* vol. 2 (Gloucester, Mass.: Peter Smith, 1967), p. 13.

16. Ibid.

17. The fullest discussion is Ernest Paolino, *The Foundations of the American Empire: William H. Seward and U.S. Foreign Policy* (Ithaca: Cornell University Press, 1973), p. 28.

18. Bancroft, *The Life of William H. Seward,* p. 68.

19. See William O. Scroggs, *Filibusters and Financiers: The Story of William Walker and His Associates* (New York: Macmillan, 1916).

20. Wood to Root, January 13, 1900, *The Papers of Elihu Root,* Library of Congress, Washington, D.C.

21. Bryan to Thomas Bailly-Blanchard, December 19, 1914, U.S. Department of State, *Foreign Relations of the United States, 1914* (Washington, D.C.: Government Printing Office, 1922), pp. 370–71.

22. "Present Nature and Extent of the Monroe Doctrine and Its Need of Restatement," June 11, 1914, Records of the Department of State, National Archives, Washington, D.C., File No. 710.11/185 1/2.

23. LaFeber, "The 'Lion in the Path,'" p. 714.

24. Quoted in Roy Flint, "The United States Army on the Pacific Frontier, 1899–1939," in Joe C. Dixon, ed., *The American Military and the Far East* (Washington, D.C.: Government Printing Office, 1980), p. 151.

25. Ray Stannard Baker and William E. Dodd, eds., *The Public Papers of Woodrow Wilson,* vol. 5 (New York: Harper and Brothers, 1972), pp. 223–38.

26. See, for example, Carl P. Parrini, *Heir to Empire: United States Economic Diplomacy, 1916–1923* (Pittsburgh: University of Pittsburgh Press, 1969); and Joan Hoff Wilson, *American Business and Foreign Policy, 1920–1933* (Lexington: University of Kentucky Press, 1971).

27. See William C. McNeil, *American Money and the Weimar Republic: Economics and Politics on the Eve of the Great Depression* (New York: Columbia University Press, 1986).

28. Quoted in Lloyd C. Gardner, *A Covenant with Power: America and World Order from Wilson to Reagan* (New York: Oxford University Press, 1984), p. 45.

29. Quoted in Ronald J. Stupak, *American Foreign Policy: Assumptions, Processes and Projections* (New York: Harper & Row, 1976), p. 188.

30. U.S. Congress, Senate, Committee on Foreign Relations, *Hearings Held in Executive Session: Legislative Origins of the Truman Doctrine,* 80th Cong., 1st Sess., 1973, p. 197.

31. Quoted in Lloyd C. Gardner, Walter F. LaFeber, and Thomas J. McCormick, *Creation of the American Empire: U.S. Diplomatic History* (Chicago: Rand-McNally, 1973), p. 458.

32. NSC-68, April 14, 1950, printed in U.S. Department of State, *Foreign Relations of the United States, 1950,* vol. 1 (Washington, D.C.: Government Printing Office, 1977), pp. 234–92.

33. Seymour Hersh, "The Price of Power: Kissinger, Nixon and Chile," *Atlantic Monthly* (December 1982): 31–58.

34. "Memorandum for Record," June 23, 1954, *The Dwight D. Eisenhower Papers,* Eisenhower Library, Abilene, Kans., Whitman File, Legislative Meetings.

■ CHAPTER 3

1. U.S. Commission on Integrated Long-Term Strategy, *Discriminate Deterrence* (Washington, D.C.: Government Printing Office, 1988), pp. 13–14.

2. For discussion of this phenomenon, see Michael T. Klare and Peter Kornbluh, eds., *Low-Intensity Warfare: Counterinsurgency, Proinsurgency, and Antiterrorism in the Eighties* (New York: Pantheon, 1988), ch. 1. See also U.S. Department of Defense, *Proceedings of the Low-Intensity Warfare Conference* (Washington, D.C.: Government Printing Office, 1986) (hereinafter, *LIC Proceedings*).

3. Frank C. Carlucci, *Annual Report to the Congress,* U.S. Department of Defense, Fiscal Year 1989 (Washington, D.C.: Government Printing Office, 1988) (hereinafter, *DOD Report FY 89*), p. 24.

4. *DOD Report FY 89,* p. 63; See also pp. 58–62, 225–30.

5. Caspar Weinberger, *Annual Report to the Congress,* U.S. Department of Defense, Fiscal Year 1985 (Washington, D.C.: Government Printing Office, 1985), p. 18. For discussion, see Gabriel Kolko, *Confronting the Third World: United States Foreign Policies 1945–1980* (New York: Pantheon, 1988).

6. For discussion, see Stephen E. Ambrose, *Rise to Globalism,* 4th rev. ed. (New York: Penguin, 1985), pp. 58–79; Richard J. Barnet, *Intervention and Revolution: The*

United States in the Third World, rev. ed. (New York: New American Library, 1980), pp. 119–56.

7. See Ambrose, *Rise to Globalism,* pp. 79–98.

8. Ibid., pp. 99–115. For the text of NSC-68, see U.S. Department of State, *Foreign Relations of the United States, 1950,* vol. 1 (Washington, D.C.: Government Printing Office, 1977), pp. 234–92.

9. For discussion, see Richard M. Freeland, *The Truman Doctrine and the Origins of McCarthyism* (New York: Knopf, 1972).

10. See I. F. Stone, *The Hidden History of the Korean War,* 2nd ed. (New York: Monthly Review Press, 1969).

11. See Ambrose, *Rise to Globalism,* pp. 132–79.

12. Maxwell D. Taylor, *The Uncertain Trumpet* (New York: Harper and Row, 1960), pp. 5–6.

13. For summary and analysis of NSAM 124 and NSAM 182, see Klare and Kornbluh, *Low-Intensity Warfare,* pp. 27–30. On Kennedy and counterinsurgency, see Richard J. Walton, *Cold War and Counter-Revolution: The Foreign Policy of John F. Kennedy* (New York: Viking, 1972). On counterinsurgency doctrine, see Douglas S. Blaufarb, *The Counterinsurgency Era* (New York: Free Press, 1977).

14. U.S. Congress, House, Committee on Appropriations, Subcommittee, *Department of Defense Appropriations for 1964,* Hearings, 88th Cong., 1st Sess., Pt. 1, 1963, pp. 483–84.

15. Taylor memorandum to Robert S. McNamara, January 22, 1964, as reprinted in the *New York Times*, June 13, 1971, p. A35.

16. On Vietnam, see George McT. Kahin, *Intervention: How America Became Involved in Vietnam* (New York: Knopf, 1986), pp. 146–235; Stanley Karnow, *Vietnam: A History* (New York: Penguin, 1984), pp. 312–473; and Gabriel Kolko, *Anatomy of a War* (New York: Pantheon, 1985).

17. For discussion, see Michael T. Klare, *Beyond the "Vietnam Syndrome"* (Washington, D.C.: Institute for Policy Studies, 1981), pp. 1–8.

18. Elmo R. Zumwalt, Jr., "Heritage of Weakness: An Assessment of the 1970s," in W. Scott Thompson, ed., *From Weakness to Strength* (San Francisco: Institute for Contemporary Studies, 1980), pp. 34, 39.

19. Interview in *U.S. News and World Report,* April 16, 1979, pp. 49–50.

20. See *Washington Post,* June 22, 1979, and *New York Times*, June 28, 1979.

21. Cited in the *New York Times*, January 24, 1980.

22. See Reagan's remarks at West Point on May 27, 1981, as reported in the *New York Times*, May 28, 1981.

23. See Klare and Kornbluh, *Low-Intensity Warfare,* ch. 4.

24. Remarks before the American Newspaper Publishers Association, Chicago, Ill., May 5, 1981 (U.S. Department of Defense transcript).

25. Richard Halloran, "Reagan as Military Commander," *New York Times Magazine,* January 15, 1984, pp. 24–25.

26. For discussion, see Klare and Kornbluh, *Low-Intensity Warfare,* ch. 1. For a compendium of Pentagon views, see *LIC Proceedings*. The landscape of LIC is further spelled out in U.S. Army Command and General Staff College, *Low-Intensity Conflict,* Field Circular 100-20 (Ft. Leavenworth, Kans., 1986) (hereinafter, USACGSC, FC 100-20).

27. *Taking the Stand: The Testimony of Lt. Col. Oliver L. North* (New York: Pocket Books, 1987), p. 12.

28. Neil C. Livingstone, "Fighting Terrorism and 'Dirty Little Wars,'" in William A. Buckingham, Jr., ed., *Defense Planning for the 1980s* (Washington, D.C.: National Defense University Press, 1984), pp. 166–67, 186.

29. Ibid., pp. 186–87.

30. *LIC Proceedings*, p. 10.

31. On current U.S. counterinsurgency doctrine, see USACGSC, FC 100-20, chs. 3–5. See also Klare and Kornbluh, *Low-Intensity Warfare*, pp. 56–62 and chs. 5 (on El Salvador) and 7 (on the Philippines).

32. See USACGSC, FC 100-20, chs. 8 and 9. See also Klare and Kornbluh, *Low-Intensity Warfare*, pp. 66–69.

33. Robert C. McFarlane, "Deterring Terrorism," *Journal of Defense and Diplomacy* (June 1985), p. 8. See also U.S. Army Training and Doctrine Command, *U.S. Army Operational Concept for Terrorism Counteraction*, Pamphlet No. 525-37 (Ft. Monroe, Va., 1984). On NSDD 138, see *Los Angeles Times*, April 15, 1984, and *Washington Post*, April 18, 1984.

34. See David C. Morrison, "The Pentagon's Drug Wars," *National Journal*, September 6, 1986, pp. 2105–7. On "Operation Blast Furnace," see *New York Times*, July 16–18 and September 24, 1986.

35. See Kolko, *Confronting the Third World*.

36. Guy Pauker, *Military Implications of a Possible World Order Crisis in the 1980s*, Report No. R-2003-AF (Santa Monica: RAND Corporation, 1977), pp. 1–4.

CHAPTER 4

1. See, for example, among proffered forms of change, Barrington Moore, Jr., *Injustice: The Social Bases of Obedience and Revolt* (White Plains, N.Y.: M. E. Sharpe, 1978), pp. 500–5; and Leon Trotsky, "Revolution and the Proletariat," in John G. Wright, *The Permanent Revolution and Results and Prospects* (New York: Pathfinder, 1970), pp. 62–68.

2. Kenneth Waltz, *Theory of International Politics* (Reading, Mass.: Addison-Wesley, 1979), pp. 170–76.

3. "It is no accident that between the Berlin Crisis and the invasion of Czechoslovakia, the principal threats to peace came from the emerging areas. The temptation to deflect domestic dissatisfactions into foreign adventures is ever present." Henry A. Kissinger, *American Foreign Policy* (New York: W. W. Norton, 1974), p. 80.

4. "The international system would be more stable and less conflictual if the North and the South had less to do with each other." Stephen D. Krasner, *Structural Conflict: The Third World Against Global Liberalism* (Berkeley: University of California Press, 1985), p. 30.

5. Roger D. Hansen, *Beyond the North-South Stalemate* (New York: McGraw-Hill, 1979), p. 284.

6. Robert O. Keohane, *After Hegemony: Cooperation and Discord in the World Political Economy* (Princeton: Princeton University Press, 1984).

7. Edward N. Luttwak, *The Great Strategy of the Soviet Union* (New York: St. Martin's, 1983).

8. Speculation that Gorbachev is stressing "a defensive nature of military preparedness" in East-West matters does not extend to "wars of national liberation." Andrew Borowiec, "Are Soviets Giving up Dogma That War with the West Is Inevitable?" *Washington Times*, November 12, 1987, pp. A1, A9.

9. Alexander Dollin, "Policy-Making and Foreign Affairs," in James Cracraft, ed., *The Soviet Union Today: An Interpretive Guide* (Chicago: Educational Foundation for Nuclear Science, 1983), p. 55.

10. Jean-Pierre Cot, "Winning East-West in North-South," *Foreign Policy,* no. 46 (Spring 1982): 3–18.

11. Jorge I. Dominguez, "U.S., Soviet, and Cuban Policies Toward Latin America," in Marshall D. Shulman, ed., *East-West Tensions in the Third World* (New York: W. W. Norton, 1986), pp. 44–77.

12. Said Amir Arjomand, "Iran's Islamic Revolution in Comparative Perspective," *Comparative Politics* 38, 3 (April 1986): 384–414; and Kathleen M. Christenson, "Myths About Palestinians," *Foreign Policy,* no. 66 (Spring 1987): 109–27.

13. Paul Bairoch, *The Economic Development of the Third World Since 1900* (Berkeley: University of California Press, 1975), p. 195.

14. Georges Lefebvre, *The Coming of the French Revolution* (Princeton: Princeton University Press, 1970), pp. xv–xvi.

15. Benjamin Ward, *The Ideal Worlds of Economics: Liberal, Radical, and Conservative Economic World Views* (New York: Basic Books, 1979), pp. 77–78.

16. Abraham F. Lowenthal, "Ronald Reagan and Latin America: Coping with Hegemony in Decline," in Kenneth A. Oye, Robert J. Lieber, and Donald Rothchild, eds., *Eagle Defiant: United States Foreign Policy in the 1980s* (Boston: Little, Brown, 1983), pp. 311–36.

17. For the record among the advanced industrial countries on some of these indexes, see Geoffrey Garett and Peter Lange, "Performance in a Hostile World: Economic Growth in Capitalist Democracies, 1974–1980," *World Politics* 38, 4 (July 1986): 517–45.

18. Stephan Haggard, "The Newly Industrializing Countries in the International System," *World Politics* 33, 2 (January 1986): 343–70; and Bela Belassa, *The Newly Industrializing Countries in the World Economy* (New York: Pergamon, 1981).

19. Sylvia Ann Hewlett, *The Cruel Dilemmas of Development: Twentieth Century Brazil* (New York: Basic Books, 1980), pp. 233–43.

20. See Robert W. Tucker, *The Inequality of Nations* (New York: Basic Books, 1977).

21. Richard E. Feinberg, "Reaganomics and the Third World," in Oye, Lieber, and Rothchild, *Eagle Defiant,* pp. 132–66.

22. David A. Lake, "Power and the Realist World: Towards a Realist Political Economy of North-South Relations," *International Studies Quarterly* 31, 2 (June 1987): 217–34.

23. Samuel P. Huntington, "Renewed Hostility," in Joseph S. Nye, Jr., ed., *The Making of America's Soviet Policy* (New Haven: Yale University Press, 1984), pp. 265–90.

24. Barry M. Blechman, Janne E. Nolan, and Alan Platt, "Pushing Arms," *Foreign Policy,* no. 46 (Spring 1982): 138–54.

25. Richard Rosecrance, *The Rise of the Trading State: Commerce and Conquest in the Modern World* (New York: Basic Books, 1986), pp. 119–33.

26. Roger Errera, "Democracies and Human Rights: The Heritage and the Challenge," *Atlantic Community Quarterly* 25, 2 (Summer 1987): 189–200, esp. 196–97; and John F McCamant, "Social Science and Human Rights," *International Organization* 35, 3 (Summer 1981): 531–52, esp. 543–47.

27. Christopher H. Pyle, "Defining Terrorism," *Foreign Policy,* no. 64 (Fall 1986): 63–78.

28. Philip Windsor, "Terrorism and International Law," *Atlantic Community Quarterly* 25, 2 (Summer 1987): 201–9.

29. Stanley Hoffman, "Requiem," *Foreign Policy,* no. 42 (Spring 1981): 3–26, esp. 3–4.

30. Ole R. Holsti and James N. Rosenau, "Consensus Lost, Consensus Regained?

Foreign Policy Beliefs of American Leaders, 1976–1980," *International Studies Quarterly* 30, 4 (December 1986): 375–410, esp. 407–8.

31. Stephen J. Solarz, "When to Intervene," *Foreign Policy,* no. 63 (Summer 1986): 20–39.

32. Bruce Russett and Elizabeth C. Hanson, *Interest and Ideology: The Foreign Policy Beliefs of American Businessmen* (San Francisco: W. H. Freeman, 1975), pp. 220–43.

33. Francis Fukuyama, "Military Aspects of U.S.-Soviet Competition in the Third World," in Shulman, *East-West Tensions,* pp. 181–211.

34. Janice Gross Stein, "Extended Deterrence in the Middle East: American Strategy Reconsidered," *World Politics* 39, 3 (April 1987): 326–52.

35. Robert M. Cutler, Laure Despres, and Aaron Karp, "The Political Economy of East-South Military Transfers," *International Studies Quarterly* 31, 3 (September 1987): 273–99, esp. 294–95.

36. Bruce R. Kuniholm, *The Origins of the Cold War in the Near East* (Princeton: Princeton University Press, 1980), pp. 383–431.

37. William R. Cline, "Resource Transfers to the Developing Countries: Issues and Trends," in William R. Cline, ed., *Policy Alternatives for a New International Economic Order: An Economic Analysis* (New York: Praeger, 1979).

38. Patrick J. McGowan and Dale L. Smith, "Economic Dependency in Black Africa: An Analysis of Competing Theories," *International Organization* 32, 1 (Winter 1978): 179–236.

■ CHAPTER 5

1. The figures used throughout this section, for regional distributions and program types, are in constant FY 1987 dollars. A detailed analysis of the changing priorities of the foreign assistance program is provided by Stanley Heginbotham, "Foreign Aid: The Evolution of U.S. Programs," Congressional Research Service Report no. 86–86 F, April 16, 1986.

2. Peter McPherson, "Security Benefits of Foreign Assistance to U.S." (Speech, U.S. AID, Washington, D.C., May 1984), p. 3.

3. *Commission on Security and Economic Assistance: A Report* (Washington, D.C.: Department of State, 1983), p. 3 (hereinafter, *Report*).

4. Ibid., p. 31.

5. Cited in James Bovard, "Free Food Bankrupts Foreign Farmers," *Wall Street Journal,* July 2, 1984, p. A18.

6. Sudhir Sen, "Farewell to Foreign Aid," *World View* 25, 7 (July 1982): 8.

7. Francis Moore Lappé, Joseph Collins, and David Kinley, *Aid as Obstacle: Twenty Questions about our Aid and the Hungry* (San Francisco: Institute for Food and Development Policy, 1981), pp. 95–96.

8. Ibid., p. 116.

9. Ibid., p. 118.

10. The reflexive response of many presidential panels and independent analysts to the problem of underdevelopment abroad is to propose another Marshall Plan—for Central America, the Philippines, or wherever. But the Marshall Plan's effect on Europe's recovery may have been less than has been traditionally assumed. See Tyler Cowen, "The Marshall Plan: Myths and Realities," in Doug Bandow, ed., *U.S. Aid to the Developing World: A Free Market Agenda* (Washington, D.C.: Heritage Foundation, 1985), pp. 61–74. In any case, Europe had developed and only needed to be "re-

constructed," whereas Third World states lack the basic legal institutions and economic infrastructure necessary to prosper.

11. Development is more complex than just a rising GNP, but economic growth is one of the easiest surrogate variables to measure. Most important, it is usually the variable employed by U.S. policymakers.

12. Alan Rufus Waters, forthcoming Heritage Foundation Backgrounder, 1989.

13. Thomas Sowell, *The Economics and Politics of Race* (New York: William Morrow, 1983), p. 240.

14. Stephen Hellinger, Douglas Hellinger, and Fred M. O'Regan, *Aid for Just Development: Report on the Future of Foreign Assistance* (Boulder: Lynne Rienner Publishers, 1988), p. 5.

15. Ibid., pp. 30–31.

16. See, for example, Doug Bandow, "The U.S. Role in Promoting Third World Development," in Bandow, ed., *U.S. Aid to the Developing World,* pp. xviii–xvi; and James Bovard, "The Continuing Failure of Foreign Aid," Cato Institute Policy Analysis no. 65, January 31, 1986. This is not to suggest that no foreign aid program has ever worked. Creation and distribution of oral rehydration packets, for example, which treat victims of diarrhea, certainly have saved lives abroad. But even well-intended health programs suffer from a variety of problems, some of which are detailed in Carol Adelman et al., "A New Rx Is Needed for World Health Care," Heritage Foundation Backgrounder no. 592, July 9, 1987.

17. Karl Maier, "Zimbabwe Creates an 'Agricultural Miracle' in Africa—But can the Continent's Newest Nation Survive it?" *Christian Science Monitor,* September 27, 1988, p. 14.

18. *Report,* p. 33.

19. For a generally excellent overview of the civil war and the role of the United States therein, see Brook Larmer's five-part series in the *Christian Science Monitor,* October 19–21, and October 24–25, 1988. The titles of the articles in order of date are "Backsliding to the Bad Old Days" (pp. 14–15); "The Shifting Battlefront" (pp. 16–17); "Papering over the Economic Divide" (pp. 16–17); "The Politics of Polarization" (pp. 16–17); and "Hard Lessons for the U.S. and the Region" (pp. 14–15).

20. For a discussion of the agricultural program, see Bovard, "The Continuing Failure," pp. 6–8. Also see U.S. Agency for International Development (AID), *Agrarian Reform in El Salvador: A Report on its Status,* Audit report no. 1-519-84-2 (Washington, D.C.: AID, 1988).

21. Larmer, "Backsliding," p. 15.

22. This is true despite the fact that, as noted earlier, enhancing the military's power in an undemocratic state is likely to increase repression. Moreover, to the extent that U.S. military aid encourages a country to devote more of its resources to defense, it is likely to grow more slowly economically. For example, one UN study found that higher military spending consistently lowered economic growth rates and that every additional dollar spent on military outlays cuts agricultural production twenty cents. Cited in Doug Bandow, "Aid That Just Buys Guns," *Wall Street Journal,* June 14, 1988, p. A34.

23. Ibid., pp. 32–33.

24. Stephen Kinzer, "U.S. Fails to Win Tough Statement Against Nicaragua," *New York Times,* August 2, 1988, p. 4.

25. Linda Feldmann, "Critics Charge US Policy Fuels Conflict in Somalia," *Christian Science Monitor,* August 10, 1988, p. 4.

26. U.S. Congress, Senate, Committee on Foreign Relations, *Report of the Senate Committee on Foreign Relations on S. 1274, No. 100-60,* 100th Cong., 1st Sess., May 22, 1987, pp. 143–66. Ironically, the Reagan administration has, however, used a country's UN voting record as one factor in determining the recommended level of aid.

■ CHAPTER 6

1. There have been six additional cases since 1983 (see Table 6.1). These episodes are not included in the statistical analysis because time constraints prevented the compilation of comparable case studies. However, preliminary assessments of the effectiveness of sanctions have been made for these cases and are shown in the table. Including these cases lowers the overall success ratio slightly, from 42 percent to 39 percent, and lowers the post-1973 ratio by only one percentage point, from 23 percent to 22 percent.

2. See Gary Clyde Hufbauer and Jeffrey J. Schott, assisted by Kimberly Ann Elliott, *Economic Sanctions Reconsidered: History and Current Policy* (Washington, D.C.: Institute for International Economics, 1985) (hereinafter, *Economic Sanctions Reconsidered*).

3. Quoted in Stephen B. Cohen, "Conditioning U.S. Security Assistance on Human Rights Practices," *American Journal of International Law* 76 (April 1982): 265.

4. Ibid.

5. *Economic Sanctions Reconsidered,* pp. 461–64. See also Cohen, "Conditioning U.S. Security Assistance," pp. 246–79.

6. Although opposition to apartheid was a factor in the imposition of sanctions, this case is considered separately from the broader U.S./UN sanctions campaign against South Africa.

7. David A. Flores, "Export Controls and the U.S. Effort to Combat International Terrorism," *Law and Policy in International Business* 13 (1981): 550. See also *Economic Sanctions Reconsidered,* pp. 453–54.

8. Twenty-one of fifty-four if the six occurring since publication of *Economic Sanctions Reconsidered* are included.

9. Unlike David A. Baldwin's study, *Economic Statecraft: Theory and Practice* (Princeton: Princeton University Press, 1985), there was no attempt to assess the role of symbolism—for both domestic and international audiences—in the use or effectiveness of sanctions. Nor is there an appraisal of the usefulness of sanctions in deterring future "bad" behavior.

10. Some cases may have more than one objective, as shown in Table 6.1. For purposes of the statistical analysis, however, such cases were classified only by the most difficult objective.

11. These results are very similar to those found in *Economic Sanctions Reconsidered*. Looking at all 103 cases, we found that sanctions contributed to a successful outcome in 53 percent of the destabilization cases, 41 percent of the modest-goal cases, a third of the military-disruption cases, and less than a fifth of other major cases.

12. As will be explored later, research conducted subsequent to *Economic Sanctions Reconsidered* suggests that financial sanctions are generally more effective than trade sanctions. For a discussion of this topic, see Kimberly A. Elliott and Gary Clyde Hufbauer, "Financial Sanctions and Foreign Policy," *Harvard International Review* 10, 5 (June/July 1988): 8–12. Unfortunately, at the time *Economic Sanctions Reconsidered* was written, no measure of dependence on various forms of finance, similar to the trade linkage variable, had been developed.

13. Baldwin, *Economic Statecraft,* passim.

14. This does not contradict the earlier conclusion that modest goals will be relatively easier to achieve. If a modest objective is also very low priority, the political will to sustain and vigorously pursue it may be lacking, especially if it is relatively more important to the target country. A similar conclusion is reported by Albert E. Hirschman, *National Power and the Structure of Foreign Trade* (Berkeley: University of California Press, 1980).

■ CHAPTER 7

1. *Intelligence: The Acme of Skills* (Washington, D.C.: Office of Public Affairs, Central Intelligence Agency, 1982), p. 28.

2. *The CIA's Secret Operations* (New York: Reader's Digest Press, 1977), p. 13.

3. Quoted in U.S. Congress, Senate, Church Committee, *Final Report,* no. 94–755, vol. 4, 94th Cong., 2nd Sess., 1976, p. 53 (hereinafter, *Church Committee Report*).

4. Commission on CIA Activities Within the United States, Nelson Rockefeller, Chairman, *Report to the President* (Washington, D.C.: Government Printing Office, 1975), p. 5.

5. *Church Committee Report,* vol 1, pp. 159–61.

6. See "The Pike Papers," *Village Voice,* February 16, 1976.

7. Harry Rositzke, "America's Secret Operations: A Perspective," *Foreign Affairs* 53, 2 (January 1975): 344–51.

8. Loch K. Johnson, *A Season of Inquiry: The Senate Intelligence Investigation* (Lexington: University Press of Kentucky, 1985), esp. chs. 22 and 23.

9. *The Iran-Contra Report* (Washington, D.C.: Government Printing Office, 1987). See also Bob Woodward, *Veil: The Secret Wars of the CIA, 1981–1987* (New York: Simon and Schuster, 1987).

10. *Church Committee Report,* vol. 1, passim.

11. U.S. Congress, Senate, Church Committee, "Alleged Assassination Plots Involving Foreign Leaders," *An Interim Report,* no. 94-465, 94th Cong., 1st Sess., 1975. See also Warren Hinckle and William W. Turner, *The Fish Is Red: The Story of the Secret War Against Castro* (New York: Harper and Row, 1981).

12. Kermit Roosevelt, *Countercoup: The Struggle for the Control of Iran* (New York: McGraw-Hill, 1979).

13. U.S. Congress, Senate, Church Committee, "Covert Action," *Hearings,* vol. 7, appendix A, "Covert Action in Chile, 1963–1973," 94th Cong., 1st Sess., 1975, pp. 144–209 (hereinafter, *Hearings*).

14. William Colby, *Honorable Men: My Life in the CIA* (New York: Simon and Schuster, 1978), p. 109.

15. Ibid.

16. Ibid., ch. 4. For a description of various episodes of election intervention, see William Blum, *The CIA: A Forgotten History* (London: Zed Books, 1987).

17. *Hearings,* p. 95.

18. Terrence Smith, "Secret CIA Propaganda Overseas" (three-part survey), *New York Times*, December 25–27, 1977.

19. In addition to Woodward, *Veil,* see also Jay Peterzell, *Reagan's Secret Wars* (Washington, D.C.: Center for National Security Studies, 1984); Thomas Powers, *The Man Who Kept the Secrets* (New York: Knopf, 1979); John Prados, *Presidents' Secret Wars: CIA and Pentagon Covert Operations Since World War II* (New York: William Morrow, 1986); John Ranelagh, *The Agency: The Rise and Decline of the CIA* (New York: Simon and Schuster, 1986); and Gregory F. Treverton, *Covert Action: The Limits of Intervention in the Postwar World* (New York: Basic Books, 1987).

20. Woodward, *Veil,* pp. 396–97.

21. The following five paragraphs are derived from Harry Howe Ransom, "The Intelligence Function and the Constitution," *Armed Forces and Society* 14, 1 (Fall 1987): 43–63.

22. President's Special Review Board, John Tower, Chairman, *The Tower Commission Report* (New York: Bantam and Times Books, 1987), p. 63.

■ CHAPTER 8

1. Although most writers refer to the Guatemalan case as a coup d'état, it is treated in this chapter as a paramilitary intervention because it involved the use of an assembled exile invasion force, which later would serve as a model for future U.S. intervention in the Third World. For an overview of this case, see Richard H. Immerman, *The CIA in Guatemala: The Foreign Policy of Intervention* (Austin: University of Texas Press, 1982).

2. See Peter Wyden, *Bay of Pigs: The Untold Story* (New York: Simon and Schuster, 1979).

3. For a debate on this point, see John Ranelagh, *The Agency: The Rise and Decline of the CIA* (New York: Simon and Schuster, 1987), pp. 362–64.

4. Quoted in Ted Galen Carpenter, "The United States and Third World Dictatorships: A Case for Benign Detachment," Cato Institute Policy Analysis no. 58, August 15, 1985, p. 7.

5. For an overview of this case, see John Prados, *Presidents' Secret Wars: CIA and Pentagon Covert Operations Since World War II* (New York: William Morrow, 1986), pp. 128–48.

6. Prados, *Presidents' Secret Wars*, p. 161. The Tibetan campaign was part of an overall destabilization program of the PRC. For a more complete description, see ibid., pp. 61–78.

7. For a discussion of these two examples, consult Prados, *Presidents' Secret Wars*, pp. 239–60 (Vietnam) and pp. 261–96 (Laos).

8. For a brief discussion of this case, see William Blum, *The CIA: A Forgotten History* (London: Zed Books, 1987), pp. 275–78.

9. John Stockwell, *In Search of Enemies: A CIA Story* (New York: W. W. Norton, 1978), p. 68.

10. Wayne S. Smith, "A Trap in Angola," *Foreign Policy*, no. 62 (Spring 1986): 73.

11. The Reagan administration did not dogmatically follow ideological criteria, as it refused to support anticommunist guerrilla insurgencies in Ethiopia and Mozambique. For a sympathetic analysis of the Reagan Doctrine, see Jeane Kirkpatrick, *The Reagan Doctrine and U.S. Foreign Policy* (Washington, D.C.: Heritage Foundation, 1985). For a critical view, see Ted G. Carpenter, "U.S. Aid to Anti-Communist Rebels: The 'Reagan Doctrine' and Its Pitfalls," Cato Institute Policy Analysis no. 74, June 24, 1986.

12. Quoted in Carpenter, "U.S. Aid to Anti-Communist Rebels," p. 1.

13. See Philip Taubman, "Soviets Hint at a Delay Past Feb. 25 Deadline for Full Withdrawal," *New York Times*, November 5, 1988, p. A1; and Henry Kamm, "Afghan Official Says Soviets Will Withdraw by Deadline," *New York Times*, November 26, 1988, p. A5.

14. For an overview of U.S. involvement, see Selig S. Harrison, "Afghanistan: Soviet Intervention, Afghan Resistance, and the American Role," in Michael T. Klare and Peter Kornbluh, eds., *Low-Intensity Warfare: Counterinsurgency, Proinsurgency, and Antiterrorism in the Eighties* (New York: Pantheon, 1988), pp. 183–206.

15. Edward Giardet, "US Afghan Policy: Mired in Success," *Christian Science Monitor*, July 12, 1988, pp. 7, 9.

16. Ibid., p. 9.

17. Ibid.

18. See Elaine Sciolino, "Tainted Cambodia Aid: New Details," *New York Times*, November 1, 1988, p. A3.

19. See Steven Erlanger, "Hanoi Foils Khmer Rouge Plan to Use Refugees," *New*

York Times, November 29, 1988, p. A4.

20. Bernard K. Gordon, "The Third Indochina Conflict," *Foreign Affairs* 65, 1 (Fall 1986): 74.

21. Chang Pao-Min, "Kampuchean Conflict: The Continuing Stalemate," *Asian Survey* 27, 7 (July 1987): 756.

22. Elaine Sciolino, "Cambodian Peace Talks End but the War Just Goes On," *New York Times* (July 7, 1983), p. A3. See also Paul Lewis, "6 Asian Nations Move to Block Khmer Rouge," *New York Times*, September 23, 1988, p. A1.

23. Andrew Meldrum, "At War with South Africa," *Africa Report* 32, 1 (January-February 1987): 28.

24. Smith, "A Trap in Angola," p. 64; and John D. Battersby, "South Africa's Foreign Minister Sees Talks at a Critical Junction," *New York Times,* July 7, 1988, p. A8; and Battersby, "South Africa Agrees to Peace Accord," *New York Times,* November 23, 1988, p. A5.

25. For text of the accords, see *New York Times*, December 23, 1988, p. A5. See also James Brooke, "Accord for a 2-Year Angola Pullout Reported," *New York Times*, September 30, 1988, p. A6.

26. Paul Lewis, "With Angry Exchanges, Accords Are Signed on Angola," *New York Times* (December 23, 1988), p. A5.

27. African nations, especially those allied to the MPLA (e.g., Nigeria), are placing greater pressure on the MPLA government to accept some form of power-sharing with UNITA. See James Brooke, "Africans Pushing for Peace in Angola," *New York Times*, September 19, 1988, p. A3. Diplomats quoted in Brooke, "Accord," p. A6.

28. Forrest D. Colburn, "Embattled Nicaragua," *Current History* 86, 524 (December 1987): 406. See also Stephen Kinzer, "Sandinista Says Colonel's Election Shows Contra's True Character," *New York Times*, July 22, 1988, p. A3.

■ CHAPTER 9

1. There is an important distinction between the use of major military actions as an instrument of foreign policy and more limited applications of force for other purposes. For example, the Mayaguez incident in 1975 and the abortive Iranian hostage rescue mission in 1980 were relatively minor military actions in which there were few underlying foreign policy objectives. Conversely, the 1983 Grenada invasion had elements of a hostage rescue—and the Reagan administration went to great lengths to portray it as such—but the principal purpose was the overthrow of a Marxist-Leninist regime. Unless specifically noted, this chapter only deals with large-scale major military enterprises that had a significant foreign policy component.

2. For detailed discussions of destabilizing U.S. tactics, see Jonathan Kwitny, *Endless Enemies: The Making of an Unfriendly World* (New York: Congdon and Weed, 1984); Richard H. Immerman, *The CIA in Guatemala: The Foreign Policy of Intervention* (Austin: University of Texas Press, 1982); John Stockwell, *In Search of Enemies: A CIA Story* (New York: W. W. Norton, 1978); and T. D. Allman, *Unmanifest Destiny: Mayhem and Illusion in American Foreign Policy from the Monroe Doctrine to Reagan's War in El Salvador* (Garden City, N.Y.: Dial Press, 1984).

3. For examples of this reasoning, see Lyndon B. Johnson, *The Vantage Point: Perspectives on the Presidency, 1963–1969* (New York: Holt, Rinehart, and Winston, 1971), pp. 232–69, 422–24, 528–31; and Richard M. Nixon, *No More Vietnams* (New York: Arbor House, 1985), passim.

4. Arthur M. Schlesinger, Jr., *The Imperial Presidency* (Boston: Houghton Mifflin, 1973), pp. 127–208; and Ted Galen Carpenter, "Global Interventionism and a

New Imperial Presidency," Cato Institute Policy Analysis no. 71, May 6, 1986.

5. Walter LaFeber, *Inevitable Revolutions: The United States in Central America* (New York: W. W. Norton, 1984), pp. 34–69; and Dana G. Munro, *Intervention and Dollar Diplomacy in the Caribbean, 1900–1921* (Princeton: Princeton University Press, 1964), passim.

6. For discussions of the domestic debate surrounding the advent of explicit U.S. imperialism, see Robert L. Beisner, *Twelve Against Empire: The Anti-Imperialists, 1898–1900* (Chicago: University of Chicago Press, 1968); and Walter Karp, *The Politics of War* (New York: Harper and Row, 1979), pp. 3–116.

7. *New York Times*, November 29, 1984, p. A5.

8. Carpenter, "Global Interventionism," pp. 6–7.

9. "Memorandum: Meeting at Blair House, July 3, 1950," Dean Acheson Papers, box 65, Harry S. Truman Library.

10. For an example of Truman's awareness of the subterfuge, see Joseph C. Goulden, *Korea: The Untold Story of the War* (New York: McGraw-Hill, 1982), pp. 105–6.

11. Callum MacDonald, *Korea: The War Before Vietnam* (New York: Free Press, 1986), pp. 13–14, 41, 60.

12. Stephen E. Ambrose, *Eisenhower: The President* (New York: Simon and Schuster, 1984), p. 466.

13. For Eisenhower's statements and message to Congress on July 15, 1958, see "United States Dispatches Troops to Lebanon," *Department of State Bulletin* 39, 997 (August 1958): 181–86.

14. Ambrose, *Eisenhower,* p. 465.

15. Johnson, *The Vantage Point,* p. 202.

16. Stephen E. Ambrose, *Rise to Globalism,* 4th rev. ed. (New York: Penguin, 1985), p. 220.

17. Discussions of the motives for the U.S. intervention include Abraham F. Lowenthal, *The Dominican Intervention* (Cambridge: Harvard University Press, 1972); and Jerome N. Slater, *Intervention and Negotiation: The United States and the Dominican Revolution* (New York: Harper and Row, 1970).

18. See the November 4, 1983, speech by State Department spokesman Kenneth Dam, reprinted in Hugh O'Shaughnessy, *Grenada* (New York: Dodd and Mead, 1984), pp. 246–54.

19. Kwitny, *Endless Enemies*, pp. 410–11; O'Shaughnessy, *Grenada,* pp. 150–51.

20. Schlesinger, *The Imperial Presidency,* pp. 177–96. For an example of similar State Department views on the scope of presidential power, see Leonard C. Meeker, "The Legality of United States Participation in the Defense of Vietnam," *Department of State Bulletin* 54, 1396 (March 1966): 484–85.

21. Sheldon L. Richman, "Where Angels Fear to Tread: The United States and the Persian Gulf Conflict," Cato Institute Policy Analysis no. 90, September 9, 1987.

■ CHAPTER 10

1. See Eric F. Goldman, *The Crucial Decade—and After: America, 1945–1960* (New York: Random House, 1961); Richard A. Melanson, *Writing History and Making Policy: The Cold War, Vietnam, and Revisionism* (Lanham, Md.: University Press of America, 1983); and Daniel Yergin, *Shattered Peace: The Origins of the Cold War and the National Security State* (New York: Houghton Mifflin, 1978).

2. See Robert Griffith, *The Politics of Fear: Joseph R. McCarthy and the Senate* (New York: Hayden, 1970); William Manchester, *The Glory and the Dream: A Narrative*

History of America, 1933–1972 (New York: Wiley, 1972); and Richard H. Rovere, *Senator Joe McCarthy* (New York: World Publishing, 1970).

3. See Godfrey Hodgson, *America in Our Time: From World War II to Nixon, What Happened and Why* (New York: Vintage, 1976).

4. See Hodgson, *America in Our Time;* Richard E. Neustadt, *Presidential Power: The Politics of Leadership* (New York: Wiley, 1976); and Arthur Schlesinger, Jr., *The Imperial Presidency* (Boston: Houghton Mifflin, 1973).

5. See Charles W. Kegley, Jr., and Eugene W. Wittkopf, *American Foreign Policy: Pattern and Process* (New York: St. Martin's, 1986); and James A. Nathan and James K. Oliver, *Foreign Policy Making and the American Political System* (Boston: Little, Brown, 1987).

6. See Richard Barnet, *Roots of War: The Men and Institutions Behind U.S. Foreign Policy* (Baltimore: Penguin, 1972); David Halberstam, *The Best and the Brightest* (New York: Random House, 1971); Godfrey Hodgson, "The Foreign Policy Establishment," *Foreign Policy*, no. 10 (Spring 1973): 3–40; and Jerry W. Sanders, *Peddlers of Crisis: The Committee on the Present Danger* (Boston: South End, 1983).

7. See Barnet, *Roots of War*; and Hodgson, *America in Our Time*.

8. See Loren Baritz, *Backfire: A History of How American Culture Led Us into Vietnam and Made Us Fight the Way We Did* (New York: Morrow, 1985); and Hodgson, *America in Our Time*.

9. See Todd Gitlin, *The Sixties: Years of Hope, Days of Rage* (New York: Bantam, 1988); and Hodgson, *America in Our Time*.

10. See I. M. Destler, Leslie H. Gelb, and Anthony Lake, *Our Own Worst Enemy: The Unmaking of American Foreign Policy* (New York: Simon and Schuster, 1984); and Ole R. Holsti and James N. Rosenau, *American Leadership in World Affairs: Vietnam and the Breakdown of Consensus* (Boston: Allen and Unwin, 1984).

11. See Sanders, *Peddlers of Crisis*.

12. See Thomas M. Franck and Edward Weisband, *Foreign Policy by Congress* (New York: Oxford University Press, 1979); Jerel A. Rosati, "Congressional Influence in American Foreign Policy: Addressing the Controversy," *Journal of Political and Military Sociology* 12 (Fall 1984): 311–33; and Schlesinger, *The Imperial Presidency*.

13. See Doris A. Graber, *Mass Media and American Politics* (Washington, D.C.: Congressional Quarterly Press, 1984).

14. See Destler, Gelb, and Lake, *Our Own Worst Enemy;* and Nathan and Oliver, *Foreign Policy Making*.

■ CHAPTER 11

1. Caspar W. Weinberger, "The Uses of Military Power," Remarks prepared for delivery to the National Press Club, Washington, D.C., November 28, 1984.

2. Weinberger's speech may be read as almost a summary of conclusions of official military summaries of the lessons of Vietnam. See Colonel Harry Summers, *On Strategy: A Critical Analysis of the Vietnam War* (New York: Dell Publishing, 1982); this work is the result of Summers' study of the war for the U.S. Army War College and was reviewed by senior army officers and other officials.

3. George Shultz, "The Ethics of Power," Address at Yeshiva University, New York, December 9, 1984.

4. Weinberger, "The Uses of Military Power."

5. Morton H. Halperin, *Bureaucratic Politics and Foreign Policy* (Washington, D.C.: Brookings, 1974), pp. 60–61.

6. Ibid.

7. Melvin R. Laird, "A Strong Start in a Difficult Decade: Defense Policy in the Nixon-Ford Years," *International Security* 10, 2 (Fall 1985): 16.

8. Pat Towell, "Reagan Defense Plan Stresses Deterring the 'Soviet Threat,'" *Congressional Quarterly Weekly Report,* April 10, 1982, pp. 795–96.

9. Quoted in Michael R. Gordon, "John Lehman: The Hard Liner Behind Reagan's Navy Buildup," *National Journal,* October 3, 1981, p. 1765. For a discussion, see John J. Mearsheimer, "A Strategic Misstep: The Maritime Strategy and Deterrence in Europe," *International Security* 11, 2 (Fall 1986): 3–57.

10. Eliot A. Cohen, "Constraints on America's Conduct of Small Wars," *International Security* 9, 2 (Fall 1984): 165.

11. Lt. Col. A. J. Bacevich, Lt. Col. James D. Hallums, Lt. Col. Richard H. White, and Lt. Col. Thomas F. Young (all U.S. Army), "American Military Policy in Small Wars: The Case of El Salvador," Paper presented at the John F. Kennedy School of Government, Harvard University, March 22, 1988, p. 22.

12. Ibid., pp. 14–15.

13. Ibid., p. 15.

14. Ibid., pp. 57–58.

15. Ibid., p. 56.

16. Ibid., pp. 29–30.

17. Ibid., pp. 67–68.

18. Ibid., pp. 69–70.

19. Ibid., p. 84. For a discussion, see pp. 79–84.

20. See Morton H. Halperin and David Halperin, "The Key West Key," *Foreign Policy*, no. 53 (Winter 1983-84): 124.

21. For a further discussion that emphasizes this point, see U.S. Congress, Senate, *Defense Organization: The Need for Change,* Staff Report to the Committee on Armed Services, 99th Cong., 1st Sess, October 16, 1985, p. 362.

22. Steven Smith, "Policy Preferences and Bureaucratic Positions: The Case of the American Hostage Rescue Mission," in David C. Kozak and James M. Keagle, eds., *Bureaucratic Politics and National Security: Theory and Practice* (Boulder, Colo.: Lynne Rienner, 1988), p. 137.

23. *Defense Organization,* p. 364.

24. This discussion draws heavily on ibid., pp. 363–68.

25. Edward Luttwak, *The Pentagon and the Art of War* (New York: Simon and Schuster, 1985), pp. 55–57.

26. Halperin, *Bureaucratic Politics,* p. 28.

27. *Defense Organization,* pp. 368–70.

28. J. William Fulbright and Seth P. Tillman, "Schultz-Weinberger Nondifferences," *New York Times*, December 9, 1984, p. E21.

■ CHAPTER 12

1. Isaac Deutscher, *What Next?* (New York: Oxford University Press, 1953), pp. 96–112.

2. Bernard B. Fall, ed., *Ho Chi Minh on Revolution: Selected Writings, 1920–1966* (New York: Praeger, 1967), p. 5. Ho's writings stress atrocities that robbed the Vietnamese of their humanity rather than abstract ideology. See esp. pp. 3–47.

3. The 1,500-year-long struggle against Chinese domination ended in 1287 when the Vietnamese routed 300,000 Mongol troops. In 1954, General Vo Nguyen Giap

evoked the memory of this battle when he defeated the French in the same region at Dienbienphu. Communism was of secondary importance. Stanley Karnow, *Vietnam: A History* (New York: Viking, 1983), ch. 3.

4. Thich Nhat Hanh, *Vietnam: Lotus in a Sea of Fire* (New York: Hill and Wang, 1967), p. 71.

5. John Mecklin, *Mission in Torment: An Intimate Account of the U.S. Role in Vietnam* (Garden City, N.Y.: Doubleday, 1965), pp. 36, 77.

6. Bruno Knoebl, *Victor Charlie: The Face of the War in Vietnam* (New York: Praeger, 1967), pp. 126, 114.

7. John Hellmann, *American Myth and the Legacy of Vietnam* (New York: Columbia University Press, 1986), p. 221.

8. John Osborne, "The Tough Miracle Man of Vietnam: Diem, America's Newly Arrived Visitor, Has Roused His Country and Routed the Reds," *Life,* May 13, 1957, pp. 156–176.

9. Bernard B. Fall, *Last Reflections on a War* (Garden City, N.Y.: Doubleday, 1967), p. 167.

10. Frances FitzGerald, *Fire in the Lake: The Vietnamese and the Americans in Vietnam* (Boston: Little, Brown, 1972).

11. Tanya Matthews, *War in Algeria: Background for Crisis* (New York: Fordham University Press, 1961), p. 20. Official French figures put Algerian fatalities of May 1945 at 1,165; the official Algerian figure is 45,000; the U.S. OSS estimates 6,000. See OSS, "Moslem Uprisings in Algeria, May 1945," *OSS Research and Analysis Report,* no. 3135, May 30, 1945, National Archives, Washington, D.C.

12. Dean Acheson, *Present at the Creation: My Years in the State Department* (New York: W. W. Norton, 1969), p. 302.

13. Robert P. Newman, "The Self-Inflicted Wound: The China White Paper of 1949," *Prologue* (Fall 1982): 141–56.

14. Among the European allies, only British Prime Minister Margaret Thatcher supported the raid on Libya, largely because of the "Falkland factor," the recognition that Britain could not have won the war against Argentina without U.S. logistic support. Joseph Lelyveld, "Intense Talks Led to Thatcher Ruling," *New York Times*, April 16, 1986, p. A14.

15. N. J. Dawood, *The Koran,* 4th ed. (New York: Penguin, 1974), Surah 28: 5, p. 75.

16. "Ganging up on Uncle Sam," *The Economist,* July 16, 1988, pp. 36–37.

17. See Michael T. Klare, "The Arms Trade: Changing Patterns in the 1980s," *Third World Quarterly* 9, 4 (October 1987): 1257–81.

18. Ibid., pp. 1278–79.

19. George Thayer, *The War Business: The International Trade in Armaments* (New York: Simon and Schuster, 1969), pp. 340, 138–41.

20. Stalin told Yugoslav Vice President Milovan Djilas: "Do you think . . . the United States, the most powerful state in the world, will permit you to break their lines of communication in the Mediterranean Sea?" Quoted in Milovan Djilas, *Conversations with Stalin* (New York: Harcourt, Brace, and World, 1962), pp. 181–82.

21. CIA special estimate, advance copy for National Security Council, March 10, 1953, "Probable Consequences of the Death of Stalin and the Elevation of Malenkov to Leadership in the USSR," p. 4, in Paul Kesaris, ed., *CIA Research Reports: The Soviet Union, 1946–1976* (Frederick, Md.: University Publications of America, 1982), reel II, frames 637–48.

22. See Uri Ra'anan, *The USSR Arms the Third World: Case Studies in Soviet Foreign Policy* (Cambridge: Massachusetts Institute of Technology Press, 1969).

23. Kenneth A. Oye, "Constrained Confidence and the Evolution of Reagan

Foreign Policy," in Kenneth Oye, Robert J. Lieber, and Donald Rothchild, eds., *Eagle Resurgent? The Reagan Era in American Foreign Policy* (Boston: Little, Brown, 1987), pp. 10–11.

24. Ibid., pp. 5–8.

■ CHAPTER 13

1. See R. J. Vincent, *Nonintervention and International Order* (Princeton: Princeton University Press, 1974).

2. See Derick W. Bowett, "The Interrelation of Theories of Intervention and Self-Defense," in John Norton Moore, ed., *Law and Civil War in the Modern World* (Baltimore: Johns Hopkins University Press, 1974), pp. 38–50; and J. L. Brierly, *The Law of Nations,* 6th ed., edited by Sir Humphrey Waldock (London: Oxford University Press, 1963), p. 402.

3. Covenant of the League of Nations (Treaty of Versailles, Part 1, Articles 1–26), done June 28, 1919, Great Britain Treaty Series No. 4 (Command No. 153).

4. Done February 20, 1928, 46 Statutes 2749, United States Treaty Series No. 814, 134 League of Nations Treaty Series 45.

5. Done December 26, 1933, 49 Statutes 3097, United States Treaty Series No. 881, 165 League of Nations Treaty Series 19.

6. Done December 23, 1936, 51 Statutes 41, United States Treaty Series No. 923, 188 League of Nations Treaty Series 31 (amending the Convention on Rights and Duties of States in note 5 supra).

7. Done December 23, 1936, 51 Statutes 116, United States Treaty Series No. 926, League of Nations Treaty Series No. 4548.

8. Done October 10, 1933, 49 Statutes 3363, United States Treaty Series No. 906, League of Nations Treaty Series No. 3781.

9. Done at San Francisco, June 26, 1945, 59 Statutes 1031, United States Treaty Series No. 933, 3 Bevans 1153.

10. Done September 2, 1947, 62 Statutes 1681, Treaties and Other International Acts Series No. 1838, 21 United Nations Treaty Series 77.

11. Done April 30, 1948, 2 United States Treaties 2394, Treaties and Other International Acts Series No. 2361, 119 United Nations Treaty Series 3, as amended by Protocol of Buenos Aires, February 27, 1967, 21 United States Treaties 607, Treaties and Other International Acts Series No. 6847, 789 United Nations Treaty Series 287, at Article 18.

12. Ibid., Article 20.

13. General Assembly Resolution 2131, 20 United Nations General Assembly Official Records, Supplement No. 14, p. 11, United Nations Doc. A/6014 (1966).

14. General Assembly Resolution 2625, 25 General Assembly Official Records, Supplement No. 28, p. 121, United Nations Doc. A/8028 (1971).

15. See the works contained in Moore, *Law and Civil War,* and Marjorie M. Whiteman, *Digest of International Law,* vol. 5 (Washington, D.C.: Government Printing Office, 1965), pp. 250–57, 276–81, 522–34.

16. See Roger Clark, "Humanitarian Intervention: Help to Your Friends and State Practice," *Georgia Journal of International and Comparative Law* 13 (1983): 211–13.

17. See L. F. L. Oppenheim, *International Law: A Treatise,* vol. 1, *Peace,* 8th ed., edited by Hersch Lauterpacht (London: Longmans, 1955), pp. 298–99.

18. Compare the views of Myres McDougal, "The Soviet-Cuban Quarantine and Self-Defense," *American Journal of International Law* 57 (1963): 597–600; and Ian

Brownlie, "The Use of Force in Self-Defense," *British Year Book of International Law* 37 (1962): 266–89.

19. Oppenheim, *International Law,* pp. 310, 319–20; and Whiteman, *Digest of International Law,* pp. 1080–87.

20. See Ian Brownlie, *International Law and the Use of Force by States* (Oxford: Clarendon, 1963), pp. 321–27.

21. Oppenheim, *International Law,* pp. 307–10; and Brownlie, *International Law,* pp. 318–320.

22. Gerhard von Glahn, *Law Among Nations: An Introduction to Public International Law,* 4th ed. (New York: Macmillan, 1981), p. 168.

23. The text of the Monroe Doctrine is reprinted as "Monroe's Seventh Annual Message to Congress," in James D. Richardson, ed., *A Compilation of the Messages and Papers of the Presidents, 1789–1897,* vol. 2 (Washington, D.C.: Government Printing Office, 1896), pp. 207–20.

24. Donald M. Dozer, ed., *The Monroe Doctrine: Its Modern Significance* (New York: Knopf, 1965), p. 4.

25. John Gerassi, *The Great Fear in Latin America* (New York: Collier Books, 1965), p. 231.

26. For elaboration, see Abraham F. Lowenthal, *The Dominican Intervention* (Cambridge: Harvard University Press, 1972).

27. "State of the Union Address," *Washington Post,* February 7, 1985, p. A16.

28. An articulate view of self-defense as a justification for U.S. actions in Nicaragua is John Norton Moore, "The Secret War in Central America and the Future of World Order," *American Journal of International Law* 80 (1986): 43–127. For my view, see Christopher C. Joyner and Michael A. Grimaldi, "The United States and Nicaragua: Reflections on the Lawfulness of Contemporary Intervention," *Virginia Journal of International Law* 25 (1985): 621–89.

29. The U.S. invasion of Grenada stands as a recent example of this predominant unilateral proclivity. See Christopher C. Joyner, "The United States Action in Grenada: Reflections on the Lawfulness of Invasion," *American Journal of International Law* 78 (1984): 131–44. For the Reagan administration's legal view, see John Norton Moore, "Grenada and the International Double Standard," in ibid., pp. 145–68.

30. Oscar Shachter, "The Right of States to Use Armed Force," *Michigan Law Review* 82 (1984): 649.

31. "U.S. Loses Rulings in Nicaragua Case," *New York Times*, May 11, 1984, p. A1. See also "Nicaragua Takes Case Against U.S. to World Court," *New York Times*, April 10, 1984, p. A1.

32. "Statement on the U.S. Withdrawal from the Proceedings Initiated by Nicaragua in the International Court of Justice," *Department of State Bulletin* 85, 2096 (1985): 64. See also William Drozdiak, "Court Asserts Jurisdiction in U.S.-Nicaragua Dispute," *Washington Post,* November 27, 1984, p. A1.

33. For elaboration, see Christopher C. Joyner, "The Reality and Relevance of International Law," in Charles Kegley and Eugene Wittkopf, eds., *The Global Agenda,* 2nd ed. (New York: Random House, 1988), pp. 88–99.

■ CHAPTER 14

1. For an analysis of U.S. involvement with Iran during World War II, see James A. Bill, *The Eagle and the Lion: The Tragedy of American-Iranian Relations* (New Haven: Yale University Press, 1988), pp. 18–26, 31–39.

2. For more details, see Barry Rubin, *Paved with Good Intentions: The American Experience in Iran* (New York: Oxford University Press, 1980), pp. 36–39.

3. For a generally positive, but frank, evaluation of the Point Four program in Iran written by its first director, see William Warne, *Mission for Peace: Point 4 in Iran* (Indianapolis: Bobbs-Merrill, 1956).

4. The most detailed study of this conflict is Richard Cottam, *Nationalism in Iran* (Pittsburgh: University of Pittsburgh Press, 1979).

5. The United States seems to have tried to dissuade Great Britain from undertaking coup attempts in 1951 and 1952. This interpretation is supported by an analysis of the various memoranda of conversations between Secretary Acheson and the British ambassador to the United States, Sir Oliver Franks. For the Acheson-Franks conversations, see *Iran White Paper,* National Security Archive, Washington, D.C., documents numbered 709–32 of Department of State typed list.

6. See Nikki Keddie, *Roots of Revolution: An Interpretive History of Modern Iran* (New Haven: Yale University Press, 1981), pp. 134–35.

7. For a detailed analysis of U.S. involvement, see Mark J. Gasiorowski, "The 1953 Coup d'Etat in Iran," *International Journal of Middle East Studies* 19, 3 (August 1987): 261–86.

8. See Richard Cottam, "American Foreign Policy and the Iranian Crisis," *Iranian Studies* 13, 1–4 (1980): 281–83.

9. Keddie, *Roots of Revolution,* p. 142.

10. For more detail on the development of U.S.-Iran relations from 1953 to 1961, see Bill, *The Eagle and the Lion,* pp. 113–27.

11. Bill, *The Eagle and the Lion,* pp. 131–51.

12. For an analysis of the shah's economic policies, see Fred Halliday, *Iran: Dictatorship and Development* (New York: Penguin Books, 1979), pp. 138–72. The land reform program is examined in Eric Hooglund, *Land and Revolution in Iran, 1960–1980* (Austin: University of Texas Press, 1982), pp. 47–99.

13. Khomeini's role during the 1963 demonstrations is described in detail in Keddie, *Roots of Revolution,* pp. 158–60. Also see Richard Cottam, *Iran and the United States: A Cold War Case Study* (Pittsburgh: University of Pittsburgh Press, 1988), pp. 130–31.

14. U.S.-Iran relations during the Johnson administration are examined in Bill, *The Eagle and the Lion,* pp. 154–80.

15. For a detailed account of arms sales to the shah during this period, see Michael T. Klare, *American Arms Supermarket* (Austin: University of Texas Press, 1984), pp. 112–23.

16. See Phebe Marr, *The Modern History of Iraq* (Boulder, Colo.: Westview Press, 1985), pp. 112–21; and Bill, *The Eagle and the Lion,* pp. 204–7.

17. The shah's intervention in Oman is described in Richard Cottam, "Arms Sales and Human Rights: The Case of Iran," in Peter Brown and Douglas Maclean, eds., *Human Rights and U.S. Foreign Policy* (Lexington, Mass.: Heath, 1979), pp. 289–90.

18. U.S. Congress, Senate, Subcommittee on Foreign Assistance, Committee on Foreign Affairs, *U.S. Military Sales to Iran* (Washington, D.C.: Government Printing Office, 1976), pp. xiii, 1–2.

19. Gary Sick, *All Fall Down: America's Tragic Encounter with Iran* (New York: Random House, 1985), pp. 25–27.

20. Sick, *All Fall Down,* pp. 22–24; and Bill, *The Eagle and the Lion,* pp. 219–44.

21. Eric Hooglund, "Government and Politics," in Helen Metz, ed., *Iran: A Country Study* (Washington, D.C.: Library of Congress, 1989), pp. 438–44; and Shaul Bakhash, *The Reign of Ayatollahs* (New York: Basic Books, 1984), pp. 69–70.

22. See Bill, *The Eagle and the Lion,* pp. 276–86, 293–96.

23. The most complete description of the efforts to resolve the hostage crisis, written from the perspective of a Carter administration official, is Sick, *All Fall Down,* pp. 195–342.

24. For more detail, see Eric Hooglund, "Reagan's Iran: Factions Behind U.S. Policy in the Gulf," *Middle East Report* 151 (March-April 1988): 29–31.

25. The Reagan administration's difficulties in trying to fit Iran into a cold war perspective are analyzed by Richard Cottam, "Iran and Soviet-American Relations," in Nikki Keddie and Eric Hooglund, eds., *The Iranian Revolution and the Islamic Republic* (Syracuse: Syracuse University Press, 1986), pp. 229–32.

26. Hooglund, "Reagan's Iran," p. 30; Cottam, *Iran and the United States,* pp. 237–42.

27. For the change in CIA Director Casey's views on Iran and the subsequent change in covert policy, see Bob Woodward, *Veil: The Secret Wars of the CIA, 1981–1987* (New York: Simon and Schuster, 1987), pp. 111–12, 407–8. For an evaluation of the presumed pro-U.S. (moderate) and pro-Soviet factions in the Iranian government, see Eric Hooglund, "The Search for Iran's 'Moderates,'" *Middle East Report* 144 (January-February 1987): 5–6.

28. For analyses of the contradictory U.S. policies toward Iran during 1985–1987, see Nikki Keddie, "Iranian Imbroglios: Who's Irrational?" *World Policy Journal* (Winter 1987–1988): 29–54; and Cottam, *Iran and the United States,* 243–45.

29. Keddie, "Iranian Imbroglios," pp. 44–47.

30. Gary Sick, "The Internationalization of the Iran-Iraq War: The Events of 1987," in Mike Gasiorowski and Nikki Keddie, eds., *Iran, the U.S. and the U.S.S.R.* (New Haven: Yale University Press, 1989).

31. For details of these incidents see the *Washington Post,* April 19 and July 4, 1988.

■ CHAPTER 15

1. Quoted from a recording of the meeting made available to me and confirmed by a participant.

2. Ibid.

3. See Joseph L. Schott, *The Ordeal of Samar.* (New York: Bobbs-Merrill, 1964), p. 62.

4. Ibid.

5. Quoted in Richard J. Kessler, "U.S. Policy Toward the Philippines," Stanley Foundation Policy Paper no. 37, June 1986.

6. U.S. Congress, House, Committee on Foreign Affairs, *Hearings on Mutual Security Act of 1958,* 85th Cong., 2nd Sess., Pt. 4, 1958, p. 566.

7. U.S. Congress, Senate, Committee on Foreign Relations, *United States Security Agreements and Commitments Abroad, the Republic of the Philippines, Hearings Before the Subcommittee on United States Security Agreements and Commitments Abroad,* 91st Cong., 1st Sess., Pt. 1, September 20, October 1–3, 1969, p. 37. Also see Raymond Bonner, *Waltzing with a Dictator* (New York: Times Books, 1987), p. 75.

8. See Scott W. Thompson, *Unequal Partners: Philippine and Thai Relations with the United States, 1965–75* (Lexington, Mass.: Lexington Books, 1975).

9. Thompson, *Unequal Partners,* p. 82.

10. Richard J. Kessler, "Marcos and the Americans," *Foreign Policy,* no. 63 (Summer 1986): 50.

11. See Thompson, *Unequal Partners,* pp. 66–67, 142; and W. Scott Thompson,

"How to Intervene in the Philippines," *Washington Post*, January 14, 1986, p. A19.

12. Interview, former senior State Department official, July 10, 1985, Washington, D.C.

13. William E. Berry, "American Military Bases in the Philippines," Ph.D. dissertation, Cornell University, 1981, p. 276.

14. Interview, former senior State Department official, November 1984, Washington, D.C. Berry, "American Military Bases," p. 301, also agrees.

15. Embassy of the Philippines, *Annual Report* (FY 1975/76), Washington, D.C., pp. 22–23.

16. Interview, U.S. State Department officials, Washington, D.C., November 1986.

17. Henry Kissinger, "America and Asia," *Department of State Bulletin* 75, 1938 (August 16, 1976): 20.

18. Handwritten note passed to me in 1986. See also Kessler, "Marcos," pp. 40–57.

19. Richard J. Kessler, "Politics Philippine Style—Circa 1984," *Asian Survey* 24, 12 (December 1984): 1209–28.

20. Interview, U.S. State Department official, November 14, 1985.

21. Written communication to me, undated, but received March 11, 1986.

22. National Security Study Directive, "U.S. Policy Towards the Philippines. Executive Summary." This document was leaked to the press by a Filipino opponent of Marcos.

23. See Richard Holbrooke, "Removal of Marcos was a Triumph for Reagan's Ad-Hocism," *Washington Post*, March 2, 1986, p. C1.

24. Personal conversation with me on November 3, 1985.

25. Interview, November 14, 1985, Washington, D.C.

■ CHAPTER 16

1. "Nicaragua has become a test case," Olds wrote in his January 2, 1927, memorandum, which advocated U.S. intervention to counter purported Mexican influence in Nicaragua's internal instability. Quoted in Richard Millett, *Guardians of the Dynasty: A History of the U.S. Created Guardia Nacional de Nicaragua* (Maryknoll, N.Y.: Orbis Books, 1977), p. 52.

2. Quoted in Ronald Steel, *Walter Lippmann and the American Century* (Boston: Little, Brown, 1980), p. 237.

3. For U.S. efforts to portray Sandino as a common criminal as opposed to a nationalist leader, see *New York Times*, July 19, 1927, p. A10.

4. For figures on the costs of the war against Sandino, see Lejeune Cummins, *Quijote on a Burro: Sandino and the Marines, a Study in the Formulation of Foreign Policy* (Mexico: no publisher, 1958), p. 68.

5. For a broader discussion of domestic reaction to the war against Sandino, see Peter Kornbluh, "U.S. Involvement in Central America: A Historical Lesson," *U.S.A. Today*, September 1983, pp. 45–47.

6. Kellogg's cable, "Strictly Personal and Confidential for General McCoy from the Secretary of State," is found in the McCoy Papers, Manuscript Division, Library of Congress. See also Millett, *Guardians of the Dynasty*, p. 88.

7. Hanna is quoted in a cable to the State Department, October 28, 1932, National Archive Record Group 59 817.1051/707 1/2.

8. See Laverne Baldwin to Secretary of State Cordell Hull, December 2, 1939,

National Archive Record Group 817.00/8736, p. 13.

9. Ibid., p. 14.

10. Ibid., p. 13.

11. Somoza is quoted in John Booth, *The End and the Beginning: The Nicaraguan Revolution* (Boulder, Colo.: Westview Press, 1982), p. 61.

12. For a discussion of how opposition to the Somoza dynasty evolved, see ibid., pp. 71–180.

13. Brzezinski's argument with Carter is taken from his diaries and is recorded in Robert Pastor, *Condemned to Repetition: The United States and Nicaragua* (Princeton: Princeton University Press, 1987), p. 162.

14. See U.S. Department of State, Pezzullo to secretary of state, Cable no. 857, "First Visit to Somoza," June 28, 1978.

15. See U.S. Department of State, Vaky to Pezzullo, Cable no. 168715, "Nicaraguan Scenario," June 30, 1979.

16. U.S. Department of State, Viron Vaky to all American Republic diplomatic posts, Cable no. 153522, June 15, 1979.

17. See Peter Kornbluh, *Nicaragua: The Price of Intervention* (Washington D.C.: Institute for Policy Studies, 1987), pp. 15–19.

18. Quoted in ibid., p. 19.

19. See Robert C. Toth and Doyle McManus, "Contras and CIA: A Plan Gone Awry," *Los Angeles Times*, March 3, 1985.

20. See McFarlane's testimony before the Iran-Contra Select Committees, May 11 and 13, 1987.

21. See U.S. Army, Training and Doctrine Command (TRADOC), "U.S. Army Operational Concept for Low Intensity Conflict," February 1986, p. 2.

22. Colonel John Waghelstein, *Military Review* 65, 2 (February 1985): 87.

23. Owen to North, "Overall Perspective," March 17, 1986. Document released during Iran-contra hearings as exhibit no. 13.

24. For quotations from the CIA's contra manual, see *The CIA's Nicaragua Manual: Psychological Operations in Guerrilla Warfare* (New York: Vintage Books, 1985).

25. Casey is quoted in Bob Woodward, *Veil: The Secret Wars of the CIA, 1981–1987* (New York: Simon and Schuster, 1987), p. 282.

26. Memorandum for Robert C. McFarlane, March 2, 1984, from Oliver L. North and Constantine Menges, "Special Activities in Nicaragua." Released as Oliver North exhibit no. 177 during the Iran-contra hearings.

27. For North's discussions with Walker, see Peter Kornbluh, "What North Might Have Wrought," *The Nation*, June 26, 1987, p. 887.

28. NSC, North to McFarlane, "Timing and the Nicaraguan Resistance Vote," March 20, 1985.

29. CIA, National Intelligence Estimate, "Nicaragua: The Outlook for the Insurgency," June 30, 1983, p. 17.

30. NSC, "Strategy on Central America," July 6, 1983.

31. Cited in Kornbluh, *Nicaragua: The Price of Intervention*, p. 116.

32. Quoted in Joel Brinkley, "Nicaraguan Army: 'War Machine' or Defender of a Besieged Nation," *New York Times*, March 30, 1985, p. A16.

33. Quoted in Michael T. Klare and Peter Kornbluh, eds., *Low-Intensity Warfare: Counterinsurgency, Proinsurgency and Antiterrorism in the Eighties* (New York: Pantheon, 1988), p. 147.

34. The NSC Planning Group report was reprinted in full. See "National Security Council Document on Policy in Central America and Cuba," *New York Times*, April 28, 1983, p. A1.

35. See NSDD 77, Management of Public Diplomacy Relative to National Secur-

ity, January 14, 1983, p.1.

36. Clark's July 1, 1983, memorandum, entitled "Public Diplomacy (Central America)," was released during the Iran-contra hearings.

37. Alfonso Chardy, "NSC Oversaw Campaign to Sway Contra Aid Vote," *Miami Herald,* July 19, 1987, p. A1.

38. See U.S. Department of State, Reich to Department of Defense, Ray Warren, "Subject: TDY Personnel for S/LPD," March 5, 1985, p. 1. This document is on file at the National Security Archive in Washington, D.C.

39. See GAO letter to Rep. Dante Fascell and Rep. Jack Brooks, September 30, 1987.

40. Quoted in Robert Parry and Peter Kornbluh, "Iran-Contra's Untold Story," *Foreign Policy,* no. 71 (Fall 1988): 27.

41. Ibid., p. 6.

42. Figures are quoted from Nicaragua memorial presented to the International Court of Justice, March 29, 1988, p. 2.

43. See coverage of Iran-contra in *Newsweek,* December 8, 1986, p. 33.

44. See *Report of the Congressional Committees Investigating the Iran-Contra Affair* (Washington, D.C.: Government Printing Office, 1987), pp. 13, 18.

45. Ibid., p. 390.

46. Alfonso Chardy, "U.S. Clout Falters in Latin America," *Miami Herald,* December 27, 1987, p. A1.

47. Stephen Kinzer and Robert Pear, "Officials Assert U.S. Is Trying to Weaken Costa Rica Chief," *New York Times,* July 31, 1988, p. A1.

48. Richard Beeston, "Shultz Admits Difficulty in Anti-Sandinista Drive," *Washington Times,* August 1, 1988, p. A1.

■ CHAPTER 17

1. President Ronald Reagan's televised speech to the nation, October 27, 1983. Reproduced in Institute of Caribbean Studies, *Documents on the Invasion of Grenada* (Rio Piedras, Puerto Rico: University of Puerto Rico, 1984), p. 28.

2. Capt. William T. DeCamp, U.S. Marine Corps, "Grenada: The Spirit and the Letter of the Law," *Naval War College Review* 34, 3 (May-June 1985): 35.

3. Tony Thorndike, *Grenada: Politics, Economics, and Society* (Boulder, Colo.: Lynne Rienner, 1985), p. 77.

4. Bruce Marcus and Michael Taber, eds., *Maurice Bishop Speaks: The Grenada Revolution, 1979–83* (New York: Pathfinder Press, 1983), p. 27.

5. Robert Pastor, "U.S. Policy Toward the Caribbean: Continuity and Change," in Peter M. Dunn and Bruce W. Watson, eds., *American Intervention in Grenada: The Implications of Operation "Urgent Fury"* (Boulder, Colo.: Westview Press, 1985), p. 22.

6. Maurice Bishop, *Selected Speeches, 1979–1981* (Havana, Cuba: Casa de las Americas, 1982), p. 13.

7. "Land of the Smoking Gun," *Time,* August 18, 1980, p. 35.

8. *The Soviet-Cuban Connection in Central America and the Caribbean* (Washington, D.C.: Department of State and Department of Defense, 1985), p. 3.

9. H. Michael Erisman, "Colossus Challenged: U.S. Caribbean Policy in the 1980s," Caribbean Studies Association Conference, St. Thomas, U.S. Virgin Islands, May 27–30, 1981, p. 18.

10. *Barbados Advocate News,* August 31, 1981, p. 1.

11. *Caribbean Insight* (London) 5, 4 (April 1982): 1.

12. See, in particular, documents 2-21, 2-26, 2-29, and 2-30 in *Grenada Documents: An Overview and Selection* (Washington, D.C.: Department of State and the Department of Defense, September 1984).

13. *Caribbean Tourism Statistical Report 1984* (St. Michael's, Barbados: Caribbean Tourism Research and Development Center, 1985), p. 66.

14. *The Guardian* (London), November 27, 1983, p. 5.

15. For a full text of the treaty, see *Bulletin of Eastern Caribbean Affairs* 7, 2 (May-June 1981): 16–82.

16. William C. Gilmore, "Legal and Institutional Aspects of the Organization of Eastern Caribbean States," *Review of International Studies* 11, 4 (October 1985): 319.

17. "Statement by the Honorable Prime Minister George Chambers to the House of Representatives of the Parliament of Trinidad and Tobago on October 26, 1983, on the Grenada Crisis." Reproduced in Institute of Caribbean Studies, *Documents on the Invasion of Grenada,* pp. 75–80.

18. Bob Woodward, *Veil: The Secret Wars of the CIA, 1981–1987* (New York: Simon and Schuster, 1987), p. 291.

19. Anthony Payne, Paul Sutton, and Tony Thorndike, *Grenada: Revolution and Invasion* (New York: St. Martin's, 1984), pp. 89–101.

20. "The Ocho Rios Declaration," *Caribbean Contact* (Barbados) 10, 8 (December 1982): 8–9.

21. Quoted in "Reagan's Mediterranean," North American Congress on Latin America (NACLA) *Report on the Americas* 11, 4 (July/August 1985): 34.

22. Anthony Payne, "The Grenada Crisis in British Politics," *The Round Table,* no. 292 (1984): 407–8.

23. *Latin American Weekly Report* (London), WR-87-50 (December 24, 1987): 8–9.

24. Anthony P. Maingot, "American Foreign Policy in the Caribbean: Continuity, Changes and Contingencies," *International Journal* 11 (Spring 1985): 325.

■ CHAPTER 18

1. Sam C. Nolutshungu, "South African Policy and United States Options in Southern Africa," in Gerald J. Bender, James S. Coleman, and Richard L. Sklar, eds., *African Crisis Areas and U.S. Foreign Policy* (Berkeley: University of California Press, 1985), p. 56.

2. African political organizations outlawed included the African National Congress and the Pan Africanist Congress.

3. For a full discussion of NSSM 39, see Mohamed A. el-Khawas and Barry Cohen, eds., *The Kissinger Study of Southern Africa: National Security Study Memorandum 39* (Nottingham: Spokesman Books, 1975).

4. Kevin Danaher, *In Whose Interest?* (Washington, D.C.: Institute for Policy Studies, 1984), p. 79.

5. Nolutshungu, "South African Policy," p. 57.

6. Henry F. Jackson, *From the Congo to Soweto: U.S. Foreign Policy Toward Africa Since 1960* (New York: Quill, 1984), pp. 157–58.

7. Chester A. Crocker, "South Africa: Strategy for Change," *Foreign Affairs* 59, 2 (1980–81): 324–25.

8. For a greater discussion, see Gwendolen M. Carter, *Continuity and Change in Southern Africa* (Los Angeles: Crossroads, 1985), p. 35.

9. As of March 1988, there were some signs, however, that the deadlock over Angola and the presence of Soviet-bloc armed forces might be ending.

10. U.S. Department of State, *A U.S. Policy Toward South Africa: The Report of the Secretary of State's Advisory Committee on South Africa* (Washington, D.C.: Department of State, 1987), p. 2 (hereinafter, *Report*).

11. Crocker, "South Africa," p. 351.

12. *Report,* p. 38.

13. Ibid., p. 8.

14. Ibid.

15. Ibid., p. 9.

16. Ibid.

17. Ibid.

18. Ibid., p. 13.

19. Ibid., pp. 12–13.

20. Ibid., p. 13.

21. Ibid.

22. Ibid., p. 15.

23. For an example of such hopeful thinking, see "Hints of Hope: Afrikaners Begin to Bend," *Time,* May 4, 1987, pp. 28–33.

24. Quoted in Study Commission on U.S. Policy Toward Southern Africa, *South Africa: Time Running Out* (Berkeley: University of California Press, 1981), p. 210. At the time, van Zyl Slabbert was talking about the role of the PFP.

25. *Time,* July 27, 1987, p. 49.

26. *New York Times*, May 8, 1987.

27. Crocker, "South Africa," p. 331.

28. Ibid., pp. 341–43.

29. Ibid., p. 344.

30. Pauline H. Baker, "Facing up to Apartheid," *Foreign Policy,* no. 64 (Fall 1986): 49.

31. Robert M. Price, "Pretoria's Southern African Strategy," *African Affairs* 83, 330 (1984): 11–32.

32. Thomas G. Karis, "South African Liberation: The Communist Factor," *Foreign Affairs* 65, 2 (Winter 1986–1987): 286.

■ CHAPTER 19

1. For an excellent discussion of containment, see John Lewis Gaddis, *Strategies of Containment: A Critical Appraisal of Post-War American National Security Policy* (New York: Oxford University Press, 1982).

2. Kenneth E. Sharpe, "The Real Cause of Iran-Gate," *Foreign Policy,* no. 68 (Fall 1987): 19.

3. Morris J. Blachman and Kenneth E. Sharpe, "De-Democratizing American Foreign Policy: Dismantling the Post-Vietnam Formula," *Third World Quarterly* 8, 4 (October 1986): 1271.

4. Cited in Sharpe, "The Real Cause," p. 28. Sharpe notes, however, that Nixon's domestic covert activities had roots in previous administrations. See Frank J. Donner, *The Age of Surveillance* (New York: Vintage, 1981).

5. Sharpe, "The Real Cause," p. 35, summarizes nicely several of these views.

6. Morton H. Halperin, "Lawful Wars," *Foreign Policy,* no. 72 (Fall 1988): 173–91.

7. See ibid., pp. 187–91.

8. Ibid., pp. 193–95, 176.

9. Ibid., pp. 193–95.

10. See Piero Gleijeses, "The Reagan Doctrine and Central America," *Current History* 85, 515 (December 1986): 401–37.

11. This is one of the major themes of Morris J. Blachman, William M. Leogrande, and Kenneth E. Sharpe, eds., *Confronting Revolution: Security Through Diplomacy in Central America* (New York: Pantheon, 1986). Quote from p. 304.

12. The discussion of El Salvador is drawn from ibid., esp. ch. 3.

13. Ibid., p. 304.

14. Quoted in Ted G. Carpenter, "The United States and Third World Dictatorships: A Case for Benign Detachment," Cato Institute Policy Analysis no. 58, August 15, 1987, p. 7.

15. Anthony Lake, "Wrestling with Radical Third World Regimes: Theory and Practice," in John W. Sewell, Richard E. Feinberg, and Valeriana Kallab, eds., *U.S. Foreign Policy and the Third World: Agenda 1985–86* (New Brunswick, N.J.: Transaction, 1985), p. 144.

16. See Paul Lewis, "U.N. Urges Soviet Pullout in Afghanistan," *New York Times*, November 11, 1987, p. A8.

17. For the various European positions concerning the Reagan Doctrine, see Evan Luard, "Western Europe and the Reagan Doctrine," *International Affairs* 63, 4 (Autumn 1987): 563–74.

18. Jonathan Kwitny, *Endless Enemies: The Making of an Unfriendly World* (New York: Congdon and Weed, 1984), p. 404.

19. This discussion of economic and military aid is taken from Blachman, Leogrande, and Sharpe, *Confronting Revolution,* ch. 14.

20. Ibid.

21. Ibid.

22. Ibid.

23. Michael T. Klare and Cynthia Arnson, *Supplying Repression: U.S. Support for Authoritarian Regimes Abroad* (Washington, D.C.: Institute for Policy Studies, 1981), p. 15.

24. William Minter, "South Africa: Straight Talk on Sanctions," *Foreign Policy,* no. 65 (Winter 1986–1987): 46.

25. For an excellent discussion, see Janice Love, "The Potential Impact of Economic Sanctions Against South Africa," *Journal of Modern African Studies* 26, 1 (1988): 91–111.

26. See, for example, Selig S. Harrison, "Inside the Afghan Talks," *Foreign Policy,* no. 72 (Fall 1988): 31–60.

27. Quoted in Ray Moseley, "Revitalized UN Gaining Praise from an Old Critic," *Chicago Tribune,* September 18, 1988, p. D4.

28. Joseph S. Nye, Jr., "Understanding U.S. Strength," *Foreign Policy,* no. 72 (Fall 1988): 106, 108.

Selected Bibliography

■ CHAPTER 1: CONCEPTS, RELEVANCE, THEMES, AND OVERVIEW

Barnet, Richard J. *Intervention and Revolution: The United States in the Third World*, rev. ed. New York: New American Library, 1980.

Feinberg, Richard E. *The Intemperate Zone: The Third World Challenge to U.S. Foreign Policy*. New York: W. W. Norton, 1983.

Girling, John L. S. *America and the Third World: Revolution and Intervention*. London: Routledge and Kegan Paul, 1980.

Gurtov, Melvin. *The United States Against the Third World: Antinationalism and Intervention*. New York: Praeger, 1974.

Gurtov, Melvin, and Ray Maghroori. *Roots of Failure: United States Policy in the Third World*. Westport, Conn.: Greenwood, 1984.

Kwitny, Jonathan. *Endless Enemies: The Making of an Unfriendly World*. New York: Congdon and Weed, 1984.

Oye, Kenneth A., Richard J. Lieber, and Donald Rothchild, eds. *Eagle Resurgent? The Reagan Era in American Foreign Policy*. Boston: Little, Brown, 1987.

Sewell, John W., Richard E. Feinberg, and Valeriana Kallab, eds. *U.S. Foreign Policy and the Third World: Agenda 1985–86*. New Brunswick, N.J.: Transaction, 1985.

Thompson, W. Scott. *The Third World: Premises of U.S. Policy*. San Francisco: Institute for Contemporary Studies, 1983.

Weatherby, Jr., Joseph, et al., eds. *The Other World: Issues and Politics in the Third World*. New York: Macmillan, 1987.

■ CHAPTER 2: THE EVOLUTION OF THE INTERVENTIONIST IMPULSE

Beale, Howard K. *Theodore Roosevelt and the Rise of America to World Power*. Baltimore, Md.: Johns Hopkins University Press, 1956.

Gardner, Lloyd C. *A Covenant With Power: America and World Order from Wilson to Reagan*. New York: Oxford University Press, 1984.

Kahin, George. *Intervention: How America Became Involved in Vietnam*. New York: Knopf, 1986.
LaFeber, Walter F. *Inevitable Revolutions: The United States in Central America*. New York: W. W. Norton, 1986.
Limerick, Patricia Nelson. *The Legacy of Conquest: The Unbroken Past of the American West*. New York: W. W. Norton, 1987.
Mead, Walter Russell. *Mortal Splendor: The American Empire in Transition*. Boston: Houghton Mifflin, 1987.
Nash, Gary B. *The Urban Crucible: Social Change, Political Consciousness, and the Origins of the American Revolution*. Cambridge: Harvard University Press, 1979.
Schmidt, Hans. *Maverick Marine: General Smedley D. Butler and the Contradictions of American Military History*. Lexington: University of Kentucky Press, 1987.
Van Alstyne, Richard W. *The Rising American Empire*. Chicago: Quadrangle Books, 1965.
Williams, William Appleman. *The Tragedy of American Diplomacy*. New York: World Publishing, 1959.

■ CHAPTER 3: THE DEVELOPMENT OF LOW-INTENSITY CONFLICT DOCTRINE

Barnett, Frank R., et al., eds. *Special Operations in U.S. Strategy*. Washington, D.C.: National Defense University Press, 1984.
Blaufarb, Douglas. *The Counterinsurgency Era: U.S. Doctrine and Performance*. New York: Free Press, 1977.
Kitson, Frank. *Low-Intensity Operations: Subversion, Insurgency, Peace-Keeping*. London: Faber, 1971.
Klare, Michael T. *War Without End: American Planning for the Next Vietnams*. New York: Knopf, 1972.
Klare, Michael T., and Peter Kornbluh, eds. *Low-Intensity Warfare: Counter-insurgency, Proinsurgency, and Antiterrorism in the Eighties*. New York: Pantheon, 1988.
Livingstone, Neil C. "Fighting Terrorism and 'Dirty Little Wars,'" in William A. Buckingham, Jr., ed., *Defense Planning for the 1980s*. Washington, D.C.: National Defense University Press, 1984.
Miles, Sara. "The Real War: Low-Intensity Conflict in Central America." *NACLA's Latin America Report* (April-May 1976): 17–48.
Osgood, Robert E. *Limited War Revisited*. Boulder, Colo.: Westview Press, 1979.
Sarkesian, Sam C., and William L. Scully, eds. *U.S. Policy and Low-Intensity Conflict*. New Brunswick, N.J.: Transaction, 1987.
U.S. Department of Defense. *Proceedings of the Low-Intensity Warfare Conference*. National Defense University, Fort Lesley McNair, Washington, D.C., January 14–15, 1986. Washington, D.C.: Government Printing Office, 1986.

■ CHAPTER 4: THE GLOBALIST-REGIONALIST DEBATE

Bairoch, Paul. *The Economic Development of The Third World Since 1900*. Translated by Lady Cynthia Postan. Berkeley: University of California Press, 1975.
Doran, Charles F. *Domestic Conflict in State Relations: The American Sphere of Influ-*

ence. Beverly Hills, Calif.: Sage, 1976.
Doran, Charles F., George Modelski, and Cal Clark, eds. *North/South Relations: Studies in Dependency Reversal*. New York: Basic Books, 1975.
Gilpin, Robert. *U.S. Power and the Multinational Corporation: The Political Economy of Foreign Direct Investment*. New York: Basic Books, 1975.
Hansen, Roger D. *Beyond the North-South Stalemate*. New York: McGraw-Hill, 1979.
Hoffman, Stanley. *Primacy or World Order: American Foreign Policy Since the Cold War*. New York: McGraw-Hill, 1978.
Krasner, Stephen D. *Structural Conflict: The Third World Against Global Liberalism*. Berkeley: University of California Press, 1985.
Meier, Gerald M. *Leading Issues in Economic Development*. 4th ed. New York: Oxford University Press, 1984.
Rosecrance, Richard. *The Rise of the Trading State: Commerce and Conquest in the Modern World*. New York: Basic Books, 1986.
Shulman, Marshall D., ed. *East-West Tensions in the Third World*. New York: W. W. Norton, 1986.

■ CHAPTER 5: ECONOMIC AND MILITARY AID

Bandow, Doug, ed. *U.S. Aid to the Developing World: A Free Market Agenda*. Washington, D.C.: Heritage Foundation, 1985.
Bauer, P. T. *Equality, the Third World, and Economic Delusion*. Cambridge: Harvard University Press, 1981.
———. *Dissent on Development*. Cambridge: Harvard University Press, 1976.
Bovard, James. "The Continuing Failure of Foreign Aid." Cato Institute Policy Analysis no. 65, January 31, 1986.
Harberger, Arnold, ed. *World Economic Growth: Case Studies of Developed and Developing Nations*. San Francisco: Institute for Contemporary Studies, 1984.
Heginbotham, Stanley. "Foreign Aid: The Evolution of U.S. Programs." Congressional Research Service Report no. 86-86 F, April 16, 1986.
Krauss, Melvyn. *Development Without Aid: Growth, Poverty and Government*. New York: McGraw-Hill, 1983.
Lal, Deepak. *The Poverty of "Development Economics."* London: The Institute of Economic Affairs, 1983.
Lappé, Frances, et al. *Betraying the National Interest*. New York: Grove Press, 1987.
Powelson, John, and Richard Stock. *The Peasant Betrayed: Agriculture and Land Reform in the Third World*. Boston: Oelgeschlager, Bunn, and Hain, 1987.

■ CHAPTER 6: ECONOMIC SANCTIONS

Adler-Karlsson, Gunnar. *Western Economic Warfare, 1947–67: A Case Study in Foreign Economic Policy*. Stockholm: Almqvist and Wiksell, 1966.
Baldwin, David A. *Economic Statecraft: Theory and Practice*. Princeton: Princeton University Press, 1985.
Barber, James. "Economic Sanctions as a Policy Instrument." *International Affairs* 55 (1979): 367–84.
Doxey, Marget P. *Economic Sanctions and International Enforcement*. 2nd ed. New York: Oxford University Press, 1980.

Hufbauer, Gary Clyde, and Jeffrey J. Schott, assisted by Kimberly Ann Elliott. *Economic Sanctions Reconsidered: History and Current Policy*. Washington, D.C.: Institute for International Economics, 1985.

Knorr, Klaus. "International Economic Leverage and Its Uses." In Klaus Knorr and Frank Traeger, eds., *Economic Issues and National Security*. Lawrence, Kans.: Regents Press, 1977.

Leyton-Brown, David, ed. *The Utility of Economic Sanctions*. London: Croom Helm, 1987.

Losman, Donald L. *International Economic Sanctions: The Cases of Cuba, Israel, and Rhodesia*. Albuquerque: University of New Mexico Press, 1979.

Olson, Richard Stuart. "Economic Coercion in World Politics: With a Focus on North-South Relations." *World Politics* 31 (July 1979): 471–94.

Wallensteen, Peter. "Characteristics of Economic Sanctions." *Journal of Peace Research* 5, 3 (1968): 248–67.

■ CHAPTER 7: COVERT INTERVENTION

Constantinides, George C. *Intelligence and Espionage: An Annotated Bibliography*. Boulder, Colo.: Westview Press, 1983.

Corson, William R. *The Armies of Ignorance: The Rise of the American Intelligence Empire*. New York: Dial Press, 1977.

Dulles, Allen. *The Craft of Intelligence*. New York: Harper and Row, 1963.

Fain, Tyrus G., Katherine Plant, and Ross Molloy, eds. *The Intelligence Community: History, Organization, and Issues*. New York: R. R. Bowker, 1977.

Godson, Roy, ed. *Intelligence Requirements for the 1980s*. 7 vols. Washington, D.C.: National Strategy Information Center (vols. 1-5) and Lexington, Mass.: Lexington Books (vols. 6-7), 1979-1986.

Marchetti, Victor, and John D. Marks. *The CIA and the Cult of Intelligence*. New York: Dell Books, 1980.

Phillips, David Atlee. *The Night Watch: Twenty-Five Years of Peculiar Service*. New York: Atheneum, 1977.

Smith, Bradley F. *The Shadow Warriors: OSS and the Origins of the CIA*. New York: Basic Books, 1983.

Treverton, Gregory F. *Covert Action: The Limits of Intervention in the Postwar World*. New York: Basic Books, 1987.

Turner, Admiral Stansfield. *Secrecy and Democracy: The CIA in Transition*. Boston: Houghton Mifflin, 1985.

■ CHAPTER 8: PARAMILITARY INTERVENTION

Elliott, David, ed. *The Third Indochina Conflict*. Boulder, Colo.: Westview Press, 1986.

Harrison, Selig S. "Afghanistan: Soviet Intervention, Afghan Resistance, and the American Role." In Michael T. Klare and Peter Kornbluh, eds., *Low-Intensity Warfare: Counterinsurgency, Proinsurgency, and Antiterrorism in the Eighties*. New York: Pantheon, 1988.

Immerman, Richard H. *The CIA in Guatemala: The Foreign Policy of Intervention*. Austin: University of Texas Press, 1982.

Kirkpatrick, Jeane. *The Reagan Doctrine and U.S. Foreign Policy*. Washington, D.C.: Heritage Foundation, 1985.
Luard, Evan. "Western Europe and the Reagan Doctrine." *International Affairs* 63, 4 (Autumn 1987): 563–74.
Peterzell, Jay. *Reagan's Secret Wars*. Washington, D.C.: Center for National Security Studies, 1984.
Prados, John. *Presidents' Secret Wars: CIA and Pentagon Covert Operations Since World War II*. New York: William Morrow, 1986.
Smith, Wayne S. "A Trap in Angola." *Foreign Policy,* no. 62 (Spring 1986): 61–74.
Stockwell, John. *In Search of Enemies: A CIA Story*. New York: W. W. Norton, 1978.
Wyden, Peter. *Bay of Pigs: The Untold Story*. New York: Simon and Schuster, 1979.

■ CHAPTER 9: DIRECT MILITARY INTERVENTION

Blechman, Barry M., and Stephen S. Kaplan, eds. *Force Without War: U.S. Armed Forces as a Political Instrument*. Washington, D.C.: Brookings, 1978.
Kahin, George M. *Intervention: How America Became Involved in Vietnam*. New York: Knopf, 1986.
Kwitny, Jonathan. *Endless Enemies: The Making of an Unfriendly World*. New York: Congdon and Weed, 1984.
Lowenthal, Abraham F. *The Dominican Intervention*. Cambridge: Harvard University Press, 1972.
MacDonald, Callum. *Korea: The War Before Vietnam*. New York: Free Press, 1986.
Munro, Dana G. *Intervention and Dollar Diplomacy in the Caribbean, 1900–1921*. Princeton: Princeton University Press, 1964.
Quandt, William B. "Reagan's Lebanon Policy: Trial and Error." *Middle East Journal* 38 (Spring 1984): 237–54.
Qubain, Fahim I. *Crisis in Lebanon*. Washington, D.C.: Middle East Institute, 1961.
Rubner, Michael. "The Reagan Administration, the 1973 War Powers Resolution, and the Invasion of Grenada," *Political Science Quarterly* 100 (Winter 1985): 627–47.
Schlesinger, Jr., Arthur M. *The Imperial Presidency*. Boston: Houghton Mifflin, 1973.

■ CHAPTER 10: THE DOMESTIC ENVIRONMENT

Baritz, Loren. *Backfire: A History of How American Culture Led Us into Vietnam and Made Us Fight the Way We Did*. New York: William Morrow, 1985.
Barnet, Richard. *Roots of War: The Men and Institutions Behind U.S. Foreign Policy*. Baltimore: Penguin, 1972.
Bernstein, Carl, and Bob Woodward. *All the President's Men*. New York: Warner, 1974.
Destler, I. M., Leslie H. Gelb, and Anthony Lake. *Our Own Worst Enemy: The Unmaking of American Foreign Policy*. New York: Simon and Schuster, 1984.
Gelb, Leslie H., with Richard K. Betts. *The Irony of Vietnam: The System Worked*. Washington, D.C.: Brookings, 1979.
Hodgson, Godfrey. *America in Our Time: From World War II to Nixon, What Happened and Why*. New York: Vintage, 1976.
Holsti, Ole R., and James N. Rosenau. *American Leadership in World Affairs: Vietnam*

and the Breakdown of Consensus. Boston: Allen and Unwin, 1984.
Melanson, Richard A. *Writing History and Making Policy: The Cold War, Vietnam, and Revisionism*. Lanham, Md.: University Press of America, 1983.
Nathan, James A., and James K. Oliver. *Foreign Policy Making and the American Political System*. Boston: Little, Brown, 1987.
Yergin, Daniel. *Shattered Peace: The Origins of the Cold War and the National Security State*. New York: Houghton Mifflin, 1978.

■ CHAPTER 11: GOVERNMENT AND THE MILITARY ESTABLISHMENT

Betts, Richard K. *Soldiers, Statesmen, and Cold War Crises*. Cambridge: Harvard University Press, 1977.
Cohen, Eliot A. "Constraints on America's Conduct of Small Wars." *International Security* 9, 2 (Fall 1984): 151–81.
Halperin, Morton H. *Bureaucratic Politics and Foreign Policy*. Washington, D.C.: Brookings, 1974.
Halperin, Morton H., and David Halperin. "The Key West Key." *Foreign Policy*, no. 53 (Winter 1983-84): 114–30.
Komer, Robert. *Bureaucracy Does Its Thing: Institutional Constraints on U.S.-G.V.N. Performance in Vietnam*. R-967-ARPA 1972. Santa Monica: Rand Corporation, 1973.
Kozak, David C., and James M. Keagle, eds. *Bureaucratic Politics and National Security: Theory and Practice*. Boulder, Colo.: Lynne Rienner, 1988.
Laird, Melvin R. "A Strong Start in a Difficult Decade: Defense Policy in the Nixon-Ford Years." *International Security* 10, 2 (Fall 1985): 5–26.
Luttwak, Edward. *The Pentagon and the Art of War*. New York: Simon and Schuster, 1985.
Ryan, Paul B. *The Iranian Rescue Mission*. Annapolis, Md.: Annapolis Naval Institute Press, 1985.
Summers, Colonel Harry. *On Strategy: A Critical Analysis of the Vietnam War*. New York: Dell Publishing, 1982.

■ CHAPTER 12: THE STRUCTURE OF THE INTERNATIONAL SYSTEM

FitzGerald, Frances. *Fire in the Lake: The Vietnamese and the Americans in Vietnam*. Boston: Little, Brown, 1972.
Garthoff, Raymond. *Detente and Confrontation: American-Soviet Relations From Nixon to Reagan*. Washington, D.C.: Brookings, 1985.
Griffith, William E. *Peking, Moscow, and Beyond: The Sino-Soviet Triangle*. Washington, D.C.: Center for Strategic Studies, 1973.
Kedourie, Elie. *Islam in the Modern World*. New York: Holt, Rinehart, and Winston, 1980.
Kennedy, Paul. *The Rise and Fall of the Great Powers: Economic Change and Military Conflict from 1500 to 2000*. New York: Random House, 1987.
Keohane, Robert O. *After Hegemony: Cooperation and Discord in the World Political Economy*. Princeton: Princeton University Press, 1984.

Klare, Michael T. "The Arms Trade: Changing Patterns in the 1980s." *Third World Quarterly* 9, 4 (October 1987): 1257–81.
Linder, S. B. *The Pacific Century*. Stanford: Stanford University Press, 1986.
Mazrui, Ali A., and Michael Tidy. *Nationalism and New States in Africa from About 1935 to the Present*. London: Heinemann, 1985.
Oye, Kenneth A. "International Systems Structure and American Foreign Policy." In Kenneth A. Oye, Robert J. Lieber, and Donald Rothchild, eds., *Eagle Defiant: United States Foreign Policy in the 1980s*. Boston: Little, Brown, 1983.

■ CHAPTER 13: INTERNATIONAL LAW

Bemis, Samuel F. *The Latin American Policy of the United States: An Historical Interpretation*. New York: Harcourt Brace, 1943.
Dinerstein, Herbert S. *Intervention Against Communism*. Baltimore: Johns Hopkins University Press, 1967.
Falk, Richard A., ed. *The Vietnam War and International Law*. Princeton: Princeton University Press, vol. 1, 1968; vol. 2, 1969; vol. 3, 1972; vol. 4, 1976.
Hart, Albert A. *The Monroe Doctrine: An Interpretation*. Boston: Little, Brown, 1916.
Lillich, Richard B., ed. *Humanitarian Intervention and the United Nations*. Charlottesville: University of Virginia Press, 1973.
Miller, Linda B. *World Order and Local Disorder: The United Nations and Local Conflicts*. Princeton: Princeton University Press, 1967.
Moore, John Norton, ed. *Law and Civil War in the Modern World*. Baltimore: Johns Hopkins University Press, 1974.
Perkins, Dexter. *A History of the Monroe Doctrine*. Boston: Little, Brown, 1955.
Thomas, A. J., and Thomas Ann. *Non-Intervention: The Law and Its Import in the Americas*. Dallas: Southern Methodist University Press, 1956.
Vincent, R. J. *Nonintervention and International Order*. Princeton: Princeton University Press, 1974.

■ CHAPTER 14: IRAN

Abrahamian, Ervand. *Iran Between Two Revolutions*. Princeton: Princeton University Press, 1982.
Bill, James A. *The Eagle and the Lion: The Tragedy of American-Iranian Relations*. New Haven: Yale University Press, 1988.
Cottam, Richard. *Iran and the United States: A Cold War Case Study*. Pittsburgh: University of Pittsburgh Press, 1988.
Halliday, Fred. *Iran: Dictatorship and Development*. New York: Penguin Books, 1979.
Hooglund, Eric. *Land and Revolution in Iran, 1960–1980*. Austin: University of Texas Press, 1982.
Ioannides, Christos. *America's Iran: Injury and Catharsis*. Lanham, Md.: University Press of America, 1984.
Keddie, Nikki, and Eric Hooglund, eds. *The Iranian Revolution and the Islamic Republic*. Syracuse: Syracuse University Press, 1986.
Ramazani, R. K. *Revolutionary Iran: Challenge and Response in the Middle East*. Baltimore: Johns Hopkins University Press, 1987.
Rubin, Barry. *Paved with Good Intentions: The American Experience in Iran*. New

York: Oxford University Press, 1980.
Sick, Gary. *All Fall Down: America's Tragic Encounter with Iran*. New York: Random House, 1985.

■ CHAPTER 15: THE PHILIPPINES

Bain, David Howard. *Sitting in Darkness: Americans in the Phillippines*. Boston: Houghton Mifflin, 1984.
Bonner, Raymond. *Waltzing with a Dictator: The Marcoses and the Making of American Policy*. New York: Times Books, 1987.
Johnson, Bryan. *The Four Days of Courage: The Untold Story of the People Who Brought Marcos Down*. New York: Free Press, 1987.
Lande, Carl H. *Leaders, Factions, and Parties: The Structure of Philippine Politics*. New Haven: Yale University Press, 1965.
Lande, Carl H., ed. *Rebuilding a Nation, Philippine Challenges and American Policy*. Washington, D.C.: Washington Institute Press, 1987.
Miller, Stuart Creighton. *"Benevolent Assimilation": The American Conquest of the Philippines, 1899–1903*. New Haven: Yale University Press, 1982.
Pringle, Robert. *Indonesia and the Philippines: American Interests in Island Southeast Asia*. New York: Columbia University Press, 1980.
Rosenberg, David A., ed. *Marcos and Martial Law in the Philippines*. Ithaca: Cornell University Press, 1979.
Shalom, Stephen R. *The United States and the Philippines, A Study of Neocolonialism*. Philadelphia: Institute for the Study of Human Issues, 1981.
Thompson, W. Scott, *Unequal Partners: Philippine and Thai Relations with the United States, 1965–75*. Lexington, Mass.: Lexington Books, 1975.

■ CHAPTER 16: NICARAGUA

Bermann, Karl. *Under the Big Stick: Nicaragua and the United States Since 1848*. Boston: South End Press, 1987.
Blachman, Morris J., William M. Leogrande, and Kenneth E. Sharpe, eds. *Confronting Revolution: Security Through Diplomacy in Central America*. New York: Pantheon, 1986.
Booth, John. *The End and the Beginning: The Nicaraguan Revolution*. Boulder, Colo.: Westview Press, 1982.
Dickey, Christopher. *With the Contras*. New York: Simon and Schuster, 1985.
Gutman, Roy. *Banana Diplomacy: The Making of U.S. Policy in Nicaragua, 1981–1987*. New York: Simon and Schuster, 1988.
Kornbluh, Peter. *Nicaragua: The Price of Intervention*. Washington, D.C.: Institute for Policy Studies, 1987.
Millett, Richard. *Guardians of the Dynasty: A History of the U.S.-Created Guardia Nacional and the Somoza Family*. Maryknoll, N.Y.: Orbis Books, 1977.
Pastor, Robert. *Condemned to Repetition: The United States and Nicaragua*. Princeton: Princeton University Press, 1987.
U.S. Congress. *Report of the Congressional Committees Investigating the Iran-Contra Affair*. Washington, D.C.: Government Printing Office, 1987.
Walker, Thomas, ed. *Reagan vs. the Sandinistas: The Undeclared War on Nicaragua*. Boulder, Colo.: Westview Press, 1987.

■ CHAPTER 17: GRENADA

Anderson, Thomas D. *Geopolitics of the Caribbean: Ministates in a Wider World*. New York: Praeger, 1984.
Ashby, Timothy. *The Bear in the Backyard: Moscow's Caribbean Strategy*. Lexington, Mass.: Lexington Books, 1987.
Crozier, Brian, ed. *The Grenada Documents*. London: Sherwood Press, 1987.
Hart, Richard. *In Nobody's Backyard*. London: Zed Press, 1984.
Lewis, Gordon K. *The Jewel Despoiled*. Baltimore: Johns Hopkins University Press, 1987.
Mandle, Jay R. *Big Revolution, Small Country: The Rise and Fall of the Grenadian Revolution*. Lanham, Md.: North-South Publishing, 1985.
Payne, Anthony. *The International Crisis in the Caribbean*. Beckenham, Kent: Croom Helm, 1984.
Payne, Anthony, Paul Sutton, and Tony Thorndike. *Grenada: Revolution and Invasion*. New York: St. Martin's, 1984.
Sanford, Gregory. *The New Jewel Movement: Grenada's Revolution, 1979–1983*. Washington, D.C.: Foreign Service Institute, Department of State, 1985.
Thorndike, Tony. *Grenada: Politics, Economics and Society*. Boulder, Colo.: Lynne Rienner, 1985.

■ CHAPTER 18: SOUTH AFRICA

Bender, Gerald J., James S. Coleman, and Richard L. Sklar, eds. *African Crisis Areas and U.S. Foreign Policy*. Berkeley: University of California Press, 1985.
Carter, Gwendolen M. *Continuity and Change in Southern Africa*. Los Angeles: Crossroads, 1985.
Carter, Gwendolen M., and Patrick O'Meara, eds. *South Africa: The Continuing Crisis*. 2nd ed. Bloomington: Indiana University Press, 1982.
Davis, Stephen M. *Apartheid's Rebels: Inside South Africa's Hidden War*. New Haven: Yale University Press, 1987.
Fatton, Robert. *Black Consciousness in South Africa*. Albany: State University of New York Press, 1986.
Hanlon, Joseph. *Beggar Your Neighbours: Apartheid Power in South Africa*. Bloomington: Indiana University Press, 1986.
Jackson, Henry F. *From the Congo to Soweto: U.S. Foreign Policy Toward Africa Since 1960*. New York: Quill, 1984.
Khawas, Mohamed A. el-, and Barry Cohen, eds. *The Kissinger Study of Southern Africa: National Security Memorandum 39*. Nottingham: Spokesman Books, 1975.
Lemarchand, René, ed. *American Policy in Southern Africa: The Stakes and the Stance*. Washington, D.C.: University Press of America, 1978.
Study Commission on U.S. Policy Toward South Africa. *South Africa: Time Running Out*. Berkeley: University of California Press, 1981.

■ CHAPTER 19: U.S. INTERVENTION IN PERSPECTIVE

Blachman, Morris J., and Kenneth E. Sharpe. "De-Democratizing American Foreign Policy: Dismantling the Post-Vietnam Formula." *Third World Quarterly* 8, 4 (October 1986): 1271–1308.

Hough, Jerry F. *The Struggle for the Third World: Soviet Debates and American Options*. Washington, D.C.: Brookings, 1986.

Lake, Anthony. "Wrestling with Third World Radical Regimes: Theory and Practice." In John W. Sewell, Richard E. Feinberg, and Valeriana Kallab, eds., *U.S. Foreign Policy and the Third World: Agenda 1985–86*. New Brunswick, N.J.: Transaction, 1985.

Nye, Jr., Joseph S. "Understanding U.S. Strength." *Foreign Policy*, no. 72 (Fall 1988): 105–129.

Parry, Robert, and Peter Kornbluh. "Iran-Contra's Untold Story." *Foreign Policy*, no. 72 (Fall 1988): 3–30.

Rubin, Barry. *Modern Dictators: Third World Coup Makers, Strongmen, and Populist Tyrants*. New York: McGraw-Hill, 1987.

Sharpe, Kenneth E. "The Real Cause of Iran-Gate." *Foreign Policy*, no. 68 (Fall 1987): 19–41.

Sharpe, Kenneth E., et al. "Security Through Diplomacy: A Policy of Principled Realism." In Morris J. Blachman, William M. Leogrande, and Kenneth E. Sharpe, eds., *Confronting Revolution: Security Through Diplomacy in Central America*. New York: Pantheon, 1986.

Index

4872